Governance and Policy in Sport Organizations

Understanding governance structures is essential for any career in sport management as it provides a "big picture" perspective on where one fits into one's organization and where that organization fits into its industry segment. Drs. Hums and MacLean are ideally suited authors who possess a wealth of experience in a variety of international sport settings as sport management researchers and practitioners. Utilizing current real-world examples, their fourth edition book equips the reader with the theoretical knowledge bases related to governance and policy development, as well as governance structures in a variety of sport industry segments.

Karen Danylchuk, Professor of Sport Management,
Western University, Canada

Now in a fully updated new edition, this textbook introduces readers to the power and politics of sport organizations. It explores the managerial activities essential to good governance and policy development, and looks at the structure and functions of individual organizations within the larger context of the global sport industry.

Reflecting the latest industry changes, it draws on a fresh selection of real-world examples to demonstrate the types of dilemmas that sport managers face every day. Professional administrators from a wide variety of sport organizations also offer their insights, giving readers a glimpse into the real concerns of sport professionals and the impact of governance and policy on their jobs. Exploring current topics, such as sport and human rights, refugees, social media, and the evolution of eSports, this practical and accessible textbook helps readers to see the big picture of the contemporary sport industry and find their place in it as future sport managers.

Complemented by a new companion website full of useful ancillary materials, this is an essential resource for all sport management students and instructors.

Mary A. Hums is Professor in the Department of Health and Sport Sciences at the University of Louisville, USA. In 2009 she was selected as the recipient of NASSM's Earle F. Zeigler Lecture award, the highest academic honor bestowed by the organization. She was a co-contributor to

Article 30.5 (Participation in Cultural Life, Recreation, Leisure and Sport) of the 2006 United Nations Convention on the Rights of Persons with Disabilities. She is currently a Senior Research Fellow for the Institute for Human Centered Design, and a NASSM Research Fellow. She received the 2010 University of Louisville Trustees Award and has been a frequent University of Louisville Red and Black Scholar-Athlete Mentor. Hums has worked at four Paralympic Games as well as one Olympic Games and Para-Pan American Games.

Joanne C. MacLean is President of the University of the Fraser Valley in British Columbia, Canada. She served as Dean of the Faculty of Health Sciences at UFV from 2012 to 2018, prior to being selected as the institution's first female President. From 2002 to 2012 she was a professor of Sport Management at Brock University, where she held the positions of department chair and interim Dean. She also has had extensive experience in the administration, governance, and human resource management of university sport within Canada. MacLean has had a long-term role administering basketball within Canada. She acted as President of the Canadian University Women's Basketball Coaches Association, Chair of the Canadian Women's National Basketball Operations Committee, and was a member of the Board of Directors of Canada Basketball from 2002 to 2008. She was named a Research Fellow of the North American Society for Sport Management in 2009.

GOVERNANCE AND POLICY IN sport ORGANIZATIONS

FOURTH EDITION

**Mary A. Hums and
Joanne C. MacLean**

Routledge
Taylor & Francis Group

LONDON AND NEW YORK

First published 2018
by Routledge
2 Park Square, Milton Park, Abingdon, Oxon OX14 4RN

and by Routledge
711 Third Avenue, New York, NY 10017

Routledge is an imprint of the Taylor & Francis Group, an informa business

British Library Cataloguing-in-Publication Data
A catalogue record for this book is available from the British Library

Library of Congress Cataloging-in-Publication Data
Names: Hums, Mary A., author. | MacLean, Joanne, author.
Title: Governance and policy in sport organizations / Mary A. Hums and Joanne C. MacLean.
Description: Fourth Edition. | New York : Routledge, 2018. | Series: Sport Management series | Includes bibliographical references and index.
Identifiers: LCCN 2017047139| ISBN 9781138086333 (Hardback) | ISBN 9781138086340 (Paperback) | ISBN 9781315111056 (eBook)
Subjects: LCSH: Sports administration.
Classification: LCC GV713 .H86 2018 | DDC 796.06/9—dc23
LC record available at https://lccn.loc.gov/2017047139

ISBN: 978-1-138-08633-3 (hbk)
ISBN: 978-1-138-08634-0 (pbk)
ISBN: 978-1-315-11105-6 (ebk)

Typeset in Sabon LT Std
by Swales & Willis Ltd, Exeter, Devon, UK

Visit the companion website: www.routledge.com/cw/hums

Contents

List of Contributors

Packianathan Chelladurai, Troy University, USA
Marion E. Hambrick, University of Louisville, USA
Sun J. Kang, Manchester University, USA
Thierry Zintz, Université Catholique de Louvain, France

Foreword

Governance organizations, which are at the apex of the organizational network in a given industry segment, serve to achieve the individual and collective goals of the member organizations. Such organizations also serve the member organizations by generating valued resources and facilitating the interactions and exchange of information among members.

Hums and MacLean have done an excellent job in identifying and describing the various organizations that govern scholastic sport, amateur sport in the community, campus recreation, intercollegiate athletics, major games in amateur sport, Olympic sport, Paralympic sport, North American professional sport, and international professional sport. It is also noteworthy that Hums and MacLean cover segments of the industry that encompass participant sport, elite sport, professional/commercial sport, and sport for individuals with disabilities.

The chapters on each of these segments are unique in their inclusion of history of the segment, the governance structures and programming within the segment, and the policy issues faced in each segment. Readers will appreciate and enjoy the presentation in each chapter of the mission statements and financial and membership aspects of the respective governance organizations. The authors have prefaced these chapters with four introductory chapters. The first chapter is a lucid introduction to the sport industry, its segments, and the concept of governance. The authors argue rightfully that students should gain insight into the "big picture" of sport governance in addition to understanding individual organizations within a segment. The second chapter is devoted to a treatise on managerial activities including planning, organizing, and decision making. The critical concepts of strategic management and policy development are dealt with separately in the third chapter. The fourth chapter is devoted to ethics in sport organizations. This is an important chapter because a major responsibility of governance organizations is to foster ethical conduct by member organizations and the individuals therein. These four introductory chapters lead nicely into the substance of the book. The book's final chapter is fittingly devoted to raising issues that will confront sport governing organizations in the future.

It is a matter of great pleasure and pride to present the credentials of the authors. The pleasure is professional in the sense that I am referring to two outstanding professionals in the field. The pride is personal and stems from the fact that my association with these scholars began as they were developing as academics. Mary Hums and Joanne MacLean were my doctoral students at the Ohio State University. They are not new to the science and art of writing scholarly papers and texts. Each has published in leading journals and each has published texts and/or chapters in texts. And each has been associated with the governance organizations about which they write. These practical experiences have provided them with the insights that they admirably bring to bear on the discussion of the governance of sport industry organizations and segments. In sum, Hums and MacLean have written an excellent text on the governance of segments of the sport industry

Packianathan Chelladurai
Distinguished Professor
School of Hospitality, Sport, and Tourism Management
Troy University
USA

As with previous editions, the fourth edition of *Governance and Policy in Sport Organizations* is designed for use in governance or policy development courses with upper-level undergraduate students, and can also be used with some graduate-level courses that introduce students to business and policy development aspects of the sport industry.

Sport management students entering the workforce will be employed in various sport industry segments. An important part of their training is learning the structure and function of the various sport organizations they will work within or interact with. Successful sport managers understand the big picture of how their sport organizations are structured. They also know what issues their organizations—and they as managers—will have to confront. This book challenges students to integrate management theory with governance and policy development practices. It discusses where the power lies in an organization or industry segment and how individual sport organizations fit into the greater industry. The book also interweaves ethical issues throughout, as sport managers need to make sure their decisions are just, fair, and inclusive.

This fourth edition of the book reflects industry changes and offers real-world examples. Numerous sport organization websites are highlighted throughout the text, to prompt in-class discussions and facilitate further research. These websites are displayed in the margins of the text and thus are easily referred to. This edition also features new Industry Portraits & Perspectives boxes, with contributions by administrators in a wide variety of sport segments, including campus recreation, Olympic and Paralympic sport, community recreation, and others. For this feature, administrators answered our questions about their jobs and their organizations to give students a glimpse into the practical concerns of sport managers and the impact of governance and policy in the sport industry.

In this edition, we continue to explore current topics such as sport and human rights; refugees and sport; use of social media by athletes, coaches, and front office staff; and the evolution of eSport. Issues such as these will continue to emerge and evolve, and this text will provide a springboard for class discussions and projects.

Knowledge of sport beyond North America is essential for A well-informed manager and is required for success in the increasingly global sport industry. Although this book focuses primarily on North American sport organizations, it presents sufficient information on international sport organizations to provide students with working models and an understanding of these organizations. For example, we highlight how North American scholastic, intercollegiate, and professional sports differ from those in other regions of the world. In this edition, contributions from the French translation of our book, by Thierry Zintz, Université Catholique de Louvain, offer additional insight into European sport organizations. In addition, our backgrounds as authors—one from the United States and the other Canada—contribute to the international scope of this book. Both of us have had hands-on experience in international sport settings as researchers and practitioners. This combination brings a unique skill set and knowledge base to the text. For example, Mary Hums is an internationally recognized researcher in the area of management issues affecting disability sport, having worked four Paralympic Games and also the Para-Pan American Games and contributes her expertise to the Paralympic Sport chapter. Joanne MacLean is an experienced University Athletic Director and served as Canada's Chef de Mission for the FISU Games, lending her experience to the chapters on Intercollegiate Athletics and Major Games in Amateur Sport.

Governance and Policy in Sport Organizations is written and organized with the goal of being teacher- and student-friendly so that instructors will be comfortable with the topic and can present the material to students in a clear, organized fashion. To this end, we now include useful information on accreditation standards, on the book's organization and pedagogy, and about the instructor materials available to adopters.

The fourth edition of this book has now been used by instructors teaching in the online format. The feedback has been very positive, as instructors have noted the organization of the chapters and the end-of-chapter questions and case studies work successfully with online students. With so many Sport Management programs adding online classes, this book fits the format well.

COSMA CURRICULAR APPLICATION

As Sport Management educational programs have continued to evolve, the previous NASSM/NASPE approval process has been phased out and new accreditation standards established. Today, Sport Management education programs can be fully accredited by COSMA— the Commission on Sport Management Accreditation. Governance is included in the COSMA documents as one of the Common Professional Components, in section 3.2 of the *COSMA Self-Study Manual*. Governance is included as a Foundation of Sport Management along with Management Concepts and International Sport.

ORGANIZATION OF THE CHAPTERS

T he book is divided into two main sections. The purpose of this division is to first establish the theoretical knowledge bases related to governance and policy development that sport managers need to operate their sport organizations on a daily basis, and then to present ways the theoretical bases play out in practical sport governance environments.

The first section, Chapters 1 through 4, presents the basics of specific managerial activities necessary for governance and policy development in sport organizations. This section includes material that is more theoretical in nature, covering an introduction to sport governance and the management functions of planning, organizing, decision making, and strategic management. Because sport managers face ethical dilemmas on a regular basis, the book devotes a chapter to ethical decision making and the importance of corporate social responsibility.

The second section of the book, Chapters 5 through 14, details the governance structures of various sport industry segments, including:

- scholastic sport
- amateur sport in the community
- campus recreation
- intercollegiate athletics
- major games
- Olympic sport
- Paralympic sport
- North American professional sport leagues
- professional individual sport
- professional sport leagues outside of North America

The content of this section is much more applied in nature. These chapters on the specific industry segments include sections on history, governance structures, and current policy issues. Organizational policies often develop as a reaction to current issues faced by sport organizations and sport managers. Because these issues change and evolve over time, for each industry segment the text presents a selection of current policy issues and the strategies that sport managers are implementing to deal with these issues. Often, such organizational policy decisions have ethical underpinnings as well. Throughout the current policy sections, the book addresses the ethical questions sport managers confront when developing policies. Each chapter also contains a case study related to the chapter content, and ethical concerns are integrated into many of these case studies.

Finally, in Chapter 15, with the goal of stimulating student thought and class discussion, we consider challenges with which sport governing bodies may have to grapple in the future.

THE BOOK'S PEDAGOGY

Each chapter includes Chapter Questions, for use either as homework assignments or for class discussion. In addition, chapters contain case studies that have been used successfully in governance classes and have proven useful for students. A new section titled, For Additional Information, has been added to each chapter as well and directs readers to links to expand on what the chapter covers. As mentioned, many of the industry segment chapters include Industry Portraits & Perspectives boxes that provide insight into the job responsibilities of and issues faced by sport managers in that segment. These boxes can be used to stimulate further discussion as readers consider the way the professionals responded to an issue and how they might respond differently. Please note, too, that for easy reference the book's frontmatter includes a table of the many acronyms that students will encounter here and in the field.

ANCILLARY MATERIALS

Ancillary materials are available to instructors with adoption of this text. These ancillary materials include an Instructor's Manual, a PowerPoint presentation, and a testbank. The Instructor's Manual contains student learning objectives, exam questions (multiple choice, short answer, and true/false, also offered in testbank form), and suggestions for additional assignments. The PowerPoint presentation focuses on key points from the chapters to help instructors deliver the material as effectively as possible. To help readers easily access the many websites cited throughout the book, the ancillary materials also include an electronic document containing active links to the sites. You may distribute this file to your students or post it on your website.

It is our hope that instructors and students will find this book to be an interesting and useful tool for learning the fundamentals of sport governance and its relationship to current policy and ethical issues facing today's sport managers. It is a book designed to help readers understand the big picture of the sport industry, and their place in it as future sport management professionals.

Acknowledgments

A book project is truly a labor of love, and it cannot be undertaken and successfully completed without a great deal of help from others. Thus, many thanks are in order.

First, special thanks to Marion Hambrick and Sun Kang, who stepped up and contributed this edition's chapter on Professional Individual Sports. Our book adopters requested this content, and we are happy to offer this excellent new chapter in response. We are delighted to be working on this new edition with a new publishing company—Routledge. It is an honor that an internationally well-respected and well-known publishing company would deem this book as worthy to undertake. We would like to thank our previous publisher, Colette Kelly, Gay Pauley, and all the good people at Holcomb Hathaway for their support and insightful comments throughout the years in getting us to the point that a fourth edition was in demand.

Our sincere thanks to the many reviewers who have offered us thoughtful, thorough, and relevant feedback for each edition, making a significant contribution to the book's usefulness. These individuals include (*for the current edition*): Craig Esherick, George Mason University; Katie Flanagan, Florida State University; Matthew Garret, Loras College; Daniel Sargeant, Lasalle College; David Walsh, University of Houston; and Loni Wilson, Keiser University; and for prior editions Chad Carlson, Eastern Illinois University; Mark Dodds, SUNY Cortland; Matthew Garrett, Loras College; Harlan L. Johnson, Bacone College; William Kuchler, Methodist University; Rachel Madsen, Niagara University; Robert P. Mathner, Troy University; Jon Oliver, Eastern Illinois University; Chad Seifried, Louisiana State University; Corri Wilson, Southern New Hampshire University; Lonni Wilson, Keiser University; Athena Yiamouyiannis, Ohio University; Gala Bank, Northwood University; Carol A. Barr, University of Massachusetts; Dennis Bechtol, Northwood University, Florida Campus; Richard C. Bell, Colorado Mesa University; Mel Brennan, Towson University; Susan Brown Foster, Saint Leo University; Karen Danylchuk, University of Western Ontario; Stephen W. Dittmore, University of Arkansas; John Harris, Kent State University; Timothy Henrich, University of the Incarnate Word; Sue Inglis, McMaster University; E. Newton Jackson, Florida State University; Darlene Kluka, Kennesaw State University; John D. McMillan, Bowling Green State University; Steven Ross Murray, Colorado Mesa University; Barry J. Nicholson, Southeast Missouri State University; Jeff Noble, Wichita

State University; Cecile Reynaud, Florida State University; James T. Reese, Ohio University; B. David Ridpath, Mississippi State University; Raymond G. Schneider, Bowling Green State University; Robert Taylor, California University of Pennsylvania; Bernadette M. Twardy, Flagler College; Susan Vail, York University; and Michael Wynn, Northwood University.

—*Mary Hums and Joanne MacLean*

I would like to specifically acknowledge my Sport Administration colleagues along the way at the University of Louisville: Evan Frederick, Chris Greenwell, Marion Hambrick, Meg Hancock, Anita Moorman, Gin Presley, Sam Schmidt, and Megan Shreffler. Without their ongoing and daily support and encouragement, as academics but more importantly as friends, this project would never have reached completion. I am especially thankful for all they have done for me here at the University of Louisville. I would also like to thank the student research assistants who helped me with this book in one or all of its editions: Sarah Williams, Seonghun Lee, Yung Chou (Enzo) Chen, Morgan Fishman, Robert Sexton, Mark Perry, Michael Clemons, and Kathleen Sipe. They put in numerous hours at the computer and in the library searching for information.

My personal thanks to Dr. Packianathan "Chella" Chelladurai for his help in inspiring me to write this textbook in the first place and even more for his valuable guidance and mentorship in my academic life. I would also like to thank all of our professional colleagues who have adopted the book and made it a success. I sincerely appreciate your support. And to all the students who read it—a big thank you! Without the students, we wouldn't have had the opportunity to write this book.

Finally, I would like to thank my family and friends here and around the world for their ongoing support and encouragement. Once again I cannot say enough about the good work of my co-author, Joanne MacLean, who is now President of the University of the Fraser Valley. Finding someone who shares a common work ethic and dedication to task on a long-term project such as this is a blessing. One of the main reasons I asked Joanne if she wanted to team with me when we initiated this project was because I knew she was a "do-er," and through each edition she has been a valuable and supportive colleague. She motivated me and kept me going on more occasions than she will ever know! I enjoy working with people like her—people who make me better.

Thanks to all of you!

—*MH*

I have been challenged by the magnitude of writing each edition of this book and want to thank the many individuals who have assisted and encouraged me. I am fortunate for the support and inquisitiveness of my students and colleagues, first at the University of Windsor and Brock University, and now at the University of the Fraser Valley. Special thanks to Dr. Eric Davis, Provost at UFV who supported my work time for completing the fourth edition. I wish to thank University of Louisville graduate student Sarah

Williams who contributed editing and suggestions to content in some of my chapters, and past graduate students Dan Hess and Bogdan Ciomaga for their hard work researching content for previous editions of the book. I am indebted to each student for the questions, suggestions, and strong attention to detail.

I continue to be grateful for my family and friends who have always encouraged and shown interest in my academic pursuits. This one's for you, Mom!

Finally, I am thankful for my co-author, Mary Hums. Dr. Hums is known around the world as an accomplished scholar, teacher, and sport manager. To me, she is all of those things while also being an inspiration and a true friend. I am honored to be her co-author.

My thanks to you all!

—JM

Credits List

ermission to reprint the following third-party material has kindly been granted by the following organizations:

Chapter 5, Exhibit 5.5: WIAA Organizational Chart (reproduced with permission from Wisconsin Interscholastic Athletic Association)

Chapter 7, Exhibit 7.3: Organizational Chart of NIRSA Board of Directors (reproduced with permission from NIRSA: Leaders in Collegiate Recreation)

Chapter 7, Exhibit 7.4: NIRSA Headquarters Organizational Chart (reproduced with permission from NIRSA: Leaders in Collegiate Recreation)

Chapter 8, Exhibit 8.4: Governance Structure of the NAIA (reproduced with permission from the NAIA National Office)

Chapter 11, Exhibit 11.4: IPC Organizational Chart (reproduced with permission from the International Paralympic Committee [IPC])

DISCLAIMER

The publishers have made every effort to contact the authors/copyright holders of works reprinted in *Governance and Policy in Sport Organizations* 4th Edition and to obtain permission to publish extracts. This has not been possible in every case, however, and we would welcome correspondence from those individuals/companies whom we have been unable to trace. Any omission brought to our attention will be redeemed in future editions.

IMAGE CREDITS

Title page:	Shutterstock/SnvvSnvvSnvv
Contents page:	Shutterstock/Beneda Miroslav
List of contributors:	Shutterstock/meunierd
Foreword:	Shutterstock/melis

Preface:	Shutterstock/SnvvSnvvSnvv
Acknowledgements:	Shutterstock/Beneda Miroslav
Credits list:	Shutterstock/meunierd
List of abbreviations:	Shutterstock/melis
Chapter 1 title page:	Shutterstock/Frank Romeo
Chapter 2 title page:	Shutterstock/BlueSkyImage
Chapter 3 title page:	Shutterstock/Monkey Business Images
Chapter 4 title page:	Shutterstock/karina
Chapter 5 title page:	Shutterstock/Aspen Photo
Chapter 6 title page:	Shutterstock/Monkey Business Images
Chapter 7 title page:	Shutterstock/Dean Drobot
Chapter 8 title page:	Shutterstock/Aspen Photo
Chapter 9 title page:	Shutterstock/Luigi Fardella
Chapter 10 title page:	Shutterstock/Hafiz Johari
Chapter 11 title page:	Shutterstock/Shahjehan
Chapter 12 title page:	Shutterstock/DebShutterstock/Wong
Chapter 13 title page:	Shutterstock/mooinblack
Chapter 14 title page:	Shutterstock/Ververidis Vasilis
Chapter 15 title page:	Shutterstock/Leonel Calara
Index:	Shutterstock/Gemenacom

Abbreviations

AAU	Amateur Athletic Union
ABA	American Basketball Association
ACC	Atlantic Coast Conference
ACT	American College Test
AD	Athletic Director
ADA	Americans with Disabilities Act
ADHD	attention deficit hyperactivity disorder
AFC	American Football Conference
AFL	American Footbali League
AFL-CIO	American Federation of Labor-Congress of Industrial Organizations
AGM	Annual General Meeting
AIAW	Association for Intercollegiate Athletics for Women
AIM	American Indian Movement
APR	Academic Progress Rate
ASAA	Alberta Schools Athletic Association
ASC	Australian Sports Commission
ASCOD	African Sports Confederation for the Disabled
ATP	Association of Tennis Professionals
BAA	Basketball Association of America
BASS	Bass Anglers Sportsman Society
BSU	Big State University
BUCS	British Universities and Colleges Sport
CBA	collective bargaining agreement
CCDBG	Child Care Development Block Grant
CCES	Canadian Centre for Ethics in Sport
CEO	Chief Executive Officer
CFAR	Council of Faculty Athletics Administrators
CGF	Commonwealth Games Federation
CIS	Canadian Interuniversity Sport

CISS	International Committee of Silent Sports
COC	Canadian Olympic Committee
CoHEASAP	Coalition of Higher Education Associations for Substance Abuse Prevention
COI	Committee on Infractions
COO	Chief Operating Officer
COSMA	Commission on Sports Management Accreditation
CPISRA	Cerebral Palsy International Sport and Recreation Association
CSR	corporate social responsibility
CU	Cornell University
DI	Division I
DI-FBS	Division I Football Bowl Series
DI-FCS	Division I Football Championship Series
DII	Division II
DIII	Division III
ED	Executive Director
EPC	European Paralympic Committee
EPL	English Premier League
FA	Football Association of England
FAR	Faculty Athletic Representative
FARE	Football Against Racism in Europe
FBS	Football Bowl Subdivision
FCS	Football Championship Division
FIA	Fédération Internationale de l'Automobile
FIBA	Fédération Internationale de Basketball Association
FIFA	Fédération Internationale de Football Association

FISEC	International Sports Federation for Catholic Schools
FISU	Fédération Internationale du Sport Universitaire
FITA	World Archery Federation/International Federation of Archery
FIVB	International Volleyball Federation
GOP	Games Organizing Committee
GPA	grade point average
HBCU	historically black college and university
HSPN	Homeschool Sportnet Incorporated
IAAF	International Association of Athletics Federation
IAAUS	Intercollegiate Athletic Association of the United States
IBSA	International Blind Sports Association
ICC	International Cricket Council
ICSD	International Committee of Sports of the Deaf
IF	International Federation
IGF	International Golf Federation
IHF	International Handball Federation
INAS-FID	International Association of Sport for People with an Intellectual Disability
IOC	International Olympic Committee
IOSD	International Organization of Sport for the Disabled
IPC	International Paralympic Committee
IPSF	International Paralympic Sport Federation
ISA	International Surfing Association
ISF	International School Sport Federation
ISHSAA	Indiana State High School Athletic Association
ISOD	International Sport Organization for the Disabled
ITF	International Tennis Federation
ITTF	International Table Tennis Federation
IWAS	International Wheelchair and Amputee Sports Federation
JCC	Jewish Community Center
KHSAA	Kentucky High School Athletic Association
LGBTQ	lesbian, gay, bisexual, trans, and queer
LOCOG	London Organizing Committee for the Olympic Games
LPGA	Ladies Professional Golf Association

MEMOS	Executive Masters in Sports Organization Management
MLB	Major League Baseball
MLBPA	Major League Baseball Players Association
MLS	Major League Soccer
MMA	mixed martial arts
MOBA	multi-player online battle arena
NACDA	National Association of Collegiate Directors of Athletics
NACAC	National Association for College Admissions Counseling
NAIA	National Association of Intercollegiate Athletics
NAIB	National Association of Intercollegiate Basketball
NASCAR	National Association for Stock Car Auto Racing
NASPE	National Association for Sport and Physical Education
NASSM	North American Society for Sport Management
NBA	National Basketball Association
NBCA	National Basketball Coaches Association
NBL	National Basketball League
NBPA	National Basketball Players Association
NCAA	National Collegiate Athletic Association
NCCAA	National Christian College Athletic Association
NEA	National Education Association
NFC	National Football Conference
NFHS	National Federation of State High School Associations
NFL	National Football League
NFLPA	National Football League Players Association
NGB	national governing body
NHL	National Hockey League
NHLPA	National Hockey League Players Association
NIA	National Intramural Association
NIAAA	National Interscholastic Athletic Administrators Association
NIRSA	National Intramural-Recreational Sports Association
NJCAA	National Junior College Athletic Association
NOC	National Olympic Committee

NPC	National Paralympic Committee
NSO	National Sport Organization
NTC	National Tennis Center
OCOG	Organizing Committee for the Olympic Games
OFSAA	Ontario Federation of School Athletic Associations
OGR	Olympic Golf Rankings
OSAA	Oregon School Activities Association
OSU	Ohio State University
PA	Players Association
PBA	Professional Bowlers Association
PBR	Professional Bull Riders
PED	performance-enhancing drug
PGA	Professional Golfers' Association
PASO	Pan American Sports Organization
R&A	Royal & Ancient (golf)
RBI	Reviving Baseball in the Inner Cities
SA	Surfing Australia
SAT	Scholastic Aptitude Test
SEC	Southeastern Conference
T&CP	Teaching and Club Professionals
UEFA	Union of European Football Associations
UFC	Ultimate Fighting Championship
UM	University of Michigan
UN	United Nations
UNESCO	United Nations Educational, Scientific and Cultural Organization
USADA	United States Anti-Doping Agency
USCAA	United States Collegiate Athletic Association
USFL	United States Football League
USGA	United States Golf Association
USLTA	United States Lawn Tennis Association
USNLTA	United States National Lawn Tennis Association
USNZ	University Sport New Zealand
USOC	United States Olympic Committee
USTA	United States Tennis Association
VANOC	Vancouver–Whistler Canada Organizing Committee
WADA	World Anti-Doping Agency
WCF	World Curling Federation
WFL	World Football League
WHA	World Hockey Association
WIAA	Washington Interscholastic Activities Association
WNBA	Women's National Basketball Association
WNBPA	Women's National Basketball Players Association
WTA	Women's Tennis Association
WWE	World Wrestling Entertainment
XFL	Xtreme Football League
YMCA	Young Men's Christian Association
YMHA	Young Men's Hebrew Association
YWCA	Young Women's Christian Association
YWHA	Young Women's Hebrew Association

Introduction to Sport Governance

Mary A. Hums
Joanne C. MacLean

The National Collegiate Athletic Association (NCAA) passes legislation granting autonomy
to the Power Five conferences. A National Football League (NFL) player gets suspended
for domestic abuse. A city's Parks and Recreation Department creates new programs
for people with disabilities and those who are overweight or obese. A campus recreation

center requires an identification card to enter the facility. The International Olympic Committee (IOC) changes the sports on the official program of the Olympic Games. The International Paralympic Committee (IPC) suspends the Russian Paralympic Committee over allegations of government- supported doping violations. These types of occurrences in the sport industry deal with issues of membership, regulation, programming, or organizational structure. All are related to governance and policy development in sport organizations. Many organizations in the industry act as governing bodies and make decisions about their everyday operations. This chapter sets the groundwork for you to see governance and policy development in action in the sport industry.

WHAT IS THE SPORT INDUSTRY?

Today's sport industry is continually expanding and evolving on a global scale. Sport is distinctive and remarkable in magnitude and influence, reaching billions of participants and followers. The mass media devote special coverage to the sporting world, recounting competitive, recreational, and leisure-time activities for a variety of age groups and participant levels. The latest stories and trends are the focus of many blogs, Twitter feeds, Instagram postings, and other forms of social media. Scholars study sport from each angle as well, including sport history, sport psychology, and sport management.

In your sport management academic career, by now you are well aware of the industry segments of this global industry, including professional sport, intercollegiate athletics, the Olympic and Paralympic Movements, recreational sport, facility management, event management, sport for people with disabilities, health and fitness, sport club management, interscholastic sport, sport marketing, and legal aspects of sport. Considering the numerous segments comprising the sport industry, what is the size and monetary value of this business we call sport?

SCOPE OF THE INDUSTRY

According to Heitner (2015), the value of the sport industry will grow from US$60.5 billion in 2014 to $73.5 billion in 2019. Media rights will comprise the greatest portion of this amount, followed by gate receipts, sponsorships, and merchandising. This is not just a North American phenomenon. Over the last five years, sport in the United Kingdom has become a £20 billion ($25 billion) industry, fueled by events such as the Olympic and Paralympic Games, Rugby World Cup, and the continued strong growth in football (soccer) (Critchlow, 2015).

Despite its size, the sport industry is a people-oriented, service-oriented industry. The importance of treating one's customers and employees in a positive and respectful manner has likely been widely discussed throughout all of your coursework. Most Sport Management courses deal with a micro approach to the industry, focusing on various specific areas such as marketing, facility management, event management, or financial issues. Governance courses, by contrast, take a macro view of sport organizations and will help you understand the big picture of how the various sport industry segments work together. Successful sport managers need conceptual skills (Chelladurai, 2014) to see the big picture, an important element in governance. Governance is more closely related to courses dealing with management, organizational behavior, or most especially, legal aspects of sport, which deal specifically with governance-related and policy-oriented issues. What, then, is the definition of *governance?*

DEFINITION OF GOVERNANCE

A common dictionary definition of *governance* is "the exercise of authority." Sometimes people mistakenly think of "governance" as meaning the "government" or elected political officials. It is much more than that. Sport managers must, of course, be aware of legislation or court decisions that affect them. In the sport industry, governance includes regulatory and service organizations. Governance is associated with power, authority, control, and high-level policy making in organizations. People involved in governance make decisions that set the tone for the entire organization.

Sport governance occurs mainly on three different levels—local, national, and international. An example of a local governance organization is the Kentucky High School Athletic Association (KHSAA) at the state level. On the national level, examples include the NFL, the National Intramural-Recreational Sports Association (NIRSA), USA Hockey, Hockey Canada, and Nippon Professional Baseball in Japan. International organizations include the IOC, IPC, Fédération Internationale de Football Association (FIFA, the international governing body for soccer), Fédération Internationale de Basketball Association (FIBA, the international governing body for basketball), and the International Association of Athletics Federations (IAAF, the international governing body for track and field, known internationally as athletics).

Governance structures within such organizations, while often similar, are not universally the same. Governance structures in North American sport differ from governance structures in European sport. For example, professional leagues in Europe use the promotion and relegation system in which basketball teams that finish at the bottom of a Division I league are relegated to Division II, while the top teams in Division II are promoted to Division I. This system is not used in professional sport leagues in North America. Even within North America, differences exist between governance structures in Canada and the United States. NCAA rules and regulations governing collegiate sport in the United States are different from the Canadian Interuniversity Sport (CIS) rules and regulations governing collegiate sport in Canada. The role of a country's government in sport also differs. Jamaica, for example, has a Ministry of Culture, Gender,

Entertainment and Sport (Ministry of Culture, Gender, Entertainment and Sport, 2017) Slovenia has a Ministry of Education, Science and Sport (Ministry of Education, Science and Sport, 2017). Again, this differs from the United States, where no federal government office exists to oversee sport in the country. Wouldn't it be interesting if the United States government had a cabinet position for a Department of Sport, similar to having a Department of State or a Department of Agriculture?

In the professional sport industry segment, Sharp, Moorman, and Claussen (2014) describe *governance* as being "roughly divided into governance of team sports by professional sport leagues and governance of individual sports by players associations operating professional tours" (p. 274). For international sport managers, according to Thoma and Chalip (1996), governance involves making effective choices among policy alternatives. They suggest three techniques sport managers can use in the international setting: ideology analysis, political risk analysis, and stakeholder analysis.

As you can see from the discussion above, sport governance is often easy to identify but difficult to define. Several authors have offered their thoughts on the subject. According to O'Boyle (2013, p. 1), governance, broadly speaking, is "The process of granting power, verifying performance, managing, leading, and/or administering within an organization." Ferkins, Shilbury, and McDonald (2009) state that sport governance is "the responsibility for the functioning and overall direction of the organization and is a necessary and institutionalized component of all sport codes from club level to national bodies, government agencies, sport service organizations and professional teams around the world" (p. 245). King (2017) acknowledges that governance includes both political and administrative aspects. For the purposes of this textbook, the authors of this book define *sport governance* as follows:

> Sport governance is the exercise of power and authority in sport organizations, including policy making, to determine organizational mission, membership, eligibility, and regulatory power, within the organization's appropriate local, national, or international scope.

We will study each element of this definition in this book.

What Is an Organization?

In order for sport governance to take shape, we must first have an organization that needs governing. Certainly, plenty of groups are involved with sport, but what truly identifies a group as an organization rather than just a group of people?

Chelladurai (2014) lists several attributes of an organization, including the following:

1. identity
2. program of activity
3. membership
4. clear boundaries

5. permanency
6. division of labor
7. hierarchy of authority
8. formal rules and procedures

To illustrate how an organization is different from just a group of people, let's attempt to apply these attributes to professional sport organizations and then to the group of people you met in college and regularly go out with on weekends.

1. IDENTITY.   Teams establish a public identity by their name, whether that name is the Cavaliers, the Lynx, the Dodgers, or Bayern Munich. Teams also have an established corporate identity separate from the players or the fans. In contrast, your group of friends usually does not have a name and is not an established business entity.

2. PROGRAM OF ACTIVITY.   A program of activity implies that an organization has a certain set of goals it wishes to achieve and that these goals are tied to its mission statement and its successful business operation. A basketball team wants to win a championship, and the people who work in its front office want to maximize revenues. A group of friends may have goals (for example, to go to an event), but it does not have a written set of goals it wishes to accomplish or a written mission statement.

3. MEMBERSHIP.   Organizations have set rules about membership. In order to play professional basketball, one would need a certain amount of experience at a certain level of play to be considered for "membership" in the league. In a group of friends the rules for membership may depend on who is mad at someone this week, whom you met at a party last week, or whom you have as your current Facebook friends.

4. CLEAR BOUNDARIES.   We know who plays on the Cavaliers or the Lynx because they have published, league-approved rosters. Any claim that "I play for the Cavaliers" can be easily verified. Groups of friends change from year to year, often from week to week or day to day, depending on who is now dating or angry at whom.

5. PERMANENCY.   True organizations have relative permanency, although the organizational members come and go. For example, Bayern Munich's current players are not the same people as when the franchise was new, but the Bayern Munich organization still exists. A group of friends also changes over time but is more likely than an organization to cease to exist as a group.

6. DIVISION OF LABOR.   Within organizations labor is divided among members. Tasks are determined, and then people are assigned to the tasks. Organizations clearly illustrate division of labor with organizational charts. The front office of a basketball team has specialization areas such as Marketing, Media Relations, Community Relations, and Ticket Sales.

However, a group of friends has no organizational chart with assigned duties, except perhaps for the designated driver.

7. HIERARCHY OF AUTHORITY.   An organizational chart also reflects an organization's hierarchy of authority. Who reports to who is clear from the lines and levels within the chart. At the top of the chart, a basketball team has a General Manager in charge of the day-to-day operations of the club; all others answer to her. In a hierarchy, people higher up are responsible for the actions of the people below them. In a group of friends, one seldom has any personal responsibility for the actions of others in the group.

8. FORMAL RULES AND PROCEDURES.   Organizations have formal rules and procedures, such as constitutions, bylaws, and operational manuals. Examples of some of these include office dress codes, policies on accepting gifts from clients, sexual harassment policies, or policies on acceptable use of organizational property. Friends don't have policy manuals outlining how the group will operate, what brand of smartphone everyone will use, or who can come along on Saturday night.

As you see from these very simplified examples, organizations are formalized entities with rules about mission, membership, structure, operation, and authority. You will read about these fundamental elements of governance in the chapters focusing on the different segments of the sport industry.

Regulatory Power

Another significant aspect of governance is that organizations have regulatory power over members, an ability to enforce rules and impose punishments (sanctions) if necessary. Different governing bodies possess this sanctioning power to different degrees. For example, the National Federation of State High School Associations, referred to as NFHS, establishes set competition rules for individual sports. Failing to follow these rules may prevent a particular school from participating in a certain event. The IOC has the power to ban athletes from competing in future Olympic Games if they test positive for performance-enhancing drugs, and Major League Baseball (MLB) can impose a luxury tax on teams whose payrolls exceed a certain amount. The NCAA determines recruiting rules for coaches, which, if violated, carry sanctions such as loss of scholarships for an ensuing season.

External and Internal Influences on Sport Organizations

Sport organizations do not exist in a vacuum. As part of the greater society in which they exist, they must anticipate changes in both their external and internal environments, preferably before they *must* react.

Chelladurai (2009) subdivides the organization's external environment into two categories: (1) the task or operating environment, sometimes referred to as the *proximal* (close) environment, and (2) the general environment, also called the *distal* (further removed) environment. Sport managers must be cognizant of what is happening in their external environments and adapt accordingly. Their internal environments are created through each organization's specific policies and procedures (Chelladurai, 2014).

As open systems with inputs, throughputs, and outputs, sport organizations are in a constant state of interaction with their various environments (Minter, 1998). Governance structures, therefore, must adapt to changes in an organization's internal and external environments. For example, as society increasingly disapproves of the use of performance-enhancing drugs by athletes, more and more sport organizations are toughening their policies and procedures regarding the use of banned substances; as a result, we see the formation of organizations such as the World Anti-Doping Agency (WADA). As another example, as more athletes at all levels are standing up for social causes, leagues and teams are responding by making sure the athletes can voice their opinions and not setting policies that would infringe on their right to free speech. These *internal* reactions to trends in the sport organization's *external* environment are made to adapt with the times.

The Five Rs of Good Governance

For a governing body to operate successfully, it must be structured in such a way that important information can flow throughout the organization and be disseminated externally to others needing this information. But what types of information are most important? According to Grevemberg (1999, p. 10), sport organizations need to be mindful of what he calls the "Five Rs":

1. *Regulations*—systems that report organizational governance structures, constitutions, legal control mechanisms, event selection criteria, and codes of eligibility, conduct, and ethics;
2. *Rules*—systems that report technical rules for the officiating and management of the respective sport's competitive events;
3. *Rankings*—systems that report and place athlete/team performances based on results and competitive criteria into numerical order from first to last place;
4. *Records*—systems that report the best performances ever accomplished by athletes/teams within competitions, time periods, or overall;
5. *Results*—systems that report the final standings and performance statistics from competitions.

If sport organizations can consistently apply the Five Rs across all their operations, they will find that governance can be consistent and efficient.

ORGANIZATIONAL UNITS AND DOCUMENTS IN SPORT GOVERNANCE

How many of you have ever taken a language class? Maybe you took Spanish or German or Arabic. When you started the class, you had to take small steps. First you learned the alphabet and then small words like numbers or food. Finally, you put together sentences and paragraphs and were able to know how to ask directions, meet new people, and find the washroom. So it is with learning governance. Governance has a certain language, with basic terms and concepts we must know in order to understand governance and the inner workings of sport organizations. In terms of sport governance, organizations are made up of distinct units with varying degrees of authority and responsibility. In addition, sport organizations usually maintain a set of documents dealing with governance structures. This section briefly introduces some of these organizational units and documents.

General Assemblies

Many sport organizations (for example, the IOC, International Paralympic Committee, NCAA, and NIRSA) are voluntary in nature. Nevertheless, these organizations employ paid staff members. The size of the headquarters staff can vary widely. NIRSA, for example, has approximately 25 employees, while the NCAA headquarters employs over 500 people. The paid staff members handle the day-to-day operations of organizations, although they are not the ones who actually govern the organizations.

The primary governing body for many sport organizations is usually called a General Assembly; it may also be called a Congress or a General Business Meeting. In many sport organizations, the members of this governing body are volunteers. According to Chelladurai and Madella (2006), "Voluntary organizations are truly political systems; power is continuously exerted by professionals and volunteers to influence decisions and actions in order to satisfy personal or group needs" (p. 84).

A General Assembly for a sport organization usually convenes on a regular basis (often yearly). The members of the General Assembly, selected in accordance with an organization's constitution and bylaws, vote as a group on legislation, rules, policies, and procedures. This type of governing body generally elects officers such as the President, Vice Presidents, and Secretary. It also utilizes several standing committees assigned specific tasks, as will be discussed later. Its meetings, or sessions, are generally conducted using a common set of rules of operation. One of the most commonly used sets of guidelines for running a meeting is called *Robert's Rules of Order* (Robert et al., 2011). Those of you who are in a fraternity or sorority may recognize these from house meetings you attended. These rules are often referred to as Parliamentary Procedure, and most organizations designate a person who is familiar with Robert's Rules as the organizational Parliamentarian. It is the Parliamentarian's job to make sure the group members properly follow Robert's Rules of Order so that discussions can proceed in an orderly manner. Meetings organized using Robert's Rules usually follow this order of events:

1. call to order
2. approval of the minutes of the previous meeting
3. committee reports
4. old business
5. new business
6. announcements
7. a call to adjourn the meeting

During the meeting, when someone wants to make a suggestion for action by the group, he makes what is called a "motion to take the action." Another person from the group must then second the motion. Then, the meeting chair allows debate on the action to begin. During this time the motion can be amended and if so, the members must then vote on the amended motion. When the debate is complete, the chair calls for a vote. Votes are taken by a count of hands, by voice, or sometimes by a paper ballot, depending on the topic. If no decision can be reached because, for example, the members need more information, a motion can be tabled—that is, set aside for action at the next meeting. When all the business of the group is complete, someone makes a motion to adjourn the meeting, and after another member seconds that motion, the meeting ends. Using these rules for the standard operation of a business meeting helps ensure fairness and enables all members to voice their opinions in an orderly manner (Introduction to Robert's Rules of Order, n.d.). Typically the agendas for General Assembly meetings and the issues on which they vote come from a body known as an Executive Committee or Management Council.

www

Robert's Rules of Order
www.robertsrules.org

Executive Committees, Governing Boards, and Management Councils

Executive Committees, sometimes called Governing Boards or Management Councils, are small subsets of an organization's General Assembly. Members of the General Assembly select a group, usually from 5 to 20 members, to serve on the organization's Executive Committee. Many believe that the Executive Committee is where the "real power" in a sport organization lies. This group usually generates the agenda action items on which the General Assembly votes. If the Executive Committee does not endorse an idea, it will almost never be brought to the General Assembly for a vote. In addition, this group meets formally more frequently, often two or three times a year, in order to deal with issues that may come up between

General Assembly meetings. It may also deal with special issues via Skype, web conferencing such as GoToMeeting.com or WebEx, conference calls, or through e-mail.

Standing Committees

Sport organizations also designate standing committees with specific responsibilities within their governance structures. The type and number of standing committees vary by organization. The World Curling Federation (WCF), for example, has committees (which they call Commissions) for the following areas:

- Finance
- Competition and Rules
- Governance
- Athletes
- Zonal
- Judicial (World Curling Federation, 2014, p. 1)

Compare the simplicity of the WCF to the standing committee structure of the much larger international governing body for football (soccer), FIFA:

- Appeal Committee
- Audit and Compliance Committee
- Beach Soccer Committee
- Bureau 2018 FIFA World Cup Russia
- Bureau for the FIFA World Cup Qualifiers
- Committee for Club Football
- Committee for Fair Play and Social Responsibility
- Committee for Women's Football and the FIFA Women's World Cup
- Compensation Sub-Committee
- Development Committee
- Disciplinary Committee
- Emergency Bureau for the FIFA World Cup Qualifiers
- Ethics Committee
- Finance Committee
- Football Stakeholders Committee
- Futsal Committee
- Governance and Review Committee
- Legal Committee
- Marketing and TV Committee
- Media Committee
- Member Associations Committee
- Organising Committee for FIFA Competitions

- Organising Committee for FIA Club World Cup
- Organising Committee for the FIFA Confederations Cup
- Organising Committee for the FIFA U-17 Women's World Cup
- Organising Committee for the FIFA U-17 World Cup
- Organising Committee for the FIFA U-20 Women's World Cup
- Organising Committee for the FIFA U-20 World Cup
- Organising Committee for the FIFA World Cup
- Organising Committee for the Olympic Football Tournament
- Players' Status Committee
- Referees Committee
- Security and Integrity Committee
- Strategic Committee (FIFA, 2017, p. 1)

Ad Hoc Committees

At times, sport organizations face issues that need to be dealt with on a short-term basis. For example, perhaps the organization is planning to host a special fundraising event or play a home game at a site other than its usual home arena. Because the event may just occur one time, the organization will assemble an *ad hoc*, or temporary, committee that is in charge of the event. Unlike standing committees that deal with ongoing concerns, once the event is over, the ad hoc committee usually ceases to exist. An ad hoc committee usually only operates for a short period of time, generally less than one year. Occasionally, a topic initially addressed by an ad hoc committee will become an ongoing concern and the organization will then establish a standing committee to address it.

Executive Staff

The people who serve on a General Assembly or Executive Council are almost always volunteers. Their business expenses may be paid, but they are not employees of the sport organization. The people who are employed by the sport organization to run the daily operations are called Executive or Professional Staff. People in these positions have titles such as Executive Director, General Manager, Marketing Director, Sport Administrator, Technical Director, or Event Coordinator. These individuals are paid sport management professionals, employed by the governing body. They work in the organization's headquarters, as opposed to volunteers who may be located anywhere in the world. For example, the Executive Staff of the NCAA works daily in offices in Indianapolis, Indiana. The Athletic Directors on NCAA committees, however, are located at their home institutions across the nation and come together only at designated times during the year. As another example, the staff of the World Archery Federation (also known as International Federation of Archery, FITA) works at the headquarters of the organization in Lausanne, Switzerland. The elected Executive Committee members, however, operate from their respective national federations and meet twice a year (Hums, MacLean, & Zintz, 2011). Similarly, the

Executive Staff for the International Paralympic Committee (IPC) work in the organization's headquarters in Bonn, Germany. They run the organization on a daily basis, planning events, handling financial matters, and marketing upcoming events. The volunteers, however, who work with a specific sport such as Ice Sledge Hockey, may be located in Canada, Norway, and the United States. They will meet together at a Sport Technical Committee meeting, for example, at a designated time and place each year or may hold a business session during the Paralympic Games.

Constitutions and Bylaws

Almost all sport organizations have documents outlining the basic functions of the organization, usually called the constitution and bylaws. An organization's constitution acts as a governing document that includes statements about the organization's core principles and values. Bylaws, also governing documents, are more operational in nature, outlining how an organization should conduct its business in terms of elections, meetings, and so on. For examples of what these types of documents include, see Exhibit 1.1, a Table of Contents from the Constitution of the Amateur Athletic Union (AAU), and Exhibit 1.2, a Table of Contents from the National Junior College Athletic Association (NJCAA).

Examples of these different organizational units and documents will be discussed throughout each of the industry segment chapters in this text.

WHY STUDY GOVERNANCE?

Given all the areas to study within the academic discipline of Sport Management, why study governance? Three main reasons come to mind: (a) you need to understand the "big picture", (b) you need to understand how governance fits within the Sport Management curriculum, and (c) you definitely will use your knowledge of sport governance in whichever industry segment you work.

Understanding the Big Picture

In studying governance, you will truly be challenged to put together all the pieces of the sport industry. As mentioned above, studying sport governance requires the ability to see the big picture, to understand how individual sport organizations fit into the greater industry, and to see the similarities and differences among the various industry segments. Sport governance also prepares you for the global sport industry you will be entering. Sport managers who lack the ability to see how their organizations fit in to the global picture guarantee the ultimate failure of their organizations. With an understanding of sport governance, you will see how the governing structures of seemingly dissimilar industry segments such as Intercollegiate Athletics and the Olympic Movement have much more in common than you would think.

ARTICLE I: Governance of the Union

A. Adoption and Amendments
   a. Adoption
   b. Amendments
      i. Presentation
      ii. Time and Form of Publication
      iii. Consideration
      iv. Urgent Amendment
      v. Language, Stylistic, Housekeeping Changes
B. Membership
   c. Conditions for Membership
   d. Categories
      i. District Member
      ii. Club Member
      iii. Individual Member
      iv. Allied Member
C. Congress
   e. Composition
      i. District Representatives
      ii. Sport Committee Representatives
      iii. The National Officers
      iv. Past Officers of the AAU
      v. Allied Member Representatives
      vi. Members-at-Large
   f. Powers
   g. Vote(s) in Congress
D. Board of Directors
   h. Composition
   i. Powers
   j. Officers
      i. Titles
      ii. Elections
      iii. Qualifications
   k. Term of Office
      i. Term Limits
   l. Duties
      i. President
      ii. Vice Presidents
      iii. Secretary
      iv. Treasurer

m. Vacancies
   i. President
   ii. First Vice-President
   iii. Second Vice-President
   iv. Secretary
   v. Treasurer
n. Emergency Powers of Officers
o. Committees
   i. Administrative Committees
      1. Finance Committee
         a. Composition
         b. Duties
      2. Insurance Committee
         a. Composition
         b. Duties
      3. Legislation Committee
         a. Composition
         b. Duties
      4. Nominations and Elections Committee
         a. Composition
         b. Duties
      5. Redistricting Committee
         a. Composition
         b. Duties
      6. Committee Structure and Procedures
         a. Chairs
         b. Meetings
   ii. National Sport Committees
      1. Chair
      2. Composition
      3. Removal/Replacement
      4. Meetings
      a. Regular
      b. Special
      5. Voting
      6. Quorum
      7. Duties
      8. Dissolution
   iii. Special Committees/Ad Hoc Committees

Source: AAU (n.d.).

exhibit 1.2 National Junior College Athletic Association Bylaws

Article I	**Membership**
Article II	**Election of NJCAA Elective Officers and Terms of Service**
Article III	**Meetings**
Article IV	**Administrative**
Article V	**Student-Athlete Eligibility**
Article VI	**Grants-in-Aid and Recruitment**
Article VII	**Member College Sport Policies and Guidelines**
Article VIII	**Procedures for Appeal**
Article IX	**Constitution and Bylaw Changes**
Article X	**Policies Governing and Awarding of NJCAA Championship Events**
Article XI	**Policies for Conducting NJCAA Championship Events**
Article XII	**Team Sport District Qualification for National Tournaments**
Article XIII	**NJCAA National Championships**
Article XIV	**NJCAA Championships**

Source: NJCAA (2016).

Governance in the Sport Management Curriculum

As the number of Sport Management academic programs has increased greatly in the past few decades, so have issues of program quality. From the very beginning, governance has been an integral part of Sport Management education. In 1987 two academic organizations, the North American Society for Sport Management (NASSM) and the National Association for Sport and Physical Education (NASPE), formed a task force to develop curricular standards (Parkhouse, 2001). Recognizing the importance of learning governance, the task force included sport governance as one of the content areas required for Sport Management programs to attain NASSM/NASPE approval. The premise was that students must be familiar with governance agencies, their authority, organizational structure, and functions.

Sport Management Training Internationally

Contributed by Thierry Zintz

Just as training sport managers in good governance practices is important in North American Sport Management programs, it is also important on the international scene. The International Olympic Committee, in collaboration with scholars from around the world, has set up training programs for managers working in the governance of National Olympic Committees (NOCs) and International Federations (IFs). The programs are offered by Olympic Solidarity and culminate in the program known as MEMOS (Executive Masters in Sports Organization Management) (IOC Olympic Studies Center, 2012).

Through this program, Olympic Solidarity provides scholarships for sports leaders supported by their NOCs and accepted by the MEMOS selection committee to take this course. It is recognized internationally and offered by a network of universities partnered with Olympic Solidarity.

MEMOS takes the form of modules, each focusing on one aspect of sport management. The key is for the participants, assisted by a tutor, to complete a project aimed at improving an aspect of the management of their organization. Through a combination of residential modules and distance learning, MEMOS allows participants to learn while continuing their work in their respective sport organizations. MEMOS is offered in English, French, and Spanish.

Source: Hums, M. A., MacLean, & J. C., Zintz, T. (2011). *La gouvernance au coeur des politiques des organisations sportives*, 1re ed., De Boeck Supérieur, Bruxelles, p. 320. Used with permission.

As Sport Management programs have continued to evolve, the NASSM/NASPE approval process has been phased out and new accreditation standards have been established.

Today, Sport Management education programs can be fully accredited by an organization known as COSMA—the Commission on Sport Management Accreditation. According to NASSM (n.d., para. 1), COSMA "is a specialized accrediting body that promotes and recognizes excellence in sport management education in colleges and universities at the baccalaureate and graduate levels." Governance is now included in the COSMA documents as one of the common professional components.

COSMA
http://cosmaweb.org/

The educational examples above and in the accompanying box illustrate the international nature of the sport industry. They also reinforce why learning about governing structures on all levels will help develop your understanding of how this worldwide industry operates.

Using Knowledge of Governance in Your Career

Understanding governance structures is important for any career in sport management. If you work at a bank, you need to know the rules for your workplace and probably some basic federal and state laws. But for the most part, especially at an entry-level position, you will not be interacting with the people who write the policies for your bank or for the broader banking industry. In sport, however, especially because of the ramifications of enforcement, you will need to be keenly aware of governance structures and issues. You will also need to understand different contexts of governance. There will be governance issues dealing with a given sport and its rules as well as governance issues dealing with the business side of sport. You will need to know where the power lies in your organization, and studying governance can help you understand this. You will need to know which governing bodies you will deal with in your industry segment. If you work in a college athletic department, you must understand how you relate to governance structures of your university, your conference, and the NCAA. In professional sport, if you deal with players associations or players unions, you will need to know how they relate to the decisions you make. In high school sport, the power rests at the state or provincial level in organizations such as the Indiana State High School Athletic Association (ISHSAA) and the Ontario Federation of School Athletic Associations (OFSAA). A recreation director in a City Parks and Recreation Department may answer to the mayor or the City Council. If you work for a sport federation such as FIBA, you will have to be knowledgeable about the federation's rules and regulations dealing with athlete eligibility.

Studying sport governance gives you a perspective on where you fit into your sport organization and where your sport organization fits into its industry segment. For example, if you work in the front office of a MLB team, you will need to understand various levels of governance in your job, from the club's front office to the League Office to the Commissioner's Office. In Olympic and Paralympic Sport, you may be involved in interactions among IFs, National Governing Bodies, NOCs, and Organizing Committees of the Olympic Games. In intercollegiate athletics, you will need to know basic NCAA compliance rules to avoid placing your school in danger of NCAA sanctions. If you work for the Commonwealth Games Federation (CGF), you will need to understand eligibility rules for athletes, so that any athletes you are responsible for do not jeopardize their eligibility. In sport, you are likely to have more direct interactions with governing bodies and policy makers than in many other industries. You need to understand who has the power and where the power lies in any sport organization you work or interact with.

Finally, the importance of sport managers acting in an ethical manner in any sport governance situation cannot be overstated. Sport managers face ethical dilemmas on a daily basis. How they deal with them is a measure of their own ethical nature and that of their organization. For this reason this textbook devotes a chapter to ethical decision making and the importance of corporate social responsibility and discusses various ethical issues sport managers may face in different industry segments.

SUMMARY

The sport industry continues to grow and develop on a global scale. Studying sport governance allows you to take a big-picture approach to this global industry. Learning about the governing structures and documents for sport organizations illustrates where power and authority exist within the industry. This area of study is sufficiently important to be discussed in the COSMA accreditation documentation, reemphasizing the importance of understanding this complex, fascinating aspect of the sport industry.

In your previous Sport Management classes, you learned about basic managerial activities and functions. For purposes of this textbook, we will focus on four of these important areas in Chapters 2 through 4—planning, decision making, strategic management and policy development, and ethical decision making. These activities are the heart and soul of the governance process and have separate chapters devoted to them, further explaining their roles in the governance of sport organizations.

The remainder of the text guides you through selected industry segments and explains how sport governance is implemented in those segments, using numerous examples to illustrate governance in action. It is our hope that you will enjoy these challenging and interesting areas of study within sport management.

case STUDY

INTRODUCTION TO GOVERNANCE

You are the Sport Director for the State Summer Games in your home state. The Games take place every year, and the program of sports and events has to be agreed upon by the Games' General Assembly two years in advance. You are part of a group designated to propose the addition of a new sport to the program. How would the organization proceed on deciding whether or not to add a new sport to the program?

1. Research the existing program for your home state and select a sport not currently a part of the program that you would like the group to consider.
2. What type of information should your group gather to help in making this decision?
3. With which organizations and governing bodies will the committee need to interact?
4. When the proposal comes to the General Assembly, describe how Robert's Rules of Order would work at that meeting in making the decision about adding a new sport to the program.

CHAPTER questions

1. Choose a sport organization and then use Chelladurai's model of organizational attributes from this chapter to define the different elements of that organization.

2. Find two sample sport organization constitutions or bylaws. Compare the two for content. Explain why you think they are different or similar.

3. Using the definition of *sport governance* from this chapter, choose a sport organization and identify the different parts of the definition in that organization.

FOR ADDITIONAL INFORMATION

1. *The International* Olympic Committee Organization: IOC. (n.d): https://www.olympic.org/about-ioc-institution

2. The Structure of the Salt Lake City Winter Olympic Games: The Olympic Movement: https://stillmed.olympic.org/media/Document%20Library/OlympicOrg/Documents/Games-Salt-Lake-City-2002-Winter-Olympic-Games/Fundamentals-and-Ceremonies/Fundamentals-and-Ceremonies-3-4-Salt-Lake-City-2002.pdf

3. Michigan State Youth Soccer Association: MSYSA. (2017). MSYSA mission statement: www.michiganyouthsoccer.org/Page721.aspx

4. SurfAid, a non-profit surfing organization's governance structure: www.surfaid.org/governance

5. WNBA Players' Association Governance: WNBPA. (2017). Leadership: https://wnbpa.com/leadership/

6. What is good governance? Sport Ireland. (2017). What is good governance: www.sportireland.ie/Governing_Bodies/Governance/What-Is-Good-Governance/

REFERENCES

AAU. (n.d.). Constitution of the Amateur Athletic Union of the United States, Inc (AAU). Retrieved from http://image.aausports.org/codebook/article_I.pdf

Chelladurai, P. (2009). *Managing organizations for sport and physical activity: A systems perspective* (3rd ed.). Scottsdale, AZ: Holcomb Hathaway.

Chelladurai, P. (2014). *Managing organizations for sport and physical activity: A systems perspective* (4th ed.). Scottsdale, AZ: Holcomb Hathaway.

Chelladurai, P., & Madella, A. (2006). *Human resource management in Olympic sport organizations*. Champaign, IL: Human Kinetics.

Critchlow, A. (2015, May 3). Britain's sport industry hitting top form. *The Telegraph*. Retrieved from www.telegraph.co.uk/finance/11580773/Britains-sport-industry-hitting-top-form.html

Ferkins, L., Shilbury, D., & McDonald, G. (2009). Board involvement in strategy: Advancing the governance of sport organizations. *Journal of Sport Management, 23*, 245–277.

FIFA. (2017). Standing committees. Retrieved from www.fifa.com/about-fifa/committees/standing-committees.html

Grevemberg, D. (1999, May). Information technology: A solution for effective Paralympic Sport administration. Paper presented at the VISTA 1999 Paralympic Sport Conference, Cologne, Germany.

Heitner, D. (2015, October 19). Sports industry to reach $73.5 by 2019. *Forbes*. Retrieved from www.forbes.com/sites/darrenheitner/2015/10/19/sports-industry-to-reach-73-5-billion-by-2019/#38894ab31585

Hums, M. A., MacLean, J. C., & Zintz, T. (2011). *La gouvernance au coeur des politiques des organisations sportives*. Traduction et adaptation de la 2e édition américaine. Bruxelles, Belgique: Groupe De Boeck.

Introduction to Robert's Rules of Order. (n.d.). Retrieved from www.robertsrules.org/rulesintro.htm

IOC Olympic Studies Center. (2012). *Post-graduate courses offering Olympic based content*. Author: Lausanne, Switzerland.

King, N. (2017). *Sport governance: An introduction*. Oxon: Routledge.

Ministry of Culture, Gender, Entertainment and Sport. (2017). Home page. Retrieved from http://mcges.gov.jm/

Ministry of Education, Science and Sport. (2017). In focus. Retrieved from www.mizs.gov.si/en/

Minter, M. K. (1998). Organizational behavior. In J. B. Parks, B. R. K. Zanger, & J. Quarterman (Eds.), *Contemporary sport management* (pp. 79–89). Champaign, IL: Human Kinetics.

NASSM. (n.d.). Program accreditation. Retrieved from www.nassm.com/InfoAbout/NASSM/ProgramAccreditation

NJCAA. (2016). 2016–2017 handbook changes. Retrieved from http://static.psbin.com/o/m/lbgilmsvmjx1cp/Online_HB_11.1.2016.pdf

O'Boyle, I. (2013). Managing organizational performance in sport. In D. Hassan & J. Lusted (Eds.), *Managing sport: Social and cultural perspectives* (pp. 1–16). Oxon: Routledge.

Parkhouse, B. L. (2001). *The management of sport: Its foundation and application* (3rd ed.). Boston, MA: McGraw-Hill.

Robert, H. M., Honemann, D. H., Balch, T. J., & Seabold, D. E. (2011). *Robert's Rules of Order newly revised* (11th ed.). Cambridge, MA: Da Capo.

Sharp, L. A., Moorman, A. M., & Claussen, C. L. (2014). *Sport law: A managerial approach* (3rd ed.). Scottsdale, AZ: Holcomb Hathaway.

Thoma, J. E., & Chalip, L. (1996). *Sport governance in the global community*. Morgantown, WV: Fitness Information Technology.

World Curling Federation. (2014). *WCF constitution*. Perth, Scotland: Author.

Managerial Functions
Related to Governance

Mary A. Hums
Joanne C. MacLean

Sport managers carry out a myriad of managerial activities and functions on a daily basis. The four functions of management have been defined as planning, organizing, leading, and evaluating (Chelladurai, 2014). Sport managers dealing with governance issues must be able to carry out all these functions, but two functions, planning and organizing, are more critical to governance than others and will be discussed in this chapter. Decision making, a subset of leading, is also essential to sport managers dealing with governance issues, and it will be discussed here as well. Sport managers perform these functions daily. This chapter provides a brief overview of these important managerial activities and their relationship to sport governance.

PLANNING

The Importance of Planning for Sport Organizations

Sport organizations need to plan because the sport industry presents a complex environment. Whether it is the Olympic Games bringing together nations or a high school softball tournament featuring local teams, the sport industry requires interaction and cooperation in order for teams, leagues, tours, and events to be successful. What are the specific purposes of planning? According to the Australian Sports Commission (2012, p. 1), planning serves to help a sport organization:

- become proactive rather than reactive—to clarify club purposes and direction;
- initiate and influence outcomes in favor of the club;
- exert more control over its destiny—deciding where it wants to be in the future;
- adopt a more systematic approach to change and reduce resistance to change;
- improve financial performance and use resources effectively;
- increase awareness of its operating environment (for example, competitors, government policy, threats);
- improve organisational control and coordination of activities;
- develop teamwork off the field.

Given these benefits of planning, why then do some people resist efforts to plan (Bryce, 2008)?

Resistance to Planning

People tend to develop comfort zones. They do things a certain way because "We've always done it that way." To these individuals, trying to implement a plan to do something different or new is a challenge they do not wish to undertake. Sometimes people who have worked with an organization for many years respond to planning initiatives with "Why should we do this? We've done this a million times before, and we know no one really looks at these things. Then five years later they ask us to do it again, and they ignore us again." Longtime employees may resist changes to operations they developed. Finally, there are those who simply lack the ability to plan and are intimidated by the process. Good sport managers make planning a priority and learn how to deal effectively with those employees who resist the importance of planning.

Types of Plans

Sport managers must be able to develop both short-term and long-term plans. They must develop timetables so projects and events will take place as smoothly as possible. *Short-term planning* refers to planning projects and events that will occur within the next one to three years. For example, with the Olympic and Paralympic Games, test events in all venues are run within a year or two of the start of the Games. At a new stadium, contracts with concessionaires and security are finalized in the year before the stadium opens.

In contrast, *long-term planning* involves planning that extends three or more years. For example, the International Olympic Committee (IOC) awards the Olympic and Paralympic Games to a host city seven years before the flame is lit to open the Games in that city. Sport teams deciding to build new stadiums must begin working with architects and contractors at least five years before the first beverage is poured at a game. Within these long-term plans, short-term plans must be implemented. Returning to our stadium example, the people who work in presentation (coordinating the music, announcements, etc., during an event) need to be able to work with the sound system (short-term planning). However, before a sound system in a venue can be checked, all the proper infrastructure for the power must be in place (long-term planning). All these plans must be carefully sequenced for the sport organization to be successful.

Long-term and short-term plans are not the only types of plans sport managers need to develop. For example, there are standing plans and single-use plans (Chelladurai, 2014). *Standing plans* refer to plans that are put in place and then referred to continuously as certain events repeat. For example, a facility manager working at a Major League Baseball team (MLB) stadium needs to have parking and traffic plans to use at every home game for the season. *Single-use plans* refer to plans developed for events that may occur just once. For example, ESPN2's College Game Day may come to your city for the first time and plans need to be made for this one-time event.

The Planning Process

Sport organizations need to follow a set process to establish effective short-term and long-term plans. For some sport organizations, this process may begin with a vision statement. Other organizations will start with a mission statement and then take the following steps (adapted from VanderZwaag, 1998):

1. vision/mission statement
2. goals
3. objectives
4. tactics
5. roles
6. evaluation

The next sections examine each step in the planning process and use examples to illustrate the different steps. The focus is on the sport organization's front-office planning, rather than on-the-field plans such as the Cleveland Indians' objective to win the World Series and the University of Notre Dame women's basketball team's objective to win the National Collegiate Athletic Association (NCAA) tournament. As a sport manager, you most likely will be working in off-the-field careers, so the focus of this chapter is on goals and objectives dealing with front-office matters such as increasing ticket sales or securing sponsorship packages. For sport organizations to effectively move into the future, they must establish both long- and short-term plans. Because sport governance issues are generally broad in nature and affect the entire sport organization, any course of action dealing with governance issues must be carefully planned.

Vision Statements

A number of sport organizations begin their planning process by developing what is known as a vision statement. According to Fernandes (2016, paras. 2 & 5), "A vision statement can be as simple as a single sentence or can span a short paragraph . . . Vision statements are future-based and are meant to inspire and give direction to the employees of the company, rather than to customers."

Vision statements are different from mission statements in that vision statements focus on the organization's future aspirations and values while mission statements focus on an organization's purpose.

The vision for the International Paralympic Committee (IPC) states "To enable Para athletes to achieve sporting excellence and inspire and excite the world" (International Paralympic Committee, n.d., para. 2). British Columbia School Sports vision is that "Students in British Columbia schools will benefit from participation in physical activity and sport" (BCSS, 2016, para. 3). As you can see, these are quite brief and aspirational in nature. Mission statements, as you will see next, are more concrete.

Mission Statements

Sport organizations are a lot like sailboats. Without a rudder to steer, it does not matter how much wind there is—the boat will not go in its intended direction. It will still float, but it will not get where the crew wants it to go. What gives a sport organization its direction?

Direction is established early in the planning process with the organization's mission statement. As previously stated, a *mission statement* focuses on an organization's purpose. More specifically, it

1. describes who we are
2. describes what we do
3. uses concise terms
4. uses language that is understandable to people inside and outside the sport organization
5. communicates the organization's purpose, philosophy, and values

A well-written mission statement does not need to be a lengthy document. It may be only 30 to 40 words, or two or three sentences long, although some organizational mission statements will incorporate a few short paragraphs. In a perfect world, a sport organization's mission statement should fit on the back of a business card. All organizational planning documents should flow from the mission statement. As you read the mission statements in this book, keep in mind they are living documents that are subject to change.

In this section we will use a minor league baseball team as an example, starting with the mission statements of existing franchises. The mission statement for the Round Rock Express (2017, paras. 1–3), a AAA minor league baseball team is:

> The Round Rock Express continues to dedicate itself to promoting America's national pastime in a safe, fun, friendly and exciting atmosphere that allows fans and players alike to enjoy the game.
>
> By employing the best staff in minor league baseball, we have continually laid a foundation that helps us take care of the three groups of people who allow us to work in and for the game we love: our fans, our sponsors and our players.
>
> We are devoted to providing all of our fans with affordable, family-friendly baseball. We offer our sponsors maximum exposure through a unique environment of marketability. Our players are given the best opportunities to achieve their goals through the exceptional facilities, qualified personnel and professional atmosphere we provide.
>
> As an organization, we, the Round Rock Express, are dedicated to this mission and we will settle for nothing less than achieving and growing these goals.

The Hagerstown Suns (2017, paras. 1–3), a single-A level team, posts the following mission statement:

> The Hagerstown Suns are committed to promoting America's national pastime while creating a safe, friendly, exciting environment for fans, sponsors and players to enjoy the game.
>
> A hard-working, innovative staff continually strives for excellence to produce an enjoyable experience for families, friends, sponsors and players. The front office members lay a strong foundation to build success.

We are dedicated to providing affordable, quality entertainment for fans of all ages. We help businesses reach the market in which they operate. We give players excellent facilities, qualified personnel and a professional environment to help them achieve their goals. We respect—and love—the game.

We, the Hagerstown Suns, will not settle for anything less than these goals as we work to make the Hagerstown community a better place through baseball.

These mission statements are relatively similar. Both clearly state that minor league baseball is about fun and affordable family entertainment. Anyone who has attended a minor league baseball game recently would agree that these statements describe what it is all about—a fun atmosphere, inexpensive food, and between-inning promotional contests for fans of all ages.

Goals

Different textbooks use differing definitions for *goals* and *objectives*. Sometimes the terms are even used interchangeably. In this textbook, however, *goals* are defined as broad, qualitative statements that provide general direction for a sport organization. "Setting goals helps define the direction that a business will take. Goals should align with your business' mission and vision statements" (Norman, 2016, para. 3). For example, a minor league baseball team may have the following goals:

Goal #1 Increase attendance

Goal #2 Increase sponsorship revenues

Objectives

As opposed to goals, which are qualitative in nature, *objectives* are defined as quantitative statements that help a sport organization determine if it is fulfilling its goals. They are measurable, realistic, and clear (Norman, 2016; Parkhouse, Turner, & Milloch, 2012). Another way to think of objectives is that they are SMART – Specific, Measurable, Achievable, Realistic, and Timely (Siddiqui, 2015). Because objectives can be measured, they are useful tools in evaluating both employee and organizational performance. To be measurable, objectives always contain quantifiable measures such as numbers, percentages, or monetary values. Objectives are tied directly to achieving specific goals. For example:

Goal #1 Increase attendance

    Objective #1 Increase game-day walk-up sales by 5 percent

    Objective #2 Increase group ticket sales by 10 percent

Goal #2 Increase sponsorship revenues

    Objective #1 Secure five new corporate sponsors

    Objective #2 Increase the value of existing sponsorships by 5 percent

Measurable objectives are important in two ways: first, they can be used in employee and organizational evaluations and, second, they are necessary because it is difficult to manage something you cannot measure!

Tactics

Once sport managers establish their goals and objectives, they must determine specifically how to achieve them. These specific how-to steps are called tactics. (Some textbooks use the term *strategies*, but to avoid confusion with strategic planning principles, *tactics* is the term used here.) *Tactics* are the specific actions sport managers take to achieve organizational objectives. For example:

Goal #1 Increase attendance

    Objective #1 Increase game-day walk-up sales by 5 percent

        Tactic #1 Add two new promotional nights (bobblehead giveaway and $1 hot dog night)

        Tactic #2 Purchase ten 30-second advertising slots on the new local country radio station

Goal #2 Increase sponsorship revenues

    Objective #1 Secure five new corporate sponsors

        Tactic #1 Have each sales rep contact ten new local corporations

        Tactic #2 Offer special first-year benefits to new sponsors (extra tickets)

Roles

After the tactics have been determined, the responsibilities for carrying out those tactics must be assigned. Roles refer to the organizational units specifically responsible for carrying out the sport organization's tactics and the behaviors needed to achieve success (VanderZwaag, 1998). For example:

Goal #1 Increase attendance

    Objective #1 Increase game-day walk-up sales by 5 percent

        Tactic #1 Add two new promotional nights (bobble-head giveaway and $1 hot dog night)

        Role Ticket Office, Marketing

Goal #2 Increase sponsorship revenues

    Objective #1 Secure five new corporate sponsors

        Tactic #1 Have each sales rep contact ten new local corporations

        Role Marketing, Sales

Evaluation

In the final step in the planning process, sport managers must evaluate the planning process to see if they are fulfilling the organization's mission statement by successfully completing the stated goals, objectives, tactics, and roles. For example:

Goal #1 Increase attendance

Objective #1 Increase game-day walk-up sales by 5 percent

Tactic #1 Add two new promotional nights (bobble-head giveaway and $1 hot dog night)

Role Ticket Office, Marketing

Evaluation Determine the actual percentage increase and compare to 5 percent target. Reward responsible employees appropriately.

Goal #2 Increase sponsorship revenues

Objective #1 Secure five new corporate sponsors

Tactic #1 Have each sales rep contact ten new local corporations

Role Marketing, Sales

Evaluation Determine the actual number of new sponsors and compare to target (five new sponsors). Reward responsible employees appropriately.

This brief example shows how the planning process flows from one step to the next. It also shows that the planning process does not consist of a number of separate, fragmented steps but rather is a seamless garment. The process is part of the big picture of the entire organization. Note, too, that all the steps in the process can be traced directly back to, and should be consistent with, the organization's mission statement.

The Role of Planning in Governance

Sport governance is complex and ever-changing. Sport organizations can be as small as a city soccer league or as massive as the Olympic and Paralympic Movements. Whatever the size of the sport organization, those in charge of the governance structures must plan accordingly. Examples of organizations that planned both well and poorly come from the Olympic Games. Local organizing committees for the Athens 2004 and the Rio 2016 Summer Games ended up running millions of dollar and euro deficits from construction cost overruns. Meanwhile, the London 2012 Olympic and Paralympic Games came in under budget. An organization without a well-thought-out and organized plan complete with a mission statement, goals, objectives, tactics, roles, and an evaluation system is destined to fail. Remember: if you fail to plan, you plan to fail.

ORGANIZING

The traditional view of organizing revolves around staffing. We usually think of establishing tasks, determining who will be responsible for those tasks, and then placing those people into a hierarchy, commonly illustrated by an organizational chart. *Organizing* can be defined as "the process of delegating and coordinating tasks and resources to achieve objectives" (Lussier & Kimball, 2009, p. 122).

An organizational chart is a diagram illustrating all positions and reporting relationships within an organization. Sport organizations vary in size. Some organizations such as a family owned paint-ball facility employ a small number of people. Large, complex organizations like the NCAA or the IOC employ hundreds of workers. Many organizations are departmentalized into subunits according to the division of labor within the organization and the responsibility of members within each subunit. Exhibit 2.1 is an example of an organizational chart subdivided by business function. Other charts can be organized by strategic business unit structure (Exhibit 2.2) or geographic region (Exhibit 2.3).

In all cases, well-established structures are important for sport organizations. According to Daft (2015), "Organizations are (1) social entities that (2) are goal directed, (3) are designed as deliberately structured and coordinated activity systems, and (4) are linked to the external environment" (p. 13). Organizational structure can be examined through the lens of organizational design as well, where "Good design takes inventory of all the tasks, functions and goals of a business, and then develops groupings and orderings of job positions, departments and individuals to best and most efficiently achieve those ends" (Feigenbaum, 2017, para. 3). This concept of organizational design indicates that structure is not only about the static set of tasks in an organization, but also about what influences the organization's culture. This structural influence can be seen in sport governance organizations. Despite their similarities, the structures of sport organizations also have elements unique to their sport industry segment.

Structural Features of Sport Governance Organizations

Governing organizations generally have several hierarchical levels of work units and subunits. Paid staff members usually maintain the organization's headquarters and take care of the day-to-day operations of the organization. As stated previously, for high school sport, these would be the paid sport managers working for a state or provincial athletic association such as the Washington Interscholastic Activities Association (WIAA). Major professional sport leagues operate league offices such as the National Basketball Association (NBA) League Office in New York City. The headquarters for the IOC resides in Lausanne, Switzerland, while the IPC is housed in Bonn, Germany. The sport managers employed in these offices have titles such as Executive Director, League Vice President, and Marketing Director. These employees keep the organization moving along, and their responsibilities include budgeting, staffing, scheduling tournaments and events, marketing, and media relations. However, this level of the organization does not typically set policies dealing with governance issues. Rather, those sport managers implement the policies determined by another level of the structure.

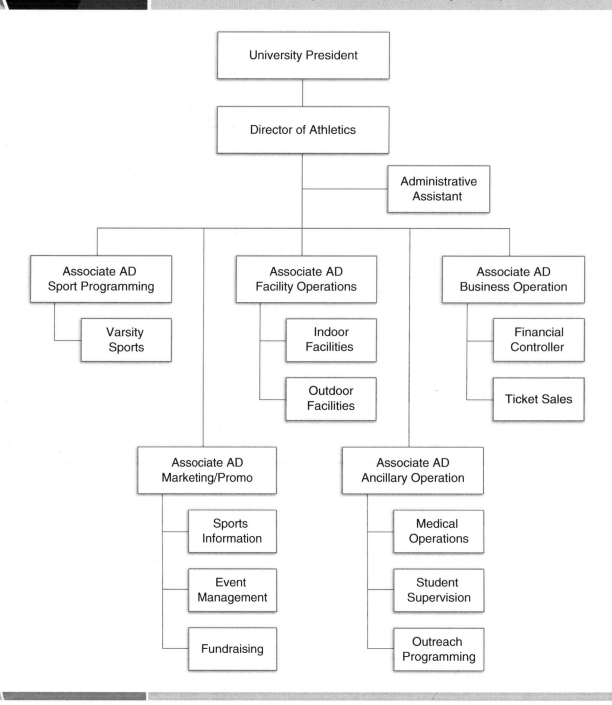

Note: AD = Athletic Director

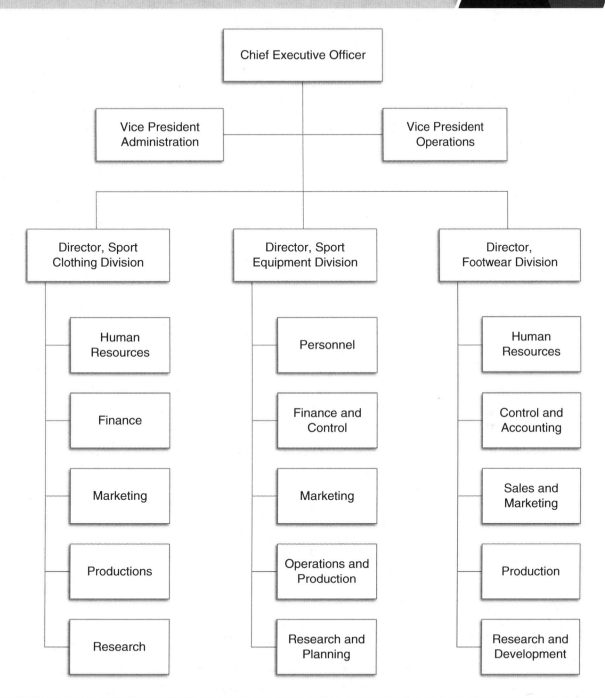

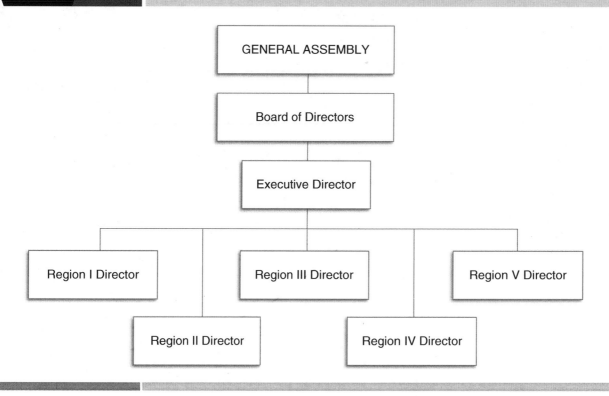

Most major sport organizations are nonprofit organizations with voluntary membership—not individual people, but institutions or nations. The membership of these organizations—not the paid staff—determines their policies, rules, and regulations. The vehicle for setting these policies usually takes the form of regularly scheduled, often annual, meetings of the membership. Sometimes called *General Assemblies* or *Annual Business Meetings*, members meet and vote to establish new policies and rules or to modify existing ones. For example, at the Winter Paralympic Games, Nordic Skiing holds its own Sport Assembly, and the voting members, each representing his or her home nation, vote on issues such as acceptable equipment modifications or the length of various races. While professional sports leagues are for profit, they still have meetings at which they make governance decisions. Every year, for example, at the Baseball Winter Meetings, representatives of minor league baseball teams vote on issues such as draft rules and stadium specifications.

These General Assemblies and Annual Business Meetings often appoint a President for the organization as well as an Executive Committee or Executive Council. Sometimes the organization needs to make adjustments between General Assembly meetings, and so it vests the responsibility and authority to do so in the hands of the President and the Executive Committee. Executive Committees also generate ideas for the Annual General Assemblies to consider. The Executive Committee for the IOC has eight members selected from the Annual General Assembly, plus the President. For most sport organizations, the true power rests in the hands of the Executive Committee. The reason for this is because the Executive Committee sets the agenda for the General Assembly. If the Executive Committee decides an action item is not worthy of going forward to the full General Assembly, the item never goes before the General Assembly for a vote. The opposite is true as well and Executive Board members may have a specific item they feel is critical to the organization and needs to go to a vote. You can clearly see here how the Executive Committee can control the direction of an entire organization because of the agenda items they favor or disfavor.

Naturally, the governance structures within each industry segment differ. This section merely gives an overview of some important organizational characteristics and shows how organizational charts for sport governance organizations contain elements different from a traditional sport front-office organizational chart. In each industry segment chapter, the organizational structures for that industry segment are explained in more detail.

The Role of Organizing in Governance

The organizational structures in any sport governing body dictate the flow of information and the setting of policies and rules and act as philosophical statements about the organization. Power is distributed differently within these structures. Sometimes power rests with the membership, and other times it rests with the Executive Committee or the President. It is important to note that the organizational charts for sport governing structures parallel traditional organizational charts with one difference: in traditional organizational charts we see people or titles in certain places; in governance structures we see governance units. This difference illustrates how governing bodies transcend individual responsibility and also shows us the big picture involved in governance.

DECISION MAKING

The decision-making process is essential in sport governance. We all make decisions every day. Some decisions are very simple. You chose what to wear to class on Monday. What did you consider when deciding what clothes to wear? You probably considered the weather, what was clean, what matched, whom you might sit next to in class, or if you had to give a presentation. Even this simplistic example shows the two basic parts of decision making—gathering and analyzing information. Sport managers must also make decisions on an everyday basis (after they decide what to wear to work).

Routine and Complex Decisions

Sport managers face a variety of decisions in the workplace, some of which are routine and some of which are not routine. *Routine decisions*, sometimes referred to as *programmed decisions*, are straightforward, repetitive, and mundane (Business Case Studies, 2012). During a Brooklyn Nets basketball game, if a toilet overflows, the decision to call Maintenance to fix it is easy. When the Athletic Director's suite at a University of Tennessee football game is running low on soft drinks (a recurring situation), the decision to order more drinks is routine.

All decisions are not so easy. Many problems are unique. Complex, nonroutine decisions are novel and referred to as *nonprogrammed decisions* (The Times 100, 2012). For example, baseball stadiums often shoot fireworks after the home team hits a home run. But suppose Stadium Operations personnel discover that some fireworks have been stolen. What types of decisions do they have to make about public safety? Which public safety departments need to be informed? What does the public need to know? Or suppose your local community is struck by a natural disaster such as the 2011 Tuscaloosa, Alabama tornado or Hurricane Sandy in 2012? Do sporting events such as high school, college, or professional games, or even the New York City Marathon go on as scheduled? What about diverting resources to those events from people who may be without power or heat? Or suppose you are a high school athletic director facing budget cuts. How do you decide which teams' budgets will be decreased and which won't, and how will you implement those decisions? These examples illustrate the complex decision-making situations sport managers face.

The Rational Model

One item is of great importance to sport managers when they make decisions: they must follow an organized, thoughtful process. Decisions of great magnitude cannot be left to chance. Rather, the sport manager's thought process must be detailed and organized. One such process, the Rational Model based on Robbins (1990), is outlined here:

1. Identify the REAL problem.
2. Identify the decision objective.
3. Gather all pertinent information.
4. Identify any hurdles.
5. Brainstorm for alternatives.
6. Narrow down the options.
7. Examine the pros and cons of each option.
8. Make the decision.
9. Evaluate the decision.

To illustrate this decision-making process, assume that you are the Athletic Director (AD) at Big State University (BSU), home of the Fightin' Saugers. Recently, a group of female athletes came to you asking to add rowing and lacrosse to your roster of women's sports. You are aware of the Title IX regulations that pertain to providing appropriate opportunities for female athletes, particularly the "proportionality" interpretation, whereby the ratio of male-to-female athletes must reflect the ratio of male-to-female students in the greater university population. Currently, the student body is 53 percent women and 47 percent men, while the Athletic Department's athlete breakdown is 35 percent female athletes and 65 percent male athletes. You know the financial implications of adding sports, but the group is also threatening legal action if the university does not do as they are asking.

Let's apply the Rational Model:

1. *Identify the REAL problem.* The real problem is that the university is not in compliance with Title IX, which guarantees equal athletic opportunities for men and women athletes.

2. *Identify the decision objective.* The decision objective is to bring the department into compliance.

3. *Gather all pertinent information.* Look at the different program areas Title IX covers, such as facilities, coaches, equipment, travel and per diem, scholarships, and so forth.

4. *Identify any hurdles.* Be aware not only of tangible hurdles, such as budgetary constraints, but also of intangible hurdles, such as people's attitudes toward women's sports.

5. *Brainstorm for alternatives.* Brainstorming emphasizes "broad and creative thinking, inviting all participants' points of view, and ensuring that all relevant aspects of an issue or question are considered" (Massachusetts Institute of Technology, n.d., para 1). The idea is to list all possible ideas now and sort through them later. In this case, the options could include adding sports without increasing the budget, asking the university for additional funding, cutting some men's nonrevenue sports to free up money, dropping football, and finding additional funding sources such as increasing sponsorship dollars, finding new donors, or increasing ticket prices for the major revenue sports. Not all the ideas may be reasonable, but when brainstorming, remember to put all ideas on the table.

6. *Narrow down the options.* Then narrow down your list of options to three or four. Let's say that the best options appear to be finding additional funding sources and dropping some men's nonrevenue sports.

7. *Examine the pros and cons of each option.* Carefully weigh the pros and cons of these options. Dropping men's sports is a quick fix in terms of budgets, but in terms of public relations, it would be a nightmare. Finding

additional sponsorship dollars is a possibility as the university is located in a major metropolitan area, but you may be limited in how much you can ask for. Increasing ticket prices will help, but the increase will be limited to how much fans will pay, and the increase will not finance the entire venture.

8. *Make the decision.* You decide on a combination approach, using the tactics of finding additional sponsorship dollars and increasing ticket prices.

9. *Evaluate the decision.* These tactics will have to be evaluated over the coming years. Once the teams are in place, BSU's Athletic Department will need to continually account for sponsorship dollars and fans' responses to increased ticket prices by measuring the impact on tickets sold.

This simplified version of a very complex decision-making process illustrates how an organized approach to decision making can help a sport manager decide on a course of action.

The SLEEPE Principle

Another decision-making method, which takes a more global view of the organization and the implications of sport managers' decisions, is called the SLEEPE Principle. The decisions sport managers make are often publicly scrutinized by the media, fans, and the general public. Therefore, when sport managers make decisions, they must be able to use their conceptual skills to see the big picture. By using the SLEEPE method, decision makers can analyze decisions, especially decisions affecting policy development or interpretation. Originally set up as the SLEEP model by W. Moore at Ohio State University in 1990, this decision-making model has since been modified (Hums, 2006; Hums & Wolff, 2017) and applied in the sport industry to help sport managers see the big picture by analyzing the many different ramifications of their decisions. The components of the SLEEPE Principle are as follows:

S—Social
L—Legal
E—Economic
E—Ethical
P—Political
E—Educational

Using this model helps sport managers understand how their decisions will be viewed in different ways by various constituencies in society. The following example will illustrate this:

You are the AD at BSU. Shortly after the regular season ended, your potential National Football League (NFL) top draft pick, star running back Austin Franklin, has been arrested and is in jail on charges of domestic violence. Your team is headed for a bowl game to determine the national championship. Of course, this story has received extensive national coverage in the press and is the talk of the bowl season. The decision you have to make, in conjunction with your head coach, is whether to allow Franklin to play in the upcoming bowl game. Let's use the SLEEPE Principle to analyze this situation:

S—SOCIAL. Look at the social ramifications of the decision: allowing Franklin to play makes the statement to society in general that domestic violence is not serious enough to warrant his not playing in the game. This decision could lead to protests by both on- and off-campus groups, including faculty, students, and alumni groups, as well as community organizations opposing domestic violence. It also suggests winning the bowl game is more important to the Athletic Department than standing up against domestic violence by athletes. However, if you do not allow Franklin to play, many fans and university supporters will be angry, especially if your team loses the game. However, you will have made a statement that BSU will not tolerate this sort of obvious unacceptable conduct.

L—LEGAL. From the legal standpoint, one may argue that Franklin should be allowed to play because he has not actually been convicted of anything yet. However, extending the definition of legal beyond just the traditional legal system, one can ask, has he violated team or university rules related to such conduct? How would a student who is not an athlete be treated by the university? If he does not play and the team loses, is it possible to hold him in some way legally responsible for the loss of revenue resulting from losing the game (Moorman & Hums, 1999)?

E—ECONOMIC. The economic ramifications for both the university and Franklin himself are as follows: allowing him to play maximizes the opportunity to win the game, meaning increased revenue for the university, especially in terms of sales of licensed products and perhaps ticket sales for the upcoming year. Keeping the team highly ranked will help with recruiting and potential future earnings. On the personal level, if Franklin plays well, he could increase his potential professional earnings. However, if he does not play, there is greater potential that BSU would lose the game, the national championship, and all the revenue streams associated with these events. Franklin's draft status could suffer, costing him money in his contract and potential endorsement deals.

E—ETHICAL. Next are the ethical considerations. Saying Franklin cannot play takes the ethical stance that domestic violence is wrong and will not be tolerated. It also says athletes are not above the law and must be held accountable for their actions. However, allowing him to play may make the ethical statement that a person is innocent until proven guilty. He has not yet been tried by a court of law, so he should not be convicted in the court of public opinion. Of all the parts of the SLEEPE Principle, this is the most complex and challenging to sport managers.

P—POLITICAL.   Politically there are a number of constituencies to consider. In this context, the term *political* is not limited to elected officials only; it is broader, including any groups or stakeholders who may exert some type of political power or influence in a given situation. In our example, if Franklin is allowed to play, the university's faculty, staff, and administration will most likely make public statements about the decision. They may exert public pressure on the school's Athletic Department. The school's conference or even the NCAA may also make statements about the decision. Since BSU is a state university, members of the state legislature may also voice their opinions. If he is not allowed to play, some of these same groups may issue supportive comments, publicly supporting and strengthening the AD's stance.

E—EDUCATIONAL.   Finally, there is the educational component to consider. Here sport managers need to reflect on what they have learned by going through the decision-making process in this situation. They have likely learned about public backlash but may also have learned about understanding what their true core values are and what values they want their department to reflect and model. Going through this complex decision-making process will inform future good practice when tough decisions arise again.

This example illustrates the complexity and public nature of many decisions sport managers face on a daily basis. Athlete misconduct, substance abuse, equity, diversity, inclusion, violence, economic challenges, and other pressing issues are present in the sport industry just as they are in general society. Because of the far-reaching ramifications of their decisions, forward-thinking sport managers must learn to examine all potential results of and reactions to their decisions before they make them.

This section outlined various decision-making models sport managers can incorporate when solving problems. Often, sport managers' decisions will be ethical in nature. Do the same decision-making models apply? To address the importance of dealing with ethical issues, Chapter 4 discusses ethical decision making.

The Role of Decision Making in Sport Governance

Sport managers dealing with governance issues are faced with decisions that have far-reaching implications. Their decisions, from simple to complex, shape the direction of the organization. The decisions sport managers make are open to public scrutiny and media discussion. As such, sport managers must make sure they have a concrete method for analyzing any decisions they need to make.

SUMMARY

Sport managers need to be able to perform the major management functions of planning, organizing, leading, and evaluating. This chapter focused on planning, organizing, and one subset of leading—decision making. It is important to have a solid foundation in these areas before further examining specific industry segments.

Planning is the basis for everything a sport manager does. Sport managers must make both short- and long-term plans. The planning process is sequential: organizational goals, objectives, tactics, roles, and evaluation all flow from the mission statement. Sport organizations are organized with different levels of responsibility. Determining the tasks an organization needs to accomplish and the people needed to accomplish those tasks is essential for organizational success. Sport managers must make decisions every day. Some of their decisions are routine; others are unique. Two structured methods to help sport managers make solid decisions are the Rational Model of decision making and the SLEEPE Principle. By mastering these important skills, sport managers can successfully conduct the business of governance and policy development in their sport organizations.

case STUDY

MANAGERIAL FUNCTIONS

You are the General Manager for the Elkhart Komets, a struggling AA baseball franchise. Playing in the old, poorly maintained Riverfront Stadium and trying to market an outdated logo (a gold star with a silver tail), you need to make some decisions on how to increase revenues. Keep in mind that this is a minor league team, and you have no control over which players you can acquire.

- Use the Rational Model of decision making to determine your course of action.

CHAPTER questions

1. Locate organizational charts for three different sport organizations. Compare and contrast the titles and structures of each. Why are some aspects similar and others different?
2. Choose one of the following:
   - minor league baseball team
   - college or university athletic department

- high school athletic department
- charity 5K run/walk
- campus recreation department
- sporting goods store

After you choose one of these sport organizations, develop the following:

a. mission statement
b. one goal
c. two objectives for that goal
d. two tactics for each objective
e. the roles for each tactic

3. For a sport organization of your choosing, identify two situations that would involve routine decision making and two situations that would involve complex decision making.

FOR ADDITIONAL INFORMATION

For more information check out the following resources:

1. Australian Sports Governance Principles: Australian Sports Commission. (2017). Sports governance principles: https://www.ausport.gov.au/supporting/governance/governance_principles
2. 2017 NHL General Manager Meeting recap: Rosen, D. (2017, March 6). General managers look to NHL's future. NHL: https://www.nhl.com/news/nhl-general-managers-look-to-future/c-287441518
3. Mission Statement and Fever Cares Initiatives of the WNBA's Indiana Fever: Indiana Fever. (n.d.) Fever Mission Statement: www.wnba.com/archive/wnba/fever/community/fever_about_us.html
4. Minor League Baseball Attendance Statistics and Ideas for Increase: Hill, B. (2014, January 10). Inside the numbers: The drawing board. MiLB: https://www.milb.com/milb/news/inside-the-numbers-the-drawing-board/c-66453294/t-185364810
5. FIFA's Finances: Where does all the money come from?: Fraser, I. (2015, May 29). FIFA's finances: Where does all the money come from? *The Telegraph*: www.telegraph.co.uk/sport/football/fifa/11635985/Fifas-finances-where-does-all-the-money-come-from.html
6. International World Games Governance: International World Games Association. (n.d.). Governance: www.theworldgames.org/contents/The-IWGA-15/Governance-1114

REFERENCES

Australian Sports Commission. (2012). Planning. Retrieved from www.ausport.gov.au/supporting/clubs/governance/planning

BCSS. (2016). Mission, vision, and values. Retrieved from www.bcschoolsports.ca/member-services/mission-vision-and-values

Bryce, T. (2008). Why we resist planning. Retrieved from http://www.articles.scopulus.co.uk/Why%20We%20Resist%20Planning.htm

Business Case Studies. (2012). Strategy theory. Retrieved from http://businesscasestudies.co.uk/business-theory/strategy/decision-making.html

Chelladurai, P. (2014). *Managing organizations for sport and physical activity: A systems perspective* (3rd ed.). Scottsdale, AZ: Holcomb Hathaway.

Daft, R. I. (2015). *Organizational theory and design* (12th ed.). Boston, MA: Cengage Learning.

Feigenbaum, E. (2017). Difference between organizational structure and design. Retrieved from http://smallbusiness.chron.com/difference-between-organizational-structure-design-3839.html

Fernandes, P. (2016, April 20). What is a vision statement? *Business News Daily*. Retrieved from www.businessnewsdaily.com/3882-vision-statement.html

Hagerstown Suns. (2017). Mission statement. Retrieved from www.milb.com/content/page.jsp?ymd=20111028&content_id=25823618&sid=t563&vkey=team4

Hums, M. A. (2006, May). Analyzing the impact of changes in classification systems: A sport management analysis model. Paper presented at the VISTA 2006 International Paralympic Committee Congress, Bonn, Germany.

Hums, M. A., & Wolff, E. A. (2017). Managing Paralympic sport organizations: The STEEPLE framework. In S. Darcy, S. Frawley, & D. Adair (Eds.), *Managing the Paralympics* (pp. 155–174). London: Palgrave Macmillan.

Hums, M. A., Moorman, A. M., & Wolff, E. (2002). Examining disability sport from a sport management perspective. *Proceedings of the VISTA 2001 Conference*, Vienna, Austria.

International Paralympic Committee. (n.d.). The IPC: Who we are. Retrieved from https://www.paralympic.org/the-ipc/about-us

Lussier, R. N., & Kimball, D. (2009). *Applied sport management skills*. Champaign, IL: Human Kinetics.

Massachusetts Institute of Technology. (n.d). Learning and development: Brainstorming guidelines. Retrieved from http://hrweb.mit.edu/learning-development/learning-topics/meetings/articles/brainstorming

Moorman, A. M., & Hums, M. A. (1999). Student athlete liability for NCAA violations and breach of contract. *Journal of Legal Aspects of Sport*, 9(3), 163–174.

Norman, L. (2016). What is the business difference between objectives and goals? Retrieved from http://smallbusiness.chron.com/business-difference-between-objectives-goals-21972.html

Parkhouse, B., Turner, B., & Milloch, K. S. (2012). *Marketing for sport business and success*. Dubuque, IA: Kendall Hunt.

Robbins, S. P. (1990). *Organizational theory: Structure, design and applications* (3rd ed.). Englewood Cliffs, NJ: Prentice Hall.

Round Rock Express. (2017). Mission statement and core values. Retrieved from www.milb.com/content/page.jsp?ymd=20100112&content_id=7908236&sid=t102&vkey=team3

Siddiqui, F. (2015). Defining the terms: Vision, mission, goals and objectives. Retrieved from https://www.linkedin.com/pulse/defining-terms-vision-mission-goals-objectives-fareed

The Times 100. (2012). Strategy theory. Retrieved from http://businesscasestudies.co.uk/business-theory/strategy/decision-making.html

VanderZwaag, H. J. (1998). *Policy development in sport management*. Westport, CT: Praeger.

Strategic Management and Policy Development

Mary A. Hums
Joanne C. MacLean

As discussed in Chapter 1, sport is an industry with considerable reach and impact on consumer-spending indices and the economy in general. Sport is acknowledged as big business, given the sheer numbers of participants, its exponential growth over the past 30 years, and the healthy percentage of the economic marketplace attributed to sport worldwide (DeSchriver, Mahony, & Hambrick, 2014). Ozanian's (1995, p. 30) comment over two decades ago still applies:

> What's all the excitement about? Sports is not simply another big business. It is one of the fastest-growing industries in the U.S., and it is intertwined with virtually every aspect of the economy . . . sports is everywhere, accompanied by the sound of a cash register ringing incessantly.

The magnitude and reach of the sport industry is important in terms of economic impact, employment opportunities, and consumer interest. The extent of the business of sport is understandable, considering the vast numbers of both participants and activities involved. The popularity of different sporting activities, for participants and spectators, provides a rationale for the proliferation of organizations delivering the business of sport. Such organizations are involved in providing entertainment (amateur and professional spectator sport) or facilities (gyms and clubs for participation); offering structures within which competitive sport is delivered (minor, scholastic, or college, and club sport leagues and championships); designing and manufacturing equipment used by all levels of participants (clothing, sporting equipment, and other apparel); and promoting and delivering sporting competitions and festivals (World Championships and Paralympic Games). These organizations can be public or private, for-profit or nonprofit. Regardless of the specifics of the business, sport as a consumer product is massive, technological advances occur daily, and focused marketing and promotion efforts are resulting in the further globalization of the sport industry (Markovits & Rensmann, 2013).

Without a doubt, the competition is fierce and the stakes high. For students interested in a career in the sport industry, learning the breadth and depth of the businesses and understanding how these organizations are strategically managed and governed is an important, early step in defining your career. According to Szymanski and Wolfe (2017), the need for effective and strategic management practices and the development of meaningful policy has never been more important for sport organizations. Therefore, the focus of this chapter is the development of business strategy, the implementation of the principles of strategic management, and the development of policy in sport organizations. Even though the 1990s and early 21st century represented a period of expansion in the sport industry, growth was impacted by the world-wide economic downturn in 2008, making the implementation of creative business strategies an imperative (Fried, DeSchriver, & Mondello, 2013). It follows, then, that strategic management is an important concept to the sport manager. Future sport managers need to ask themselves:

- Is there a link between the macro approach (assessing the organization as a whole) to strategic management and what a manager does as an individual?
- Will strategic management enable managerial activities to be more successful in defining and setting policy for the organization?
- Is it important to understand strategic management and policy development in order to understand the governance of a sport organization and its pursuit of effectiveness?

The answer to each question is a resounding "Yes." This chapter provides further insight into the importance of strategic management and policy development for sport organizations.

STRATEGIC MANAGEMENT

trategy refers to the plans and actions implemented to achieve a goal in the most efficient and effective manner. Strategy is a common tool used by organizations as a whole or in part to achieve a goal or gain some advantage. Chapter 2 described *tactics* as the specific steps that need to be followed to implement the strategy. You might consider strategy an organization's game plan. Sport is the perfect example to illustrate the concept because strategy is a normal part of competitive sports. A coach develops a game plan or strategy based on her team's strengths and weaknesses in comparison to the competition. The plan, of course, is to negate the opposition's strengths and find ways to capitalize on the strengths of one's own team. Managers of organizations seek these same results. They set goals and strive to realize them through a series of tactics or steps that will help the organization reach a goal. Strategy, then, is an important component in the management of an organization because it helps paint a picture of where the organization is headed. Again, tactics relate to the specific steps used to carry out the broader game plan. Let's focus our attention on the development of overall organizational strategy by first defining *strategic management.*

Defining Strategic Management

The terms *strategic management*, *business strategy*, and *organizational strategy* are often used synonymously to refer to both a purpose and a plan of action enabling an organization to reach its goals (Belcourt & McBey, 2015). For the purpose of this text, we will use the term *strategic management.* According to Pearce and Robinson (2014), strategic management

- involves decisions and action plans evolving from the organization's mission;
- takes into account both the internal and the external environment;

- involves both short- and long-term objectives (tactics) and plans;
- requires strategic choices in budget resource allocation with respect to tasks, people, structures, technologies, and reward systems.

To summarize, strategic management involves the planning, organizing, leading, and evaluating of an organization's strategy-related decisions and actions (Pearce & Robinson, 2014). On a larger scale, the term *corporate strategy* refers to global strategy for the larger *corporation*, an entity that may include several smaller businesses. Thus, a strategy can be developed in a global organizational sense to deal with corporate-wide plans (corporate-level strategy); it can deal with factors impacting the main organizational mission (business- or management-level strategy); or it can be implemented to enable specific managerial functions such as planning or decision making (functional-level strategy) (Pearce & Robinson, 2014). See Exhibit 3.1.

For example, Pacers Sports & Entertainment Ltd is the parent company managing the Indiana Pacers and WNBA Fever basketball franchises. The organization's corporate strategy might involve a focus on growing the games of basketball by encouraging grassroots development and opportunities for participation and strengthening the fan base for these teams. The business-level strategy of the Pacers and Fever might include a commitment to a certain budget to hire staff and run programming, thereby encouraging the accomplishment of the corporate goals. Partnerships with other sport delivery groups and contributions to both facilities and program development might result. The outcome of these investments will strengthen the functional-level strategies, such as delivering hoops programs for kids such as the Junior Pacers Program, by helping to develop a following in a particular sport, widening the fan base, and enabling marketing activities that promote ticket sales. Each level of strategy is critically important and contributes to the overall success of the organization. Then tactics such as advertising, acquiring facilities, managing risk, and developing rules and regulations are employed to enact the overall strategy.

exhibit 3.1	Defining Levels of Strategy

Type of Strategy	Definition
Corporate-Level Strategy	General, overall strategic planning for the entire organization and all its business
Business-Level Strategy	Specific, individualized strategic planning for individual products or services
Functional-Level Strategy	Specific, individualized strategic planning concepts implemented by personnel

Strategic management often occurs as a result of some environmental factor impacting the operation of the organization and its ability to achieve defined goals. Specifically, strategy involves creating mission, goals, and objectives statements, along with action plans (tactics) accounting for both the organization's environment and its competition (Masterman, 2014). With an ultimate goal or several goals in mind, the organization's decision makers will maneuver activities and decisions based upon factors in the organization's environment to achieve them. Strategic management is dynamic, both short and long term in nature, and sometimes results in structural changes to organizational arrangement.

In his seminal book, Mintzberg (1988) offered the five Ps of strategy as a way to understand the meaning of strategic management. He suggested that strategic management involves the following:

1. *Planning*: setting a course of action to deal with a situation.
2. *Purpose*: actions that are sometimes deliberate and other times emergent that deal with change and opportunity.
3. *Ploy*: some specific maneuver to deal with an issue.
4. *Position*: the location of the organization relative to its business and competitors.
5. *Perspective*: the culture or perspective of the organization.

Remember that organizational strategy involves not only goals and objectives but also the tactics by which goals are achieved (Mintzberg et al., 2013). The chief executives and board members of the organization commonly develop business strategy.

Although defining specific business strategy is important, it is not more important than executing the strategic management plan. According to Belcourt and McBey (2015), this is accomplished by

1. defining the vision or clear purpose
2. converting the vision to measurable objectives
3. defining a plan to achieve the end goal
4. implementing the plan
5. measuring the results and revising the plan based upon actual versus planned events

The flow of information leading to strategic action involves looking backward and forward prior to assessing the current organizational environment. Managers will evaluate historical, current, and forecasted data in light of the values and priorities of the organization's stakeholders (Pearce & Robinson, 2014). Stakeholders are usually subdivided groups of professionals, volunteers, and customers who have an interest in the product or service being developed.

To be effective, an organization must create a good fit between its strategy, organizational structure, and governance plan (Parent, O'Brien, & Slack, 2012). This means the managerial activities related to governance discussed in Chapter 2 are critical to success. If those sport managers responsible for planning, organizing, and decision making are not cognizant of their environment and in tune with the mission and action plans of the organization, then outcomes are bound to be ineffective. Consider the negative results likely to occur if the United States Olympic Committee (USOC) were to work at cross-purposes with the national governing bodies (NGBs). The result of divergent policy or unacknowledged shifts in the environment could lead to chaotic, illogical management illustrated by inconsistent decision making, poor planning, and inadequate organization. For instance, suppose the USOC were to establish a common policy dictating how athletes were selected for the Olympic Teams but not effectively accounting for the differences between selecting an individual athlete in swimming versus a team sport athlete in basketball. The end result might involve selecting the wrong athletes and might well be illustrated by decreased medal performances at the Olympic Games.

Planning and organizing are critical components of the process, because determining goals and the means to achieve them (tactics) are core items of strategic management. After all, it's hard to achieve success if you cannot define it and the steps needed to achieve it. Developing policies that empower action are equally vital. However, perhaps even more important to the concept of strategic management is strategic decision making. Knowing what to do at the right time is a critical component of strategic management.

Strategic Decision Making

As discussed in Chapter 2, decision making is the act of deciding a course of action based on the available alternatives related to a particular issue. Strategic decision making attaches a global organizational perspective to individual decisions. Strategic decision making usually involves top management decisions related to substantial resources. The long-term prosperity of the organization may even be affected, as strategic decisions sometimes have enduring effects. Strategic decision making involves forecasting both the environment and the effects of a particular decision in the acquisition of long-term goals. Normally, several alternatives and "if–then" scenarios are played out to gain perspective on the results of the decision. Strategic decision making is employed in an attempt to ensure the most profitable decision is made. Follow-up evaluations are used to promptly correct negative outcomes that might accrue once a decision is made. Examples of common strategic decisions in sport organizations include developing partnerships with sponsors or other organizations, long-term planning, establishing the organizational brand, and dramatic shifts in programming.

Decision making in sport organizations is among the manager's most important functions (Chelladurai, 2014). Although some decisions will be routine and repetitive with precedent and policy defining the decision choices, others will involve unique situations with little in the way of established guidelines to assist the decision maker (Taylor, 2017). Given the magnitude and importance of the outcome to the entire organization, some decisions require business strategy. In each case, a procedure for framing and solving the problem is critical to ensure a well-thought-out decision. In line with the Rational Model of decision making presented in Chapter 2, Chelladurai (2014) summarizes strategic decision making in the following steps:

1. defining the problem
2. listing all possible alternatives, taking into consideration the internal and external organizational environments
3. assessing the pros and cons of the alternatives
4. considering the global and the long-term impact of the alternatives
5. selecting the best course of action

Step 4 is included in order that the best and most strategic decision for the overall organization is considered, emphasizing the importance of strategy in sport management.

Good decisions are made when the data are accurate and the means of using them are appropriate. In business, finding and analyzing information and gaining insight from the data to guide decision making is referred to as *analytics*. While coaches and athletes have traditionally used sport statistics to guide decision making in games and events, more recently analytics has been emphasized in managing the sport organization. For example, sport marketing has become a highly data-driven process, and organizations use consumer demographics and perceptions obtained from surveys, download choices, or other research to develop strategies to enhance the consumption or use of certain products. Sport managers define their general market by using data on size (e.g., numbers of customers), trading radius (e.g., distance customers will travel), demographics (e.g., male vs. female customers, age, income, etc.), psychographics (e.g., personal likes and dislikes), and future trends (e.g., impact of changing game times). Data obtained from sales records, customer comments, account records, complaints, and online interactions may be used in decision making. Organizations may also intentionally source such data through customer questionnaires, mystery shoppers, focus groups, and computerized surveys. Using data from websites and social networking sites gathered via technology also plays an important role in decision making.

The Importance of Strategy in Sport Management

Sport organizations must embrace strategic management practices to maximize their potential for several reasons:

1. TO PLAN EFFECTIVELY. Strategy is extremely important because sport organizations have historically had reputations for ineffective planning. Many amateur sport groups developed informally and were dominated by volunteer, nonprofessional staff. When the stakes are high, poor management can mean not getting to the medal podium or losing a billion-dollar product line. It is accepted that planning is the foundation of effective strategic management.

2. TO CAPITALIZE ON OPPORTUNITIES. Capitalizing on opportunity is enhanced by the tenets of strategic management. A turbulent environment can result in a warp-speed, frenetic business climate. Only those organizations with a strategy and an understanding of alternatives will truly capitalize on the opportunities. Suppose that you manage a privately owned fitness club and that you, the owner, and the three investors who provided the original capital to start the club have engaged in regular meetings, charting strategy for the current and future activities of the club. Now suppose that you receive an inside tip that your main competitor who runs three local clubs is about to sell the business. Having a strategic management plan that includes designs for acting relative to both future acquisitions and outselling the competition might well enable you to merge your business with your competitor's. In the absence of such strategic management and planning, you may be ill equipped to make such a decision or to make it in a timely manner. Capitalizing on this opportunity is critical, given the competition among sport organizations for customers, fans, athletes, and consumers.

3. TO MAKE EFFECTIVE DECISIONS. An organization charting a specific course of action is most likely to make effective decisions. Strategic management will enable strategic decision making by keeping the organization in tune with environmental realities and reducing internal resistance to change.

4. TO ENHANCE THE MANAGER'S ENTREPRENEURIAL ROLE. Many years ago Mintzberg (1975) described four decisional roles of a manager that are still useful today: entrepreneur, disturbance handler, resource allocator, and negotiator. The sport organization with a clear business strategy has the greatest potential of enhancing the manager's entrepreneurial role, encouraging the development or acquisition of innovative goods and services, and effectively managing organizational change.

In addition to strategic management, effective sport organizations are administered through effective policy. Strategic management involves specific action or patterns of action. The ultimate goal of this action is to achieve objectives defined by the organization while respecting the guiding principles and policies of the organization. Let's turn our attention now to the definition of policy, the importance of policy in the governance of sport organizations, and the concept of policy development.

POLICY

All organizations deal with different types of difficult situations, often issues related to human resources, service delivery, risk management, or finance. The issue could result from deviating from the strategic business plan, straying from past practice, or confronting some new, uncharted ground. It may be difficult or tricky, the answer may not be immediately clear, and the potential consequences could be far-reaching within the organization. Sport organizations require policy in the areas of finance, human resources, facility use and control, equipment, travel, public relations, promotion, and other items related to managing risk. For example, travel is a pressure point in college athletics. How will the college Athletic Director (AD) react when an athlete asks to travel to a particular road game on his own? Should this concern the administrator? Are there larger issues to consider? Will granting the request set a precedent? Would it matter if the athlete were to travel with his parents as opposed to his girlfriend? Who would be responsible in the event of an accident? How will the athlete's coach view the situation? Each of these questions, and possibly others defined by the college risk manager and insurance carrier, provides the framework for developing policy to deal with this issue. Let's take a further look at defining policy and answer the questions posed above.

What Is a Policy?

Policies are broad guidelines or procedures an organization follows as it moves toward its goals and objectives. Policies are normally general, written statements providing a framework for enabling decisions while allowing employees some flexibility and discretion in problem solving. These guiding statements are meant to provide common direction for all facets of the organization. It is important to understand that policies are different from objectives, strategies, procedures, or philosophy (Houlihan, 2017; see Exhibit 3.2). Policies have wide ramifications and are formal expressions of an organization's standing decisions on important, often recurring, issues. They are different from procedures, which are established to guide the work of an individual or a division within the organization. Policies are also different from goals, objectives, and tactics. They emerge from the organization's philosophy by creating a framework for resolving issues directly and consistently. Effective policies evolve over time in reaction to the environment within which the organization exists. For example, college athletic departments often have a fiscal responsibility policy that prevents its divisions from spending beyond their budgets. The policy does not dictate how or on what items to spend, but rather creates a bottom line principle specific to the importance of only spending within the means of the organization. As significant savings occur, the policy might be amended to allow quarterly reports on budget savings to reallocate funds to a list of items not funded in the original budget. Over time, this practice might be

| *exhibit* | **3.2** | Definition of Terms Related to Policy Development |

Philosophy	A set of beliefs used to guide decision making.
Policy	General, usually written statements emerging from an organization's philosophy that express its position on important, recurring issues and used to guide decisions and enable consistent decision making.
Goal	Broad, qualitative statements that provide general direction for an organization (see Chapter 2).
Objective	Quantitative statements that help an organization determine if it is fulfilling its goals (see Chapter 2).
Strategy	A plan to bring about a goal or solution to a problem in the most efficient and effective manner.
Procedure	A step-by-step sequence of activities implemented in order to achieve a task.

changed slightly so that the savings remain within the original department budget to further encourage fiscal responsibility to managers concerned with losing part of their original resources.

Organizations rely upon policy and precedent (or past practice) to solve problems fairly and consistently. In the earlier example of the athlete who wishes to travel by his own means to the college game, the AD will likely rely on a college policy or a departmental policy for an answer to help ensure consistency when another athlete asks. Check out the website of the Athletics Business Office at the University of Notre Dame for an excellent example of a Team Travel Policy. It illustrates that the administrator will be concerned with the following:

- the college's responsibility for the safety and the behavior of athletes when traveling
- the coach's wishes about team cohesion and togetherness
- the athlete's understanding of his responsibilities and expectations
- the circumstances and rationale surrounding the request

In such a case, the Department of Athletics may approve the policy shown in Exhibit 3.3 regarding athletes traveling to competitions. In its policy, the department defines an expectation that athletes will travel with their team, but it acknowledges that there are circumstances in which this may not be possible and that such cases will be dealt with on an individual basis. The definition of those circumstances will then be left to the discretion of those involved. Perhaps the athlete has an exam that will not permit him to leave with the team but is able and willing to drive on his own and arrive in time for the game. A parent might be at the game and want to take her

It is expected that athletes will travel to and from athletic contests with their teammates on carriers provided by the College. In the event an athlete wishes to make alternate travel plans, he or she must obtain the form "Permission for Alternate Travel Plans—Varsity Athletes" from the Athletic Office. This form requests information regarding the intended mode of transportation and a rationale for the request. Permission may be granted on a case-by-case basis only when the form is signed off by both the head coach and the Athletic Director. Permission requests must be made 48 hours prior to travel.

son home for the weekend afterward. Together, the case-by-case decisions begin to establish a precedent. An example of the athlete permission form is presented in Exhibit 3.4.

The Importance of Policy in Sport Organizations

Developing policies permitting effective decision making has never been more important for sport organizations, especially given their current size and complexity. Rapid growth over the past decade coupled with an increase in the complexity and business orientation of sport organizations have made it necessary to expand managers' decision-making responsibilities. This trend toward decentralized decision making means effective policy development is crucial. A policy manual can be an invaluable tool that helps personnel to deal quickly and effectively with issues. Policies also promote fair, equitable decisions supported by rationales that are both reasonable and easy to understand. Policies encourage consistency, ensuring the same answer to a problem is applied between organizational units and over time. Perhaps even more important, policy development enables the organization to link its mission statement and management strategy to its operations, ensuring the business strategy is implemented through overall policies and tactics. Let's consider this point in more detail.

Suppose you become the AD for a college competing in Division III of the National Collegiate Athletic Association (NCAA). You are in the leadership role for directing the department. The athletics mission statement might be "to provide student-athletes opportunities for the pursuit of excellence in a broad range of competitive athletics." You need to ensure that department policies are developed that link to the pursuit of the mission relative to how you operate (management strategy) on a day-to-day basis. The mission clearly reflects the need to offer as many sports as possible and to operate them at the highest possible competitive level in order to win. Policies about funding, recruiting, program breadth, competitive schedules, excellent facilities, and so on will help to link the management *exhibit* **3.4** Sample Athlete Permission Form

Department of Athletics

**Statement of Personal Responsibility for Alternative
Travel Arrangements Chosen by Student–Athletes**

REQUEST   Date:_____

I (_____) request permission to _____

_____

_____

and will not **travel with / return with** the _____ **prior to / following**
                (circle one)   (team)   (circle one)

the contest played at _____
                                                        (location/opponent)

on _____.
            (date)

If my request is approved, I will assume all the responsibilities for my travel, conduct, and well-being while traveling
to and/or from the contest. I will not hold the college liable in any way for any harm or injury I may suffer, or for any
loss or damage to my property that may occur during this journey.

_____ Date:_____
(Signature of student making request)

Address: _____ _____

_____

_____

Telephone: _____ Birth Date: _____

_____

Permission Granted by Department of Athletics

_____   _____
(Athletic Director)   (Coach)

Date: _____   Date: _____

and business strategies. Your college wants to offer lots of sport opportunities and to operate them at the highest competitive level. The steps necessary to achieve these goals require following specific tactics. For instance, your tactic might include having a balance of sports that use both indoor and outdoor facilities, with no more than four sports sharing any one facility. This tactic ensures that each team's competitive schedules and necessary practice times can be accommodated.

Remember, too, that sport organizations are held to standards of fairness and principle as defined by law. Policies provide for a systematic framework that aids in decision making. For example, a gender-equity policy may call for an equal number of competitive sport opportunities for females as there are for males within the athletic program. When decisions are being made relative to adding or dropping sports, this policy helps to guide the discussion. Of course, this does not ensure the policy is legally defensible, but it does promote actions based upon reasoned statements of organizational intent, developed for a purpose.

Developing Policy

Armed with an understanding of what a policy is and why it is important, let's now turn our attention to developing policy. *Policy development* is an ongoing process through which a framework for decision making is developed relative to issues broadly encountered throughout the organization. Policy is developed on recurring issues or problems and is usually directed to guiding decision making around critical organizational resources such as finances and personnel (Hoye, Nicholson, & Houlihan, 2010). Policy areas are those parts of an organization's operation where important decisions have surfaced and several alternative actions are possible. The stakes connected to the issues are high; thus the organization forms policy to solve a problem or take a stand on an issue that is likely to recur. Issues or problems that arise, especially those issues that are recurring or that impact a large proportion of organization members or activities, frequently result in the development of policy. Thus policies are active, living documents that can change in response to changes in the environment of the organization.

Policy development is affected by the institutional context of the organization and its actors (Houlihan, 2017). Institutional context involves the political, sociological, cultural, fiscal, ethical, legal, and technological environments within which policy is developed by the actors (employees, volunteers, parents, participants, etc.) of the organization. For a college athletic department, these are factors within the department, within the university, and from the wider external environment including alumni and the community. Consider the example of gender equity in college sport: this became a political and legal issue with the passing of Title IX in the United States when the federal government passed into law that no person shall be excluded from participation in sport on the basis of sex. Therefore policy to ensure that opportunities exist for both genders was affected by the wishes of politicians, on the basis of the citizens of society, to be fair in delivering opportunities for both women and men. Such policy certainly has fiscal implications, and is influenced on the basis of the cultural values, norms, and beliefs of a society with broader views than those valuing only male sport opportunities. A wide variety of individual forces influence policy development.

Since policies are meant to clarify actions, embed fairness within operations of what and how things are done, and to help manage risk, it is understandable that policies result from issues that arise. Ultimately, a policy guides the actions of all members of the organization facing a particular issue or dilemma, speeding decision making, and unifying the thinking of managers and subordinates.

An effective way to develop policy and to be strategic about it is through the case method analysis for understanding the problem and properly framing the issue (King, 2017; VanderZwaag, 1998). Essentially, the case method analysis is a procedure for looking at a problem, collecting information to assess the available options for solving the problem, and then choosing the alternative most closely aligned with the strategy and philosophy of the organization. This method involves four main steps, as outlined in Exhibit 3.5.

As an example for using the case method analysis outlined, let's consider Major League Soccer (MLS) in the United States and Canada:

1. **Define the problem.** MLS executives have been aware that soccer, or football as the sport is known around the world, is highly popular worldwide, but does not draw the same fan or media following as other professional leagues in North America, such as the NFL (National Football League), NHL (National Hockey League), NBA (National Basketball League), PGA (Professional Golfers' Association), and LPGA (Ladies Professional Golf Association). In a strategic move, MLS executives decided that increasing the league market share was an issue for the league to strategically manage and that its impact on MLS was a major problem for realizing potential levels of profit.

2. **Collect information and formulate options.** Those same executives spent considerable time studying the other leagues including England's Premier League (EPL), identifying ways and means for increasing MLS North American profits through team expansion, player acquisitions, promotion and publicity, television, merchandising, and stadium capacity.

3. **Evaluate the options.** Evaluate the pros and cons, as well as the potential impact of each of the options identified above.

4. **Choose the favored option and define the action.** MLS executives identified and pursued player acquisition as a means for increasing the exposure for soccer within the North American professional sport market

(Step 4) and thus as a strategic move to increase profit. As an example, in 2007 David Beckham was enticed to join the MLS's Los Angeles Galaxy. The impact of his playing for an MLS team was immediate for virtually all MLS teams in terms of ticket sales, merchandising, and television revenues. Leander Schaerlaeckens (2017, para. 30) from Yahoo! Sports reflects on the enduring impact of the MLS strategy:

> Since Beckham's signing, MLS has grown from 13 teams to 22 for the 2017 season. The Designated Player rule has been expanded and there were no fewer than 50 of them last year. Salaries and TV ratings are up. Regular season attendance has jumped from an average of 15,504 in 2006 to 21,629 in 2016, across far more teams. There are now more than twice the number of stadiums built either specifically for soccer or designed to accommodate it. Toronto FC paid an expansion fee of $10 million; the next round of new teams, when the league grows to 26, and then 28, will pay $150 million and perhaps upwards.

At the end of each industry segment chapter in this book, a case study gives you an opportunity to deal with real-life policy issues confronting sport managers working in that industry segment. After reading the cases, you may wish to refer to Exhibit 3.5 and follow the steps presented to frame your response to the case.

Once policy is defined, it must be communicated within the organization and properly enforced. This is possible only by developing clearly delineated, written policy (refer to Exhibit 3.5) and a procedure for communicating the policy throughout all levels of the organization. Such a procedure includes the specific communication method (face-to-face meetings, e-mail, or written memo) and the timing for announcing and clarifying the policy, and it identifies exactly who announces what. Commitment and understanding from every level of the organization are necessary for organizational policy to serve its intended purpose. In addition, the developed policy needs to be affiliated with the mission, business pursuits, strategy, and environment of

---

Case Method Analysis Steps for Developing Policy | *exhibit* **3.5**

1. Define in detail the issue and the facts describing the scope of the problem and its impact on the organization.

2. Collect and assess information on both sides of the issue. What are the options for action?

3. Evaluate how and to what extent each of these options will ultimately affect the organization.

4. Choose the favored option for the solution and specifically define the action. This, then, becomes the written policy statement.

the sport organization. Policies need to remain current and closely aligned with the strategic management activities of the overall management process. In fact, policies play an important role in strategy implementation.

STRATEGIC MANAGEMENT ACTIVITIES AND POLICY DEVELOPMENT

In Chapters 1 and 2 you were introduced to managerial activities related to governance. Planning, organizing, and decision making are actions carried out by sport managers at the *micro*, or departmental, level of analysis. These actions are considered everyday activities performed as the functions of management. The alternative to the micro level of analysis is the *macro* approach to managing the organization. A macro orientation looks at those issues impacting the organization as a whole, assessing things from the perspective of the larger, more complex structure. The content presented earlier in this chapter takes on a macro perspective by investigating the concepts of strategic management and policy development, two concepts that embrace the organization as a whole.

It is important to understand the link between the macro and micro levels of managerial activities guiding an organization. In essence, the managerial activities carried out at the micro level of analysis (planning, organizing, decision making) provide information for the construction of the business strategy and policy development occurring at the macro level of organizational activity. Departmental activities such as planning, organizing, and decision making provide fundamental information for defining organizational strategies. The business strategies then contribute a foundation from which organizational policy is derived. This process should be viewed as a dynamic operation in which information flows both ways in response to the changes that occur in the organizational environment (Exhibit 3.6). Policies empower the action of strategic management.

---

exhibit **3.6** The Macro and Micro Levels of Management Interaction

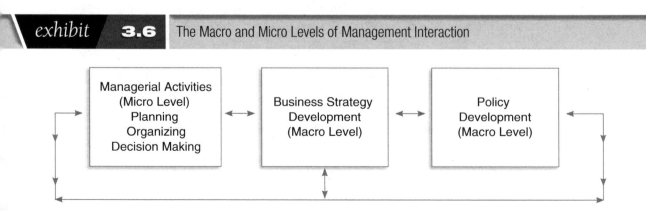

The interaction of three factors—managerial activities, strategy, and the size; technology; and environment of the organization's structure—is the primary determinant of organizational design (Griffin, Phillips, & Gully, 2017). The structure of an organization reflects the division of labor and the hierarchy of authority and power that exists to maximize the use of available resources (O'Brien & Gowthorp, 2017). The actual structural configuration of the organization can be analyzed from several different perspectives, including (1) its size and shape as depicted on the organizational chart, (2) how it operates via decision making, specialized tasks, and procedures, and (3) the responsibility and authority accorded its members (Griffin, Phillips, & Gully, 2017). The chapters that follow describe the governance structures present in several different sport industry segments from these perspectives.

SUMMARY

Sport pervades society, and sports is big business. Organizations delivering the business of sport have grown in response to the interest and economic impact of the sport industry. Accordingly, the importance of effective management has emerged, and the concept of strategic management for sport organizations has evolved. Business strategy involves the development of purposeful plans, actions, and decisions that enable an organization to reach its goals. The strategic level of management involves global, organization-wide strategy dealing with issues that have important financial or human resource consequences for the organization as a whole. Such factors are related to the mission of the organization and are affected by the organizational environment. Strategy involves the creation of mission, goals, and objective statements, along with tactics. Strategy should enable action and decision making as well. Strategic decision making means making the right decision at the right time. Strategic management and decision making are critically important for sport organizations in the pursuit of their organizational goals. Strategy encourages planning, capitalizing on opportunities, and overall competitiveness.

Strategic management is enabled through policy development. A policy is a written statement providing guidelines to solve recurring problems fairly and consistently. Policy is written for issues broadly impacting the organization and its constituent groups. They provide for equitable decision making that can be enacted throughout the organization on a consistent basis. Policy is developed using case method analysis: collecting the facts of the issue, defining and evaluating the options for action, selecting the favored option, and developing the written policy statement.

Including issues of strategy links the micro level of analysis of the organization (the managerial functions of planning, organizing, and decision making) to the macro perspective (strategic management and strategic decision making). The effective sport organization will be structured to embrace both concepts in the pursuit of its organizational goals.

caseSTUDY

POLICY DEVELOPMENT

As a high school AD you supervise a large sport program (19 sports) and are determined to be fair to each of the teams. Your problem: six sports (girls field hockey, boys football, and boys and girls soccer, lacrosse, and archery) require practice and game time on the only outdoor field you have.

■ Follow the steps in Exhibit 3.5, culminating in writing a policy that (a) covers the use of the field by your teams (you are not in a position to drop any sports), (b) describes the boundaries for using fields off school property, and (c) manages the political situation of the Football Booster Club demanding sole use of the field and the School Principal's concern for safety of participants leaving the field to go home in the dark.

CHAPTER questions

1. Suppose you are sitting in an interview for a management position with your favorite professional sport organization. One member of the interview panel says: "The business of sports is fiercely competitive. We have to be very strategic in our management decisions. Tell us what strategic management means to you." List five answers you would provide, given your understanding of this chapter.

2. Consider the following statement: *timing is everything in strategic decision making.* Is this statement true? Why, or why not? How do you know the best time to make a decision?

3. Use your device to look up a sports policy for one of your favorite teams. Identify three strengths and weaknesses of the policy, and explain your position within a class discussion.

4. You are the manager of Campus Recreation at a small, Division III college. Your boss asks you to create a policy for the department that will guide decisions for whether women can play on men's intramural teams and vice-versa. First write a policy statement on this issue, and then list and explain the factors of the environment that influenced the policy you developed. Discuss your ideas with a classmate.

FOR ADDITIONAL INFORMATION

For more information check out the following resources:

1. Steps in the policy development process from Leo Isaac: www.leoisaac.com/policy/top132.htm
2. Henry, I. P. & Ko, L. M. (Eds.) (2013). *Handbook of sport policy*. London: Routledge.
3. David Beckham's Impact on MLS: https://ca.sports.yahoo.com/news/david-beckhams-impact-on-american-soccer-endures-a-decade-after-landmark-mls-signing-081645640.html
4. USA Swimming Safe Sport Handbook http://www.metroswimming.org/safety/Safe-Sport-Handbook-FINAL.pdf
5. Comparing Sports Policies in Economically Developed Countries: https://ecpr.eu/Filestore/PaperProposal/7bd9c6bb-0ce4-4e72-874c-57453de55d70.pdf
6. World Anti-Doping Policy: The Code: https://www.wada-ama.org/en/what-we-do/the-code

REFERENCES

Belcourt, M., & McBey, K. J. (2015). *Strategic human resources planning* (6th ed.). Scarborough, Canada: Nelson Thomson Learning.

Chelladurai, P. (2014). *Managing organizations for sport and physical activity: A systems perspective* (4th ed.). Scottsdale, AZ: Holcomb Hathaway.

DeSchriver, T. D., Mahony, D. F., & Hambrick, M. E. (2014). Finance and economics in the sport industry. In P. Petersen, & L. Thibault (Eds.), *Contemporary sport management* (5th ed.). Champaign, IL: Human Kinetics.

Fried, G., DeSchriver, T., & Mondello, M. (2013). *Sport Finance* (3rd ed.). Champaign, IL: Human Kinetics.

Griffin, R. W., Phillips, J. M., & Gully, S. M. (2017). *Organizational behavior: Managing people and organizations* (12th ed.). Retrieved from https://www.cengage.com/c/organizational-behavior-managing-people-and-organizations-12e-griffin.

Houlihan, B. (2017). Sport policy and politics. In R. Hoye & M. M. Parent (Eds.), *The Sage handbook of sport management* (pp. 183–201). London: Sage.

Hoye, R., Nicholson, M., & Houlihan, B. (2010). *Sport and policy: Issues and analysis*. Oxford, UK: Butterworth-Heinemann.

King, N. (2017). *Sport governance: An introduction*. London: Routledge.

Markovits, A. S., & Rensmann, L. (2013). *Gaming the world: How sports are reshaping global politics and culture*. Princeton, NJ: Princeton University Press.

Masterman, G. (2014). *Strategic sports event management* (3rd ed.). New York: Routledge.

Mintzberg, H. (1975). The manager's job: Folklore and fact. *Harvard Business Review*, 53, 49–61.

Mintzberg, H. (1988). *In the strategy process*. Englewood Cliffs, NJ: Prentice Hall.

Mintzberg, H., Lampel, J., Quinn, J., & Ghoshal, S. (2013). *The strategy process: Concepts, context, and cases* (5th ed.). Englewood Cliffs, NJ: Prentice Hall.

O'Brien, D., & Gowthorp, L. (2017). Organizational structure. In R. Hoye & M. M. Parent (Eds.), *The Sage handbook of sport management* (pp. 39–61). London: Sage.

Ozanian, M. K. (1995, February 14). Following the money: FW's first annual report on the economics of sports. *Financial World, 164,* 26–27, 30–31.

Parent, M., O'Brien, D., & Slack, T. (2012). Organizational theory and sport management. In L. Trenberth & D. Hassan (Eds.), *Managing sport business: An introduction* (pp. 99–120). New York: Routledge.

Pearce, J. A., & Robinson, R. B. (2014). *Strategic management: Planning for domestic and global competition* (14th ed.). Toronto, Canada: McGraw-Hill Education.

Schaerlaeckens, L. (2017). *David Beckham's impact on American soccer endures a decade after landmark MLS signing.* Retrieved from https://ca.sports.yahoo.com/news/david-beckhams-impact-on-american-soccer-endures-a-decade-after-landmark-mls-signing-081645640.html

Szymanski, M., & Wolfe, R. A. (2017). Strategic management. In R. Hoye & M. M. Parent (Eds.), *The Sage handbook of sport management* (pp. 24–38). London: Sage.

Taylor, T. (2017). Human resource management. In R. Hoye & M. M. Parent (Eds.), *The Sage handbook of sport management* (pp. 62–84). London: Sage.

VanderZwaag, H. J. (1998). *Policy development in sport management.* Westport, CT: Praeger.

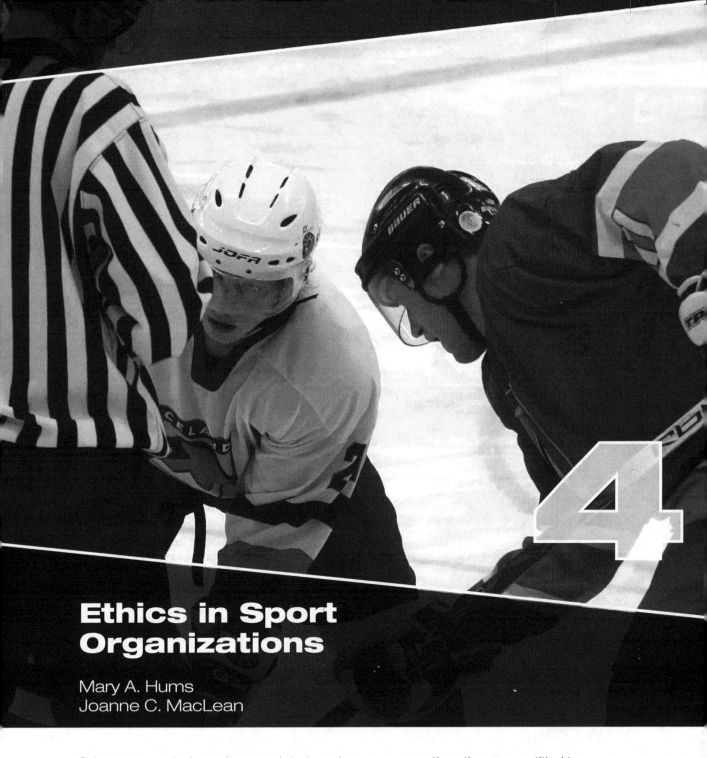

Ethics in Sport Organizations

Mary A. Hums
Joanne C. MacLean

Sales representatives alter receipts to get more money than they are entitled to. Managers lie to their bosses about using company-owned cars. Bosses lie to their employees about company policies. Politicians appoint family members without following proper procedures. Accountants alter the books to cover up questionable spending practices. Major corporations are forced to close down because of income mismanagement. Large manufacturers violate the human rights of their workers. Wealthy government officials ignore the needs of their lower income level constituents to line their pockets with financial support from political action committees. Organizations use production processes and build facilities that are not environmentally friendly. Such negative news from the corporate and political worlds calls into question the ethics we see practiced in business and industry on a daily basis.

It is of the essence that leaders in sport organizations behave in an ethical manner. Leaders set the tone for their sport organizations. We need leaders with formal authority in sport organizations, but more so, according to Dov Siedman, author of the book *How* and CEO of LRN (quoted in Friedman, 2017, paras. 13–14), what really makes any organizational system work, is

> "when leaders occupying those formal positions—from business to politics to schools to sports—have moral authority. Leaders with moral authority understand what they can demand of others and what they must inspire in them. They also understand that formal authority can be won or seized, but moral authority has to be earned every day by how they lead. And we don't have enough of these leaders." In fact, we have so few we've forgotten what they look like. Leaders with moral authority have several things in common, said Seidman: "They trust people with the truth—however bright or dark. They're animated by values—especially humility—and principles of probity, so they do the right things, especially when they're difficult or unpopular."

The world of sport is a place where we want to believe in fair play and good conduct. But is this world somehow immune to the ethical issues confronting managers and business-people in general society? Unfortunately, the answer is "No," as is illustrated by the following examples:

- A National Football League (NFL) team is accused of altering the air in play-off game footballs.
- National Collegiate Athletic Association (NCAA) football players participate in sexual violence and their coaching staff supports them.
- Major League Baseball (MLB) players use banned substances to improve performance.
- A state high school athletic association policy on transgender athletes forces those athletes into competing under their incorrect gender.
- Fans shout racial slurs at opposing players.

- International officials accept bribes to swing the votes for the selection of a host city for the World Cup.

- Investigations reveal state-sponsored systematic doping programs which protect "dirty" athletes.

- A well-known international gymnastics coach is accused of sexual misconduct involving athletes.

Sadly, these types of incidents appear with regularity in the sports pages and are often the lead stories on the evening sports broadcasts. All the above scenarios involve behavior that is considered unethical. As sport managers, you will confront situations that will present you with ethical dilemmas. How, then, should you respond to them?

SPORT AS A MIRROR OF SOCIETY

Every society faces its own unique issues, including violence, substance abuse, domestic abuse, racism, sexism, homophobia, ableism, economic downturns, differential treatment based on religion, bullying, and corporate cheating. These issues also appear in all levels and facets of industry, including the sport industry. It has been said that sport is a mirror, a microcosm, or reflection of society, not just in the United States, but other nations as well (Eitzen & Sage, 2009; Gargan, 2015; Gibbs, 2016; Maguire & Nakayama, 2006). It should come as no surprise, therefore, that sport managers face the same issues.

According to DeSensi and Rosenberg (2010, p. 2), the following are ethical considerations for sport managers:

- professionalism
- equity
- legal and financial management
- personnel concerns
- governance and policies
- league and franchise issues
- matters of social justice

Notice that one of the points above mentions governance. Many of the ethical considerations listed above have obvious parallels as societal issues. So how do these societal issues manifest themselves in sport? The simple diagram in Exhibit 4.1 illustrates how societal issues are reflected in sport.

The first example depicted in the model is social activism. People as a whole are becoming more aware of social issues present in society and are making public statements about them. Look no further than the Black Lives Matter movement or the 2017 Women's March on Washington DC. Sport figures are now standing up for just causes as well. While the most notable

exhibit   **4.1**   Societal Issues Reflected in Sport

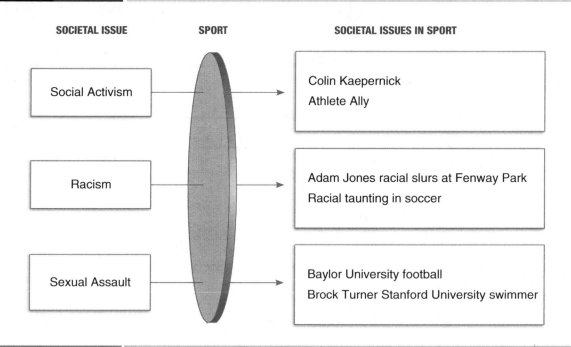

athlete to take this brave step was the great Muhammad Ali, others have since followed suit. NFL quarterback Colin Kaepernick led the way with his decision to kneel during the US national anthem as a statement against the treatment of African Americans. Hudson Taylor founded Athlete Ally as a group to stand up for the rights of the lesbian, gay, bisexual, trans, and queer (LGBTQ) community (Athlete Ally, 2017). Athletes are finding their voice and realizing the powerful platform they have to exert influence in society.

The second example shown in Exhibit 4.1—racism—still exists in society, as evidenced by the need for the Black Lives Matter Movement. In sport, we saw Baltimore Orioles outfielder Adam Jones experience racial slurs at Fenway Park (Perez, 2017). Black players are still regularly being taunted in international football, despite the best efforts of international governing bodies to curb the behavior (Reuters, 2015).

The third example illustrated in Exhibit 4.1 is sexual assault, a daily occurrence in society, often depicted by the media on television and in films. Sexual assault, the societal issue, appears on the left-hand side of the model. As the issue is filtered through sport, we see, the disaster that is Baylor University football and the systematic cover-up of coaches and administrators to protect players at the expense of the survivors (Schnell, 2017). Another example is the case of Brock Turner, the Stanford University swimmer who raped a woman and was convicted but granted a lenient sentence by the judge (Rocha & Mejia, 2016).

This diagram could include other examples, but its purpose is not to provide a comprehensive list. Rather, its purpose is to ask, "As sport managers, when we are confronted by these issues, how will we respond?" Responding to these incidents is never easy, because sport managers feel pressure from many constituencies to do the right thing. But what is "the right thing," and more important, how should a sport manager decide on carrying out "the right thing"? Remember, too, as mentioned in Chapter 2, the decisions sport managers make will be publicly scrutinized by the media, fans, and casual readers of the news. As a sport manager, you will be faced with ethical dilemmas on a regular basis. But will you know how to recognize an ethical dilemma?

ETHICS DEFINED

Where do ethical codes in sport management emanate from, and who is responsible for ethical behavior? The United Nations Educational, Scientific and Cultural Organization (UNESCO) (2017) has a Code of Sports Ethics and states that responsibility for ethical behavior lies with those who are involved with sports for children and young adults including (a) governments at all levels and the agencies that work with them; (b) sports and sports-related organizations including sports federations and governing bodies; and (c) individuals including parents, teachers, coaches, referees, officials, sport leaders, athletes who serve as role models, administrators, journalists, doctors, and pharmacists. Clearly, sport managers in general and those working specifically in sport governing bodies are responsible for ethical behavior. While this may sound far away from you as you read this book, ultimately it means as a sport manager you will be responsible for ethics in your sport organization. All sport managers are responsible for ethical behavior, and the higher one moves up in the organization the greater that responsibility becomes. As Lussier and Kimball (2009) point out, "An organization's ethics are the collective behavior of its employees. If each employee acts ethically, the actions of the organization will be ethical, too. The starting place for ethics, therefore, is you" (p. 35).

How does a sport manager recognize when and where ethics will come into play? Sport managers face certain issues and considerations that require ethical analysis. Some of these include (Hums, Wolff, & Morris, 2012):

- non-discrimination/equity in sporting participation
- fair play
- inclusive facilities and equipment
- protection against abuse and violence
- safety and security
- sport-related labor conditions
- employment and hiring practices
- right to due process

- access to information
- freedom of speech
- right to privacy
- environmental violations
- displacement of persons for sporting events
- access and availability of resources/financial spending

Often, when people think of sport ethics they think of conduct and fair play *on* the field. As stated by the Council of Europe Committee of Ministers (2010, p.1), "the ethical considerations that underpin fair play are not an optional element but an essential component to all sporting activities." Fair play extends to the management of sport as well. From the information above, it is obvious that ethics and ethical concerns spill over into the business aspects of sport. The business venue is where sport managers will encounter myriad ethical issues and dilemmas.

ETHICAL DILEMMAS

 hat is an ethical dilemma? According to Mullane (2009, pp. 2–3), an *ethical dilemma* occurs:

> when important values come into conflict, and the decision maker
> (the leader, in many cases) must make a choice between these
> values . . . To further complicate things, ethical dilemmas usually
> involve multiple stakeholders (those affected by the ultimate decision),
> and the outcome is marred by uncertainty.

According to Wallace (2012), a manager faces a significant ethical conflict when the following exist: "(1) significant value conflicts among differing interests, (2) real alternatives that are equally justifiable, and (3) significant consequences to stakeholders in the situation" (Definition section). For example, a star athlete is arrested for driving while intoxicated one week before the final game for the league championship. Should the player be allowed to play?

- Are value conflicts present? Some people would say the athlete should not play because of the arrest; others would say he has been arrested but not convicted, so let him play.
- Do real alternatives exist that are equally justifiable? Real alternatives may include playing the athlete, not playing the athlete at all, or limiting playing time.
- Are there significant consequences to stakeholders, including owners, sponsors, or investors? If the athlete does not play and the team loses the championship, significant revenue could be lost; if the athlete does play, negative publicity will be significant.

When faced with an ethical dilemma, what is a sport manager to do? What should guide the sport manager when making a decision about an ethical dilemma like this?

ETHICAL DECISION-MAKING MODELS

As discussed in Chapter 2, a sport manager must have an organized and sequential method for making decisions. It is no different when the problem is ethical in nature. The literature on ethical decision making is loaded with different models for managers to use (Low, Ferrell, & Mansfield, 2000). Some very practical models and guidelines have been suggested (Lipschutz, 2013; McDonald, 2001; Thornton, Champion, & Ruddell, 2012; Zinn, 1993). These models examine a variety of factors and involve multiple steps. For our purposes, we will identify a straightforward model sport managers can apply in the workplace. The model presented below by Hums, Barr, and Guillion (1999, p. 64) and Hancock and Hums (2011) is an adaptation of Zinn's model:

1. **Identify the correct problem to solve.** When making any type of decision, the decision maker must first identify the *real* problem. Identifying a symptom of the problem and acting on that will not resolve the problem itself.
2. **Gather all pertinent information.** Good decision makers try to be as informed as possible. Is it realistic to think you can gather every piece of information needed? Probably not, but sport managers need to make a good faith effort to find all the information possible to guide them in their decision making.
3. **Explore codes of conduct relevant to one's profession or to this particular dilemma.** More and more sport organizations are developing codes of conduct. Take a look at codes from yours and other sport organizations to see if they provide guidance for your decision.
4. **Examine one's own personal values and beliefs.** We all come to the workplace with our own unique sets of values. Be sure you understand your values and how they could impact your decision. This does not mean every decision has to be in line with your own values. It means you must be keenly aware of your own values and how they may influence your decision.
5. **Consult with peers or other individuals in the industry who may have experience in similar situations.** Sport managers throughout the industry are facing increasing numbers of ethical issues. Perhaps some trusted colleagues have faced a similar dilemma. Talk with them to discuss how they went about solving the issue.
6. **List decision options.** Good decision makers learn to look at as many options as possible so they can make the best choice.

7. **Look for a win–win situation if at all possible.** This is a difficult but critical step. Ethical dilemmas arise when there are questions about the right thing to do. Try to make a decision that maximizes the outcome for the parties involved.

8. **Ask the question, "How would my family feel if my decision and how and why I arrived at my decision appeared on the Internet tomorrow?"** Remember, as a sport manager, your decisions will be publicly analyzed and criticized. Be sure you have done all the right things in making your decision and that there is nothing about your decision you could not be up front about.

9. **Sleep on it.** Do not rush to a decision. In other words, think hard about the situation and the options and consequences you face. You need to make a well-thought-out decision.

10. **Make the best decision possible, knowing it may not be perfect.** At some point, you will have to make your decision. Knowing you have followed the steps listed above will help you reach the best decision possible. In ethical decision making, reasonable people will often reasonably disagree over decisions.

11. **Evaluate the decision over time.** Often overlooked by managers, it is important to reflect on the decision later to see how it is working, or how changes could be made to improve upon it. This step is especially important if the issue or a similar one arises again.

Another useful decision-making technique for examining ethical decisions is the SLEEPE Principle (presented in Chapter 2). This model helps the sport manager look at the big picture before making a decision. Ethical decisions, by their very nature, are bound to have far-reaching and complex ramifications. The SLEEPE Principle helps a sport manager think in broad terms about the ramifications of ethical decisions. In addition, this model has ethical considerations already built in as the second *E* in SLEEPE. Regardless of which model a sport manager chooses to use, each provides a structure to help make decisions (Hums, 2006, 2007).

Up to this point, we have concentrated mainly on ethical situations and how individual sport managers will respond to them. Now we must expand that view and look at sport organizations as a whole and their corporate stance on ethical issues. One way to assess the ethical nature of a sport organization is to examine what kind of "citizen" the sport organization represents. This idea of a sport organization as a "citizen" can be looked at through the concept of corporate social responsibility (CSR).

CORPORATE SOCIAL RESPONSIBILITY

C*orporate social responsibility* is a term that often appears in business ethics literature. What does it mean to be a responsible corporate citizen? In general, CSR is a management concept whereby companies integrate social and environmental concerns in their business operations and interactions with their stakeholders. CSR is generally understood as being the way through which a company achieves a balance of economic, environmental and social imperatives ("Triple-Bottom-Line Approach"), while at the same time addressing the expectations of shareholders and stakeholders. (UNIDO, n.d., para 1)

Another definition offered by Rankin (2017a, para. 1) states that "CSR encourages companies to be more aware of their impact on society. Its focus can be wide ranging, addressing issues such as education, health, gender inequalities and the environment." Post (2017, para. 16) quotes Susan Hunt Stevens, founder and CEO of employee engagement platform WeSpire, "[CSR] often represents the policies, practices and initiatives a company commits to in order to govern themselves with honesty and transparency and have a positive impact on social and environmental wellbeing." While speaking out using the voice of CSR on the side of just causes may come at a business cost, the bigger question to ask is "What is the cost of remaining silent?" (Price, 2017, p. 2).

Sport management researchers have begun to study the topic of CSR in sport (Babiak & Trendafilova, 2011; Babiak & Wolfe, 2009; Bradish & Cronin, 2009) and have called for sport managers to be more aware of the power of sport to do good (Darnell, 2012; Hums, 2010; Hums & Hancock, 2012; Hums & Wolff, 2014; Thibault, 2009). Social responsibility should become part of who you are and how you do your job on a daily basis once you become a sport manager. It helps to have a few ideas on how to make sure your sport organization acts in a socially responsible manner.

How can CSR be measured? There is no singular measure of good citizenship because by its very nature it can be ascertained only from the perspectives of multiple stakeholders. One of the earliest and still often cited measurements of CSR comes from Carroll (1991), who explained how corporations can operate at four different CSR levels:

1. economic—focus only on economic concerns
2. legal—follow the letter of the law
3. ethical—follow the spirit of the law
4. philanthropic—act as a leader in promoting CSR

He examined corporations and the levels where they existed relative to various organizational stakeholders, including owners, customers, employees, the community, and the public at large (Carroll, 1991). The economic level represents the lowest level of CSR, and the philanthropic represents the highest level of CSR. The concept of CSR is usually applied in business settings; rarely has Carroll's model been applied in a sport industry setting.

Applying CSR in a Sport Setting

For our purposes, let's examine a college athletic department and its compliance with Title IX. By law, a college athletic department can comply with Title IX by meeting any one prong of the so-called three-prong approach:

1. proportionality—having the same percentage of female athletes and female undergraduates
2. a continuing history of expanding athletic opportunities for women
3. demonstrating success in meeting the interests and abilities of female students (Carpenter & Acosta, 2004, pp. 14–15)

Given this information about Title IX compliance, let's apply the four levels of the CSR model to an intercollegiate athletic department.

1. ECONOMIC LEVEL. If the department is operating at the economic level, this means it is most interested in achieving purely financial goals. Here the Athletic Department would basically ignore Title IX, doing nothing to comply until forced to do so by outside influences. Using the logic that complying with Title IX is too costly, the Athletic Department would not take any steps to comply with the law unless it became costlier not to comply.

2. LEGAL LEVEL. If the Athletic Department operates at the legal level, it will attempt to meet the minimum legal criterion for compliance. At this stage, organizations strive to meet legal minimums and basically follow the letter of the law. Most certainly it would only attempt to fulfill one of the three prongs currently used to determine compliance. Since Title IX is not a quota system, this Athletic Department may rely on the so-called proportionality rule. It may make the case for continuing progress in developing opportunities for female athletes, or it could show it is meeting the needs and interests of the female student population. Athletic departments at this level are likely to drop men's sports to be in compliance, a quick and efficient way to come into minimum compliance with the proportionality prong. These same departments may state the reason for dropping the sports was because they needed more resources for women's sport, when in fact the reason was the football "arms race," a football program's increased need for expenditures to keep up with competing teams.

3. ETHICAL LEVEL. The Athletic Department operating at the ethical level would follow not just the letter of the law, but the spirit of the law as well. The department would not just meet but may exceed the legal minimums because it values providing equal opportunities for women. The department would add emerging sports that attract female participants, such as rowing or lacrosse. Rather than dropping men's sports, the department would find alternative sources of funding or ways to redirect the budget so that female opportunities are increased without adversely affecting opportunities for males.

4. PHILANTHROPIC LEVEL.   Athletic departments operating at the philanthropic level become active advocates for Title IX. They develop model programs for compliance and strive to fulfill all three prongs of the law, instead of the minimal one prong for compliance. These departments actively offer help to athletic departments at other universities as those departments work to comply with Title IX. By presenting their programs as models and perhaps acting in a consultative mode to help other institutions comply with the law, athletic departments can operate at the philanthropic level.

Sport Organizations and Corporate Social Responsibility in Practice

More and more sport organizations, governing bodies, and clubs are beginning to integrate elements of CSR into their everyday business operations (Rankin, 2017b). For example, Nike (much maligned for its labor practices, including unsafe working conditions and low wages) issued its 2014–2015 *Sustainable Business Report*. The company's four main approaches are to work to minimize their environmental footprint, transform manufacturing, unleash human potential, and work on governance and policy (Nike, n.d.). The Sunderland Football Club was awarded the Best Corporate Social Responsibility Scheme at the 2016 Football Business Awards. The English football club has a relationship with the Foundation of Light. "The Foundation of Light is the corporate social responsibility programme of Sunderland Athletic FC. The multi-award winning Foundation was established in 2001 and works across the North East of England with a strategy to 'Involve. Educate. Inspire'" (sportanddev Community, 2016, para. 9).

The International Olympic Committee (IOC) includes several examples of CSR in its required documents for cities bidding to host the Olympic and Paralympic Games. For example, the 2018 Candidature Acceptance Procedure contains suggestions on Olympic Games Impact and on Sustainable Development (IOC, 2009). The IOC's policy document Agenda 2020 includes numerous recommendations for CSR related topics such as including sustainability in all aspects of the Olympic Games, strengthening the sixth fundamental principle of Olympism which deals with anti-discrimination, complying with basic principles of good governance, increasing transparency, and strengthening ethics (IOC, 2014). For the 2012 London Games, sustainability was part of the plan from the start, and included areas such as carbon management, sustainable transport, food vision, and waste management (London 2012, n.d.).

Major professional sport organizations also act in a socially responsible manner. For example, the National Football League (NFL) has its annual Walter Payton Man of the Year Awards. "Each team nominates one player as its Man of the Year who is then eligible to win the national award. These players represent the best of the NFL's commitment to philanthropy and community impact" (NFL, n.d., p. 7) The Ladies Professional Golf Association (LPGA), Women's National Basketball Association (WNBA), and Major League Baseball (MLB) all work with the Susan G. Komen Breast Cancer Foundation. MLB's Reviving Baseball in the Inner Cities

(RBI) program has grown over the last few years. Many universities support local community activities through programs such as the University of Notre Dame's partnership with its campus Center for Social Concerns, where athletes get involved with projects on campus, in the local community, and in other areas around the country.

Codes of ethics vary in content, length, and complexity. Exhibit 4.2 offers a sample code of ethics from the National Federation of State High School Associations (2017). Exhibit 4.3 shows the table of contents of the

---

exhibit **4.2** National Federation of State High School Association Coaches Code of Ethics

The function of a coach is to educate students through participation in interscholastic competition. An interscholastic program should be designed to enhance academic achievement and should never interfere with opportunities for academic success. Each student should be treated with the utmost respect, and his or her welfare should be considered in decisions by the coach at all times. Accordingly, the following guidelines for coaches have been adopted by the NFHS Board of Directors:

- The coach shall be aware that he or she has a tremendous influence, for either good or ill, on the education of the student and, thus, shall never place the value of winning above the value of instilling the highest ideals of character.
- The coach shall uphold the honor and dignity of the profession. In all personal contact with students, officials, athletic directors, school administrators, the state high school athletic association, the media, and the public, the coach shall strive to set an example of the highest ethical and moral conduct.
- The coach shall take an active role in the prevention of drug, alcohol and tobacco abuse.
- The coach shall avoid the use of alcohol and tobacco products when in contact with players.
- The coach shall promote the entire interscholastic program of the school and direct his or her program in harmony with the total school program.
- The coach shall master the contest rules and shall teach them to his or her team members. The coach shall not seek an advantage by circumvention of the spirit or letter of the rules.
- The coach shall exert his or her influence to enhance sportsmanship by spectators, both directly and by working closely with cheerleaders, pep club sponsors, booster clubs, and administrators.
- The coach shall respect and support contest officials. The coach shall not indulge in conduct which would incite players or spectators against the officials. Public criticism of officials or players is unethical.
- The coach should meet and exchange cordial greetings with the opposing coach to set the correct tone for the event before and after the contest.
- The coach shall not exert pressure on faculty members to give student special consideration.
- The coach shall not scout opponents by any means other than those adopted by the league and/or state high school athletic association.

Source: NFSHSA (2015).

International Olympic Committee Code of Ethics

Preamble

A Fundamental Principles

B Integrity of Conduct

C Integrity of Competitions

D Good Governance and Resources

E Candidatures

F Confidentiality

G Reporting Obligation

H Implementation

Source: IOC. (2016). IOC code of ethics. Retrieved from https://stillmed.olympic.org/media/Document%20Library/ OlympicOrg/IOC/What-We-Do/Leading-the-Olympic-Movement/Code-of-Ethics/EN-IOC-Code-of-Ethics-2016.pdf

IOC Code of Ethics (IOC, 2016). Whether the code is long or short, concise or complex, what is most important is that sport organizations are beginning to develop codes of ethics appropriate for use in their segment of the industry.

ETHICS AND SPORT GOVERNANCE ORGANIZATIONS

Why is it important to include a chapter in this book about ethics? Individual sport managers and sport organizations look to their governing bodies for guidance on a wide range of topics, including legal issues, safety issues, and personnel issues—and ethical issues such as good business practices.

Sport governing bodies can set the tone from the top down regarding ethical issues. The stance taken by a governing body will influence decisions you make as a sport manager in any organization under that governing body's umbrella. An example of this relationship is the effect on International Federations and National Sports Organizations when the IOC makes a ruling on banned substances. State and provincial high school athletic associations are taking stronger stances on tobacco use by minors, so individual schools are also instituting such programs. Governing bodies' rulings on ethical issues will hopefully result in behavioral changes and choices by their constituencies as well.

Sport managers need to understand the effects of their decisions and the number of people affected by their decisions (Crosset & Hums, 2015). According to DeSensi (2012, p. 130):

> Is it too much to expect of sport managers that they become ethically, morally and socially responsible professionals? My response is no; I believe they should be at the forefront of this issue . . . The moral climate of sport has always been in need of improvement, and who better than sport managers to assume this responsibility?

Knowing you will face ethical dilemmas, you will need to employ an ethical decision-making model to deal with them. You will have the opportunity to consider ethical questions in some case studies in this book. You will shape the culture of your organization, impacting its ethical climate and its stance on being a good corporate citizen. In other words, the driving force for a sport organization's level of CSR rests with its employees and, most certainly, with its managers. That means you!

SUMMARY

We see numerous examples of ethical dilemmas in society today. The sport industry is part of that greater society; therefore, we encounter ethical issues and dilemmas in the sport industry as well. When sport managers are faced with ethical dilemmas, they have to make decisions about them. To make sound decisions, sport managers must follow a systematic ethical decision-making process.

When examining ethics, examine ethical activity on the organizational as well as on the individual level. One measure of ethics in a sport organization is CSR, whether it is reflected in a sport organization's stance on a particular issue, its involvement in charitable community events, or its adoption of a code of ethics.

Finally, it is important to examine ethics in the context of governance because of the influence governing bodies have over individual sport organizations. By exhibiting ethical behaviors at the top levels, governing bodies set the ethical tone for their membership.

case STUDY

ETHICS

1. Use the ethical decision-making model we just discussed in class to deal with the following situations:

   a. You are the Director of the Tiger Athletic Fund, the fund-raising arm of your NCAA Football Bowl Subdivision (FBS) school,

Central City University. One of your major long time donors, Ray Mosswell, whose name adorns the football practice facility, recently made a significant investment in a construction company owned by an international business with an abysmal human rights abuse record, having recently been tied to human trafficking. Needless to say, the story made national headlines and has lit up social media. It is time to renew his annual donation to Tiger Athletics.

b. You are the Athletic Director (AD) at Marion Heights College. A big baseball fan, you often go to the games and the players know and respect you. One of the players, Matt, comes to your office and asks to speak with you privately. Matt is a highly skilled player who is projected to be taken in the early rounds of the draft. Breaking into tears, he tells you, "I had to go to the doctor last week and I found out that I am HIV+ and I don't know what to do. But please, please, don't tell Coach . . . don't tell Coach . . ."

c. You are the AD at Big State University, a successful NCAA D-I basketball program. Members of your men's basketball team approach you with a request. They would like to wear warm-up shirts that read "Black Lives Matter" before the next game which is against your biggest traditional rival, Western State University. The game falls at the same night where the local police union is scheduled to be honored at halftime. The players have already talked to the head coach, who supports their actions for this game.

d. You are the Assistant Director of Scholastic Marketing for adidas. It has come to your attention that numerous high school accounts which you manage still use Native American mascot names which many people feel are offensive. Recently, you received a letter from the American Indian Movement (AIM) indicating that if adidas continues to supply schools using these mascots with their products, they will call for a national boycott of the brand. You know that Native Americans' annual buying power exceeds $90 billion and many of those dollars could go to sporting equipment and apparel.

CHAPTER questions

1. Using the model presented in Exhibit 4.1, choose three additional societal issues and illustrate how they are seen in sport.

2. Place the sport organizations/persons listed below on the CSR continuum. Provide examples as to why you placed them where you did. Remember, an organization/person can be in more than one place on the model. For example, if Lance Armstrong were on this list, one could say at times he belongs on the Economic level due to his wanting to win at all costs by doping and yet he could be on the Leadership level due to his work in raising funds to fight cancer.

NCAA   Colin Kaepernick
IOC   LaVar Ball
NFL   LeBron James
New England Patriots   Adam Silver

3. Find codes of conduct or codes of ethics from three different sport organizations, each from a different industry segment. Compare the three for similarities and differences. Create and prepare to defend the content of your own code of conduct statement in a class discussion.

4. Some organizations have a charitable arm for CSR initiatives, but their business practices may still seem less than ethical. Can Carroll's model be applied to such organizations? Consider whether and how an organization's business practices might be offset by its philanthropic efforts.

FOR ADDITIONAL INFORMATION

For more information check out the following resources:

1. Four Ways to Foster Ethics in College Athletics: Plante, T. G. (2015, October 1). Four ways to foster ethics in college athletics. *Psychology Today*: https://www.psychologytoday.com/blog/do-the-right-thing/201510/four-ways-foster-ethics-in-college-athletics

2. YouTube: Patagonia's Fair Trade Documentary: https://www.youtube.com/watch?v=y4zn5h5TboU

3. Building corruption-free sport organizations: A Managerial Framework: Hums, M. A.: www.playthegame.org/upload/mary_hums_-_building_corruption_free_sport_organizations.pdf

4. The NFL and the Community: Community Programs: www.nfl.com/community

5. NBA Cares: The NBA Cares Commitment: www.nba.com/nba_cares/keyissues.html

6. World Sports and Social Responsibility: Bentley, R. (2013, August 25). World sports and social responsibility. *Huffington Post*: www.huffingtonpost.com/robert-bentley/world-sports-and-social-r_b_3491020.html

REFERENCES

Athlete Ally. (2017). Our story: A straight ally stands in solidarity with the LGBT community. Retrieved from https://www.athleteally.org/about/

Babiak, K., & Trendafilova, S. (2011). CSR and environmental responsibility: Motives and pressures to adopt green management practices. *Corporate Social Responsibility and Environmental Management*, 18(1), 11–24.

Babiak, K., & Wolfe, R. (2009). Determinants of corporate social responsibility in professional sport: Internal and external factors. *Journal of Sport Management*, 2(6), 717–742.

Bradish, C., & Cronin, J. J. (2009). Corporate social responsibility in sport. *Journal of Sport Management*, 23, 691–697.

Carpenter, L. J., & Acosta, R. V. (2004). *Title IX.* Champaign, IL: Human Kinetics.

Carroll, A. B. (1991, July/August). The pyramid of corporate social responsibility: Toward the moral management of organizational stakeholders. *Business Horizons*, 39–48.

Council of Europe Committee of Ministers. (2010). Code of sport ethics. Retrieved from https://www.coe.int/t/dg4/epas/resources/texts/Rec(92)14rev_en.pdf

Crosset, T., & Hums, M. A. (2015). Ethical principles applied to sport management. In L. P. Masteralexis, C. A. Barr, & M. A. Hums (Eds.), *Principles and practice of sport management* (5th ed., pp. 131–148). Burlington, MA: Jones and Bartlett.

Darnell, S. C. (2012). *Sport for development and peace: A critical sociology.* London: Bloomsbury Academic.

DeSensi, J. (2012). The power of one for the good of many. In A. Gillentine, R. E. Baker, & J. Cuneen (Eds.), *Critical essays in sport management* (pp. 125–132). Scottsdale, AZ: Holcomb Hathaway.

DeSensi, J., & Rosenberg, D. (2010). *Ethics and morality in sport management* (3rd ed.). Morgantown, WV: Fitness Information Technology.

Eitzen, D. S., & Sage, G. H. (2009). *Sociology of North American sport* (8th ed.). Boulder, CO: Paradigm Publishers.

Friedman, T. (2017, June 21). Where did "We the People" go? *New York Times.* Retrieved from https://www.nytimes.com/2017/06/21/opinion/where-did-we-the-people-go.html?action=click&pgtype=Homepage&clickSource=story-heading&module=opinion-c-col-right-region&region=opinion-c-col-right-region&WT.nav=opinion-c-col-right-region&_r=0&login=email

Gargan, M. (2015, November 19). Sport holds up a mirror to society. *Irish Catholic.* Retrieved from https://www.irishcatholic.com/sport-holds-up-a-mirror-to-society/

Gibbs, L. (2016, June 4). Muhammad Ali: The original activist-athlete. Retrieved from https://thinkprogress.org/muhammad-ali-the-original-activist-athlete-a13ac939f310

Hancock, M., & Hums, M. A. (2011). Participation by transsexual and transgender athletes: Ethical dilemmas needing ethical decision making skills. *ICSSPE Bulletin*, 68. Retrieved from http://connection.ebscohost.com/c/articles/95769419/participation-by-transsexual-transgender-athletes-ethical-dilemmas-needing-ethical-decision-making-skills

Hums, M. A. (2006, May). Analyzing the impact of changes in classification systems: A sport management analysis model. Paper presented at the VISTA 2006 International Paralympic Committee Congress, Bonn, Germany.

Hums, M. A. (2007, June). The business of the Paralympic Games: Economics and ethics. Paper presented at 7th International Conference on Sports: Economic, Management and Marketing Aspects, Athens, Greece.

Hums, M. A. (2010). The conscience and commerce of sport: One teacher's perspective. *Journal of Sport Management*, 24, 1–9.

Hums, M. A., & Hancock, M. (2012). Sport management: Bottom lines and higher callings. In A. Gillentine, B. Baker, & J. Cuneen (Eds.), *Critical essays in sport management: Exploring and achieving a paradigm shift* (pp. 133–148). Scottsdale, AZ: Holcomb Hathaway.

Hums, M. A., & Wolff, E. A. (2014, April 3). Power of sport to inform, empower, and transform. *Huffington Post.* Retrieved from www.huffingtonpost.com/dr-mary-hums/power-of-sport-to-inform-_b_5075282.html?utm_hp_ref=sports&ir=Sports

Hums, M. A., Barr, C. A., & Guillion, L. (1999). The ethical issues confronting managers in the sport industry. *Journal of Business Ethics*, 20, 51–66.

Hums, M. A., Wolff, E. A., & Morris, A. (2012). Human rights in sport checklist. In K. Gilbert (Ed.), *Sport, peace, and development* (pp. 243–254). Champaign, IL: Common Ground.

IOC. (2009). 2018 candidature acceptance procedures. Retrieved from https://stillmed.olympic.org/media/Document%20Library/OlympicOrg/Documents/Host-City-Elections/XXIII-OWG-2018/Candidature-Acceptance-Procedure-for-the-XXIII-Olympic-Winter-Games-2018.pdf

IOC. (2014). *Olympic Agenda 2020: 20+20 recommendations.* Lausanne, Switzerland: Author.

IOC. (2016). IOC code of ethics. Retrieved from https://stillmed.olympic.org/media/Document%20Library/OlympicOrg/IOC/What-We-Do/Leading-the-Olympic-Movement/Code-of-Ethics/EN-IOC-Code-of-Ethics-2016.pdf

Lipschutz, R. (2013, August 1). Ethics corner: Resolving ethical dilemmas. NASW-IL News. Retrieved from http://naswil.org/news/chapter-news/featured/ethics-corner-resolving-ethical-dilemmas/

London 2012. (n.d.). Sustainability. Retieived form https://www.olympic.org/sustainability

Low, T. W., Ferrell, L., & Mansfield, P. A. (2000). Review of empirical studies assessing ethical decision making in business. *Journal of Business Ethics*, 25(3), 185–204.

Lussier, R. N., & Kimball, D. C. (2009). *Applied sport management skills*. Champaign, IL: Human Kinetics.

Maguire, J. A., & Nakayama, M. (2006). *Japan, sport and society: Tradition and change in a globalizing world*. London: Routledge.

McDonald, M. (2001). A framework for ethical decision-making: Version 6.0 Ethics shareware. Retrieved from www.ethics.ubc.ca/upload/A%20Framework%20for%20Ethical%20Decision-Making.pdf

Mullane, S. P. (2009). Ethics and leadership—White Paper. Coral Gables, FL: University of Miami Johnson Edosomwan Leadership Institute.

NFL. (n.d.) Beyond the game. Retrieved from www.nfl.com/static/content/public/photo/2017/03/24/0ap3000000795087.pdf

NFSHA. (2015). Coaches code of ethics. Retrieved from www.nfhs.org/nfhs-for-you/coaches/coaches-code-of-ethics/

Nike. (n.d.). Sustainable innovation. Retrieved from http://about.nike.com/pages/sustainable-innovation

Perez, A. J. (2017, May 19). Orioles' Adam Jones on racist slurs at Fenway: "It's point blank disgusting". *USA Today*. Retrieved from https://www.usatoday.com/story/sports/mlb/orioles/2017/05/19/orioles-adam-jones-racist-slurs-fenway/101873618/

Post, J. (2017, April 3). What is corporate social responsibility? Retrieved from www.businessnewsdaily.com/4679-corporate-social-responsibility.html

Price, S. (2017, Feb. 8). What CEOs need to know as we enter a new era of corporate activism. *Forbes*. Retrieved from https://www.forbes.com/sites/susanprice/2017/02/08/what-ceos-need-to-know-as-we-enter-a-new-era-of-corporate-activism/2/#5bf6e43c40c6

Rankin, N. (2017a). Sport and corporate social responsibility. Retrieved from https://www.sportanddev.org/en/article/news/sport-and-corporate-social-responsibility

Rankin, N. (2017b). Sport and CSR: Lessons learnt. Retrieved from https://www.sportanddev.org/en/article/news/sport-and-csr-lessons-learnt

Rocha, V., & Mejia, B. (2016, June 10). Stanford swimmer convicted of sex assault lied about never partying, documents show. *Los Angeles Times*. Retrieved from www.latimes.com/local/lanow/la-me-ln-stanford-rape-case-documents-release-20160610-snap-htmlstory.html

Reuters. (2015, May 12). FIFA steps up racism surveillance for 2018 qualifiers. Retrieved from www.reuters.com/article/us-soccer-fifa-racism-idUSKBN0NX19O20150512

Schnell, L. (2017, Feb. 3). How many more sickening Baylor details does college football needs before it changes? *Sports Illustrated*. Retrieved from https://www.si.com/college-football/2017/02/03/baylor-sexaul-assault-scandal-art-briles-assistants

sportanddev Community. (2016). Social responsibility recognised at Football Business Awards. Retrieved from https://www.sportanddev.org/en/article/news/social-responsibility-recognised-football-business-awards

Thibault, L. (2009). Globalization of sport: An inconvenient truth. *Journal of Sport Management*, 23, 1–20.

Thornton, P. K., Champion, Jr., W. T., & Ruddell, L. S. (2012). *Sports ethics for sport management professionals*. Sudbury, MA: Jones & Bartlett.

UNESCO. (n.d.). Education: Physical education and sport. Retrieved from www.unesco.org/new/en/social-and-human-sciences/themes/physical-education-and-sport/

UNIDO. (2017). What is CSR? Retrieved from www.unido.org/csr/o72054.html

Wallace, D. (2012). Definition of an ethical dilemma. Retrieved from https://www.scribd.com/doc/56047818/Definition-of-an-Ethical-Dilemma

Zinn, L. M. (1993). Do the right thing: Ethical decision making in professional and business practice. *Adult Learning*, 5, 7–8, 27.

Scholastic Sport

Mary A. Hums
Joanne C. MacLean

On any given Friday night in the fall, the air is filled with the sounds of fans screaming, helmets pounding, and bands playing. On Saturdays in winter, the ball bounces off the court, and skates glide over the ice. In the spring, the starter's gun marks the beginning of the 100-meter dash, and we hear the familiar sound of softballs and baseballs being hit and caught. On fields, courts, and rinks everywhere, it is time for the weekend ritual—high school sports. All across the land, young athletes compete for their schools, their communities, and themselves. Many of you remember those days, no doubt. This chapter will focus on high school sport, a sizable section of the sport industry involving thousands of schools and participants.

Although it may surprise you, this is a primarily North American model. In many nations of the world, young people compete for their local municipality's club teams, not for their high school teams. For example, a young athlete living in Hamburg, Germany, will play field hockey for the local sports club, not for Hamburg High School. The high school may not even field any teams, since the schools do not compete against each other in sports like schools in North America. In Munich, a talented young football (soccer) player might compete on a developmental team of the Bayern Munich professional football club. The best young athletes are generally selected early for development by professional clubs. In other countries, high school students participate in sport on the local level—and sometimes even on the national level—as with the Koshien national high school baseball championship in Japan. While most of this chapter focuses on the North American model, remember that this is not the only competitive model for youth sport. "The opportunity provided by member schools to girls and boys to represent their school and community through participation in interscholastic athletics is a privilege to young people in American education" (PIAA, 2017, para. 1). How, then, did it happen that North American high school sport developed into the product we see today? To understand this evolution, let's take a look at the history and evolution of sport in high schools.

HISTORY OF HIGH SCHOOL SPORT

The history of high school sport is long and storied. It began simply to develop healthy habits in youngsters and has gained widespread popularity among spectators, with important steps along the way. For purposes of this textbook, we will examine mainly how the governance of high school sport evolved.

Early Development

In the late 1800s, sport was seen as a vehicle to help solve societal ills, such as delinquency and poor health, so schools began to promote sport (Seymour, 1990). In its early days, high school sport was initiated, organized, and operated by students, similar to the way intercollegiate sport started. Also like intercollegiate sport, the need for adult supervision and direction soon became apparent, because the supervising adults did not care for the direction that high school sport was heading. To uphold a certain moral image, administrators felt it necessary to extend their authority over interscholastic sport. In the 1890s, the popularity of high school football soared, and its abuses mirrored those of college sport at the time—overemphasis on winning, using ineligible players, and mismanagement of finances (Rader, 1999).

By the time the 15th Conference on Academies and High Schools met in 1902, faculties controlled sport in several states, and the Conference issued basic recommendations on faculty control of interscholastic sport. Around the same time, state high school associations began to form (Covell, 2015). In the early 1900s, rules were put in place for high school athletes that defined minimum course loads and satisfactory progress in school, as well as participation eligibility certification. These rules were a progression from those outlined by the Michigan State Teachers' Association's Committee on High School Athletics in 1896 (Forsythe, 1950). As athletics became more integral in a student's academic experience, government-funded educational institutions assumed increased control over the governance of high school athletics (Vincent, 1994).

Development of the National Federation of State High School Associations (NFHS)

In 1920, representatives of five Midwestern states—Illinois, Indiana, Iowa, Michigan, and Wisconsin—met in Chicago to discuss concerns about collegiate and non-school sponsorship of high school events. The result was a plan to ensure the well-being of high school student-athletes in competitive situations. These five state associations banded together to form the Midwest Federation of State High School Athletic Associations. Eventually, more state associations joined this group, and in 1923 they changed their name to the National Federation of State High School Athletic Associations (NFHS, 2016b). By the 1930s, the group assumed responsibility as the rules-writing and rules-publishing body for high school sports. The organization grew throughout the 20th century, adding members until 1969, when all 50 states and the District of Columbia belonged. In the 1970s, the fine arts were added under the organization's umbrella, and the term *Athletic* was removed from the organization's name. The official name became the "National Federation of State High School Associations," as it remains today, and since 1997 the organization has gone by the abbreviation "NFHS" (NFHS, 2017).

Organizational development continued from the 1980s to the present, with increased educational programming, incorporation of debate and spirit programs, and ongoing rules interpretations and publications. In 2000, the NFHS moved its headquarters to Indianapolis, Indiana (NFHS, 2015a).

Development of High School Sport in Europe

Contributed by Thierry Zintz

In Europe, school sport evolved from the formation of numerous clubs and sports associations. In many cases, extracurricular sports activities were extended by the creation of clubs involved in competitions organized by sports federations. Alongside school sports, organized on sectarian basis (such as Catholic education based on religious beliefs), political parties in many countries created Christian, liberal, or socialist sport organizations to compete in events organized by sports federations.

By the 1930s, Catholic educational institutions in Europe created the International Sports Federation for Catholic Schools (FISEC). This federation, which organizes international competitions, the FISEC Games, grew gradually, opening to include the Americas and the Middle East. Its religious basis, however, limited its development to countries with a network of Catholic educational institutions.

During the 1960s, international sports contacts between schools of all networks multiplied. The number of competitions, as well as the number of schools, continued to increase. This resulted in the effort to coordinate these events as part of an International School Sport Federation (ISF). The ISF is not specifically linked to networks of educational institutions but organizes world competitions in different sports.

Its mission statement indicates:

The ISF is the International Federation of official school sport organisations in the different countries or of representative organisations where there is no official one. It organises international competitions in different sporting disciplines and encourages contests between school students with a view to promoting better mutual understanding. It seeks close collaboration with the school authorities of member countries, with the international sporting federations concerned, and with international organisations having similar aims. (ISF, 2017)

The ISF features competitions in traditional team sports such as basketball, football, handball, and volleyball as well as the individual sports such as athletics, badminton, cross-country, gymnastics, orienteering, skiing, swimming, and table tennis (ISF, 2017).

The ISF is a true movement associated with learning, aimed at raising awareness, and promoting official recognition of good sport and education in schools. The ISF hopes, through its actions, to enable boys and girls to cultivate the ideas of mutual understanding and fair play. It is interesting to note the differences and similarities between North American high school and high school sport around the world. Whenever one looks at high school sport, however, one thing is clear—there are myriad benefits to young people participating.

Source: Hums, M. A., MacLean, J. C., & Zintz, T. (2011). *La gouvernance au coeur des politiques des organisations sportives*, 1re ed., De Boeck Supérieur, Bruxelles, p. 320. Used with permission.

Value of High School Sport Today

The values and benefits of high school sport have been well defined by its advocates. For example, the mission statement of the Colorado High School Activities Association states, "In pursuit of educational excellence, the Colorado High School Activities Association strives to create a positive and equitable environment in which all qualified student participants are challenged and inspired to meet their highest potential" (CHSAA, 2016, p. 1). The organization goes on to explain how its members will implement this mission:

- – Act as an integral component of the educational process.
- – Administrate, interpret, and seek compliance with the CHSAA Bylaws as needed to promote fair play within Colorado activities and athletics.
- – Provide diverse and equitable opportunities for participation that encourages all qualified students to take part in the activity/athletic experience.
- – Provide an environment that enhances personal development through sporting behavior, character education, teamwork, leadership, and citizenship while increasing values that partner the educational standards of the State of Colorado.
- – Recognize the outstanding accomplishments of Colorado athletes, teams, coaches, and administrators through our academic and activity awards programs. (p. 1)

As another example, the New Hampshire Interscholastic Athletic Association (NHIAA, 2014, para. 1) states, "The mission of the New Hampshire Interscholastic Athletic Association, as the leader of high school athletics, is to ensure fair play in competition and equal opportunity in interscholastic programs." As a final example, the South Carolina High School League mission (SCHSL, n.d., p. 1) is to "provide governance and leadership for interscholastic athletic programs that promote, support, and enrich the educational experience of students."

For all these reasons, high school sport has become an important component of many students' total educational experience. To make sure worthwhile activities happen in a well-planned and organized environment, governance structures must be in place.

GOVERNANCE

Scholastic sport governance occurs on a number of different levels. As mentioned previously, at the national level there is the NFHS, which includes members from the United States and Canada. But unlike some national-level sport governing bodies, this is not where the real power lies as the NFHS is a service organization. In high school sport the real power and authority rest at the state level, where the regulatory power lies. According to Wong (1994), "the power and authority in high school athletics are in the individual state organizations, which determine the rules and regulations for the sport programs and schools within that state" (p. 22). There is also governance on the local level, meaning the school or school district. Let's look at the organizational structures at these different levels and the scope of their authority.

www

Colorado High School Activities Association
http://rcasey.wpengine. netdna-cdn.com/wp-content/ uploads/bylaws/2016-17-bylaws.pdf

www

New Hampshire Interscholastic Athletic Association
www.nhiaa.org

www

South Carolina High School League
www.schsl.org

National Federation of State High School Associations

The NFHS (2015a) is a member-governed, nonprofit national service and administrative organization of high school athletics and fine arts programs in speech, debate, and music. From its offices in Indianapolis, the NFHS serves its 50-member state high school athletic and activity associations, plus those of the District of Columbia. The organization publishes playing rules for 16 sports for boys and girls and provides programs and services that its member state associations can use in working with the 18,500 member high schools and approximately 11 million young people involved in high school activity programs (NFHS, 2015a).

From this information, it is important to note two main points. First, the NFHS is considered a service organization. In contrast to the National Collegiate Athletic Association (NCAA), which has strong sanctioning power over members, the purpose of the NFHS is to provide services to its members. Also, the NFHS is not involved solely in athletic competition. Subgroups within the NFHS include not only the National Federation Coaches Association, the National Federation Officials Association, and the National Interscholastic Athletic Administrators Association (NIAAA), but also the National Federation Interscholastic Speech and Debate Association, the National Federation Interscholastic Music Association, and the National Federation Interscholastic Spirit Association. Thus, the organization has a broad base across many high school extracurricular activities. This textbook, however, focuses on those aspects of the NFHS dealing directly with interscholastic athletics.

Mission

The mission statement of the NFHS (presented in Exhibit 5.1) states that its purpose is to promote activities that contribute positively to a student's educational experience. Also apparent is that the organization seeks to develop students into people who will be contributing members of society due to the good lessons they learned from their sport experience. From this mission statement it is clear that high school sport is meant to help students achieve educational goals.

Membership

Who belongs to the NFHS? NFHS membership is made up of state associations, not individuals. The active members of the National Federation of State High School Associations are the 50 state high school athletic/activity associations, plus the District of Columbia. There are also affiliate members, including associations in the US territories, Canada, and other neighboring nations (NFHS, 2015c). The affiliated members from outside the US include Canadian School Sport Federations from Alberta, British Columbia, Manitoba, New Brunswick, Nova Scotia, Ontario, Prince

National Federation of State High School Associations
www.nfhs.org

NFHS Coaches' Association
http://www.nfhs.org/coaches/

NFHS Officials' Association
www.nfhs.org/officials/

National Interscholastic Athletic Administrators Association
http://www.niaaa.org

School Sport Canada
wwwschoolsport.ca/

Mission Statement

The National Federation of State High School Associations serves its members, related professional organizations and students by providing leadership for the administration of education-based interscholastic activities, which support academic achievement, good citizenship and equitable opportunity.

We believe:

Participation in education-based interscholastic athletics and performing arts programs:

- Enriches each student's educational experience.
- Promotes student academic achievement.
- Develops good citizenship and healthy lifestyles.
- Fosters involvement of a diverse population.
- Promotes positive school/community relations.
- Is a privilege.

The NFHS:

- Promotes and protects the defining values of education-based interscholastic activity programs in collaboration with its member state associations.
- Serves as the recognized national authority on education-based interscholastic activity programs.
- Serves as the pre-eminent authority on competition rules for education-based interscholastic activity programs.
- Promotes fair play and seeks to minimize risk for student participants through the adoption of national competition rules and delivery of programs and services.
- Delivers quality educational programs to serve the changing needs of state associations, school administrators, coaches, officials, students and parents.
- Provides professional development opportunities for NFHS member state association staff.
- Promotes cooperation among state associations to advance their individual and collective well-being.

Source: NFHS (2016b).

Edward Island, Quebec, and Saskatchewan. Other affiliates include Guam and the Bahamas, and several state independent schools athletic associations (eg., North Carolina and Georgia) (NFHS, 2015c).

Financials

How does the NFHS finance itself? Approximately one third of the organization's income comes from sales revenue (NFHS, 2016a). In addition, the organization earns funds from educational programs; membership dues and professional organizations; contributions, royalties, and sponsors; meetings and conferences; and a few lesser sources. How is the money spent? The major expense categories for the NFHS are salaries and benefits, educational and professional development, professional organizations, rules making, and publications (NFHS, 2016a).

Organizational Structure

The organizational structure of the NFHS indicates that the membership drives the governance of the organization. As illustrated in Exhibit 5.2, the member state associations form the base of support for the chart. The National Council is the legislative body of the NFHS and is responsible for enacting amendments to the constitution and bylaws in addition to other duties. The National Council consists of one representative from each member state association. The National Council meets two times a year and each member state association has one vote. The Board of Directors of the NFHS is made up of 12 members, one from each geographic section and four additional at-large members. The board is empowered to conduct the business of the NFHS, including activities such as approving the annual budget, overseeing the investment and management of all funds, and establishing the standing rules and special committees (NFHS, n.d.). The next group involved in the governance of the NFHS is the 18-member Executive Staff, the organization's paid employees, including an Executive Director and Directors of Sports and Sports Medicine; Sports and Student Services; Publications and Communications; Sports, Events, and Development; Performing Arts and Sports; Information Services; Coach Education; and Sports and Officials. Several Assistant Directors and a Chief Operating Officer are also employed, as well as a General Counsel to handle legal questions and issues. Finally, as with most organizations, a series of committees work in designated areas, such as the National Athletic Directors Conference Advisory Committee, Citizenship/Equity Committee, Technology Committee, general committees, designated Sports and Activities Committees, and special committees (NFHS, n.d.).

State High School Athletic Associations

Each state has its own high school athletic association. As you will see, they have different names. In the United States, for example, we see the Georgia High School Association, Idaho High School Activities Association, Indiana High School Athletic Association, Maine Principals' Association, Texas University Interscholastic League, and the Wisconsin Interscholastic Athletic Association. In Canada we see the Alberta Schools Athletic Association (ASAA), and the Ontario Federation of School Athletic Associations. Despite their different names, these organizations share common missions and authorities.

California Interscholastic Federation
www.cifstate.org/landing/index

Hawaii High School Athletic Association
www.sportshigh.com/

Illinois High School Sports
www.illinoishighschoolsports.com/

Massachusetts Interscholastic Athletic Association
www.miaa.net/miaa/home?sid=38

New York State Public High School Athletic Association
www.nysphsaa.org/

University Interscholastic League
www.uiltexas.org/athletics/sports

Wisconsin Interscholastic Athletic Association
https://www.wiaawi.org/

National Federation of State High School Associations Organizational Chart — *exhibit* **5.2**

ORGANIZATIONAL CHART

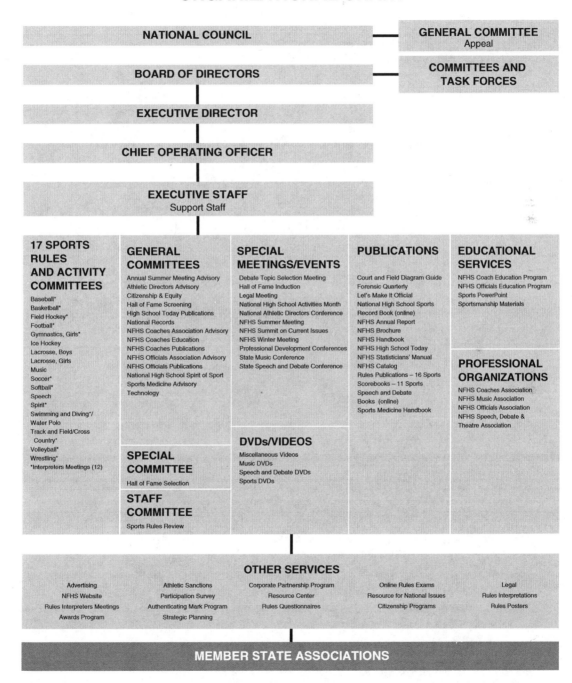

NATIONAL COUNCIL

GENERAL COMMITTEE
Appeal

BOARD OF DIRECTORS

COMMITTEES AND TASK FORCES

EXECUTIVE DIRECTOR

CHIEF OPERATING OFFICER

EXECUTIVE STAFF
Support Staff

17 SPORTS RULES AND ACTIVITY COMMITTEES

Baseball*
Basketball*
Field Hockey*
Football*
Gymnastics, Girls*
Ice Hockey
Lacrosse, Boys
Lacrosse, Girls
Music
Soccer*
Softball*
Speech
Spirit*
Swimming and Diving*/
Water Polo
Track and Field/Cross
   Country*
Volleyball*
Wrestling*
*Interpreters Meetings (12)

GENERAL COMMITTEES

Annual Summer Meeting Advisory
Athletic Directors Advisory
Citizenship & Equity
Hall of Fame Screening
High School Today Publications
National Records
NFHS Coaches Association Advisory
NFHS Coaches Education
NFHS Coaches Publications
NFHS Officials Association Advisory
NFHS Officials Publications
National High School Spirit of Sport
Sports Medicine Advisory
Technology

SPECIAL COMMITTEE

Hall of Fame Selection

STAFF COMMITTEE

Sports Rules Review

SPECIAL MEETINGS/EVENTS

Debate Topic Selection Meeting
Hall of Fame Induction
Legal Meeting
National High School Activities Month
National Athletic Directors Conference
NFHS Summer Meeting
NFHS Summit on Current Issues
NFHS Winter Meeting
Professional Development Conferences
State Music Conference
State Speech and Debate Conference

DVDs/VIDEOS

Miscellaneous Videos
Music DVDs
Speech and Debate DVDs
Sports DVDs

PUBLICATIONS

Court and Field Diagram Guide
Forensic Quarterly
Let's Make It Official
National High School Sports
Record Book (online)
NFHS Annual Report
NFHS Brochure
NFHS Handbook
NFHS High School Today
NFHS Statisticians' Manual
NFHS Catalog
Rules Publications – 16 Sports
Scorebooks – 11 Sports
Speech and Debate
Books (online)
Sports Medicine Handbook

EDUCATIONAL SERVICES

NFHS Coach Education Program
NFHS Officials Education Program
Sports PowerPoint
Sportsmanship Materials

PROFESSIONAL ORGANIZATIONS

NFHS Coaches Association
NFHS Music Association
NFHS Officials Association
NFHS Speech, Debate &
Theatre Association

OTHER SERVICES

Advertising	Athletic Sanctions	Corporate Partnership Program	Online Rules Exams	Legal
NFHS Website	Participation Survey	Resource Center	Resource for National Issues	Rules Interpretations
Rules Interpreters Meetings	Authenticating Mark Program	Rules Questionnaires	Citizenship Programs	Rules Posters
Awards Program	Strategic Planning			

MEMBER STATE ASSOCIATIONS

Source: NFHS (2015b).

State high school associations serve several important functions. First, they are the regulatory bodies for high school sport in a particular state. As noted earlier, the power in high school athletics resides on this level. According to Sharp, Moorman, and Claussen (2010), "Authority to govern interscholastic athletics within a state is granted to the state association by the state legislature or by judicial decision. Each state's high school athletic association is responsible for implementing and enforcing regulations governing interscholastic athletics participation of the member high schools" (p. 324). This statement clearly establishes that the regulatory power in high school sport governance lies at the state level. Second, they are responsible for organizing state championships, always the highlight of the year for any sport. Finally, they maintain the educational philosophy for high school athletics in their respective states.

State-level governance is often vested with power from the state legislature. State associations have the authority to revoke eligibility for individual students and to disqualify schools from participating in events if the schools break state association rules. In disputes about eligibility and other questions about the interpretation of rules, the US state high school associations are named in any resulting lawsuits. The reason for this is that in most cases the state association has been found to be a state actor (Altman, 2010), that is, an organization working as if it were empowered by the government to act. You may remember from your Legal Aspects of Sport class that this makes state associations subject to the requirements of the United States Constitution. Whenever a high school athlete feels his or her constitutional rights have been violated because of an association's rule, that athlete names the high school association in the suit. Thus when state associations craft policies, they must be mindful not to enact policies or procedures that could be construed as infringing on a student's fundamental rights, such as the right to due process if a student is denied eligibility for some reason.

Mission

As mentioned earlier, while the associations' names differ from state to state, common ideals are reflected in each association's mission statement. Sample mission statements from the Oregon School Activities Association (OSAA) and the Ohio High School Athletic Association are presented in Exhibits 5.3 and 5.4, respectively. While these mission statements are somewhat different, one can see similarities between them. Shared themes include the place of athletics in an educational setting, the values and benefits students derive from high school sport, and the provision of service to their members.

Oregon School Activities
Association
www.osaa.org

Membership

High school associations generally are voluntary, nonprofit organizations whose members are the public and private secondary schools in that

Mission Statement of the Oregon School Activities Association

exhibit **5.3**

> The mission of the OSAA is to serve member schools by providing leadership and state coordination for the conduct of interscholastic activities, which will enrich the educational experiences of high school students. The OSAA will work to promote interschool activities that provide equitable participation opportunities, positive recognition and learning experiences to students, while enhancing the achievement of educational goals.

Source: OSAA (2012). Reprinted with permission

Mission Statement of the Ohio High School Athletic Association

exhibit **5.4**

> The Ohio High School Athletic Association's mission is to regulate and administer interscholastic athletic competition in a fair and equitable manner while promoting the values of participation in interscholastic athletics as an integral part of a student's educational experience. The OHSAA represents its member schools by recognizing and promoting academics, the safety of participants, good citizenship and lifelong values as the foundation of interscholastic athletics.

Source: OHSAA. (n.d.) Our mission. Retrieved from http://ohsaa.org/AboutOHSAA

particular state. In some cases, junior high schools and middle schools may also belong to the association. The size of each association varies, depending on the number of high schools in the state. The membership of high school associations is similar to that of the NCAA, where institutions (high schools), not individual people, are the members of the organization.

Financials

The sources of funding for athletic associations vary by state. The Georgia High School Association's primary source of revenue is state tourneys/playoffs, followed by corporate partnerships, and then community coach registrations. Its main expenses are state/tourneys/playoffs and salaries and wages (GHSA, 2016). The Washington Interscholastic Athletic Association indicates its largest revenue source is state tournament revenue and then fees from member schools. The largest expense items are operations related and state-wide activities (WIAA, 2013). In Florida:

www

Arizona Interscholastic Association
www.aiaonline.org

Nebraska School Activities Association
www.nsaahome.org

the primary source of funding for the FHSAA [Florida High School Athletic Association] is derived from the FHSAA State Championship Series, followed by corporate partnerships and fees for services (such as certification and training of game officials) . . . The FHSAA does not receive revenue from member schools regular season games, nor does it receive any direct tax funding, state revenue or federal funding. (FHSAA, 2017, para. 4)

The Kentucky High School Athletic Association includes financial issues in its Strategic Plan. The specific strategies in this document include the following:

Strategy 1.1 Pursue an aggressive fundraising and promotional strategy seeking additional ancillary revenue for the Association while protecting existing programs.

Strategy 1.2 Continue the practice of fiscal restraint and management controls over the current business operations of the Association.

Strategy 1.3 Exercise control and optimize usage of Association funds.

Strategy 1.4 Analyze event structures and financial management practices. (KHSAA, 2006a, pp. 9–10)

As budgets become tighter, associations must come up with more creative means of financing their programs. This topic will be discussed in more detail later in the chapter.

Organizational structure

STATE ASSOCIATIONS. During the year, an Executive Committee or Board of Directors meets to deal with any ongoing issues. The Executive Committee is made up of Superintendents, Principals, and Athletic Directors (ADs) from various high schools around the state. In addition, paid Executive Staff members work in the association headquarters year-round. These headquarters are usually located in the capital of the state. This provides a central location for members and also access to state elected officials and education policy makers. While the titles may vary, often the highest-ranking paid staff member is called the Commissioner or the Executive Director. There are also several Associate or Assistant Commissioners or Associate or Assistant Executive Directors, each of whom has distinct responsibilities for certain sports and other areas, such as eligibility, rules interpretation, officials, coaches' clinics, sportsmanship and ethics programs, and trophies and awards. The organizational chart for the Wisconsin Interscholastic Athletic Association is presented in Exhibit 5.5.

www

Tennessee Secondary School Athletic Association

www.tssaa.org

www

Wisconsin Interscholastic Athletic Association

https://www.wiaawi.org

exhibit **5.5** WIAA Organizational Chart

WISCONSIN INTERSCHOLASTIC ATHLETIC ASSOCIATION
Committee Organization
A charter member of the NFHS in 1923

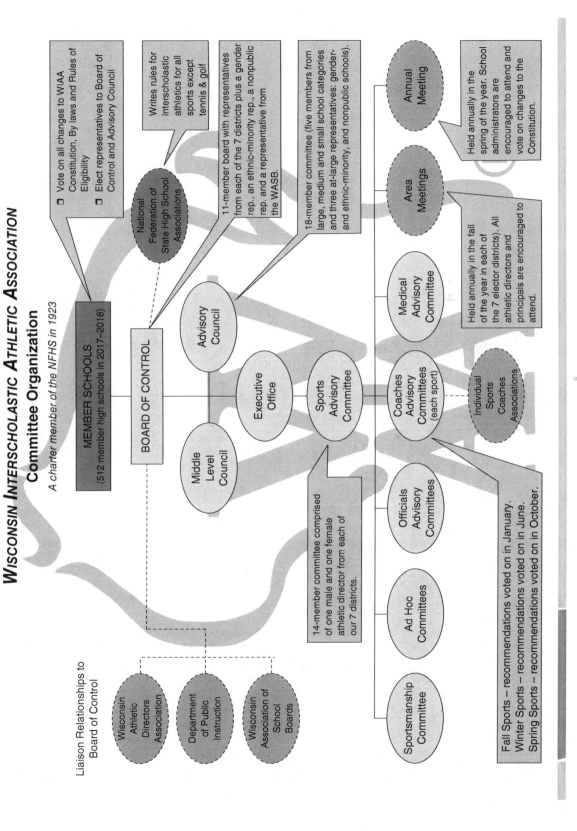

Liaison Relationships to Board of Control

MEMBER SCHOOLS (512 member high schools in 2017–2018)

- Vote on all changes to WIAA Constitution, By laws and Rules of Eligibility
- Elect representatives to Board of Control and Advisory Council

National Federation of State High School Associations

Writes rules for interscholastic athletics for all sports except tennis & golf

11-member board with representatives from each of the 7 districts plus a gender rep., an ethnic-minority rep., a nonpublic rep., and a representative from the WASB.

18-member committee (five members from large, medium and small school categories and three at-large representatives: gender and ethnic-minority, and nonpublic schools).

BOARD OF CONTROL

Advisory Council

Executive Office

Middle Level Council

Sports Advisory Committee

Coaches Advisory Committees (each sport)

Individual Sports Coaches Associations

Medical Advisory Committee

Officials Advisory Committees

Ad Hoc Committees

Sportsmanship Committee

Annual Meeting

Area Meetings

Held annually in the spring of the year. School administrators are encouraged to attend and vote on changes to the Constitution.

Held annually in the fall of the year in each of the 7 elector districts). All athletic directors and principals are encouraged to attend.

14-member committee comprised of one male and one female athletic director from each of our 7 districts.

Fall Sports – recommendations voted on in January. Winter Sports – recommendations voted on in June. Spring Sports – recommendations voted on in October.

Wisconsin Athletic Directors Association

Department of Public Instruction

Wisconsin Association of School Boards

SCHOOL DISTRICTS.   School districts have various responsibilities, including dealing with high school athletic programs in a limited fashion. For example, local school boards approve all employee contracts, including approving coaches' and athletic directors' contracts. It is important again to note that school district responsibilities differ from state to state. For example, in Indiana, coaches' salaries come from the same general fund as teachers' salaries in that district. Therefore, the school district decides on salaries for coaches from that pool of money. This is not true in all states. In terms of facility construction, decisions on funding sport-related facilities may also be approved by the school district. For example, if a school district decides to fund a gymnasium, the gymnasium is not built just for athletics. It is part of a project benefiting the physical education program, and athletics would share the facility. Finally, school districts may also organize capital campaigns to fund individual projects. Sometimes, depending on the success of the campaign and the immediate needs of the school district, the money raised may or may not go to improving athletic facilities, such as renovating a track or developing an exercise room at a particular school (D. Sullivan, personal communication, June 29, 2002).

INDIVIDUAL SCHOOLS.   Each high school has someone who serves as the AD. Sometimes this person also works as a coach, although that is not ideal. According to Covell (2015), the responsibilities and tasks of the AD include:

- hiring, supervising and evaluating coaches;
- coordinating nearly all facets of contest management, including the hiring and paying of officials and event staff; setting . . . training and disciplinary policies; determining . . . budgets; and associated fund-raising;
- determining and verifying game scheduling and athlete eligibility;
- transmitting relevant publicity; and
- handling public relations. (p. 158)

For all of these tasks, the average high school AD's salary varies from state to state:

> While Texas leads the way in number of administrators, it has a relatively low annual mean wage of $77,440; West Virginia has the lowest at $64,130. New Jersey and New York are on the opposite end of the spectrum averaging $120,130 and $118,570, respectively. Other factors, such as your qualifications, degrees and performance can move you up the scale. Entry level salaries are typically in the $50,000 to $60,000 range. (Firth, 2017, para. 2)

The AD is the person who puts forward coaching candidates for the school board's approval. In some states the AD must also have current teaching certification credentials. In Canada, the setup is usually slightly different. High schools do not have separate AD positions. The head of the Physical Education Department usually acts as the AD.

In addition, the Principal has influence in this area as well. The AD reports directly to the Principal on any matters concerning budget, scheduling, or personnel. If there are conflicts within the department that the AD cannot resolve, that responsibility may fall to the Principal.

CURRENT POLICY AREAS

A number of policy areas are prominent in the governance of high school athletics, including eligibility, risk minimization, amateurism, gender equity, participation by athletes with disabilities, homeless high school athletes funding, and home schoolers. Sport managers working in this industry segment must be aware of the constantly changing tides of public opinion about issues surrounding school-age children and young adults as these will impact their policy-making decisions. Several of these issues result from legal challenges to existing or proposed policies. As pointed out earlier in the chapter, because state associations are considered state actors, they cannot violate any students' fundamental rights. The same is true for public school employees, including coaches and athletic directors. Students who believe their rights have been violated can initiate a lawsuit against a coach, an AD, a local school board, and the state high school athletic association. The outcomes of these cases can directly affect policies in high school sport, as sometimes the courts mandate that an association change a rule that violated a student's rights.

Eligibility

The policy area receiving the majority of attention is eligibility. Some of you may have attended a high school where an athlete was denied the opportunity to play for a particular reason—maybe his grades were not high enough, or maybe she moved in from a different school district. Perhaps you knew a student who took an eligibility case to the legal system. First, you must remember that playing high school sport is *not* a right guaranteed by law. Attending school until you are a certain age is your right, but participating in interscholastic sport is *a privilege, not a right* (Sieck, 2015; Tilley, 2012). According to Colles and Williams (2010), "Participation is voluntary, and more important, a privilege in the reasoning of the courts, which may be extended at the discretion of the school board" (p. 473). However, even though athletic participation is a privilege, it cannot be taken away arbitrarily. Sport governing bodies must still ensure due process is followed in any decisions they make about eligibility otherwise they may end up in litigation. Remember, state associations are state actors, and while their actions are not supposed to violate anyone's constitutional rights, sometimes they do, resulting in litigation. Eligibility discussions most often relate to questions of ethics, academic eligibility, public versus private schools, transfer rules, and age limits for participation.

Ethics and Eligibility Rules

Eligibility rules in general generate some interesting ethical questions. For example, a high school athletic association may have certain rules about "No pass, no play." While this seems acceptable on the surface, what is the effect on academically struggling students for whom sport is the primary motivation to stay in school? If that chance is taken away, are they more likely to drop out? Although transfer rules are based on the educational premise that a student learns best by staying in the same school for an academic career, should students be "punished" for family problems that may result in relocation to another school district? It is important to make sure the outcome of such rules is, in fact, as fair as possible to the student.

Academic Eligibility

All high school associations have policies governing academic eligibility. The reason for this is clear. High school sports are meant to be an extension of a student's educational experience.

According to the Kentucky High School Athletic Association (KHSAA, 2014, p. 8), a number of reasons exist for academic eligibility standards:

(1) interscholastic athletic activity programs are an extension of the classroom, and academic standards help ensure the balance between participation in the activity and appropriate academic performance;

(2) interscholastic athletic and activity programs assist in the educational development of all participants;

(3) academic standards promote the objective of graduation from the institution and that student participants are truly representing the academic mission of the institution;

(4) overall, academic standards promote educational standards, underscore the educational values of participating in activities, encourage appropriate academic performance and allow the use of interscholastic participation as a motivator or improved classroom performance;

(5) participants in the interscholastic athletic program are expected to be student-athletes;

(6) high school sports are not intended to be a "farm team" for college and professional sports, but a complementary activity to the total learning experience.

A focus of discussion in this area is the so-called "No pass, no play" rule (Hayward, 2014). While the specifics differ from state to state, basically this type of rule makes players ineligible to participate for a set number of weeks if they do not meet certain academic standards. For example, students who fail a class in a given term may be ineligible to play sports the following term. Proponents indicate that such rules keep students focused on academics rather than athletics. For athletes seeking college scholarships, these rules also help them stay on a course to meet the NCAA Eligibility Center standards (see Chapter 8). Opponents of such rules mention that for some students, being able to play sports is what motivates them to stay in school, and without the opportunity to participate, those students may drop out. Opponents also point out that this rule may lead students to choose a less-challenging curriculum so they do not put themselves in academic jeopardy. Some states and districts are now revisiting and modifying these rules.

This matter is determined in a simple way in most European countries. Zintz says:

> Being enrolled in and regularly attending classes in a school of secondary education is a primary criterion for eligibility. The second category is age, which cannot of course be waived. When these two conditions are met, the student is eligible to participate in school sport competitions. (Hums, MacLean, & Zintz, 2011, p. 105)

Transfer Rules

High school associations have transfer rules for various reasons. Transferring schools is generally not easy on high school-age students, either educationally or socially. If you have ever transferred schools, you may remember the difficulties of making new friends, having new teachers, and learning new rules. In this way, transfer rules work to maintain the ideal of students starting and ending their academic careers in the same school. According to Angelico (2013, para. 2), the Colorado High School Athletic Association states:

> One of the primary objectives of the CHSAA is to ensure that student athletes are just that: students—and then athletes. As we all know, there is much documentation regarding that changing schools and curriculums is not a positive thing for a student's academic progress. Curriculums do not always match up well enough for a smooth transition when changing schools.

Transfer rules have the goal to keep students from moving from school to school for nonfamily reasons. In other words, these rules are in place to keep students from simply enrolling in whichever school has a successful sports program or a well-known coach. School district boundaries are drawn to ensure fair distribution of students across districts. These distributions are tied to the amount of funding the districts receive from the state. Students "jumping" out of district to play sports interrupt this balance.

Another reason for transfer rules is to deter coaches from recruiting students away from other schools. High school athletes, especially the talented ones, have enough pressure on them already. People are wondering where they will go to college, sport apparel companies may already be approaching them, and they still have to maintain their grades for eligibility. Attempting to recruit these students to rival high schools only adds another layer of pressure to their lives.

Risk Minimization

Participating in any sport or physical activity carries with it some element of risk of injury. That is just the nature of such activities. Responsible sport managers know, however, that it is their job to keep participants as safe as possible, particularly if those participants are children or minors. High school sport administrators have been given a series of directives from the National Federation to help them minimize risk in certain sports. For example, in baseball, pitch limits and required rest periods have been established. Blindside blocking and the pop-up kick in football have been defined and penalties established if players attempt these actions. In swimming new rules have been adopted for safer approaches to diving and foot contact rules on the blocks during relay exchanges. Other sports and activities including lacrosse and spirit squads have also established new rules with the safety of high school athletes in mind.

Amateurism

By definition, high school sport means amateur sport. "A student who represents a school in an interscholastic sport shall be an amateur in that sport. An amateur is one who engages in athletic competition solely for the physical, mental, social and pleasure benefits derived therefrom" (NFHS, 2017, para. 7). In other words, for high school athletes, sport should be for participation and enjoyment, not a job. Sport should be an extension of the educational mission of the school.

Basically, is it in the best interest of the student to leave high school to go directly into the professional ranks? According to Kerr-Dineen (2016), here are the odds of a high school athlete making to the pro level:

Football	1 in 4,233
Men's basketball	1 in 11,771
Women's basketball	1 in 13,015
Baseball	1 in 659
Men's ice hockey	1 in 598
Men's soccer	1 in 5,768

For the favored few who actually have the talent and the maturity, professional sport can be an option. But what about those who accept the impractical notion that sport is their "way out"? Coaches and athletic directors need to provide realistic information and advice to students who harbor unrealistic hopes and expectations. These numbers are, of course, behind the NCAA's (2011) ad campaign about the number of athletes going pro in something other than sports.

Gender Equity

Whenever we hear the term *gender equity*, one phrase should come to mind immediately—Title IX. Although most of the publicity generated around Title IX during its 40+ year existence has involved college athletics, this piece of legislation also applies to high school sport. The full title of this historic legislation in the United States is Title IX of the Educational Amendments of 1972. It reads as follows: "No person in the United States shall, on the basis of sex, be excluded from participation in, be denied the benefits of, or be subjected to discrimination under any education program or activity receiving Federal financial assistance" (Carpenter, 2010, p. 540).

While great progress has been made for girls in high school sport, there is still work to be done. The National Women's Law Center (2015, paras. 2–4) pointed out some of the following:

> Schools are providing about 1.3 million fewer chances for girls to play sports in high school as compared to boys. In 1972, only 295,000 girls competed in high school sports, a mere 7.4 percent of all high school athletes, compared to 3.67 million boys. By the 2013–2014 school year, the number of girls had swelled to 3.27 million, while the number of boys was 4.53 million.

> Girls of color in particular receive far fewer opportunities to play school sports than white girls, white boys, and boys of color.

> Three quarters of boys from immigrant families are involved in athletics, while less than half of girls from immigrant families are.

The courts have repeatedly been asked to rule on different aspects of Title IX legislation, and in 2002 the Bush administration formed a special committee to examine the enforcement, guidelines, and interpretation of the law. Sport managers working in scholastic sport must be aware of any policy interpretations of Title IX issued by the US Department of Education so they can ensure their schools are in compliance with the law. These same sport managers must be vigilant and proactive in the face of policy challenges affecting Title IX that may result from administrative directives when parties in power change. The administration elected in the US in 2016 has already taken steps to roll back some Title IX coverage, particularly in regard to transgender students (Wilson, 2016). Here you need to reflect back on the discussions of ethical issues facing sport managers presented in our book chapter on ethics. Sport managers have the ethical obligation to stand up for just causes. In this case, this means being ready to defend Title IX from actions that may result in fewer participation opportunities for high school students.

Discussions about gender equity and fairness in participation opportunities will continue, even as the courts and legislative agencies interpret and reinterpret the laws. The importance of sport participation for girls cannot be overstated. Benefits from participation include greater academic success, increased career opportunities, responsible social behaviors, health benefits, and improved mental health and personal skills (National Women's Law Center, 2015). As outlined in Chapter 4, athletic administrators should consider how they respond to Title IX in terms of corporate social responsibility and whether they are providing opportunities not just because the law mandates it but also because it is the right thing to do.

Participation by Athletes with Disabilities

As mentioned earlier in the section on eligibility, athletes with disabilities have successfully challenged age limit rules that restrict their full access to participation in high school sport. Beyond that, athletes with disabilities are now gaining opportunities to participate more equally alongside their classmates.

Most notably was a young track athlete from Maryland, Tatyana McFadden. McFadden, born in Russia with spina bifida, attended Atholton High School and wanted to compete on the school's track team. A wheelchair racer who had won silver and bronze medals in the 2004 Paralympic Games in Athens, Greece, McFadden was initially blocked from participation. She won the right to compete with able-bodied athletes in track meets after she successfully sued the Howard County Public School System in federal court in 2006. Ultimately, Maryland passed the landmark Fitness and Athletics Equity for Students with Disabilities Act in 2008 (Graham & Seidel, 2010):

> The Maryland Public Secondary Schools Athletic Association changed its laws to accommodate those athletes. New language was added . . . to the MPSSAA [Maryland Public Secondary Schools Athletic Association] bylaws, allowing students with disabilities to participate in school sports programs as long as they meet preexisting eligibility requirements, are not ruled to present a risk to themselves or others, and do not change the nature of the game or event. (Graham & Seidel, 2010, para. 1&2)

McFadden has since gone on to be one of the most medalled athletes in the Paralympic Games, having won multiple gold, silver, and bronze medals, including four golds at the Rio 2016 Summer Paralympic Games.

Other states are now following Maryland's lead in providing opportunities for high school athletes with disabilities. According to *The Chicago Tribune* (2012, p. 1):

The Illinois High School Association will launch a pilot program to host state finals for student-athletes with disabilities in cross-country, bowling, swimming and track and field, the organization announced Monday.

The two-year pilot program will begin immediately, and parallel events will run at the state finals during the upcoming school year.

Additional states that have set up various programs for high school athletes with disabilities include Arizona, Florida, Kentucky, Nebraska, New Hampshire, Ohio, and Rhode Island among others.

Opportunities for high school students with disabilities took an enormous step forward with the issuance of a Dear Colleague Letter from the Department of Education (DOE) early in 2013; the letter can be found on the government link in the margin. Hailed as the "Title IX for people with disabilities" (Elliott, 2013), the DOE's guidelines stress that students with disabilities must be treated equitably with regard to interscholastic sport participation opportunities. In summary:

> On January 24, 2013 the Office for Civil Rights issued a Dear Colleague Letter clarifying a school's obligations under the Rehabilitation Act of 1973 to provide extracurricular athletic opportunities for students with disabilities. It creates a clear road for how schools can integrate students with disabilities into mainstream athletic programs and create adapted programs for students with disabilities. (Active Policy Solutions, 2013, p. 1)

Participation opportunities made available by schools to allow students with disabilities to participate in athletics to the greatest extent possible can include:

- *Mainstream programs*—school-based activities that are developed and offered to all students.
- *Adapted physical education and athletic programs*—programs that are specifically developed for students with disabilities.
- *Allied or unified sports*—programs that are specifically designed to combine groups of students with and without disabilities together in physical activities.

This Dear Colleague Letter represents a watershed moment for young athletes with disabilities.

Homeless High School Athletes

We need to acknowledge the fact that homelessness in the US is an important social issue. According to the National Alliance to End Homelessness (2017, para. 2), "In January 2016, 549,928 people were homeless on a given night in the United States. Of that number, 194,716 were people

www

Dear Colleague Letter
www2.ed.gov/about/
offices/list/ocr/letters/
colleague-201301-504.html

in families . . . On that same night, there were 35,686 unaccompanied homeless youth, roughly seven percent of the total homeless population." Typically, people end up homeless as a result of an unanticipated financial situation such as a medical emergency, car accident, or death in the family. While many are able to bounce back with support from public assistance, many others are not. When looking at the numbers and who is affected, it is obvious the children make up a large percentage of homeless people. Who exactly is considered homeless? One useful definition, used by the Jefferson County (KY) Public Schools, is

> the McKinney-Vento definition of homelessness among students. It identifies homeless students as those who lack a fixed, regular and adequate nighttime residence. This means not every student considered homeless in Louisville is sleeping on the street or in shelters . . . In fact, nearly 70 percent of the school district's homeless students are living with family, friends or relatives . . . Despite that, they still lack the consistency and stability a student needs to succeed in the classroom. (Ryan, 2015, paras. 9–10)

After an in-depth six-month investigation, Sports Illustrated recently presented a feature on homeless student-athletes (Axson, 2014). They followed the lives of three homeless high school athletes, telling their stories. The link for the video entitled "Young, Gifted and Homeless" is included on the reference page at the end of this chapter (Sports Illustrated, 2014).

It is fact that many high school athletic directors and coaches will have homeless student athletes somewhere on a team's roster, regardless of school location—urban, rural, or suburban. The goal is to work with these student athletes and their families in the most respectful way possible. Remember, high school sport is an extension of one's high school education, so coaches and ADs can, and must, play a role in improving the lives of these students. Working together with local social service agencies and school systems is necessary. The time has come, however, for state athletic associations, coaching associations and athletic administration groups to determine the best course of action here as well. Again, as this book threads the importance of ethical decision making throughout the chapters, this topic presents a pivotal opportunity for sport managers to choose to do the right thing for students and for their communities.

Funding

As with all other aspects of education, high school athletics face enormous budgetary pressure. Only a handful of sports generate any income, mostly from ticket sales and concessions. Some athletic programs have booster clubs, made up mostly of parents and alumni, who donate their time and money to help sustain the programs. As mentioned earlier in the chapter, revenue flows into high school associations from various sources, including membership dues, gate receipts, corporate sponsorships, and private donations. Some high school associations are creating new and unique ways to generate funds to ensure their sport programs are financially secure. High school programs are becoming increasingly reliant on sponsorships/corporate donations, broadcast rights, and even crowdfunding.

State associations as well as individual high schools are also turning to corporate sponsors. Go to any state high athletic association web pages and you will see sponsor logos everywhere. Some examples include USBank and Farmers Mutual (Nebraska), Spalding and Nike (California), Les Schwab Tires and Jimmy Johns (Utah), Alabama Power and Coca-Cola (Alabama), Spectrum Sports and Price Chopper (New York), and Musco Sports Lighting and Vanderbilt Sports Medicine (Tennessee). Sponsors range from local companies to national corporations and can include product categories such as banks, sporting goods, or grocery stores. High school sport as seen as a solid wholesome marketing opportunity across a variety of consumer goods and services.

Individual high schools also seek corporate sponsorship money as well. Lakewood, Ohio secured a $320,000 local naming rights deal from First Federal for a stadium used by Lakewood High School and also St Edward's High School. Noblesville High School in Indiana secured a $575,000 stadium naming rights deal from Hare Chevrolet (Koba, 2012). The school district in Katy, Texas, signed a 10 year, $2.5 million naming rights deal with Academy Sports + Outdoor (Smith, 2016). Not all high school sponsorship deals are this large, of course. Many times the gifts are a few thousand dollars or some value-in-kind from local businesses. Even these small amounts add up to help high school athletes have the opportunity to participate. It is important, however, that schools choose their sponsors wisely. One could question the selection of a fast-food restaurant as a sponsor, for example, given the obesity epidemic among young people, and certainly alcoholic beverage companies would not be acceptable and neither would local establishments who choose to discriminate against any group of people.

Then there is crowdfunding. According to Wolf (2015, para. 5), "Thousands of young athletes and their parents, coaches and schools are turning to the web—and by extension their friends, family and strangers—to try to make up the difference between ever-shrinking budgets and the hefty cost associated with summer and high school sports." A visit to the GoFundMe (2017) Sports Fundraising page reveals the following language:

Rally Support

Root on your favorite youth team or get support for a charity ride or marathon. Whether you need equipment or sponsors, a GoFundMe crowdfunding campaign can make it happen.

Equip Your Team

No matter the sport—from football and basketball to soccer and baseball—a successful GoFundMe campaign can help you get your team into the competitive spirit.

Easy Crowdfunding

Cheerleading uniforms? Little league travel costs? Intramural fees? GoFundMe is the perfect solution to any kind of financial challenge for your favorite hobby or club. Keep the focus on playing, not fundraising.

Why GoFundMe?

- Athletes, parents, and fans can start crowdfunding in minutes
- Sports campaigns have raised millions of dollars on GoFundMe
- Faster and easier than traditional fundraisers
- No deadlines or goal requirements
- 5-minute email support, 24/7

Certainly the pressure of finding new alternative funding sources is increasing daily. When seeking corporate sponsors, athletic administrators should research the reputation and products of a potential corporate sponsor. The school's and the corporation's images will be intertwined, so associating with ethical business partners is of the utmost importance.

Home Schoolers

An interesting ongoing debate continues around the issue of whether or not home-schooled students should be eligible to compete in high school athletics. In the United States, close to two million children and young adults are home schooled annually. What happens when home schoolers decide they want to play organized high school sports? With the occasional exception, most home school settings cannot offer competitive high school-level athletic opportunities, particularly for team sport athletes, so home schoolers who wish to play must make their request to the local public high school they would have attended or, sometimes, to a local private school. Of course, the first athlete who may come to mind is quarterback Tim Tebow, a product of home schooling prior to his college career at the University of Florida. Tebow played high school football for Nease High School in Ponte Vedra Beach, Florida, while being home schooled.

What policies come into play in this situation? This very complex governance and policy area involves the state legislatures, state high school activities associations, occasionally local school districts, and sometimes even the court system. First, there is no one piece of federal legislation in the United States relative to home schooling. In other words, decisions on all matters involving home schoolers are left up to the individual states to decide. No wonder there is so much confusion in this area.

portraits + perspectives

TONY BUTLER, *Athletic Director,*

St Francis School, Louisville, KY

I am the Athletic Director at St Francis School in Louisville, KY. My major responsibilities are extensive. I am responsible for hiring and firing coaches, scheduling, event management, and roster management.

High school sports are an interesting part of the sport industry. Administrators face just about as many policy issues as our larger counterparts at the collegiate level. There are some limitations in monitoring and numerous questions that go along with creating new policy on the high school level. Most policy issues have been handed down to each individual school and include drug testing and performance-enhancing drugs, smaller numbers of multi-sport athletes, influence of outside coaches, and sportsmanship of coaches, athletes, and more so parents. There are other issues like transfer rules for high school sports and kids playing up. For my school, the top two of these issues are sportsmanship and transfers.

The Kentucky High School Athletic Association (KHSAA) has a rule that forces kids to sit out a year after transferring unless they meet one of ten exceptions set forth by the Association. This rule was implemented well before my time as a high school athletics administrator. Originally it was implemented to curb recruiting of kids from one high school to another and mirrored the collegiate transfer rule. But the rule is harsh and keeps kids from playing any sport at their new school for a full year. While it makes sense on one hand, it's tough because a high school student only has four years of eligibility. The rule was created to manage adults but it truly penalizes the kids.

Sportsmanship is an increasingly important topic for athletic administrators. More and more the sense of entitlement is creeping into athletic programs. Parents who think their kids are elite expect athletic department staff to do so much more for their kids. Kids pick up cues from parents and then act in a similar fashion. Getting parents and kids to understand the overall value of participation is a major challenge for athletic administrators.

My school has worked hard on trying to change a few policies over the years. Submission of policy changes to the transfer rule has been one of the major concerns. Suggestions to change the rule have been submitted but too many people are reluctant to accept any changes.

In Kentucky, schools have a choice in whether they want to join the state association, the KHSAA. The state association staff includes a Commissioner, Associate Commissioners, IT, Marketing, General Counsel, and a few other positions. Each member school appoints a delegate to represent the school at an annual delegate assembly. There is also a 20-person Board of Control, filled by specific delegates throughout the state along with Kentucky Department of Education (KDE) personnel. The structure is solid and ensures anyone who has an issue to raise will have the opportunity for their voice to be heard. Each year the KHSAA holds a delegate assembly where representatives from schools around the state have the opportunity to submit proposals for changes and to pitch their ideas to the entire group. The group then votes for each proposal. While the fact that everyone has a voice is a benefit, it can also be a drawback as well. The overall size and diversity of the group can be a major challenge. While everyone may have an equal voice, having a large number of voices makes change tough.

The major challenge with most policy changes is the cost associated with monitoring. Drug testing is a major issue but the cost of testing is something most schools cannot work into their budgets. Numerous privacy concerns revolve around this testing that are scary for schools to consider. This is an issue we will continue to deal with into the future.

HSPN
www.hspn.net

As of 2017, home schoolers from 34 states were allowed to play high school sport, with criteria for participation varying by state (Home School Legal Defense Association, 2011). This is not to say, however, that there is not some common ground in the discussion. Homeschool Sportnet Incorporated (HSPN) is an organization that considers itself "America's Source for Homeschool Athletics" (HSPN, n.d.). Its mission is presented in Exhibit 5.6.

The issue of home schoolers' eligibility highlights the complex interaction between high school sport governing bodies, state legislations, and the court system (Hums, 1996). Home schooling is a policy area that cuts across several governance levels—local, district, and state. At each level, sport managers need to understand the ethical considerations of letting or not letting home schoolers participate. Is it fair to deny home schoolers the chance to play when their families pay taxes that fund public education? Is it fair for home schoolers to take regularly enrolled students' positions on teams? And what educational message is sent when it is acceptable for home schoolers to play sports with, but not go to school with, other students? Questions continue to emerge and policy continues to evolve in this area as home-schooled students in different states seek the opportunity to participate (Ojalvo, 2012).

---

exhibit **5.6** Mission Statement of the HSPN

1. To support homeschool parents, athletes, coaches, teams and organizations through means of an interactive web-site, newsletters, workshops and free postings.
2. To provide national athletic events for homeschool students in a Christian environment through the use of venues that are designated as Christian sites and well-known for high ideals.
3. To encourage new start-up teams as well as established organizations by our online materials and articles.
4. To offer homeschool teams the best-fit resources from reliable partners in areas such as sports insurance, uniforms, fund raising, web-site support, college recruitment and more.
5. To showcase the talent of homeschool athletes by means of our National Homeschool Scoreboard, n-Perspective Stats Manager, [and] Sports Ticker.
6. To develop a national convention and leadership council.

Source: HSPN, Mission Statement, n.d.

SUMMARY

S port governance takes place at a variety of levels, from international to national to state to local. Remember that the real power in scholastic sport lies with the state associations, although at times the courts will mandate their activities if any policies violate students' fundamental rights. The rules-setting and regulatory powers truly reside in these associations. The NFHS acts as a service organization for its state members. School districts, principals, and athletic directors can set rules on their levels, but they must be in accord with the state rules. In the United States, high school associations have repeatedly been identified as state actors and therefore subject to the US Constitution for their actions.

The types of governance and policy issues scholastic sport administrators must deal with are vast and complex. The governance decisions they make when setting policy will interact with state as well as federal legislative bodies and laws such as Title IX. They will often come in contact with the judicial system as well, and so they must be prepared for their decisions to be questioned in courts of law. Despite these considerations, scholastic sport administrators have the opportunity to provide programming that has a positive impact on the lives of thousands of young athletes. It is an exciting and personally fulfilling segment of the sport industry.

caseSTUDY

SCHOLASTIC SPORT

You are the AD at Middletown High School. Recently, your wrestling coach, Coach Sullivan, came to you for help involving one of his athletes, a senior transfer student wrestler named Michael. Coach Sullivan had noticed Michael always seemed to be the last one to leave and often seemed to be wearing the same clothes almost every day. He became aware that when the other boys on the team talked about going home or going out to eat after practice, Michael never really joined in the conversations. Everyone did know that Michael's father was absent from his life, and his family at home consisted of his mom and a younger brother, a sophomore named Allen. Although Michael mostly kept to himself, this afternoon after practice he finally confided in Coach Sullivan—home for Michael was a shelter. In fact, he and his family were homeless, and had been bouncing from shelter to shelter for the past five to six months. Fall was rapidly coming to a close, and winter in central Illinois could be pretty brutal.

1. What can you and Coach Sullivan do to assist Michael? Who do you need to contact to activate school/community resources to help out? Use the decision-making model we learned earlier in the semester to determine a course of action to take.

2. Homelessness among youth in the United States is at an all-time high. What social responsibility do sport organizations (e.g., a sport governing body) have in addressing this social issue? What can state high school athletic associations specifically do to aid in cases like this?

3. At times it seems sport is just a trivial pursuit or form of entertainment. What role can sport managers and their organizations play in the lives of people who are homeless? How can these roles vary among the managers of (a) a high-profile professional sport team, (b) a Division I athletic department, or (c) a YMCA (Young Men's Christian Association)?

CHAPTER questions

1. How does the North American model of adolescent sport participation differ from that in other countries? What do you consider the advantages and disadvantages of this model compared to others?

2. Where does the main power lie in high school sport? Why?

3. High school sport has a number of goals, including education and participation. Should one of these goals be the preparation of college athletes?

4. One emerging source of funds for high school sport is corporate sponsorship. What are the pros and cons of high school athletic departments pursuing corporate sponsors?

FOR ADDITIONAL INFORMATION

1. Home Schooled Students in Kentucky High School Sport: www.tristatehomepage.com/news/home-schooled-students-to-play-ky-high-school-sports-soon

2. 2018's Best High Schools for Athletes in America: https://www.niche.com/k12/search/best-public-high-schools-for-sports/

3. IMG Academy Homepage: https://www.imgacademy.com

4. Washington Catholic Athletic Conference Homepage: http://wcacsports.com/landing/index

5. YouTube: A Day in the Life of a Travis High School Football Player: https://www.youtube.com/watch?v=n8zyKDl5ZMQ

6. Title IX in High School Sport: AAUW. (n.d). Know the score: Investigate Title IX compliance in high school athletics: www.aauw.org/resource/title-ix-compliance/

REFERENCES

Active Policy Solutions. (2013). Overview: Disability in sport dear colleague letter. Retrieved from www.activepolicysolutions.com/news-resources/

AIA. (n.d.). About AIA. Retrieved from www.aiaonline.org/about/index.php

Altman, S. (2010). State action. In D. J. Cotton, J. T. Wolohan, & T. J. Wilde (Eds.), *Law for recreation and sport managers* (5th ed., pp. 418–427). Dubuque, IA: Kendall-Hunt.

Angelico, P. (2013). Transfer rule ensures athletics don't play a role in decision to change schools. *CHSAA Now.* Retrieved from http://chsaanow.com/2013-08-28/transfer-rule-ensures-athletics-dont-play-role-decision-change-schools/

Axson, S. (2014). SI cover: Young, gifted, and homeless. *Sports Illustrated.* Retrieved from https://www.si.com/more-sports/2014/10/14/homeless-athletes-sports-illustrated-cover

Carpenter, L. (2010). Gender equity: Opportunities to participate. In D. J. Cotton, J. T. Wolohan, & T. J. Wilde (Eds.), *Law for recreation and sport managers* (4th ed., pp. 538–547). Dubuque, IA: Kendall-Hunt.

Chicago Tribune. (2012). IHSA launches state finals pilot program for disabled athletes. Retrieved from http://articles.chicagotribune.com/2012-06-11/sports/ct-spt-0611-prep-ihsa-pilot-state-finals-for-disabled_1_ihsa-student-athletes-state-finals

CHSAA. (2016). Constitution of the Colorado High School Activities Association. Retrieved from http://rcasey.wpengine.netdna-cdn.com/wp-content/uploads/bylaws/2016-17-bylaws.pdf

Colles, C., & Williams, J. (2010). Voluntary associations and eligibility issues. In D. Cotton & J. Wolohan (Eds.), *Law for recreation and sport managers* (5th ed., pp. 471–482). Dubuque, IA: Kendall-Hunt.

Covell, D. (2015). High school and youth sport. In L. P. Masteralexis, C. A. Barr, & M. A. Hums (Eds.), *Principles and practice of sport management* (5th ed., pp. 151–172). Burlington, MA: Jones & Bartlett.

Elliot, P. (2013, January 25). Sports are a civil right for the disabled, US says. Retrieved from https://www.yahoo.com/news/sports-civil-disabled-us-says-050851263--politics.html

FHSAA. (2017). Finance and accounting. Retrieved from http://www.fhsaa.org/departments/finance-accounting

Firth, M. (2017). How much money does a high school athletic director make? Retrieved from http://work.chron.com/much-money-high-school-athletic-director-make-13226.html

Forsythe, L. L. (1950). *Athletics in Michigan schools: The first hundred years.* Englewood Cliffs, NJ: Prentice Hall.

GHSA. (2016). GHSA 2016–2017 budget. Retrieved from www.ghsa.net/sites/default/files/documents/financials/GHSA-Budget-2016-17.pdf

GoFundMe. (2017). Sports fundraising: Impact a life today! Retrieved from https://www.gofundme.com/sports-fundraising

Graham, G., & Seidel, J. (2010, March 25). Public schools open sports to athletes with disabilities. *Baltimore Sun.* Retrieved from http://articles.baltimoresun.com/2010-03-25/sports/bal-va.rule25mar25_1_athletes-mpssaa-disabilities-act

Hayward, L. (2014, December 24). No pass no play heads into fourth decade. *Midland Reporter-Telegram.* Retrieved from www.mrt.com/sports/article/No-Pass-No-Play-heads-into-fourth-decade-7419312.php

Home School Legal Defense Association. (2011, May). State laws concerning participation of homeschool students in public school activities. Retrieved from www.hslda.org/docs/nche/Issues/E/Equal_Access.pdf

HSPN. (n.d.). Home page. Retrieved from http://www.hspn.net/homeschool-sports.asp

Hums, M. A. (1996). Home schooled students' opportunities to participate in interscholastic sport: Legal issues and policy implications for secondary education. *Journal of Legal Aspects of Sport, 6*(3), 169–177.

Hums, M. A., MacLean, J. C., & Zintz, T. (2011). *La gouvernance au coeur des politiques des organisations sportives.* Traduction et adaptation de la 2e édition américaine. Bruxelles, Belgique: Groupe De Boeck.

ISF. (2017). History & Mission. Retrieved from http://isfsports.org/history-mission

Kerr-Dineen, L. (2016, July 27). Here are your odds of becoming a professional athlete (they're not good). *USA Today*. Retrieved from http://ftw.usatoday.com/2016/07/here-are-your-odds-of-becoming-a-professional-athlete-theyre-not-good

KHSAA. (2006a). 2007–2011 Kentucky High School Athletic Association strategic plan. Retrieved from www…khsaa.org/strategicplan/20072011/20072011strategicplan.pdf

KHSAA. (2006b, January 10). KHSAA Public/private update. Retrieved from www.khsaa.org/news/20052006/nr011006.pdf

KHSAA. (2014). By-law 5. Minimum academic requirement. Retrieved from https://khsaa.org/handbook/bylaws/20142015/bylaw5.pdf

Koba, M. (2012, December 9). High school sports have turned into big business. Retrieved from www.cnbc.com/id/100001024

National Alliance to End Homelessness. (2017). Snapshot of homelessness. Retrieved from www.endhomelessness.org/pages/snapshot_of_homelessness

National Women's Law Center. (2015). The battle for equity in athletics in elementary and secondary schools. Retrieved from https://nwlc.org/wp-content/uploads/2008/06/bge_elementary_and_secondary_schools_8.11.15.pdf

NCAA. (2011). Estimated probability of competing in athletics beyond the interscholastic level. Retrieved from www.ncaa.org/about/resources/research/estimated-probability-competing-college-athletics

NFHS. (2015a). About us. Retrieved from www.nfhs.org/who-we-are/aboutus

NFHS. (2015b). *Annual report* 2013–2014. Retrieved from https://www.nfhs.org/media/1014511/2013-14-annual-report_website.pdf

NFHS. (2015c). State association listing. Retrieved from www.nfhs.org/resources/state-association-listing

NFHS. (2016a). *Annual report*. Indianapolis, IN: Author.

NFHS. (2016b). *NFHS handbook 2016–2017*. Indianapolis, IN: Author.

NFHS. (2017). Eligibility results. Retrieved from www.nfhs.org/EligibilityResults/Home/Index?year=2014&state=TX

NFHS. (n.d.). National Federation of State High School Associations: Take part. Get set for life. Retrieved from www.nfhs.org/media/885655/nfhs-company-brochure.pdf

NHIAA. (2014). NHIAA strategic plan 2014–2019. Retrieved from www.nhiaa.org/ckfinder/userfiles/files/NHIAAStrategicPlan2014-2019.pdf

NYSPHSAA. (2017). Life of an athlete. Retrieved from www.nysphsaa.org/Educational-Programs/Life-of-an-Athlete

OHSAA. (n.d.). Our mission. Retrieved from http://ohsaa.org/AboutOHSAA

Ojalvo, M. E. (2012). Should home schoolers be allowed to play public school sports? *New York Times*. Retrieved from http://learning.blogs.nytimes.com/2012/02/10/should-home-schoolers-be-allowed-to-play-public-school-sports/

OSAA. (2016). 2016–2017 Oregon School Activities handbook. Retrieved from www.osaa.org/docs/handbooks/osaahandbook.pdf

PIAA. (2017). Introduction. Retrieved from www.piaa.org/about/introduction.aspx

Rader, B.C. (1999). *American sports: From the age of folk games to the age of televised sports* (4th ed.). Upper Saddle River, NJ: Prentice Hall.

Ryan, J. (2015). JCPS is addressing student homelessness despite dwindling funds. Retrieved from http://wfpl.org/jcps-addressing-student-homelessness-despite-dwindling-funds/

SCHSL. (n.d.). Constitution. Retrieved from http://schsl.org/wp-content/uploads/2017/06/5Constitution.pdf

Seymour, H. (1990). *Baseball: The people's game*. New York: Oxford University Press.

Sharp, L. A., Moorman, A. M., & Claussen, C. L. (2010). *Sport law: A managerial approach* (2nd ed). Scottsdale, AZ: Holcomb Hathaway.

Sieck, B. (2015, April 20). A house divided: Home school students on high school sports teams. Retrieved from https://www.nfhs.org/articles/a-house-divided-homeschool-students-on-school-sports-teams/

Smith, C. (2016, Dec. 21). The new Katy stadium naming rights eal grades out better than you might imagine. *USA Today*. Retrieved from http://usatodayhss.com/2016/

the-new-katy-stadium-naming-rights-deal-grades-out-better-than-you-might-imagine

Sports Illustrated. (2014). Young, gifted, and homeless. *[YouTube]*. Retrieved from https://view.yahoo.com/show/sports-illustrated-video/clip/60699826/young-gifted-homeless

Tilley, M. (2012, February 8). A privilege, not a right. *New York Times*. Retrieved from https://www.nytimes.com/roomfordebate/2012/02/08/should-home-schoolers-play-for-the-high-school-team/a-privilege-not-a-right

TSSAA. (1999). TSSAA: History, facts, and figures. Retrieved from http://tssaa.org/about/history/

Vincent, T. (1994). *The rise of American sport: Mudville's revenge*. Lincoln: University of Nebraska Press.

WIAA. (n.d.). What is the WIAA? Why was it established? Retrieved from https://www.wiaawi.org/aboutwiaa.aspx

WIAA. (2013). Washington Interscholastic Athletic Association annual budget: Fiscal year 2013–2014. Retrieved from www.ghsa.net/sites/default/files/documents/financials/GHSA-Budget-2016-17.pdf

Wilson, R. (2016, November 11). Trump administration may back down from title IX, but campuses won't. *Chronicle of Higher Education*. Retrieved from www.chronicle.com/article/Trump-Administration-May-Back/238382

Wolf, J. (2015, July 28). As budgets dwindle, high schools and youth sports teams turn to crowdfunding. *USA Today*. Retrieved from http://usatodayhss.com/2015/as-budgets-dwindle-high-schools-and-youth-sports-teams-turn-to-crowdfunding

Wong, G. M. (1994). *Essentials of sport law*. Westport, CT: Praeger.

Amateur Sport in the Community

Mary A. Hums
Joanne C. MacLean

The term *amateur sport* describes a diverse set of individual and group sporting activities engaged in by millions of people worldwide. Different people play for different reasons. Enjoyment, group affiliation, fitness, healthy living, and the joy of competition are among the most prominent motivations. Amateur athletes do not get paid for their efforts.

Rather, a great many amateur sporting activities involve participants who volunteer to play. Participants range from young children to senior citizens to people with disabilities, and their involvement is usually in addition to their primary responsibilities with jobs or schools. Amateur sports include highly competitive events like National Collegiate Athletic Association (NCAA) playoffs and the Little League Baseball World Series, and they also include less-competitive activities such as organized beach volleyball jamborees and father–daughter golf events. At times, extensive media coverage presents the glitz and glitter of highly competitive amateur sporting activities, such as high school and college championship games, but a local weekend beach volleyball tournament with thousands of participants may go unnoticed. As sport management students you need an understanding of how community amateur sport entities are organized and governed because many of you will, at some point in your career, either be in a leadership position in such organizations or work with these events in some capacity as a volunteer or paid staff member. You may be responsible for setting policy and ensuring the effective pursuit of organization goals in this extensive segment of the sport industry.

Organizations delivering amateur sport in the community for youth and adults are both numerous and offer a variety of activities. In fact, amateur sport in the community has a rich history and an abundance of community structures delivering opportunities for participation. The organizations that govern and establish policy for amateur sport are normally categorized as public or nonprofit. To begin this chapter we will discuss how amateur sport for members of the community first developed and became organized.

HISTORY OF COMMUNITY AND YOUTH SPORT

The roots of modern day amateur sport in North America might be traced to the villages and towns of rural Britain during the industrialization of the 18th and 19th centuries (Kidd, 1999). Mechanization in farming and other industries resulted in the migration of workers from the countryside to cities, and later to North America. Traditionally, farm workers competed in folk games and other precursors to today's athletic events. Although such activities were scarce in overcrowded cities where an expectation of longer work weeks was the norm, games and active forms of recreation continued to be played in elite, all-male schools (Morrow & Wamsley, 2009). As sport for the elite became more popular and better organized, an interest in participating quickly spread to upper-class girls and women and to working-class boys and men. In a similar way, participating in amateur sport emerged and gained momentum in many parts of the world.

In the United States and Canada, adaptation of British sports and development of new games began in the early 1800s. Native people were accomplished runners, climbers, swimmers, and canoeists, and they participated in many tests of skill and strength. Settlers from England and other parts of Europe brought their own games and tried the indigenous games they found on their new shores as well. While working-class men and women had little leisure time to devote to athletic contests, they still participated and spectated during holidays and other special events. By the mid-19th century, North Americans were engaging in a wide variety of athletic contests. An increase in population, the changing nature of work in an increasingly mechanized industrial world, and decreased working hours provided increased leisure time and paved the way for the development of public and nonprofit sport organizations.

Public Sport Organizations

As the urban population increased during the mid- to late-19th century, housing density amplified in urban centers. Municipal activities and private sporting clubs were scrutinized by local governments. Originally, their interest was in regulating leisure practices. Governments declared public holidays, dedicated land for parks and sporting activities, and enacted laws prohibiting activities they considered immoral or improper, such as racing and gambling on Sundays. Municipalities subsidized sport competitions such as rifle shooting and banned the rowdiness and immorality thought to be associated with highly publicized prizefights. As the numbers and types of activities and publicity increased, generating a greater number of eager participants, public sport organizations developed. Minor sport leagues were formed. Such leagues were managed by groups of individuals who set schedules, adapted and enforced rules and regulations, and promoted and publicized events such as baseball, football, rugby, and track and field. The leagues frequently led to the development of municipal groups, where teams were assembled from the top local talent to represent the entire community. Such a team would then enter into competition by challenging another team from a nearby town. While travel was difficult and kept to a minimum in the early days, teams often endured substantial travel distances in an effort to reap the glory of victory for their hometowns. Competitions between teams from different communities led to the development of sport festivals and jamborees, the precursors to today's state games in the United States and provincial games in Canada. As sport gained interest and became organized by community groups, the need for more opportunities and diversity in sport offerings soon resulted in the development of nonprofit sport organizations.

Nonprofit Sport Organizations

A *nonprofit sport organization* delivers programs and services for a particular sport or group with no intent to gain profit. These types of organizations range from very small (Portland's Rose City Hockey all girls club) to large professionally run associations (the North Texas Youth Football Association). Nonprofit sport organizations emerged as an alternative to programs such as recreational sport leagues run by city recreation departments, and in addition to those programs developed with the express intent of making money. In the beginning, nonprofit organizations filled the gap in programming between the two and provided opportunities for participation in sporting events regardless of class or financial background. For-profit organizations offered programming based on business strategies, inevitably providing only the most popular activities. It was impossible for public recreation departments to offer all possible types of sports. Therefore, interested individuals formed their own organizations according to their own interests. Nonprofit sport organizations emerged all over North America for sporting interests as diverse as waterskiing and bicycling, walking, and badminton.

Public and nonprofit sport organizations began developing organizational structures, constitutions, positions of leadership with duties and responsibilities, and programs. What are the governance structures for these types of organizations, and how do they develop policy?

GOVERNANCE

As illustrated by the history of community sport, amateur athletic organizations are structured in a manner consistent with their purpose and mission. While private for-profit ventures exist (such as climbing gyms, gymnastic centers, and figure-skating clubs), most amateur sport in the community is publicly run with funding from some level of government or delivered by nonprofit service organizations. What types of groups fall within these categories, and how are they organized to deliver amateur sport within the community? The following sections will identify the mission, funding, membership, and organizational structure of community amateur sport organizations.

The Governance of Public Sport Organizations

The three main types of public sport organizations delivering amateur sport in our communities are:

1. city parks and recreation departments
2. recreational sport leagues
3. state games and provincial games

City Parks and Recreation Departments

City parks and recreation departments have traditionally housed community sport, recreation, and physical activity programs. Cities provide a wide

www

North Texas Youth Football Association

http://leaguelineup.com/welcome.asp?url=ntyfa

www

Climbing Gym Example: Urban Ascent Rock Climbing Gym, Boise Idaho

www.urbanascent.com

Gymnastic Center Example: Gold Medal Gymnastics Center, Long Island NY

www.gmgc.com

Figure Skating Club Example: Ann Arbor Figure Skating Club, Michigan

www.annarborfsc.org

array of services to their citizens, including utilities such as sewers, water, and gas and electric. Cities also provide public transportation and care for infrastructures such as roads and bridges. In addition to these basic services, many cities also take it upon themselves to offer a wide array of sport and recreation facilities.

MISSION. City parks and recreation department mission statements are as varied as the activities they offer. They usually include themes such as opportunities for leisure-time activities, learning and playing in a safe environment, provision of a wide variety of facilities, and statements of inclusivity and support for diversity. Two sample mission statements, one of the Parks and Recreation Department of the City of Houston and one of the City of Toronto, are presented in Exhibits 6.1 and 6.2.

MEMBERSHIP. Generally these programs are open to any and all residents of a particular city. Established policies deal with participation by nonresidents and guests. The people who take part in physical activities offered by city parks and recreation programs have a wide variety of activities to choose from, including offerings such as swimming, soccer, softball,

WWW

Houston Parks and Recreation Department
www.houstontx.gov/parks/

City of Fairway, Kansas Parks and Recreation Department
www.fairwaykansas.
org/index.asp?Type=B_
BASIC&SEC=%7B84B2
4DE6-A1E6-4451-B790-
04DD2CBB3AAE%7D

Mission Statement of the City of Houston Parks and Recreation Department	*exhibit* **6.1**

To enhance the quality of urban life by providing safe, well maintained parks and offering affordable programming for our community.

Source: City of Houston (2017).

Mission Statement of the City of Fairway, Kansas Parks & Recreation Department	*exhibit* **6.2**

It is the mission of the Fairway Parks and Recreation Department to create recreational opportunities for growth and enhancement by developing diverse services and programs that promote citizen involvement and a strong sense of community while striving to increase the social, cultural, and physical well-being of its residents and visitors.

Source: City of Fairway, Kansas (2017).

fitness programs, martial arts, tennis, hiking and biking trails, and many others. Activities are not limited to the traditional team sport offerings, as departments try to keep up with trends by offering popular activities. For example, the City of Seattle Parks and Recreation (SPR) Department manages the following:

a 6,414-acre park system of over 485 parks and extensive natural areas. SPR provides athletic fields, tennis courts, play areas, specialty gardens, and more than 25 miles of boulevards and 120 miles of trails. The system comprises about 12% of the city's land area. SPR also manages many facilities, including 26 community centers, eight indoor swimming pools, two outdoor (summer) swimming pools, four environmental education centers, two small craft centers, four golf courses, an outdoor stadium, and much more. (City of Seattle, 2017)

FINANCIALS.   Because these facilities and staff are provided by the city, city residents' tax money underwrites a good portion of the costs. As a result, some facility use and programming may be offered free of charge, for example, swimming at the neighborhood public pool. Other services may require a fee, for example, a city-sponsored softball league may require teams to pay an entrance fee to cover the costs of umpires, field maintenance, and softballs for each game.

The size of a city parks and recreation budget will vary from city to city. For example, the City of Kissimmee, Florida, had a 2017 budget of $6,761,906, which came from ad valorem taxes, impact fees, sales tax, grants, and a utility surcharge (City of Kissimmee, 2017). A much smaller city, Snellville, Georgia, budgeted for $783,150 in expenses in 2017 (City of Snellville, 2017).

ORGANIZATIONAL STRUCTURE.   A city parks and recreation department is one of numerous departments within the organizational structure of a city. Exhibit 6.3 shows how parks and recreation fits into the overall organizational chart for the large city of San Diego, California. Exhibit 6.4 illustrates how the organizational chart for the City Parks and Recreation Department can become very complex in larger cities like San Diego. By contrast, the parks and recreation department for a smaller city (population 65,000) such as Loveland, Colorado, is presented in Exhibit 6.5.

Recreational Sport Leagues

Recreational sport leagues provide opportunities for regular participation in sport for both children and adults. Leagues might be established by an interested group of individuals who wish to play basketball on a regular basis, or they may be run by community recreation staff in city parks and recreation facilities. Leagues are commonly available in a wide variety of sports, like football, baseball, hockey, curling, volleyball, soccer, and bowling. Most recreational sport leagues are considered a public service.

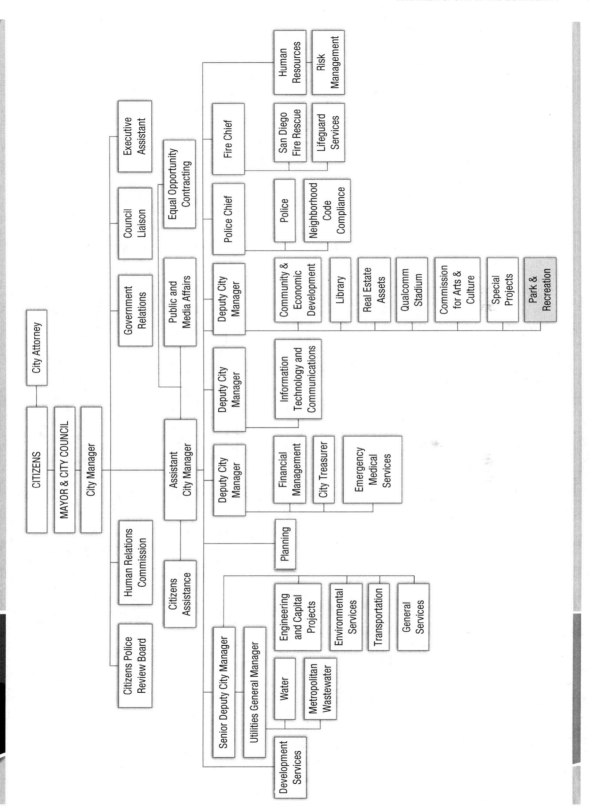

Source: City of San Diego (2017a).

exhibit **6.4**   Organizational Chart for the City of San Diego Park and Recreation Department

City Council

Mayor/Chief Executive Officer

Citizens

Chief Operating Officer

Assistant Chief Operating Officer

Park & Recreation Director

Park & Recreation Assistant Director

Administrative Services
- Financial Management
- Grants
- Training Office

Community Parks I
- Geographic by council district 1, 2, 5, 6 and 7
- Community parks
- Recreation centers
- Neighborhood parks
- Mini parks
- Joint use operations
- After school programs
- Mt. Hope Cemetery
- Naval Training Center Community Park
- Downtown parks

Community Parks II
- Geographic by Council District 3, 4, 8 and 9
- Community parks
- Recreation center
- Neighborhood parks
- Mini parks
- Joint use operations
- After school programs
- Therapeutic Recreation and Senior Services
- Aquatics
- Volunteer Coordination

Developed Regional Parks
- Balboa Park
  - Maintenance
  - Public facility maintenance
  - Special events
- Mission Bay Park
  - Maintenance
  - Special events
- Beach Maintenance
- Shoreline Parks
- Citywide Maintenance Services
  - Mowing
  - Sweeping
  - Aquatic Features
- Park Forestry
  - Irrigation
- Park Rangers
  - Balboa Park
  - Mission Bay Park
  - Community Parks
- Presidio Hill
  - Maintenance
  - Historic and Cultural Management

Open Space

Maintenance Assessment Districts (MADs)
- Open Space Maintenance
- Open Space Regional Park Management
- Mission Trails Regional Park
- Otay Valley Regional Park
- Tecolote Canyon
- Marian Bear
- Rose Canyon
- Penasquitos Canyon Preserve
- Black Mountain Open Space
- San Diego River Park
- Citywide Open Space Coordination
- Citywide Trails Planning and Management
- Multiple Special Conservation Program (MSCP) Compliance
- Maintenance Assessment Districts (MADs)
- Street Median Maintenance

Golf Operations
- Balboa Park Municipal Golf Course
- Mission Bay Municipal Golf Course and Practice Center
- Torrey Pines Municipal Golf Course

Source: City of San Diego (2017b)

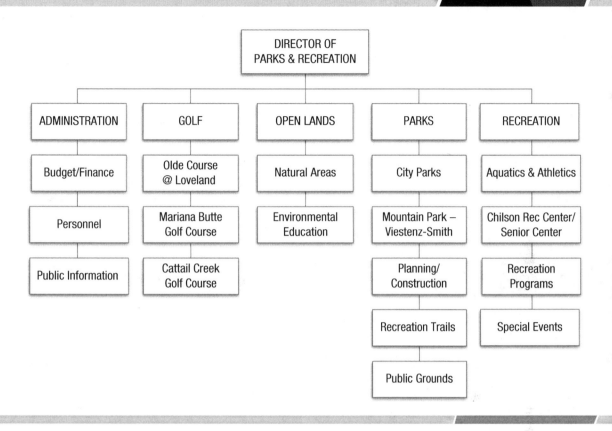

Organizational Chart for the City of Loveland, Colorado, Parks & Recreation Department / *exhibit* 6.5

Source: City of Loveland, Colorado (2017).

They are organized to provide individuals the opportunity to participate in their sport of choice.

MISSION. A recreational sport league's mission statement will likely include some language about what sport the league is delivering and at which level of competition. The league may be highly competitive or designed with more of a recreational focus on fun. Fair play, respect, and ethical conduct are common components of recreational sport league mission statements. See Exhibits 6.6 and 6.7 for the mission statements of the Boise Nationals Timbers soccer club, in Boise, Idaho, and of the Glencoe Baseball Association in Glencoe Park District, Illinois.

MEMBERSHIP. Recreational sport leagues are organized for a vast array of participants. Some activities target children and youth groups, other leagues

Boise Nationals Timbers
www.boisenationalstimbers.com

Glencoe Baseball Association
http://glencoebaseball.org

| exhibit | 6.6 | Mission Statement of the Boise Nationals Timbers Soccer Club |

We strive to develop players of character as we focus on our six core values of:

EXCELLENCE–CHARACTER–COMMITMENT–
TEAMWORK–SPORTSMANSHIP–FUN.

Our mission is to be exceptional people developing the best players with the best character.

Source: Boise Nationals Timbers (2017).

| exhibit | 6.7 | Mission Statement of the Glencoe Baseball Association, Illinois |

The Glencoe Baseball Association's (GBA's) primary Mission is to provide an environment for Glencoe youth to have an enjoyable, safe, team-oriented, and community based experience while learning and playing the game of baseball. At the same time, the GBA is committed to teaching our youth the life lessons of good sportsmanship and teamwork. Through the game of baseball, the GBA intends to help youth to set and work towards common goals and to build character, leadership ability, and confidence.

Source: Glencoe Baseball Association (2017).

are run specifically for teens and young adults, and still others include adults, both young and old. Leagues might be gender specific or co-ed.

FINANCIALS. Funding for recreational sport leagues is often provided through municipal sources and supplemented by league fees charged to each participant. The salaries of administrators designing and delivering the league may be paid through municipal departments. The costs of facilities are also borne by the community. Often, participants will pay a small fee to generate some revenue toward paying for administrative costs, officials, and equipment. Of course, the "pay for play" fee could be more substantial if the particular sport has expensive requirements, such as ice rental for hockey leagues. The major expense categories for minor sport leagues include facility rental, officials, purchase of equipment, and promotion and publicity.

ORGANIZATIONAL STRUCTURE. A group of officers is usually elected to help organize and govern the activities of the league. These voluntary positions might include a President, Vice President, and Chairs of a few committees specific to the particular sport. For example, one might expect a Beach Volleyball League to be governed by a League Executive Committee that comprises the President, Vice President, Chair of Scheduling, and Chair of Facilities. The President runs meetings and provides overall direction and leadership, while the Vice President might be responsible for league promotion, complaints, and discipline. The Scheduling Chair develops and communicates all league scheduling, and the Facilities Chair schedules event locations and coordinates with facility staff for equipment and any necessary personnel. The elected members of the Executive Committee develop policy, and these administrators debate issues and ideas regarding league operation at the Annual Meeting. Policy might be required to guide the league activities in each of the major areas of responsibility and to incorporate where, when, and how the games are played.

State Games and Provincial Games

State games (US) and provincial games (Canada) are amateur sport festivals held every year or two. Individuals and teams may have to qualify to attend the games by successfully advancing through regional competitions, by gaining entry through a lottery, or on a first-come, first-served basis. These games are usually multisport events, held in both summer and winter. For example, the Iowa Games Annual Sport Festival is held in winter and summer locations each year. Over 60 summer and 26 winter sports are organized for both adult and youth athletes, reaching 14,000 summer and 4,000 winter participants. The Iowa Games are a multisport festival of Olympic-style competition for Iowa's amateur athletes, and in this case age, ability, and gender are not considered criteria for participation.

Iowa Games
http://iowagames.org

MISSION. The mission of state and provincial games focuses on delivering well-organized amateur sport competition for athletes of a variety of ages within the region. The idea of the games is to offer citizens the opportunity to compete, gain experience, and come together in a festival atmosphere. The games are usually multisport and designed for participants, coaches, officials, spectators, volunteers, and sport managers—an experience for everyone. See Exhibit 6.8 for the mission statement of the Iowa Games.

MEMBERSHIP. The members of summer or winter games hosted by a U.S. state or Canadian province include mostly participants and volunteers. The organization does not have a group of individual members outside the

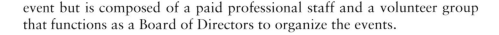

exhibit **6.8** Mission Statement of the Iowa Games

> The mission of the Iowa Games is to provide sports and recreation opportunities for all Iowans through Olympic-style festivals, events, and programs.

Source: Iowa Games (2017).

event but is composed of a paid professional staff and a volunteer group that functions as a Board of Directors to organize the events.

FINANCIALS.   State and provincial games are funded through both public and private sources, entry fees, and money raised through sponsors and marketing initiatives. The Iowa Games, for example, is a project of the Iowa Sports Foundation made possible because of the financial support from "corporate sponsorships, donations, grants and entry fees" (Iowa Sports Foundation, 2017).

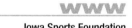

Iowa Sports Foundation
www.iowasportsfoundation.org

ORGANIZATIONAL STRUCTURE.   The paid staff usually comprises an Executive Director, one or more Directors of Sports, Event Operations, and Finance, and a number of assistant positions that help to organize specific components of the games. The Board of Directors, all volunteers, includes a Chair or President, Vice President, Treasurer, Secretary, and a number of board members who may be responsible for specific aspects of the events. The organizational structure of the Iowa Games is presented in Exhibit 6.9.

The Governance of Nonprofit Organizations Involved in Community Sports

The term *nonprofit* aptly describes many community organizations involved in sport. They are organizations developed to deliver activities and services with no intent of making a profit. This type of organization may be large or small and may have a simple or an intricate organizational structure. Prominent examples of nonprofit amateur sport organizations include the Y, formerly the Young Men's Christian Association (YMCA), the Young Women's Christian Association (YWCA), the Boys & Girls Clubs, and the Jewish Community Centers (JCC). Other local nonprofit community groups also provide opportunities for amateur sport.

Organizational Structure of the Iowa Games

exhibit   6.9

PAID PROFESSIONAL STAFF

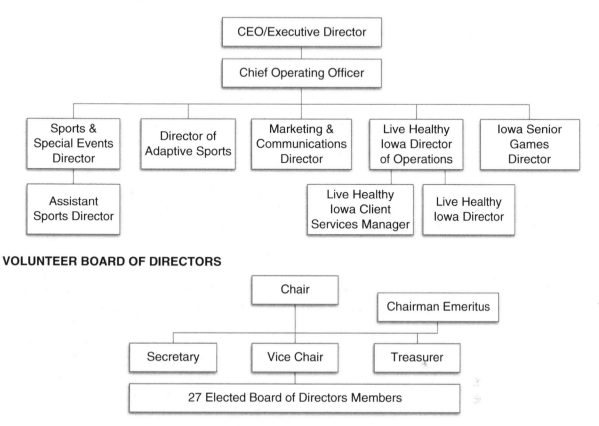

VOLUNTEER BOARD OF DIRECTORS

Source: Iowa Games (2017). Reprinted with permission.

The Y (Formerly YMCA)

Ys are service organizations, collectively the largest nonprofit community organization in the United States (The Y, 2017). The organization recently rebranded by shortening its name to "The Y" as a way of emphasizing its programs' impact on youth and healthy living. The name change resulted from more than two years of research orchestrated by the national YMCA of America, which revealed that most people do not understand the organization's activities and mission. Ys provide programming for children and adults, for men and women of all races, abilities, ages, and incomes. They have a significant history in basketball, volleyball, and racquetball, and were the original leaders in camping and fitness, as well as in providing

Y
http://ymca.net

children with swimming lessons (The Y, 2017). The Ys serve more than 45 million people in 119 countries around the world; there are more than 2,700 Ys located in the United States alone.

MISSION. A large component of the Y's mandate is delivered via amateur sports programs, including leagues, instructional classes, family nights, youth sports programming, mentoring, and exchange programs. Each Y strives to nurture the healthy development of children and teens, strengthen families, and make the community a better place. The mission involves the development of the "whole body" through programs that often incorporate physical activity. The rebranded organization focuses its activities on youth development, healthy living, and social responsibility. See Exhibit 6.10 for the mission statement of the Y.

MEMBERSHIP. Ys are a part of community life in neighborhoods and towns across North America. In the United States over 9 million youth and 13 million adults enjoy their services each year. Several types of memberships are available, along with the ability to join only specific programs or groups.

FINANCIALS. Each local Y is an independent, charitable, nonprofit organization required to pay dues to a National Association. Of the total revenue the National Association collects per year, approximately 31 percent comes from program fees, 32 percent from memberships, 19 percent from charitable contributions, 6 percent from resident camping and living quarters, 12 percent from government contracts and grants, and 1 percent from miscellaneous sources (The Y, 2017). No one is turned away for inability to pay.

ORGANIZATIONAL STRUCTURE. Ys have volunteers and professional, full-time, paid staff who help set policy that is then implemented by both employees and volunteers. Most operate with a volunteer Board of Directors, steered by an Executive Committee elected from Board members. Other committees work on specific types of programs or initiatives, like youth sports,

---

exhibit **6.10**   Mission Statement of the Y

The Y is a community service organization which promotes positive values through programs that build spirit, mind, and body welcoming all people, with a focus on youth.

Source: Y (2017a)

clubs and camps, and family nights. The local board has jurisdiction over the development of policy for the independent Y, as long as the independent Y meets the following requirements as outlined in the national constitution (The Y, 2017):

1. Annual dues are paid by the local Y to the national office, the Y of the USA.
2. The Y refrains from any practices that discriminate against any individual or group.
3. The national mission is supported.

Other decisions, including programs offered, staffing, and style of operation, are the purview of the local Y (The Y, 2017). The organizational structure of a typical Y is shown in Exhibit 6.11.

YWCA

The YWCA seeks to respond to the unique needs of community, through advocating for justice, health, human dignity, freedom, and care of the environment. It has been working to raise the status of women since it was founded in 1894 (YWCA, 2017a). The YWCA aims to provide safe places for girls and women no matter what their situation. The YWCA USA is focused on three high-impact areas: (1) racial justice and civil rights, (2) empowerment and economic advancement for women and girls, and (3) health and safety of women and girls (YWCA, 2017a).

www

YWCA
www.ywca.org

MISSION. The YWCA is committed to a strategic framework of consultation and collaboration with YWCAs around the USA, and reflects the YWCA's legacy as a pioneering organization that squarely confronts social justice issues to make lasting, meaningful change (YWCA, 2017a). The organization's mission is to eliminate racism, empower women, stand up for social justice, help families, and strengthen communities.

MEMBERSHIP. Worldwide there are more than 25 million members in 120 countries, including 2.3 million members and participants in 225 local associations in the United States. The YWCA is one of the oldest and largest women's organizations in the nation, serving women, girls, and their families.

FINANCIALS. The total net assets of YWCA USA per year are almost $60 million. Of this amount, revenues accrue from government grants, public support (individuals, foundations, and corporations), membership fees, and program service fees (YWCA, 2017a). The YWCA engages online giving; gifts of stocks, bonds or mutual funds; donation of a vehicle; planned giving through estates, and corporate giving via Amazon Smile, where you can designate that 0.5 percent of your purchases is donated (YWCA, 2017a).

exhibit **6.11** Local Y Typical Organization Chart

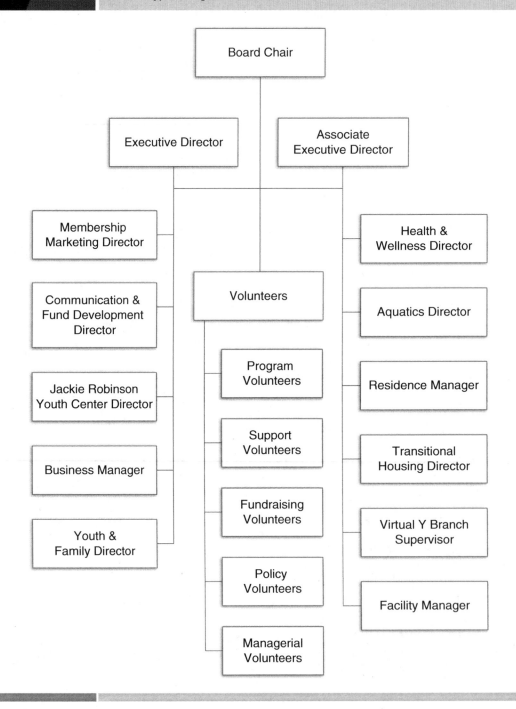

ORGANIZATIONAL STRUCTURE.   The national office is charged primarily with conducting advocacy at the national level and for marketing and branding. At the YWCA Annual Meeting in May 2012 a transition from the prior regional structure to a national federated structure was approved, followed by the adoption of new bylaws in November 2012:

> The goal of the new organizational structure is to leverage the collective strength of local YWCAs and the national organization as a national movement. Under the new structure, YWCA USA provides a range of technical assistance and capacity-building services to local YWCAs, safeguard the integrity of the YWCA brand, and maintain a strong national presence that will position the iconic, multi-tiered organization for increased stability and sustainability for the future.
>
> (YWCA, 2017b, para. 9)

All members of the YWCA USA are eligible to attend an Annual Meeting and any Special Meetings called to elect Board members and conduct business. Voting is conducted through two votes afforded all the members of Local Associations. The Board of Directors manages the affairs of the national YWCA, focusing on mission programs, national advocacy, member communication, branding, and strategic collaboration. Local YWCAs manage their own programming and personnel, and areas critical to their mission.

Boys & Girls Clubs

The Boys & Girls Clubs of America is a national association of community boys and girls clubs. Such clubs offer programs and services to promote and enhance the development of boys and girls in a safe, healthy environment. Sports programming is one component of the services provided by Boys & Girls Clubs.

www

Boys & Girls Clubs of America
www.bgca.org

MISSION.   The Boys & Girls Clubs of America acts to provide boys and girls with the following:

- a safe place to learn and grow
- the opportunity for ongoing relationships with caring adult professionals
- life-enhancing programs, opportunities, and character-building experiences
- hope and opportunity

The Boys & Girls Clubs of America strives to provide opportunities for young people, especially those from disadvantaged backgrounds. See Exhibit 6.12 for its mission statement.

JIM DOREMUS, *CEO, Concord Family YMCA,*

Concord, NH

As the Chief Executive Officer (CEO) for the Concord Family YMCA, I am responsible for the Y's operation and performance including operationalizing the organizational vision, developing strategic and operational plans, creating and implementing fiscal development and management strategies, public relations and marketing, administering programs, and Board development.

Our mission promise is to strengthen the foundation of the community through a focus on youth development, healthy living, and social responsibility. We serve over 10,000 people annually with the assistance of 130 employees, over 400 volunteers, and more than 40 partnerships with local groups and organizations. The Concord Family YMCA is a full-facility Y that provides direct and indirect financial assistance valued at just under $600,000 on an annual operating budget of $3.1 million.

For the past several years I have been involved in statewide (New Hampshire) public policy advocacy for early childhood education. During the 2017 New Hampshire Legislative session my participation intensified and I became part of a leadership group, referred to as the Smart Start Campaign, which advocated for increased funding for early childhood education initiatives. The Smart Start Campaign established a short-term goal of increased funding in New Hampshire's biannual budget for the state's portion of the Child Care Development Block Grant (CCDBG) and a longer term goal of creating advocacy capacity across the state for future early childhood education policy initiatives.

CCDBG funding requires each state to provide matching dollars (roughly a 1:1 match). The CCDBG produces tremendous value in two ways. First, it reduces the barrier for low-income families by making childcare affordable. In a society where there is increasing evidence of an "opportunity gap," quality childcare is considered one of the primary interventions that levels the socioeconomic playing field for low-income families, enabling children be better prepared for public school and more likely to succeed in later life. Second, the CCDBG is instrumental in helping low-income parents remain in the workforce, which helps their families achieve and maintain long-term financial stability. Our Y serves many individuals who benefit from the CCDBG.

All YMCAs are members of a federated model of governance led and managed by Y-USA. There are approximately 860 YMCA associations throughout the United States which are subject to national membership criteria. All YMCAs are incorporated nonprofit organizations. More than 2,700 YMCA facilities in 10,000 communities serve about 22 million people across the United States. From its inception, local autonomy has been one of the YMCA's foundational themes.

Y-USA provides a robust formal support structure for Ys covering all aspects of individual YMCA governance and operations. This includes resource staff dedicated for each individual Y, the availability of national resource staff as experts in specific topic areas (i.e. Human Resources, Financial Development, Marketing, Board Governance, etc.), and expansive professional development and training. In addition, there is an equally robust informal support network among YMCA employees and volunteers with a universally held expectation for sharing information on both successes and failures among our Y colleagues.

The major challenge associated with the Y's federated model of governance is securing uniformity and buy-in with individual YMCA associations for nationwide initiatives. Y-USA does not have the authority to mandate decisions; rather it relies on upon engagement, education, and persuasion in order to successfully implement new initiatives. While this dynamic often works, it is a time-consuming process that may prohibit the Y as a national movement from capitalizing on some opportunities.

The two most important policy issues for the YMCA both now and in the future are what is referred to as Mission Challenges—attacks on its nonprofit status, and becoming a truly diverse and inclusive organization nationwide. Communities across the country are changing rapidly when it comes to dimensions of diversity: the increase in median age; the growing number individuals of different abilities, faiths, gender identity, and sexual orientation who are making their voices heard in larger numbers; and the world is becoming smaller, ensuring that no event is isolated. Moving forward, The Y will face these challenges while continuing to provide valuable services on the community level.

| Mission Statement of the Boys & Girls Clubs of America | *exhibit* | 6.12 |

> The mission of the Boys & Girls Clubs of America is "to enable all young people especially those who need us the most, to reach their full potential as productive, caring responsible citizens."

Source: Boys & Girls Clubs of America (2017).

MEMBERSHIP. Nearly 4 million youth participated in programs at over 4,200 clubs in the United States, with the gender breakdown at approximately 55 percent male and 45 percent female (Boys & Girls Clubs of America, 2017). The clubs provide a variety of unique sport programming, tournaments, and the JrNBA and JrWNBA programs. Clubs are located in schools, youth centers, public housing, and are located within cities, rural communities, and on Native lands. Other specialized learning programs, such as the Athletic Director University program, teach youngsters leadership skills to organize and administer their own leagues, clubs, and teams.

FINANCIALS. Boys & Girls Clubs are nonprofit organizations. Revenues to run programming, hire staff, and maintain facilities come from membership dues, private donations, corporate funding, and community partnerships such as the partnership with United Way. Membership rates are kept to a minimum ($10 to $50 per year), and no one is turned away from programming because of an inability to pay. On average, about $500 is spent per youth in a given year.

ORGANIZATIONAL STRUCTURE. There may be as many as 25 clubs in a region, each operating with a small professional staff and many volunteers. The Boys & Girls Clubs of Metro Atlanta, for example, are organized with a large Board of Directors who are volunteers from the community elected to oversee the strategic operations of the organization (Boys & Girls Clubs of Metro Atlanta, 2017). The board is elected and is composed of ten unit board presidents from regions within the geographical area and 41 board members (Boys & Girls Clubs of Metro Atlanta, 2017). The Board of Directors and the association members are responsible for developing policy, such as the policy regarding the division of revenues between each of the metro clubs. Policy may determine that the use of revenues collected by individual clubs be defined without restriction by the club, but that revenues distributed to individual clubs by the overarching Atlanta parent group be used in specific areas such as programming, professional staff, and facilities.

www

Boys & Girls Clubs of Metro Atlanta
www.bgcma.org/

The organizational structure of a typical Boys & Girls Club is shown in Exhibit 6.13.

exhibit   **6.13**   Typical Board of Directors for a Boys & Girls Club of America

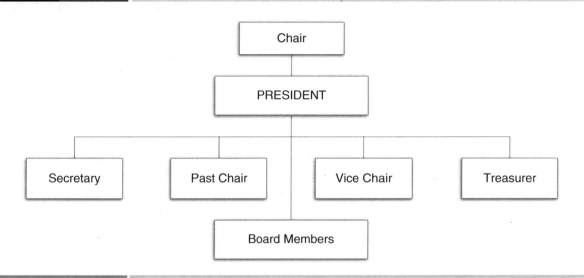

Jewish Community Centers

www
Jewish Community Center
Association of North
America
www.jcca.org/

Jewish Community Centers (JCCs) are nonprofit organizations under the authority of the Jewish Community Center Association of North America, an umbrella organization including more than 350 JCCs, Young Men's Hebrew Associations/Young Women's Hebrew Associations (YMHAs/YWHAs), and campsites in the United States and Canada (JCCA, 2017a). The Jewish Community Center Association offers a wide range of services and resources to help its affiliates provide educational, cultural, social, Jewish identity-building, and recreational programs for people of all ages and backgrounds.

Each year the JCC Association puts together a sporting festival for Jewish teens known as the JCC Maccabi Games. These games are an Olympic-style sporting competition held each summer on multiple sites in North America and is the largest organized sports program for Jewish teenagers in the world (JCCA, 2017a). In addition, the JCC Association helps sponsor the Maccabiah Games, which is essentially the quadrennial Jewish Olympic Games and is held in Israel the year following the Summer Olympic Games.

www
JCC Maccabi Games
www.jccmaccabigames.org/

MISSION. JCC programs, services, and connections are intended to support a diverse and thriving Jewish people—and as appropriate, the broader community—in making fulfilling and healthy life choices and in which Jewish wisdom is valued; differences are respected; communities are built; creativity is encouraged, and aspirations are realized in exciting and powerful new ways (JCCA, 2017a). The Jewish Community Center of Greater Baltimore, the nation's first JCC, defines its mission to promote and strengthen Jewish life and values through communal programs and activities for individuals and families (JCC of Greater Baltimore, 2017).

MEMBERSHIP. The JCC Association serves more than 350 JCCs, YM/YWHAs, and campsites in North America reaching an estimated 2 million people annually. Each of these organizational members pays annual dues to the association. The association offers its members a wide range of services and resources in educational, cultural, social, Jewish identity-building, and recreational programs for people of all ages and backgrounds (JCCA, 2017a).

Individual JCCs offer memberships in various categories. The choices include individual memberships, family memberships, senior memberships, and some local JCCs even offer full community memberships.

FINANCIALS. In 2015, the JCC Association of North America operated with total liabilities and net assets of almost $24 million. Revenues came from the following sources: JCC dues (41 percent), program revenue (27 percent), NFC and federation support (8 percent), foundation grants (15 percent), corporate sponsorship (4 percent), and earnings from investments (5 percent). Association expenses included: program enrichment services (18 percent), community consultation services (17 percent), professional leadership (7 percent), management and finance (21 percent), marketing and communications (6 percent), Jewish education (23 percent), financial resource development (5 percent), and services to the military (3 percent) (JCCA, 2017b).

In 2016, the JCC of San Francisco had operating revenues of more than $34 million that were derived from the following sources: contributions, government grants, program revenue, center membership, ancillary services, investments, special events, and other income. Expenses included programs, management, building repairs and improvements, and fundraising (JCC of San Francisco, 2017a).

ORGANIZATIONAL STRUCTURE. The JCC Association of North America is organized with an Executive Committee and a Board of Directors. The Executive Committee, formed by elected officers, consists of a President, a Chair, seven Vice-Chairs, a Secretary, two Associate Secretaries, and seven Honorary Chairs. The Board of Directors is very large, consisting of 84 members (JCCA, 2017a). The JCC Association has three North American offices, as well as one in Jerusalem, Israel. The North American offices are located in New York City; Austin, Texas; and St. Paul, Minnesota.

The JCC of San Francisco is led by an Executive Director and an executive staff, a group of elected officers, and a volunteer Board of Directors. Along with the Executive Director, the elected officers include a President, a Vice-President, a Treasurer, and a Secretary. The volunteer Board of Directors is also large, consisting of 25 members (JCC of San Francisco, 2017b).

www

JCC of San Francisco
www.jccsf.org

Community Groups

Many individuals and groups run nonprofit organizations for sport and physical activity. These may be community based but not run by community government agencies such as city parks and recreation departments, and they usually focus on a single sport or physical activity. Community groups such as the Pacers and Racers Running and Walking Group located in New Albany, Indiana, and the Mountain View Masters Swim and Social Club located in Mountain View, California, have organized themselves to participate in activities related to their sport. The San Juan Sledders Snowmobile Club of Durango, Colorado, is another example of a small nonprofit amateur sport organization. This group marks and grooms winter trails in the area, encouraging their use for multiple outdoor winter sports such as dogsledding, cross-country skiing, snowshoeing, and snowmobiling. The Traverse City Curling Club in Michigan was opened in 2014 as a nonprofit community sport organization when more than 500 people showed up for curling demonstrations and practice.

MISSION. The mission of a nonprofit community-based amateur sport organization involves delivering a particular activity by providing facilities and related services, such as arranging for individual participation or competition. Many community groups involve leagues or clubs through which regular activities are scheduled. Encouraging safe, ethical conduct and a good learning environment for all participants is a common theme. The mission statement of the Dallas Nationals Baseball Club is presented in Exhibit 6.14.

MEMBERSHIP. Volunteers run community nonprofit amateur sport organizations. Members of the organization are solicited to help organize the activities. In turn, they gain the benefit of services such as events, tournaments, and championships. Membership dues are usually collected on a yearly basis.

www

Pacers and Racers Running and Walking Group
www.pacersandracers.com/running-group/

San Juan Sledders Snowmobile Club
https://www.sanjuansledders.com

exhibit **6.14**   Mission Statement of the Dallas Nationals Baseball Club

The DALLAS NATIONALS BASEBALL CLUB mission is to prepare young men for the next level of competition both on and off the diamond. Our coaches and staff are selected specifically to improve baseball skills and knowledge; however, since there is more to life than baseball, we will also work to build character at every opportunity.

Source: Dallas Nationals Baseball Club (2017).

FINANCIALS.   Nonprofit community groups are typically funded through participant membership fees, sponsorship, and other methods of fundraising. They may also be eligible for grants extended by municipal government agencies or private foundations. For example, a "fun run" organized by a city running club might involve municipal support (facilities and race-day logistics), sponsorships (printing costs, post-race refreshments, and awards), and a small entry fee to cover the costs of race T-shirts.

ORGANIZATIONAL STRUCTURE.   Depending on its size, a community sport organization might be loosely configured or highly structured. A smaller organization such as the San Juan Sledders Snowmobile Club might have a small Executive Committee consisting of a few members in positions such as the President, Vice-President, and Treasurer. Other members of the group are then given tasks, but often they hold no specific titles. More often, the President will provide overall leadership, and the members of the group will complete tasks for specific events. An expectation exists for a fair division of labor among all group members. Once initial policy is established for managing the events, the group focuses on service as opposed to being a rules-making or sanctioning body. Conversely, in a larger organization such as the Dallas Nationals Baseball Club, a structured managerial group may provide leadership, with a President, several Vice Presidents, and a number of Committee Chairs.

CURRENT POLICY AREAS

A number of policy areas are prominent for managers of amateur sport organizations in the community. It is important that policy be defined for each of the areas described in this section because the issues are critical to the effective delivery of amateur sport, especially as related to children and children's programming. Effective policy enables effective decision making.

Fundraising

Policy enabling decision making for fundraising is a prominent issue for amateur sport organizations in the community. Community-based amateur sport organizations rely on raising capital for both programming and infrastructure. Public sport organizations compete with every other level of social programming for funding, and government grants often fall short of their needs. As important as fundraising is to public sport organizations, policy that enables effective financial management is even more important with nonprofit sport organizations. Managers in the nonprofit sector are continually concerned with maintaining strict measures for raising money, along with ensuring that budgets are balanced and spending is effective and shared among as many programs as possible. For instance, the Boys & Girls Clubs of America rely heavily on donations from both the private and the public sectors. While it takes money to run a Boys & Girls Club (about $500 per youth per year), the alternative costs of keeping a young adult in jail for a year is many times higher. The fundraising policy areas receiving most of the attention are the following:

1. IDENTIFYING FUNDING SOURCES. Most organizations set specific policies that identify sources of funds worth pursuing. Virtually all solicit private donations, government grants, and corporate sponsorships. Specific policy might list donors in order of priority based on which are most likely to enter a partnership and in specific categories of new contacts to pursue. In addition, such policy will certainly outline categories of unacceptable sources of funding. For instance, no Boys & Girls Club would solicit funds from a tobacco company. On the contrary, the club will work hard to disassociate unhealthy practices such as smoking from the club's programming for children and teenagers. The policy might also define special-event types of fundraising (charity dinners, silent auctions, golf tournaments, etc.), and set some parameters on exactly what events will be hosted and what goals will define success.

2. SOLICITING DONATIONS AND SPONSORSHIPS. Other policies will define exactly how donations and sponsorships are solicited and by whom. Will potential donors be called, contacted by mail or e-mail? Will the club website be used to initiate fundraising? How will money be received, and how will records be kept? Developing effective policy will answer questions such as these.

3. SERVICING AND MAINTAINING DONOR RELATIONSHIPS. Ensuring donors and sponsors are "serviced" is very important as well. This means giving back to the donor or sponsor. Once programming has support, every effort must be made to inform, involve, and thank the sponsors for their involvement. Courtesy and reciprocity are critical to building relationships and are the best ways to maintain donor or sponsor involvement from year to year. Newsletters, invitations to see programs in action, thank-you letters from participants, and summarized information outlining the positives resulting from the donation are all effective means of servicing. The Boys & Girls Clubs of America use an extremely prominent National Board of Governors and Officers as well as alumni in their fundraising efforts. Members of these groups include Condoleezza Rice, Ken Griffey Jr, Jennifer Lopez, and Denzel Washington.

Inactivity of Youth

Currently, the inactivity of youth generally and the declining numbers of participants in amateur sport have been targeted as trends that community-level sport programs can help reverse. Policy is often set to deal with recurring issues and to enable decision making to effect change regarding such issues. All too often, children and youth are less physically active than is optimal for health and wellness because of the prevalence of passive activities, such as video and computer games. Research shows that girls' participation in sport and physical activity declines between ages 5 and 12 (Women's Sports Foundation, 2017) and that team sports by both boys and girls have suffered declining participation numbers. Another large drop in participation occurs at the high school age, where perceived barriers to participation include lack of time, inaccessible or costly facilities, focus on technology-related activities, and body image issues (CAAWS, 2017).

Some community-based amateur sport organizations are setting policy to ensure that programming exists for all youth age groups. The goal is to provide a variety of fun-filled, supportive sport and physical activity experiences for youth. Such policy promotes development skills and healthy lifestyles and improves self-esteem. For example, some municipalities have enacted policies to ensure opportunities exist for age-group participants in sports that require the use of already overbooked areas and fields. At times, the policies specify participation for particular groups, such as a girls- or boys-only activity. In many community amateur athletic organizations, such as the City of Columbus, Ohio Recreation and Parks Department, T-ball programs and Little League Baseball are offered for girls as well as boys. Beyond gender, issues of race, ethnicity, disability, and urban vs. rural further complicate the issue of youth inactivity. The reasons impacting this issue are complicated and involve a mix of societal issues such as culture, income, family responsibilities, and the impact of technology.

Technology and Social Media

Technology and social media have changed the sports' world in many ways. Technology has become an integral part in virtually all aspects of sport, including equipment, coaching, facilities, officiating, and spectating. Social media is a source of information for fans, but also for athletes, parents, coaches, and businesses. In an instant, up-to-date information can be communicated to vast numbers of people. Unfortunately, the use of technology and social media can also easily and quickly spread false information, rumor and innuendo, and extend opinion on behalf of an organization. Policy development to ensure consistent, appropriate use of technology for fair competition and positive use of social media in amateur sport is now an imperative for community sport organizations.

www

Technology in Sports
www.topendsports.com/
resources/technology.htm

The Business Side of Sports
https://businesssideofsports.
com/2016/03/10/

Parental Involvement

Parental involvement has been a major topic of youth sport over the past several years (Center for Sports Parenting, 2017). Stories of parents being "muzzled" or banned from events are too frequently presented in the media. Adult misbehaviors have become more commonplace: splashing hot coffee in the face of an official; verbally abusing officials, coaches, and kids; and fighting, threatening, and other forms of confrontations.

According to Dan Bylsma, former National Hockey League (NHL) player and once coach of the Pittsburgh Penguins and Buffalo Sabres, two questions must be answered: why have parents become so invested in the progress of their children in sports to the exclusion of other arguably more important endeavors, such as academics? And why does this parental involvement contradict what is best for the child? Amateur sport in the community is about fun, teamwork, dedication, and respect for authority. Excessive parental involvement in amateur sport, especially involvement that overshadows other important aspects of growing up, such as doing homework and chores and gaining experience in a number of activities, teaches children the wrong lessons. Consider the values a child learns when *thousands* of dollars are spent on hockey travel by a parent who would not consider spending tens of dollars on a math tutor (Atkinson, 2014).

If the purpose of youth sports is to have fun, increase athleticism, and learn the value of teamwork and discipline, then some adults are teaching the wrong lessons. Sport managers and program administrators are working to reverse such involvement by setting policy that curtails "parental over-involvement." Examples include spectator codes of conduct, parental contracts agreeing to acceptable conduct and involvement, and conferences and seminars for parents. The City of Henderson and the Nevada Parks and Recreation Department, for example, encourage parents to get involved and stay involved in amateur sports. They have been proactive by setting policy to educate all participants' parents, which is enacted through YouthFirst, a youth sports orientation program for parents (YouthFirst, 2017). The orientation has been developed by the University of Nevada, Las Vegas, and is designed to encourage parental involvement, emphasize fun, and boost participant retention. The intent is to curb violence in youth sports by orienting all parents to their role, the coach's role, and to what parents can do to foster continued participation by their kids. The program requires parents to complete a certification quiz and sign a code of conduct (YouthFirst, 2017).

Amateur sport groups in the community are well advised to have policy governing parental involvement. Research suggests that parents can have a profound impact on the experience of youth sport participants and that top-down policy to address issues in parental behavior is warranted by sport organizations (Elliott & Drummond, 2015). Dan Doyle (2013, p. 319) suggests that "parents must help young athletes understand the meaning of gamesmanship as it applies to their sport(s), and that maintaining one's integrity begins with adhering not only to the rules of the sports, but to the spirit of the rules."

Violence in Sport

Violent behaviors associated with amateur sport are not restricted to parents. Overly aggressive and violent acts by participants and spectators are regularly reported in the media. This includes both physical and verbal acts

www

Center for Sports Parenting
www.sportsparenting.org

Institute for International Sport
https://www.
internationalsport.org

www

YouthFirst
www.youthfirst.us

of aggression. Reducing sport violence involves curtailing both athlete and spectator aggression. Policies dealing with reducing athlete violence strive to achieve the following:

- provide proper, nonaggressive role models for young athletes
- develop rules that allow low tolerance for acts of violence
- apply severe and swift penalties for violence involving the actions of athletes, referees, and coaches
- apply severe and swift penalties for coaches who support and promote violent or aggressive play
- remove stimuli that provoke aggression
- organize referee, coach, parent, and athlete workshops
- provide ample positive reinforcement for appropriate displays of behavior in sport
- teach and practice emotional control (Kids First Soccer, 2017)

Amateur athletic organizations can curtail spectator violence through policies that deal with the following items:

- banning alcoholic beverages
- making it a family affair
- ensuring that the media are not contributing to the buildup of tension
- focusing on achieving excellence rather than fighting the enemy
- fining unruly spectators (Kids First Soccer, 2017)

Kids First Soccer Club
http://www.
kidsfirstsoccerclub.com

For example, administrators of the Saint Barnabas Health Care System in New Jersey set policy to curb violence in sport by developing the Rediscovering Youth Sportsmanship program. The key elements of the program are training and education sessions for parents, coaches, officials, facility managers, and sport administrators that provide a system of boundaries, positive reinforcement, and sanctions for certain behaviors, delivered through videos, pledges, surveys, and rewards (Mariconda & Mariconda, 2004). Another example is SafeSport, a program developed by the US Center for SafeSport that aims to foster a national sport culture of respect and safety. SafeSport attempts to equip sport organizations with tools to address problems before abuse occurs (SafeSport, 2017). For example, a recreation facility may institute an Anti-Violence Policy to raise awareness among spectators and parents of their role in creating a positive environment and to give volunteers and staff the mandate and power to deal with violent and antisocial behavior. Such a policy may define *violent behavior* as the following:

- loud verbal assaults
- intimidation and threats
- aggressive actions such as approaching another individual or throwing articles
- striking another individual
- attempting to incite violence

SafeSport Program
https://safesport.org/

Policy will dictate that individuals engaging in any of the above activities are immediately ejected from the facility by designated leaders and banned from the facility for a period of time defined by the recreation facility staff.

Selecting Youth Sport Coaches

Positive Coaching Alliance
www.positivecoach.org

Good programming for kids depends on having suitable supervision and instruction, typical roles of the coach. Almost 4 million volunteer coaches work with more than 40 million young athletes in the United States alone (Positive Coaching Alliance, 2017). Unfortunately, the large number of volunteer coaches required sometimes results in the hiring of untrained, unprepared coaches. Experts have determined that some 90 percent of youth sports coaches have little to no training (American Coaching Academy, 2008). Far more dangerous is the potential for placing a pedophile or some other criminal in contact with children and youth. To ensure this does not happen, all sport organizations need to use specific criteria for hiring youth coaches and should utilize reference and criminal-background checks before hiring them. All sport organizations must have a personnel policy that contains procedures and requirements for youth sport coaches and volunteers that includes items such as the following:

- required coach training and background
- background information disclosure
- police record check
- coaching expectations and code of conduct
- coaching your own child
- understanding the goals and objectives of the association
- feedback on coaching performance
- dismissing a coach
- an individual's right to appeal

SUMMARY

Thousands of amateur sport organizations are community based. Their mandate is to provide opportunities for sport participation, and such organizations provide a broad spectrum of sports for a broad range of age groups. Such organizations can be categorized as public or nonprofit, depending on their purpose and type of funding. Amateur sport at the community level has a rich history and is considered one of the foundations of a society in which happiness, health, and well-being are central. Such organizations include leagues, groups, clubs, special-interest groups, and organizations such as The Y.

The managers of community-based amateur sport organizations deal with a wide variety of governance and policy issues. Funding is a key area, because fundraising is at the core of the operation of the organization. Programming dependent on funding and interest and the inactivity of youth are areas of concern and policy development. Inappropriate conduct or interference by parents and violence are other current policy issues confronting sport managers in amateur sport. Despite these issues, community-based sport managers provide programming that positively impacts the lives of millions of participants. It is an exceptionally important component of the sport industry.

case STUDY

UNBECOMING CONDUCT IN YOUTH SPORT

As the Director of Children's Sport Programming for the town of Clarington, you are organizing a Soccer League for girls and boys from six to ten years old. Experience tells you that the parents and kids of Clarington are a competitive group. At the winter hockey leagues several groups of parents were banned, and suspensions for violent behavior were common among the participants. In an effort to be proactive and eliminate such behaviors in the Soccer League, you have developed a Code of Conduct for both participants and spectators.

1. Describe your Code of Conduct for directing the behavior of
   (a) participants, (b) parents, and (c) general spectators.
2. How do you plan to communicate the Code of Conduct?
3. How do you plan to enforce the Code of Conduct?
4. How might you go about getting both participants and spectators to buy in to the Code?
5. What ethical dilemmas might you face implementing the policy, and how will you solve them?

CHAPTER questions

1. What is the difference between a public and a nonprofit sport organization? How do the governance structures of the two categories differ? Why do different types of recreational sport organizations exist? With a partner, use your device to look up local examples of each a

public and nonprofit sport organization. Debate with your partner which structure better fits the needs of the organization, and why.

2. Using the Internet, locate a community sport organization, for example, your community's Little League Baseball organization. With which category of those mentioned in this chapter does it most closely align? Summarize its governance structure by describing the following: mission, financials, membership, and organizational structure. As a class, compare some of the different organizations searched by students, and identify the components of a well-governed community sport organization from the examples you researched.

3. You have just been voted President of the Shippigan Social Softball Association. Your organization provides opportunities for competition for adults to play co-ed softball, and nearly 700 participants are members of 36 teams. You are dismayed by the recent conduct of both participants and spectators on and off the field, and no policy exists to establish expected behaviors. Address these concerns by doing the following: (a) develop a policy of expected behaviors for participants and spectators; (b) define an overall program of education to ensure that the policy and reasons behind it are well understood; (c) define a list of sanctions for violating the policy; and (d) decide on a course of action to help you to convince your Executive Committee that the policy is important and that it needs to be implemented next season.

FOR ADDITIONAL INFORMATION

For more information check out the following resources:

1. Sports Networker: How Technology is Affecting Sports: www.sportsnetworker.com/2010/05/12/how-technology-is-affecting-sports/

2. Become a Certified Coach: The American Coaching Academy: http://americancoachingacademy.com/certification/

3. Top Sports League Software Products: www.capterra.com/sports-league-software/

4. Australian Sports Commission. (2015). *Mandatory sports governance principles*. Canberra, Australia: Australian Sports Commission.

5. Three Social Media Lessons for Community Sport: https://sportsmarketingnetwork.wordpress.com/2015/09/08/three-social-media-lessons-for-community-sport/

6. Older people, sport and physical activity (SportScotland): https://sportscotland.org.uk/documents/research_reports/older_people_report_final.pdf

REFERENCES

American Coaching Academy. (2008). Experts say 90% of youth sports coaches have little to no training, thus putting their athletes at risk. Retrieved from www.prweb.com/releases/sports/coaching/prweb907124.htm

Atkinson, J. (2014). How parents are ruining youth sports. Retrieved from https://www.bostonglobe.com/magazine/2014/05/03/how-parents-are-ruining-youth-sports/vbRln8qYXkrrNFJcsuvNyM/story.html

Boise Nationals Timbers. (2017). Idaho's Oldest & Most Successful Soccer Club. Retrieved from https://www.boisenationalstimbers.com/about-us/

Boys & Girls Clubs of America. (2017). Who we are and what we do. Retrieved from www.bgca.org/

Boys & Girls Clubs of Metro Atlanta. (2017). Boys & Girls Clubs of Metro Atlanta—A positive place for kids. Retrieved from www.bgcma.org

CAAWS. (2017). Facts and stats. Retrieved from www.caaws.ca/facts-and-stats/

Center for Sports Parenting. (2017). CSP. Retrieved from www.sportsparenting.org/

City of Fairway, Kansas. (2017). Parks and Recreation mission statement. Retrieved from www.fairwaykansas.org/index.asp?Type=B_BASIC&SEC=%7B84B24DE6-A1E6-4451-B790-04DD2CBB3AAE%7D

City of Houston. (2017). Overview of the Parks Department. Retrieved from www.houstontx.gov//parks/aboutus.html

City of Kissimmee, Florida (2017). Annual operating budget. Retrieved from www.kissimmee.org/home/showdocument?id=4608

City of Loveland, Colorado. (2017). Organizational chart: Parks & Recreation Department. Retrieved from www.ci.loveland.co.us/departments/parks-recreation/administration/organizational-chart

City of San Diego. (2017a). City of San Diego organization. Retrieved from https://www.sandiego.gov/sites/default/files/allcity.pdf

City of San Diego. (2017b). Parks and Recreation Department. Retrieved from https://www.sandiego.gov/sites/default/files/legacy/park-and-recreation/pdf/prorgchart.pdf

City of Seattle. (2017). Seattle parks & recreation. Retrieved from www.seattle.gov/parks/about-us

City of Snellville. (2017). General Fund—budget for fiscal year 2017. Retrieved from www.snellville.org/budget-finance

Dallas Nationals Baseball Club. (2017). About us: Our mission. Retrieved from www.dallasnationals.com/page/show/1293582-about-us

Doyle, D. (2013). *The encyclopedia of sports parenting*. New York: Skyhorse Publishing.

Elliott, S., & Drummond, M. (2015). The (limited) impact of sport policy on parental behaviour in youth sport. A qualitative inquiry into junior Australian football. *International Journal of Sport Policy and Politics*, 7(4), 519–530.

Glencoe Baseball Association. (2017). GBA mission statement. Retrieved from www.glencoebaseball.org/about-gba/overview-and-mission-statement/

Iowa Games. (2017). Iowa Games mission statement. Retrieved from www.iowagames.org/about

Iowa Sports Foundation. (2017). What is the Iowa Sports Foundation? Retrieved from http://Iowasportsfoundation.org/About

JCC of Greater Baltimore. (2017). JCC mission statement. Retrieved from www.jcc.org/know-j/history/mission-vision

JCC of San Francisco. (2017a). Annual report and financial statements. Retrieved from https://www.jccsf.org/the-center/who-we-are/annual-report-financial-statements/

JCC of San Francisco. (2017b). Who we are. Retrieved from https://www.jccsf.org/the-center/who-we-are/

JCCA. (2017a). About us. Retrieved from http://jcca.org/about-us/leading-the-movement

JCCA. (2017b). JCCA annual report 2015. Retrieved from http://jcca.org/about-us/annual-reports/

Kidd, B. (1999). *The struggle for Canadian sport*. Toronto: University of Toronto Press.

Kids First Soccer. (2017). Aggression and violence in sport. Retrieved from www.kidsfirstsoccer.com/violence.htm

Mariconda, J., & Mariconda, A. (2004). Rediscovering youth sportsmanship. Retrieved from https://www.astm.org/DIGITAL_LIBRARY/STP/PAGES/STP11614S.htm

Morrow, D., & Wamsley, K. (2009). *Sport in Canada: A history*. Oxford, UK: Oxford University Press.

Positive Coaching Alliance. (2017). The power of positive. Retrieved from www.positivecoach.org

SafeSport. (2017). Welcome to SafeSport, where every athlete is safe, supported and strengthened through sport. Retrieved from https://www.safesport.org/

San Juan Sledders Snowmobile Club. (2017). The San Juan Sledders Snowmobile Club. Retrieved from www.sanjuansledders.org

Women's Sports Foundation. (2017). Retrieved from https://www.womenssportsfoundation.org/support-us/do-you-know-the-factors-influencing-girls-participation-in-sports/

The Y. (2017). Welcome to YMCA.net. Retrieved from www.ymca.net/organizational-profile/

YouthFirst. (2017). YouthFirst: Parents learning about youth sports. Retrieved from www.youthfirst.us

YWCA. (2017a). YWCA USA—what we do. Retrieved from www.ywca.org/site/c.cuIRJ7NTKrLaG/b.9360119/k.7BA2/Our_Mission_in_Action.htm

YWCA. (2017b). FAQs. Retrieved from www.ywca.org/site/c.cuIRJ7NTKrLaG/b.7515903/k.ADCE/FAQ.htm

Campus Recreation

Mary A. Hums
Joanne C. MacLean

Campus recreation is the umbrella term used to describe a myriad of recreation and leisure activity programming on university and college campuses throughout North America. Recreation departments exist on virtually every college and university campus where students attend classes. This segment of the industry has extensive facilities and numbers of personnel, and many of you may want to include Campus Recreation Departments in your career plans. Understanding the organization, governance, and policy issues pertinent to this extensive segment of the sport industry will help you prepare for management positions located on college campuses or within umbrella organizations helping to lead the campus recreation industry.

Historically, college and university administrators have accepted responsibility not only for the education but also for the general welfare of their students. When the promotion of health and well-being was identified as critical for student welfare, Campus Recreation Departments became essential components of institutions of higher learning. In general, the mandate of the Campus Recreation Department is to offer opportunities to participate in both programmed and open-facility recreational activities. This mandate gained momentum because college campuses are often community oriented and can accommodate and serve large populations of students, faculty, and staff members. Today, Campus Recreation Departments aim to enrich student life and are often considered tools for recruiting and retaining college students.

The size of Campus Recreation Departments varies depending upon the campus setting and the size of the institution; however, their purpose is often strikingly similar. Campus recreation provides opportunities to engage in sport and leisure activities. The prime target audience of such programming is the student body. However, programming is usually also accessible to faculty and staff members and sometimes their families. In addition, many activities are made available to the community at large (Wallace Carr et al., 2013). The basic premise underlying campus recreation programming is enjoyment and promotion of a healthy lifestyle through physical activity. The missions and visions of such programs (as referred to in Chapter 2) are represented by slogans such as "Life in Motion," "Engage, Educate, and Empower," "Live Play! Learn," "Recreation, Fitness, and Fun . . . Steps to Life Long Activity," and "Active Living for Health and Happiness."

Many Campus Recreation Department mission statements link the importance of campus facilities to the operation of recreational programming. In addition, the vision of the Campus Recreation Department involves inclusivity, since it operates as a vital part of the university community at large. The mission and vision of Campus Recreation Departments often include a set of values as summarized in Exhibit 7.1.

With this basic understanding of campus recreation, let's look at the roots of Campus Recreation Departments, why they were developed, and how they are organized and governed nationally.

	exhibit **7.1**
A Summary of the Typical Values of a Campus Recreation Program	

Access for all	Provide opportunities for a wide diversity of interests, age groups, abilities, including individuals with a disability.
Customer satisfaction	Develop a friendly, knowledgeable staff and clean, safe, accessible, and attractive facilities.
Awareness	Employ promotional strategies to ensure programs and services are well communicated to new and current participants.
Mutual respect	Ensure a welcoming environment, and promote opportunities for activity in an environment of respect.
Diversity	Create an environment embracing individual differences and reflecting campus diversity.
Variety	Provide opportunities reflecting the diverse interests of the campus community.
Fun	Ensure enjoyment is the mainstay of each programming area.
Development	Provide opportunities for students to guide the programming and gain valuable leadership and management skills.
Evaluation	Maintain a cutting-edge set of programs and facilities reflecting current trends and interests.
Advocacy	Advocate for lifelong movement and an active campus.
Wellness	Model and inspire lifestyles that encourage lifelong health and well-being.
Innovation	Integrate cherished traditions with new and original opportunities for fun and learning.
Stewardship	Our obligation to our community to protect valued resources through the responsible planning, management, and use of economic, environmental, and intellectual resources.
Leadership	Strive to be leaders in the recreational sports profession, in student development and in enhancing the educational environment of the University.
Holistic	Incorporate our University's concept of mind, body, and spirit in all facets of our pursuits.
Collaboration	Commitment to fostering relationships by partnering with students, campus departments, and community organizations to support projects and events.

THE HISTORY OF CAMPUS RECREATION

Recreation and leisure activities undoubtedly contributed to the early growth of competitive athletics (Langley & Hawkins, 2004). The interest in playing, learning to engage in new activities, or simply getting active is well documented in the history of sport and the pursuit of good health. Early on, goals were likely pure enjoyment, opportunities to socialize with friends, and relief from the boredom of work, study, or everyday life. If physical activity is viewed as a continuum from informal play and recreation that is not necessarily competitive to formal and institutionalized competitive sport (LaVoi & Kane, 2014), it is easy to understand that the early history of recreation on campus is interwoven with campus sport as we know it today.

The First Campus Recreation Programs

Early sport and leisure activities originated with English sport clubs and German gymnastics. Around the midpoint of the 19th century, North Americans were looking for opportunities to be physically active other than in highly competitive sports or in the rigid routine of gymnastics. This interest in pursuing physical and recreational activities and sport was naturally present on college campuses. The campus was an ideal setting for spontaneous games, with divisions already defined by academic class, major, or residence housing. The term *intramural*, used to describe the first programs of campus recreation, comes from the Latin words for "within" (*intra*) and "wall" (*murus*), that is, within the walls of an organization (Franklin, 2013).

Competition between different classes soon became commonplace. Colleges and universities embraced the notion that programming for leisure and recreational pursuits, along with competitive athletics, was an important component in the overall education and well-being of their students. In 1904, Cornell University (CU) developed a system of what is known today as instructional sport for students not participating at the varsity level. During the next decade the surge of student interest in recreational sports resulted in the development of a department to manage such student programming. The Ohio State University (OSU) and the University of Michigan (UM) each defined organized intramural departments in 1913 (Mueller & Reznik, 1979). CU quickly followed, along with other colleges and universities in the United States and Canada.

A Rationale for Campus Recreation

When considering the history of higher education, intramural sport is perhaps one of the oldest organized campus activities (Wallace Carr et al., 2013). Campus recreation emerged as a formal department on campus and recreational programming subsequently experienced extensive growth and popularity for several reasons. A significant factor in legitimizing campus recreation occurred in the early part of the 20th century. In 1918, the National Education Association (NEA) in the United States coined the phrase "worthy use of leisure time" as one of the Seven Principles of Education (Colgate, 1978). In essence, the idea of capitalizing on one's leisure time became a tenet of an effective education. Greater meaning was attached to educating the whole person and to the importance of out-of-classroom educational experiences (Smith, 1991). Over time, the notion that healthy individuals are active, involved, and accomplished in activities of both mind and body became another cornerstone supporting the need for open recreation and intramural programming on campus. As the world became more technologically sophisticated, the amount of leisure time increased and the demand for recreational activities on campus continued to grow. Recreational activities were social in nature and offered opportunities both for affiliation with one's classmates or roommates and for friendly competition for bragging rights associated with pride in that group's accomplishment.

Each of these reasons for the establishment and growth of the Campus Recreation Department remains today. In addition, the extensive facilities for recreation and the breadth of such programming in today's university are drawing cards for potential students. Students and their parents are naturally drawn to those institutions with excellent facilities and programs, providing a natural link between the Campus Recreation Department and the overall mission of the university. Research indicates that student retention is favorably influenced by getting students involved in extracurricular activities such as those housed within campus recreation (Henchy, 2011; Huesman et al., 2009; Kuh et al., 2011). Finally, and perhaps most important, campus recreation programs began to flourish because of student interest. The student body's interest has grown over the years, leading to a proliferation of facilities and program offerings. In 1928, UM was the first institution to devote a building primarily to intramurals (Mueller & Reznik, 1979). Today, many campuses have complete facilities solely dedicated to recreational use.

The Formation and Evolution of National Intramural-Recreation Associations

Following World War II, while athletic and physical education groups were holding annual meetings and looking to associate with one another for a variety of purposes, recreation programmers were without such opportunities. To fill this void in the United States, Dr William N. Wasson of Dillard University in New Orleans engaged a research study to compare intramural programs at black Colleges, resulting in participating HBCUs forming the National Intramural Association (NIA) in 1950. The mandate of the NIA was to provide an association for professionals working in college and university intramural sports programs in the United States to share ideas, develop policy, and encourage professional development. In 1975, the NIA membership voted to change its name to the current National Intramural-Recreational Sport Association (NIRSA). The membership felt NIRSA more aptly described the expanded and diversified role of recreation departments on college campuses. Such units organize and deliver programming far beyond the boundaries of intramural sports, and the scope and mission of NIRSA has expanded phenomenally to what is currently an extensive national association. Given that NIRSA was founded by African American leaders, it is fitting that inclusion and diversity are fundamental values of NIRSA that endure today. In 2012 NIRSA officially expanded its name to *NIRSA: Leaders In Collegiate Recreation* in order to promote and communicate the organization's diverse and holistic approach to collegiate recreation. The governance structure of NIRSA is described later in this chapter.

The next section describes the governance structure of NIRSA in further detail and defines how Campus Recreation Departments are organized on college and university campuses.

GOVERNANCE

Municipal and state organizations exist as umbrella organizations with which Campus Recreation Departments may affiliate on a local level. This section examines the national association to which most campus recreation professionals in the United States and Canada belong. We answer the following questions about NIRSA: what is the mission of this organization? How is it funded? Who are its members? How is the organization structured?

National Intramural-Recreational Sports Association

National Intramural Recreational Sport Association
http://nirsa.net/nirsa

NIRSA Championship Series
http://play.nirsa.net/ nirsa-championship-series/

MISSION.   The purpose of NIRSA has expanded greatly since it was founded in 1950. The organization identifies five areas of business: *we grow, we discover, we connect, we lead, we play* (NIRSA, 2017a). Beyond intramurals, areas of interest include aquatics, integrated wellness and fitness, informal recreation, instructional programs, outdoor recreation, programs for people with disabilities, special events, sport clubs, extramurals (regional and national sports tournaments), and student leadership and development. NIRSA strives to provide its members with research, teaching, presenting, and publishing opportunities as well. NIRSA is a nonprofit professional association dedicated to promoting quality recreational sports programs. The association is equally committed to providing continuing education and career development for recreational sport professionals and students. NIRSA's mission statement is presented in Exhibit 7.2.

MEMBERSHIP.   Today, NIRSA has an extensive reach and membership across North America, but this was not always the case. From the first organizational meeting in 1950 that included 20 individuals from 11 historically black college and university (HBCU) schools, the association now boasts a membership of over 4,500 professionals and students from colleges, universities, correctional facilities, military installations, and parks and recreation departments. NIRSA initiatives and programming reach millions of recreational sport enthusiasts, including an estimated

NIRSA Mission Statement

exhibit **7.2**

> NIRSA is a leader in higher education and the advocate for the advancement of recreation, sport, and wellness by providing educational and developmental opportunities, generating and sharing knowledge, and promoting networking and growth for our members.

Source: NIRSA (2017b).

8.1 million college students. NIRSA also reaches professionals and students in Canadian schools, colleges, and universities and in 2017 added Canada as the seventh region of its network.

Membership is offered at ten separate designations: institutional, professional, professional life, student, student leadership, retired, honorary, and state association categories, as well as the associate level for commercial organizations who provide products or services to the organization and state association level. Within each category NIRSA offers many opportunities to get involved. With its sole focus on the advancement of intramural-recreational sport programs and their professionals and students, NIRSA provides access to program standards, a code of ethics, an extensive resource library, career opportunity services, and the Sports Officials' Development Center. In addition, NIRSA's message is delivered to professionals through state and regional conferences, symposia and workshops, and the Annual National Conference and Exhibit Show. NIRSA Institutional Members represent large and small and public and private two- and four-year colleges and universities. For those with an institutional-level membership, access is provided to nationally sponsored programs and events ranging from individual and team sport events to fitness and wellness exhibitions and special publications. An example of a mission that extends across the association's mandate is the NIRSA Natural High program, an alcohol and drug awareness program, which lead to the Coalition of Higher Education Associations for Substance Abuse Prevention (CoHEASAP).

WWW

Coalition of Higher Education Associations for Substance Abuse Prevention (CoHEASAP) www.collegesubstance abuseprevention.org/

FINANCIALS. NIRSA is a nonprofit organization. However, material and financial growth led the organization to reorganize into three independent legal entities, each of which has a significant role in managing NIRSA finances. In addition to the parent NIRSA organization, the NIRSA Foundation and the NIRSA Services Corporation were formed (NIRSA, 2017c).

NIRSA has approximately 4,500 individual and organization members. Membership fees constitute a major source of funding. The NIRSA Foundation is also a not-for-profit organization mandated to support the NIRSA mission; it receives donations to NIRSA. The NIRSA Services

Corporation is the taxable, business-oriented component of NIRSA. It was established to receive revenues from advertising, sponsorship, sales of licensed goods, intramural championships, and sport club championships (NIRSA, 2017c).

ORGANIZATIONAL STRUCTURE.   In 2010 NIRSA began a governance transition process that streamlined the number of positions on the Board of Directors (see Exhibit 7.3), and identified the Board's role in visionary leadership. The Board is composed of seven members, including the following elected positions: President, President Designee, President-Elect, Annual Director, and three At-Large Directors. The individuals elected to these positions hold one- to three-year terms, staggered to ensure continuity on the Board of Directors from year to year. The Board is assisted by a nonvoting position of Secretary. The Board is responsive to the members of the organization, and works in concert with the Member Network and the Assembly.

The Member Network is the primary vehicle for member communication, representation, networking, and professional development. It is

exhibit 7.3   Organizational Chart of the NIRSA Board of Directors

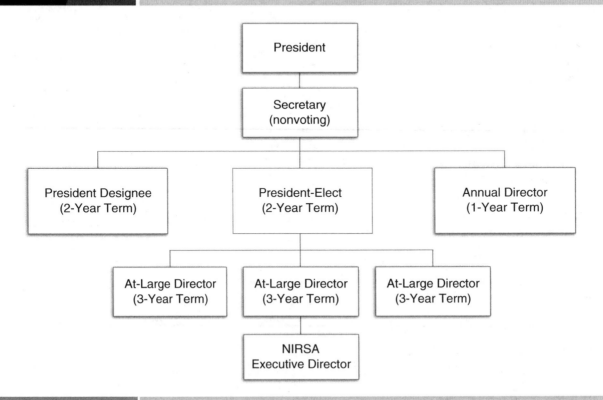

Source: NIRSA (2017c).

comprised of one region representative from each NIRSA region, one student leader from each NIRSA region, the NIRSA Student Leader, the Past-President's Member Network representative, one member of the Board of Directors, and the Chair of the Member Network. The NIRSA Assembly is described as a "forward-thinking think-tank" that facilitates the germination of ideas and national discussion in order to ensure contemporary relevance and knowledge sharing. Its membership is at the discretion of the Board of Directors, and is meant to be a broad representation of NIRSA's constituencies including individuals working in the profession, students, a Past-President's representative, and members with expertise in areas of current and strategic interest to the profession

The Executive Director (ED) of NIRSA, the only paid officer of the association, answers to the Board of Directors and is responsible for the daily activities of the organization. The NIRSA National Center, located in Corvallis, Oregon, has a professional staff grouped into the following activity areas Executive, Professional Development, Finance, Operations, Membership, Philanthropy, NSC, Sales, Sports, Marketing, and Information Technology. Each area is lead by a Director or Senior Director. Approximately 35 individuals are employed in managerial positions at NIRSA Headquarters. The NIRSA Headquarters organizational chart is shown in Exhibit 7.4.

NIRSA is primarily a service organization, dedicated to continuing education for its members and the promotion of quality recreational sport programs. NIRSA provides its members with knowledge, ideas, and community for solving problems. Its prime policy role is the development of program standards for events and activities within recreation programs. Ensuring the safety of participants and quality of programming has been one focus of such policy development. Another focus has been the development of codes of ethical practices for professionals and participants within recreational sport settings.

Campus Recreation Department Structure

Virtually every college and university in North America has a Campus Recreation Department. The campus is viewed as a community, and the pursuit of fitness and play through sport is an important part of any community operation for promoting good health and happiness.

MISSION. The structure and function of the Campus Recreation Department is directly linked to the unit's mission and goal statements, which are based upon participants' and clients' goals. A typical mission statement for a Campus Recreation Department might read: "We are committed to providing the finest programs and services in order to enrich the university learning experience and to foster a lifetime appreciation of and involvement in recreational sport and wellness activities for our students, faculty, and staff." For sample mission statements, see Exhibit 7.5.

exhibit 7.4   NIRSA Headquarters Organizational Chart

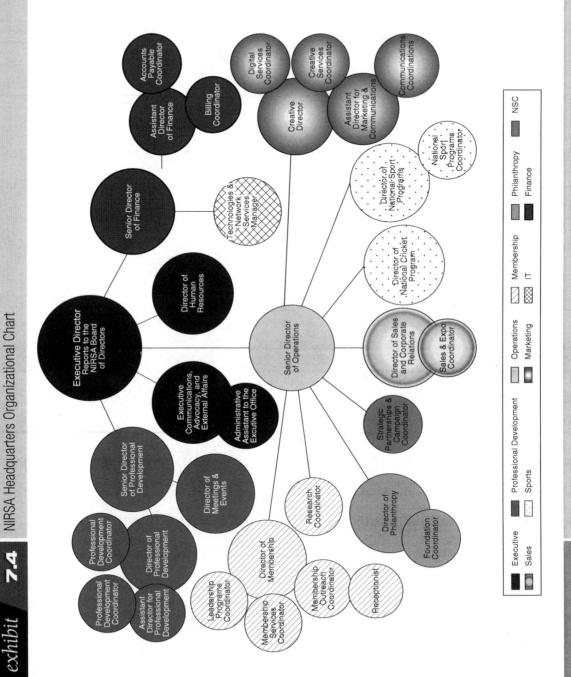

Legend:

- Executive
- Sales
- Professional Development
- Sports
- Operations
- Marketing
- Membership
- IT
- Philanthropy
- Finance
- NSC

Source: NIRSA (2017d). Reprinted with permission.

Example Mission Statements for Campus Recreation Programs *exhibit* **7.5**

WWW

UIC Campus Recreation
http://recreation.uic.edu/
mission-vision-and-values/

OSU Recreational Sports
https://recsports.osu.edu/
who-we-are

Arkansas University Recreation
http://urec.uark.edu/

University of Illinois at Chicago

> UIC Campus Recreation serves the diverse student body and university community by enhancing learning and promoting healthy lifestyles through quality facilities, programs, and services. We promote teamwork, professionalism, enthusiasm and excellence while supporting student development through programs and opportunities that strengthen leadership skills.

The Ohio State University, Columbus, Ohio

> Our mission is to engage the university community in physical and wellness activities by offering the finest collegiate recreation programs, services, staff and facilities.

University of Arkansas, Fayetteville, Arkansas

> Our mission is to engage and enhance the University of Arkansas community through diverse recreational, social and wellness opportunities.

Sources: University of Denver (2012), Southern Polytechnic State University (2012), UCLA (2012).

MEMBERSHIP.   As mentioned previously, the constituents of a modern campus recreation program include the students, faculty, and staff. However, this group may well be broadened to include alumni, families of faculty and staff, and community members interested in recreation opportunities (Wallace Carr et al., 2013).

FINANCIALS.   The financial operations of the small versus the large Campus Recreation Department will vary. Some institutions support programming and facilities through central budgets housed in Student Life. Revenue might be generated through varsity athletic budgets or through academic Physical Education, Kinesiology, or Health Sciences budgets. Budgetary support ranges from full to partial funding by the institution; more commonly, university budgets provide one of several sources of the overall recreation budget. Another common source of revenue for recreation is a compulsory recreation fee charged to every university student to help support student programs and facilities. Such fees are collected in addition to

WWW

University of Illinois at Chicago Campus Recreation
http://recreation.uic.edu/

The Ohio State University Recreational Sports
https://recsports.osu.edu/

University of Arkansas Recreation
http://urec.uark.edu/

tuition and other compulsory academic and nonacademic fees at the beginning of each semester or quarter. Another revenue source includes "pay for play" fees collected from the participants in a league, class, or special event. Budgets also often include revenue components including rentals, facility membership or daily-use fees, advertising, and other marketing initiatives. In this case, the operation is run on a break-even basis, equating operational and program spending to the revenues generated through some combination of the sources defined above.

Other campus recreation programs are run as *profit centers*. Many institutions, regardless of size, have built multi-million-dollar facilities to service the needs of their current constituents. This proactive stance recognizes the role campus facilities can play in attracting and retaining future students, faculty, and staff. Profit centers generate revenue to offset the costs beyond those related to operations, for example, to pay a facility mortgage. Often, using the facility involves a membership fee. Students may pay through the recreation fee charged within the tuition package, and faculty and staff may be required to pay monthly membership fees. Opportunity for memberships may also be extended to alumni, family members, and community users on separate fee schedules. The proposal for building such a facility sometimes involves a student referendum for an additional building fee that might extend from as few as 5 years to as many as 20 years. In this case, an additional facility or building fee is charged to all students.

Some institutions look beyond their students to additional sources of revenue to build recreation facilities. An alternative model for financing the construction or renovation of facilities involves developing partnerships. In such cases, the university partners with the community, with local governments, or with the private sector to raise capital. Agreements for use and profit allocation are developed in return for building capital. The facility is run as a business with market rates charged for use. The Director of Recreation must ensure certain profit levels are maintained through memberships and sources of program revenue. Significant sources of revenues in the millions of dollars can accrue from rental payments, instructional programs, and sport camps, to name a few.

Many institutions are also seeking corporate sponsors to fund sport leagues and specific programs. For example, the University of Nebraska's intramural program is funded by Raisin Cane's chicken and their promotional materials are on their website, shirts, calendars, and flyers.

ORGANIZATIONAL STRUCTURE. The structure of the Recreation Department is also partially determined by its size. A small college may have a fairly simple organizational structure due to fewer constituents, limited facilities, smaller levels of programming, and less need for full-time staff. However, a large college will have a complex organizational structure that provides extensive levels of programming for multiple constituents through state-of-the-art facilities. Let's have a look at the administration and operation of two examples.

Small Recreation Programs

Consider a small, private college with 900 students and 75 faculty and staff members situated in a rural community of 5,000 people. It is possible the only constituents of the campus recreation program are students and a few faculty or staff. In this case recreation may be housed within a larger unit of Athletics and Recreation, so that the continuum of competitive and non-competitive activity, along with the management of facilities, is combined within one department led by an individual with the title of Manager, Coordinator, or Assistant Director. Campus recreation thus coexists within a larger administrative unit responsible for varsity athletics and facilities; this alignment encourages an equitable distribution of resources (financial, physical, and human); good communication between multiple users of the same facilities; and effective, seamless delivery of the many physical activity options available to the participants. The head administrator of the overall operation, usually called the Director, is charged with maintaining some balance between the competitive and noncompetitive programming units.

In such cases, the Campus Recreation Manager may be the only full-time employee with direct responsibilities for recreational programming. She may have an assistant but often manages the area alone, with support from the Director and from employees who manage the facilities. In small programs it is easy to comprehend the large role students play in organizing and delivering the campus recreation program. Of necessity, in the beginning such programming was student run, and recreational programming today is still largely student run (Brown, 1998). Full-time university employees direct the overall program, set policy, and manage finances, but the actual development and delivery of programming is led by students. This fact is certainly celebrated by colleges and universities, where administrators wholly applaud the concept of "for the students, by the students." These programs allow students to gain valuable management and leadership skills. Clearly, these students have their finger on the pulse of their classmates' interests when it comes to assessing programming. It is not uncommon to have 50 student leaders in both paid and volunteer positions as supervisors, officials, and event managers even within a small campus recreation program. Student leaders help govern the program as well, often by way of management teams and advisory councils that feed information to the full-time university employees. For example, student-led committees dealing with areas such as intramurals, participant conduct, special events, clubs, and officials may report through the Student Supervisors' Council to the Campus Recreation Manager. Student input and leadership is the foundation of the program. In this case, student employees and supervisors, along with the Manager of Recreation, are likely to be heavily involved in the development and implementation of policy. The Director of Athletics and Recreation and any departmental coordinating council or management team will also play a role in confirming policy. An example of the administrative structure for a small college is presented in Exhibit 7.6.

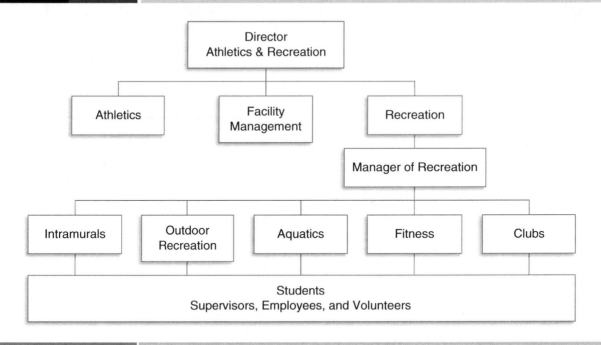

Large Recreation Programs

The scope of a large campus recreation program can differ significantly from that of the small college presented above. Many colleges and universities have significant student, faculty and staff, and alumni populations. Some are housed in large urban centers. In such cases, the administration and operation of the Campus Recreation Department is generally large and complex, with many full-time professional staff and several programming divisions. Consider, for example, a large public university with an enrollment of 50,000 students. The Department of Recreation may be led by a Director who is the administrative head reporting to a Vice President or Provost responsible for Student Life (see Exhibit 7.7), or it may be led by an Associate Athletic Director responsible for recreation, in which case campus recreation is once again linked to the Department of Athletics (see Exhibit 7.8).

In either case, the structure of the Campus Recreation Department is extensive and is compartmentalized into several operational and management areas based on the defined programming. Students help run the respective areas through positions in each of the programs areas of delivery, and a large professional staff manages the department. Associate Directors responsible for different types of programming are common, each reporting directly to the head administrator. The different programming areas depend on the campus constituents and their needs and environment. The following areas

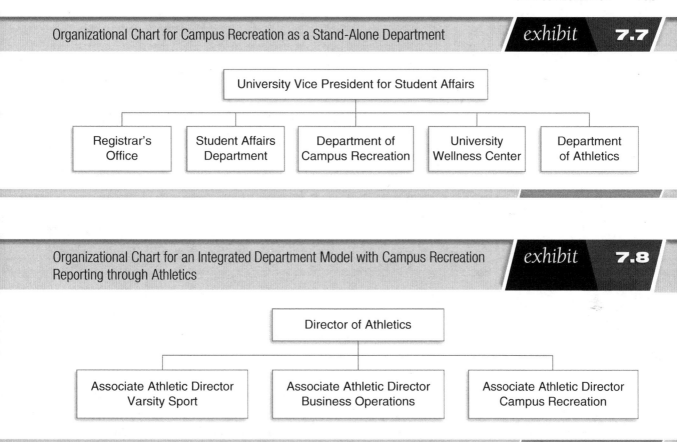

Organizational Chart for Campus Recreation as a Stand-Alone Department   *exhibit* **7.7**

University Vice President for Student Affairs

| Registrar's Office | Student Affairs Department | Department of Campus Recreation | University Wellness Center | Department of Athletics |

Organizational Chart for an Integrated Department Model with Campus Recreation Reporting through Athletics   *exhibit* **7.8**

Director of Athletics

| Associate Athletic Director Varsity Sport | Associate Athletic Director Business Operations | Associate Athletic Director Campus Recreation |

are most common: Intramural Sport, Extramural Sport, Outdoor Adventure, Sport Clubs, Fitness and Wellness Activities, Special Events, Community Programming including Sport Camps, Instructional Programming, Aquatics, Dance, Martial Arts, Family Recreation, Informal Recreation, Adapted Recreational Sports, Equipment Rentals, Facility Operations, Marketing, Technology, Business Operations, and Student Personnel. Depending on the scope of programming, each major area may operate as a separate department, with its own central office and administrative staff.

Advisory committees composed of students, faculty and staff members, alumni, retirees, and designated area (intramural sports, residence halls, fraternities, and sororities) representatives provide input to a wide spectrum of programming and management issues. The deliberations of these committees contribute to policy development that might ultimately funnel to the Director of Recreational Sports, for example, a policy regarding penalties imposed on teams that are late or fail to show up for an intramural event. To erase such practices, a policy is developed to fine the offending team and impose a ban on competition for teams with further offenses. Such policy is common in intramurals today. Another level of advisory committee, perhaps called the Advisory Committee on Recreational Sports, takes on the responsibility for overall issues of program and facility equity and direction. This Advisory Committee may be led by the Director of Recreational Sport. It meets regularly and may be composed of several faculty members appointed by the College Faculty Senate, an equal number of students appointed by the Student Association(s), and a representative from central administration, perhaps appointed by the Office of the Vice President for Student Affairs. The Advisory Committee plays a role in policy development, usually considering issues of overall program magnitude, equity, finance, future directions, and public relations. An organizational chart of a complex Campus Recreation Department in a large university setting is presented in Exhibit 7.9.

exhibit **7.9**   Organizational Chart for a Typical Campus Recreation Department for a Large University

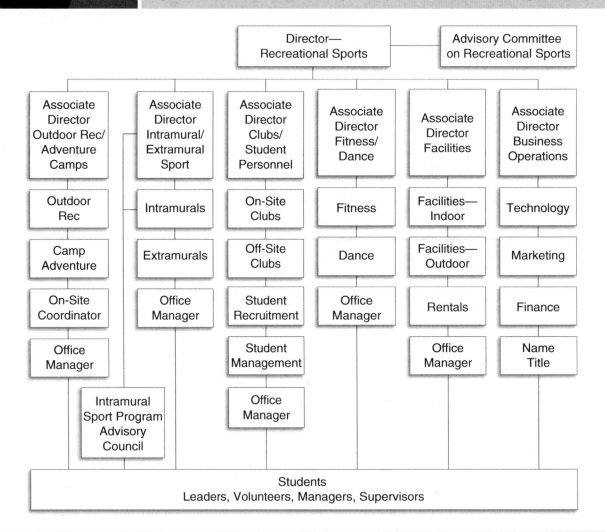

PROGRAMMING IN CAMPUS RECREATION

Regardless of the size of the Campus Recreation Department or its system of funding, an important issue on every campus involves the scope of programming. When the question of scope arises, almost without exception, the one-word answer is *extensive*. Campus recreation programs certainly live up to the "something for everyone" theme, with offerings ranging from intramural team sport leagues to instructional activities to wellness programs to events for special populations. Even small programs run by a single professional staff member with limited access to facilities can deliver extensive campus recreation programs.

Campus recreation began as intramural sport, and this area still draws strong interest today. Intramurals include not only team sports normally run in leagues but also individual sports. Intramurals encompass men-only, women-only, and co-ed leagues in virtually every sport of student interest.

Sport Clubs are also popular. Clubs are student-run organizations that provide in-depth opportunities to learn and participate in a particular activity. The extensive array of possibilities ranges from archery to bowling to fencing to racquetball to ultimate disc. Each club is formed, developed, governed, and administered by students. Student leadership and continuity is a key to success. Rules and regulations and administrative assistance are usually provided by the Campus Recreation Department. Furthermore, most Sport Clubs belong to governing bodies that define rules and regulations specific to their sport. These clubs may be recreational or competitive in nature, and Competitive Sport Clubs generally compete on a national level against other universities.

Instructional activities include classes in fitness, dance, yoga, "learn to" activities, certification courses, and facility time for self-directed activities. Self-directed activities involve sport for fitness and fun, such as individual weight training or lane swimming, pickup basketball, tennis, or health and safety courses.

Extramural sports are also gaining in popularity and include both Sport Clubs and intramural competitions. *Extramural sport* refers to structured participation between groups on different campuses. For example, the intramural champion may be invited to a state or national event (such as NIRSA basketball championships or state flag football regional events). The emphasis is still on fun, but competition is part of the event. Participants may engage in each of the areas mentioned above in traditional team and individual sports.

Another popular area of campus recreation programming is the pool. Aquatic activities range from self-directed lane fitness swimming to learn-to-swim to aqua-fitness programming. Aqua-fitness classes take place in the water and usually follow the same formats as regular fitness activities. Intramural inner tube water polo is also popular with participants and new special events, such as WipeOut! mirroring the TV action show, are being offered on some campuses.

When the fitness industry exploded in North America in the 1970s, demand for aerobic classes, yoga, spin, and fitness classes soon peaked on campus, and the trend continues today. The public has become better informed of the health benefits and personal satisfaction associated with recreation and leisure activities, so campus recreation has expanded its wellness offerings with such classes as nutrition, aromatherapy, reflexology, tai chi, Pilates, and power yoga. Events for individuals with disabilities (for example, wheelchair basketball) or to populations of international students (for example, a cricket festival) are also commonly offered.

Most of the activities and events described above take place indoors. The final area of campus recreation programming involves outdoor recreation and adventure activities. This includes activities in the great outdoors to take advantage of the lakes, mountains, and forest terrain of the surrounding area. Cycling, kayaking, canoeing, hiking, mountain biking, and scuba diving are popular pursuits, with classes for beginners to advanced participants. Outdoor adventure activities usually include an element of risk, such as outdoor rock climbing, an extreme triathlon, or open-water kayaking. Such outdoor programming lead by trained students and professionals is generally organized into three areas of the department: trips, outdoor education, and equipment rental.

It is easy to understand why campus recreation programmers have coined the slogans "Something for everyone" and "We do more than just play games." They clearly live up to these mottoes, providing an extensive and diverse array of recreation and leisure time activities. The sheer breadth of programming can be a "pressure point" for the Campus Recreation Director. Policy issues also require the attention of campus recreation providers, and some key policy areas are discussed next.

CURRENT POLICY AREAS

Policy is defined as the guidelines or procedures an organization follows in an effort to achieve its overall goals. Like any other department in an institution of higher education, the recreation unit must develop and update policy. The Campus Recreation Director leads the debate on issues of policy, gathering input from both full- and part-time recreation employees and participants. Some issues are impacted by policy enacted by the institution or the Athletic Department. Some of the current policy areas that impact campus recreation leaders today are discussed in this section.

Funding

The Sport Manager—perhaps any kind of manager—is always concerned with finances. What are our sources of funding? Are we maximizing our avenues of funding, and are we spending efficiently? Is the cost–benefit ratio of our programming effective? Can we justify our choices?

MARK WILLIAMS, *Director, Campus Recreation,*

University of Notre Dame

As the Director I lead, supervise, and manage the RecSports Department. I am responsible for leading the efforts related to creating and implementing the department's strategic vision for recreation, wellness, and safety through program development, facilities management and operations, services, and staffing. I am asked to establish and execute all strategic oversight for the department in terms of staffing, budgeting, and initiatives or programs. I have the overall responsibility for the hiring, training, supervision, and performance management of all departmental staff including all full time staff, instructors, club coaches, interns, and student staff members. And I am a member of the Student Development senior leadership team within the Division of Student Affairs.

Important policy issues confronting campus recreation today include risk management, participant safety, and the holistic well-being of students. RecSports professionals are currently developing policies and procedures related to concussion management. We offer interhall tackle football, men's and women's lacrosse, and men's ice hockey as intramural sports to name a few. These sports, and our men's and women's boxing program along with 48 other club sports, all have concussion-related needs. We are further developing these policies and procedures for these programs to inform, educate, and assist in participants' recovery if they ever experience any type of concussion-related injuries. We require participants who play contact sports to review concussion-related materials and become familiar with our policies and procedures that require participants to engage in our "return to play" process.

I believe that Student Affairs should be the organizational home for campus recreation. Like many of the other areas in Student Affairs, campus recreation looks to educate students in a holistic manner (total person). We try to create programs and activities that engage their minds, bodies, and spirits. Our focus is to educate and instruct participants on how to create a road map of physical and mental well-being that they may use in their lives beyond their time on campus. Other departments, like Athletics and Physical Education, may focus more on competition and/or education and other attributes specifically related to their core values. The Student Affairs governance model, on the other hand, encourages the student to engage in a myriad of activities that stimulate and cultivate skills related to leadership, character formation, vocational discernment and recreation/fun.

Campus recreation challenges are often financial in nature but these challenges can be overcome through collaboration to provide the best possible opportunities for all students. Athletic and academic departments may have more funding available and in some instances may have priority over facility usage. Policies that deal with inclusion and transgender students will likely become more prevalent in campus recreation. For example, institutions receiving state funding and/or that are governed by state legislatures that permit the exclusion of students who identify as transgender from participating present a very challenging policy issue for Campus Recreation Departments. Campus recreation as a whole should be as inclusive as possible to serve the entire student body. How do you care for and provide services for all students when there are laws that prohibit you from doing just that—caring for all students?

The other area I think presents a challenging policy issue was one I commented on earlier—how do schools work to educate and support students with concussion-related injuries. The NFL [National Football League] and NCAA [National Collegiate Athletic Association] are both working to find ways to improve safety protocols for athletes involved in high-impact sports. Both have funding, medical, and logistical support that campus recreation programs lack even though campus recreation programs tend to have more athletes participating in programming. I think dealing with this issue may be a policy and procedural challenge in the future from both a financial and student care perspective.

Certainly, the campus recreation administrator is required to implement effective financial management policy.

One regularly discussed issue involves financing a broad program. How do we define what activities or events should be offered, and how do we ensure the financial support exists in the form of human and physical resources to deliver an effective program? Remember, colleges and universities are about excellence, and the delivery of excellent service and programming is a cornerstone of the Campus Recreation Department's mandate. Campus recreation leaders deal with this issue by setting policy around the viability of program offerings. Program managers conduct research to gather participants' views on the effectiveness of their programs. On an annual basis, the Director then charts hard data on participant numbers in specific activities and longitudinal participant trends. This information feeds the decision-making process by providing the leaders with quantitative information about what is of interest to participants and how they view the quality of the current offerings. Then administrators consider other relevant parameters, such as availability of funds and facilities, in their decision-making formula. The Campus Recreation Director needs to research questions such as the following:

- Do we have the facilities to support a particular endeavor?
- Are we willing to enter into a "pay for play" scheme in order to collect funds to rent extra facilities?
- How much interest must support a decision to add programming on a "pay for play" basis?
- Which activities are core support activities; that is, activities covered entirely by the campus recreation budget?
- Which events are run on a break-even basis only, requiring registration dollars and other mechanisms of funding in order to support the program?

These types of questions, plus others specific to a particular institution, will help the Campus Recreation Department set financial management policy.

Competition for Limited Facilities

Campus recreation is often in competition with other programming. The Physical Education, Athletics, and Summer Camps departments often vie for the same facility and equipment use. These competing units may even exist within the same department or faculty. When facilities are shared, leaders must develop policy that balances the needs of all areas. The Campus Recreation Director needs to take a proactive leadership role, advocating for the implementation of such boundaries. Otherwise, some of those interested in becoming active will have no opportunities. The recreation administrator needs to be armed with good information when policy is negotiated. Participant numbers, student numbers, activity interests and levels, and knowledge of user preferences are important. Setting procedures for priority status and for bumping programs is necessary to prevent interruptions to planned activities and to avoid user conflicts.

Activity Trends

Defining which activities to offer, mentioned above as an issue in funding campus recreation programs, is an important area in policy development. Interest in specific leisure and recreation activities tends to blow with the wind. Fads and trends are normal in recreation, and they shift quickly. Campus recreation leaders need to have their fingers on the pulse of shifting interests, and they can gather the information they need through three important mechanisms. First, they can administer participant and non-participant questionnaires to collect interests, likes, and dislikes. Second, Recreation Department student employees can gather informal data about interests and patterns of behavior. Finally, sport leaders can observe behaviors to learn where people are recreating, what events are popular, what events fail to draw participants, what the competition is up to, and who the competition is. Through program evaluation managers can gather information needed to make appropriate changes. This is critically important to meet the interests and needs of constituent groups, which are ever evolving and sometimes change radically. Ensuring that facility development includes adaptable space for multiple uses is a key planning issue given that participation fads change. After all, the campus recreation program is nothing without participants.

Access

While having a large base of participants is important to the mission of the campus recreation program, participation, normally referred to as *participant eligibility*, is restricted. The Campus Recreation Director and his advisors are required to set eligibility policy based upon their unique environment and departmental goals. Normally, intramural and extramural sports are accessible only to the institution's currently registered students (both full- and part-time). Instructional and special-event programming may be open to faculty and staff members and their families, alumni, and community members. Other programming may have a priority listing for first-come, first-served entrance into leagues or events. To manage access, administrators of the department set policy stipulating who is eligible for a particular program. They may go so far as to create a priority listing for some activities. They may close other activities to only a certain set of the possible participant constituents. Some participants may enroll for free, while others pay fees depending on the mission of the Campus Recreation Department and of the university at large. It is important, however, that such policy is clearly communicated to participant groups and staff.

In addition to establishing participant eligibility, the Campus Recreation Department must also enforce rules limiting access to facilities and events. For example, employees must consistently check identification (ID) cards so only eligible participants enter a facility. When participants forget their ID cards, disagreements and confrontations often develop. Establishing clear policies for handling such situations helps maintain program safety and integrity.

Event Management

Recreation on today's university campus is often a huge enterprise, and consumers' expectations for excellence have kept pace with the diverse approach to programming and multi-million-dollar facilities. Students, their parents, and members of the community expect the highest quality in service and environment. To satisfy everyone's expectations, campus recreation administrators must create policy regarding event management.

Recognizing the need to develop policy may seem like common sense. However, consider the roots of the campus recreation program: "for the students, by the students." Even today, mostly student employees and student volunteers deliver recreation programs. Therefore, it is important that full-time managers of the Campus Recreation Department establish policy to define standards of event management. These may involve timelines and standards for physical setup, expectations of student managers and officials, rules for the use of logos and department letterhead, requirements concerning marketing and sponsorship, guidelines for decision making and problem solving, emergency response plans and other items related to managing risk, and media liaison and reporting of results. Of course, other issues connected to event management and requiring policy development will arise. Thus, risk management becomes particularly important to an effective and efficient Campus Recreation Department.

Risk Management

Campus Recreation Directors must be concerned with risk management (Zabonick, 2016). Of course, some risk is associated with crossing the street or playing a game of baseball. One may be run over by a speeding car or hit on the head by the baseball. Society attempts to minimize the possibility of being run over by a car by posting speed limits, building sidewalks, and setting up traffic lights and stop signs. Similarly, recreation administrators attempt to minimize risk in physical activity by requiring participants to wear protective equipment, ensuring that participants are taught proper techniques, and strictly enforcing safety rules. If the baseball player is hit in the head with a ball, hopefully her helmet will protect her. It is impossible to eliminate risk; the challenge is to manage the risk. In other words, the recreation professional is responsible for setting up and delivering programs that reduce overt risks and communicate other levels of risks to participants. According to Zabonick (2016), to achieve this, policy is required to create a culture of risk management. Managers need to:

- develop a written risk-management plan to show evidence of proactive prevention
- keep accurate and detailed records on participants and injuries that occur
- ensure that the rules of play are properly enforced and communicated
- train and certify leaders in the areas they teach and supervise
- ensure proper supervision of areas needing supervision and restrict access to some unsupervised areas
- check equipment regularly to ensure it is in good working order
- require paperwork that provides for lists of participants, identification information, and possibly health information
- develop and communicate emergency response procedures
- train event leaders in first aid and cardiopulmonary resuscitation (CPR)
- develop and implement informed consent forms and health-related questionnaires for all but the very minimal risk activities (Miller, 1998)

For example, an aerobics class should be led by a trained, certified instructor. He should have a class list, and participants should be required to complete a medical screening questionnaire such as the Physical Activity Readiness Questionnaire (PAR-Q) to identify any potential risk factors. In another activity, such as an outdoor adventure trip in white-water kayaking, medical clearance may be required, and program leaders will use waiver forms to have participants acknowledge the risks involved and to take responsibility for such risk. Waivers and informed-consent forms are commonly employed and should be a required component of the policy surrounding risk management for the Campus Recreation Department, especially where off-site travel or high-risk activities are involved.

www

PAR-Q
https://www.nasm.org/
docs/pdf/nasm-cpt-par-q.
pdf?sfvrsn=2

**Sports Waiver for Minors,
University of Florida**
http://recsports.ufl.edu/
images/uploads/docs/
sc-participant-waiver-minor_
distributed.pdf

Medical Issues

Pre-activity screening is important when dealing with medical conditions. However, it will not prepare employees in a Recreation Department for the acute medical emergencies that may result during sporting events and other physical activities. Many programs are considering or creating concussion protocols for intramural and sport club participants. Of course, it is inevitable that one player will step on another's foot while playing intramural basketball and sprain or break an ankle. The Campus Recreation Department must have set policy on procedures to help the injured participant. Having emergency supplies and equipment on-site is important, and many college recreation facilities have automated external defibrillators in case of cardiac incidents. Having an emergency action plan and trained supervisors who know what to do is also critically important.

Some activities require collecting and keeping information on-site in the event of an emergency. The group leaders on a daylong cycling tour should have information on a participant who is allergic to insect stings, including medical insurance information and contact numbers and names. Leaders must also be trained in managing information and protecting the privacy of participants. Generally, all student employees are mandated to have FERPA (Family Educational Rights and Privacy Act) training given their handling of sensitive information. Medical information needs to be collected and collated into a manageable, perhaps laminated form that can be tucked into a side-saddle or a fanny pack. Having on-site information and knowing what to do in the event of an emergency are critical areas for policy development and a clear responsibility of the Recreation Department in terms of employee training.

Recreational Opportunities for Individuals with Disabilities

The most critical issue with respect to recreational opportunities for students with disabilities is gaining an accurate demographic picture of who has needs and defining those needs (Martinez, 2017). To achieve this, campus recreation professionals must set policy enabling the collection of important information regarding maximizing opportunity for students with disabilities. This is readily achieved through a Disabled Student Advisory Council, which sets a schedule for defining appropriate activities, defines a mechanism for publicizing activities and facility schedules, creates opportunities for training with respect to facilities and equipment, and provides ongoing leadership in the assessment of the effectiveness of the overall effort. Colleges and universities across the US must work harder to provide recreational programming designed specifically for individuals with disabilities. Martinez (2017) found four themes relative to successfully including disabled students in recreational programming in a study examining 14 Big Ten Universities: (1) website information and ease of navigation for disabled programming, (2) appropriate use of language that is inclusive to disabled students, (3) access to facilities and accessibility information, and (4) support for accessibility and inclusion. Intramural sports like sit-down volleyball, beep ball, and goal ball are gaining in popularity. Fitness spaces should now be geared towards being accessible with machines that are adaptable or cater directly to disabled patrons.

SUMMARY

Recreational programming is thriving on college campuses. Universities have embraced the notion that higher education involves much more than lectures and exams and that the quality of student life is an important concern. The Campus Recreation Department helps to promote the overall goals of the institution by offering student activities that promote health, happiness, and affiliation. The diversity of programming is often extensive and usually student led. As a result of the considerable recreational scheduling on the college campus, several organizations have been established at the community, state or provincial, and national levels to promote recreation and offer recreation leaders sources of both professional development and practical resources. The largest national association is NIRSA in the United States. It includes elected recreation officials from state associations, many of whom are campus recreation professionals and students.

The Campus Recreation Department can be organized as a unit with a small number of professional staff, housed within the university Athletics Department, or it can function as a stand-alone unit within the Student Affairs operation of the university, with many departments led by recreation professionals employed on a full-time basis. In either case, the organizational structure will rely on an extensive group of student employees and student volunteers who deliver a vast array of programming. Recreation professionals manage the affairs of the department by defining mission, vision, and goals; by managing facility operation and finances; and by setting and enforcing policy. Many policy areas draw the attention of the Campus Recreation Department leaders, from defining how the unit is funded and maximizing funding sources to program offerings and participant eligibility to access for people with disabilities. The Campus Recreation Department plays an extensive role in the delivery of recreational opportunities for the constituents on the modern university campus.

case STUDY

FACILITY DEVELOPMENT

As the newly hired Assistant Director of Campus Recreation at Big State University, your first assignment is to upgrade program offerings in your new facility. You have the following facilities:

- 1 gym—big enough for eight basketball courts
- 1 pool measuring 25 meters
- 1 cardiovascular room with treadmills and stationary bikes
- 1 weight room with free weights and a weight-machine system
- 2 activity rooms with 10-foot ceilings
- 4 multipurpose grass fields

Your student body enrollment of 18,000 includes many nontraditional students, and residence halls coexist with fraternities and sororities on campus.

1. What programs would you set up? What times would you schedule activities for? Leagues versus tournaments? How would you decide which activities to drop and which to add?

2. How would you go about getting funding for your programs? Whom would you ask?

3. Where would you get building and program staff? What would you include in their training program?

4. How would you ensure that your programs and facilities fairly and effectively provide for all your users?

5. Your programs must meet local and national standards. Which organizations would you join, and how would you go about ensuring that your programming reflected the best practices around the country?

CHAPTER questions

1. Using the Internet, search for the committee structure of NIRSA. Build an organizational chart of the committees showing how they link together and where they report. How are the ideas generated and the problems solved at the committee level turned into policy? Trace and describe one example of such policy development by reading the committee meeting minutes as posted on the Web.

2. Investigate the campus recreation program at your institution. How is it structured, and how is policy developed? Who has the authority to make decisions? How is the program financed? How would you go about creating a new program activity?

3. Varsity athletics and campus recreation often compete for facilities and resources on campus. Develop an organizational structure with the best chance of downplaying this internal rivalry.

FOR ADDITIONAL INFORMATION

For more information check out the following resources:

1. A further look at Campus Recreation around the world: Kozechian, H., Heidary, A., Saiah, A., Heidary, M. (2012). Campus recreation worldwide: A literature review. *International Journal of Academic Research in Business and Social Sciences*, 132–139: http://www.hrmars.com/admin/pics/692.pdf

2. You Tube: Campus Recreation Risk Management demonstrated by the University of Arizona: https://www.youtube.com/watch?v=wC8mHapwXkY

3. Jobs in Collegiate Recreation and Beyond: NIRSAs Blue Fish Jobs: http://careercenter.bluefishjobs.com/

4. Facilities matter: Ranking Student Recreation Centers: www.bestcollegereviews.org/features/the-25-most-amazing-campus-student-recreation-centers/

5. An excellent overview of Campus Recreation as a component of Student Life: Robert Morris University: http://studentlife.rmu.edu/campus-recreation

6. Higher Ed Live podcast with host Tony Doody: Trends in Campus Recreation: http://higheredlive.com/trends-in-campus-recreation/

REFERENCES

Arkansas University (2017). Recreation mission statement. Retrieved from http://urec.uark.edu/

Brown, S. C. (1998). Campus recreation. In J. B. Parks, B. Zanger, & J. Quarterman (Eds.), *Contemporary sport management* (pp. 139–154). Champaign, IL: Human Kinetics.

Colgate, J. A. (1978). *Administration of intramural and recreational activities: Everyone can participate.* New York: John Wiley.

Franklin, D. (2013). Evolution of campus recreational sports: Adapting to the age of accountability. In NIRSA Publication, *Campus Recreational Sports: Managing Employees, Programs, Facilities, and Services.* Champaign, IL: Human Kinetics.

Henchy, A. (2011). The influence of Campus Recreation beyond the gym. *Recreational Sports Journal*, 35(2), 174–181.

Huesman, R., Brown, A., Lee, G., Kellogg, J., & Radcliffe, P. (2009). Gym bags and mortarboards: Is use of campus recreation facilities related to student success? *Journal of Student Affairs Research and Practice (NASPA Journals)*, 46(1), 49–71.

Kuh, G. D., Kinzie, J., Schuh, J. H., & Whitt, E. J. (2011). *Student success in college: Creating conditions that matter.* San Francisco: Wiley.

Langley, T. D., & Hawkins, J. D. (2004). *Administration for exercise-related professions* (2nd Ed.). Toronto: Thomson/Wadsworth.

LaVoi, N. M., & Kane, M. J. (2014). Sociological aspects of sport. In P. M. Petersen & L. Thibault (Eds.), *Contemporary sport management* (5th ed., pp. 426–449). Champaign, IL: Human Kinetics.

Martinez, A. X. (2017). How inclusive are campus recreation programs? Retrieved from www.nchpad.org/1504/6460/How~Inclusive~are~Campus~Recreation~Programs~

Miller, R. D. (1998). Campus recreation risk management. *NIRSA Journal*, 22(3), 23–25.

Mueller, P., & Reznik, W. (1979). *Intramural-recreational sports programming and administration* (5th ed.). New York: John Wiley.

NIRSA. (2017a). NIRSA – Leaders in Collegiate Recreation. Retrieved from www.nirsa.net/nirsa

NIRSA. (2017b). Our Mission. Retrieved from www.nirsa.net/nirsa/about/mission-vision/

NIRSA. (2017c). About NIRSA. Retrieved from www.nirsa.net/nirsa/about/

NIRSA. (2017d). NIRSA Headquarters Team Organizational Chart. Retrieved from www.nirsa.net/nirsa/contact/headquarters-staff/#;Lightbox[ac81a715d8a8358fe12]/0

Ohio State Recreational Sports. (2017). Who we are: Mission. Retrieved from http://recsports.osu.edu/who-we-are

Smith, P. (1991). Positioning recreational sport in higher education. In R. L. Boucher & W. J. Weese (Eds.), *Management of recreational sports in higher education* (pp. 5–12). Madison, WI: WCB Brown & Benchmark.

University of Illinois at Chicago (2017). Campus recreation mission statement. Retrieved from http://recreation.uic.edu/mission-vision-and-values/

Wallace Carr, J., Robertson, B., Lesnik, R., J., Potter, C. J., & Ogilvie, L. (2013). Unique groups. In *Introduction to recreation and leisure* (2nd ed.). Champaign, IL: Human Kinetics.

Zabonick, R. (2016). A culture of risk management. Retrieved from www.campusrecmag.com/a-culture-of-risk-management/

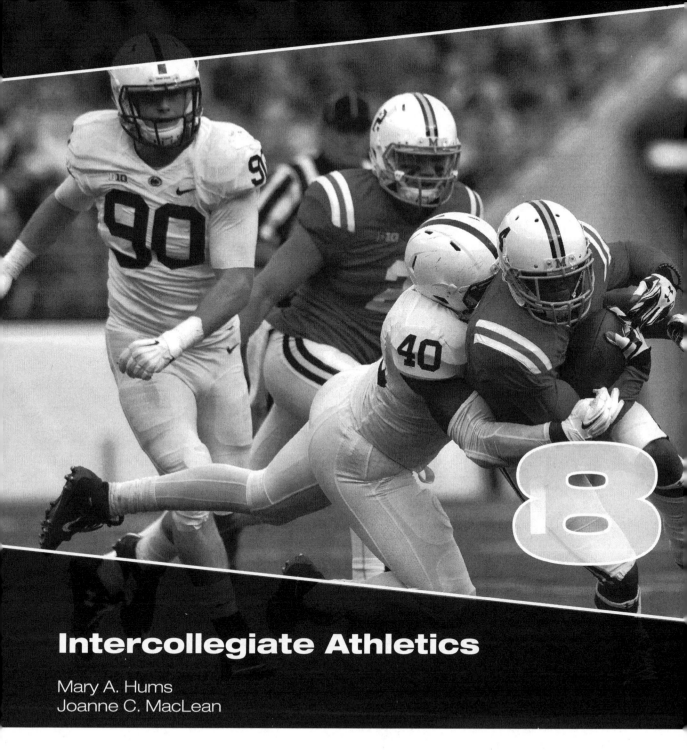

Intercollegiate Athletics

Mary A. Hums
Joanne C. MacLean

Click on a college website, open a newspaper, or turn on the television and you will immediately see the interest in North American college athletics. National championship events such as "The Final Four" are known worldwide. The spectacle of college sport will likely continue to grow and endure the test of time, due in part to the mass media's role in strengthening its appeal by bringing events and personalities directly into our homes. The appeal is strongest in the United States, but colleges and universities in many countries around the world also sponsor competitive athletic opportunities for their students. In the United States and Canada, colleges and universities support extensive competitive athletic programs. This type of competition is commonly known as *intercollegiate athletics.*

The appeal of intercollegiate athletics is unquestionable and at the same time paradoxical. From one perspective, the loyalty of cheering college students with painted faces, fully caught up in the excitement of events and intense rivalries, sometimes with national distinction at stake, is completely understandable. But viewed from another perspective, intercollegiate athletics is woven with problems. From the consumer viewpoint, the quality of play may not compare with professional leagues. In addition, a long history of abuses, excesses, and cheating has plagued intercollegiate athletics, challenging the very core concepts of sport in general and amateurism specifically. Ideals such as fairness, honesty, character development, competitive balance, and the dual role of the student-athlete have been questioned. In some cases the very existence of such an enterprise in connection with an educational institution has been called into question. Some of these issues, along with the huge costs of programming, have resulted in some schools dropping programs. In order to manage in times of fiscal restraint brought about by decreased resources and increased costs and to comply, or at least to project the image of compliance with Title IX legislation—the federal law that prohibits sex discrimination in education—some colleges have resorted to dropping teams. For example, in 2015 the University of Tennessee (UT)-Chattanooga dropped men's indoor and outdoor track and field teams, a surprising move given the long history of the program (Shahen & Heron, 2015). UT-Chattanooga is just one example of dozens of Division I schools who have eliminated men's teams like wrestling, gymnastics, and swimming in order to comply with Title IX (Thomas, 2011a). However, the reality of discontinuing sports in order to comply with Title IX is perhaps masking the real issue of poor fiscal decision making on behalf of Athletic Department personnel. Football teams may lose millions of dollars and yet no one suggests dropping football. Unfortunately, the financial decisions intentionally supported by colleges are sometimes labelled Title IX issues, when in reality, Title IX is about fairness of opportunity for both men and women. As well, some institutions have also been padding women's rosters with practice players who never compete, in order to increase the proportion of women reportedly involved in intercollegiate athletics (Thomas, 2011b). Yet despite these and many other issues, consumer enthusiasm for intercollegiate athletics continues to grow as evidenced by ticket sales and television revenues (Meyer & Zimbalist, 2017).

Growth serves as the perfect one-word descriptor of 21st-century college athletics in the United States. Interest in supporting the local team gathered momentum to a point where now more than a thousand colleges and universities offer intercollegiate sport in the United States alone. Fueled by this momentum, the sheer magnitude of intercollegiate athletics may be one reason for its enduring and expanding appeal.

Different perspectives provide different insights into this phenomenal growth. A historian might suggest that the leadership of President Theodore Roosevelt and a group of college presidents provided the original momentum for the growth of college athletics when they intervened in college football to promote more extensive rules and safety requirements in 1905. A sociologist might identify the place of sport in American society and the feelings of personal success and hometown pride when the local college team wins (MacGaffey, 2013). A psychologist might point to improved psychological health with individuals identifying strongly with a local sport team (Wann, 2006). The economist might suggest that colleges and universities need the revenue generated by athletics, whether from television, recruiting students, or developing and managing the image of the institution. Other viewpoints exist, but one thing is sure: intercollegiate athletics is a major component of the sport industry of North America.

This chapter focuses on the many differences between the governance of organizations delivering collegiate sport in the United States (the National Collegiate Athletic Association [NCAA] and the National Association of Intercollegiate Athletics [NAIA], and Junior, Small and Christian Colleges) such as size, financial capacity, committee structures, scope of operations, sports supported, and rules and philosophy. Distinctions also exist in the governance and policy development between collegiate sport organizations in other countries around the world. Although collegiate sport exists in a number of countries worldwide, and athletes from these organizations represent their countries at the World University Games (Federation Internationale du Sport Universitaire [FISU] Games; see Chapter 9), their college sport programs may differ substantially from those in the United States. For instance, the British Universities and Colleges Sport (BUCS) has 157 member universities, while University Sport New Zealand (USNZ) has nine member universities, compared to the larger NCAA which has over 1,280 members. Some countries within Africa and South America may have very limited sport offerings, with emphasis on sports unknown or less popular in North America, such as footvolley (mix of football and beach volleyball), jujitsu, biribol (volleyball in a swimming pool), and running events. The big business nature of American collegiate sport fueled by considerable fan interest and television reach (and revenue) is not necessarily mirrored in other countries around the world. U Sports, the organization governing university sport in Canada, has far smaller membership of only 56 institutions and concomitant economic impact. The organizations that manage sport and create the governance structures and policy for operations are unique to the settings, political environments, and historical events of each location. Therefore, the umbrella organizations delivering collegiate sport in countries around the world vary significantly in their size, capacity, programs, rules and regulations, and structures.

Let's turn our attention now to the governance of collegiate athletics in the United States. Exactly how is it organized? How are rules made, and who decides the issues of the day? A brief look at the history and evolution of intercollegiate sport will answer those questions.

HISTORY OF AMERICAN INTERCOLLEGIATE ATHLETICS

www

British Universities and Colleges Sport (BUCS)
www.bucs.org.uk/ homepage.asp

University Sport New Zealand (USNZ)
www.universitysport.org.nz/

U Sports
https://usports.ca/en

Often the largest and most popular events are born of the humblest beginnings, and this is exactly the case with intercollegiate athletics. The idea for athletic competition did not come from educators, nor was it a part of the curriculum. Rather, it originated with the student body.

The Beginning

College athletics began as recreational activities organized by students to meet their desire for both physical and social activities (Davenport, 1985). Although faculty members were not involved, they accepted the idea that students needed some diversions from classroom activity. It is easy to understand how college athletics developed. Two groups of students got together to play a game in the late afternoon sun; later, over dinner, the victors boasted of their success. Perhaps their classmates listened in and decided to show up for the next game to cheer on their friends. Next, for even more bragging rights, the victorious group then challenged the college in the next town. This, basically, is the story of the first intercollegiate competition, when a crew (rowing) race was organized between Harvard and Yale in 1852 (Scott, 1951).

Original Events

The next organized intercollegiate activity was baseball. The first baseball game was between Amherst College and Williams College in 1859 (Davenport, 1985). Such student-led activities gained significant interest among spectators and some notice from college faculty and administration. Administration noticed that winning athletic contests helped recruit students to campus and provide some positive attention for the college. Only ten years later, on November 6, 1869, the first intercollegiate football game was played between Rutgers and Princeton (Davenport, 1985). Challenges for competition became more and more common. This growth was not always viewed positively, however. Administrators were concerned about the unproductive nature of athletic contests, and significant resistance was voiced against the emerging popularity of intercollegiate football.

Despite the attitude of some university administrators, tremendous interest in collegiate football was evident by the 1890s. A win-at-any-cost mentality developed, and to please the spectators in the overflowing college grandstands, players and coaches without affiliation to the college were inserted in the lineup. Street brawls became common after games:

> In 1893 New York was thrown into a virtual frenzy by the annual Thanksgiving game between Yale and Princeton. Hotels were jammed . . . Clergymen cut short their Thanksgiving Day services in order to get off to the game in time. Clearly, football had arrived. (Rudolph, 1990, p. 375)

Sports were becoming so popular on college campuses that they were likened to small business enterprises (Davenport, 1985).

Birth of College Sport Organizations

Up to this point, college athletic activities were organized and operated by students, and merely tolerated by the university administration. But it was becoming evident that athletic teams served as a unifying function of the college. Heroes emerged; public interest grew, as did the public relations opportunities. All of these factors, along with the potential for revenue generation, resulted in university administrators changing their position. College presidents and their inner circles realized successful sports teams could generate additional resources for their cash-strapped institutions, as well as draw both political favor and alumni support. College administrators, especially college faculty members, moved to take over management and control of athletic programs. Athletic department personnel as we know them today did not exist.

On January 11, 1895, an historic meeting of faculty representatives was held in Chicago to develop eligibility and participation rules for football. This was the inaugural meeting of the Intercollegiate Conference of Faculty Representatives, forerunner to the Big Ten (Davenport, 1985). Soon thereafter, personnel in other regions of the United States also met and copied many of the rules developed at this initial meeting. Faculty exercised control over schedule development and equipment purchase. Playing rules and regulations were enforced, and some eligibility and financial restrictions were put in place.

About the same time, an alarming number of football players were seriously injured as a result of popular practices such as gang tackling and mass formations. In 1905, 18 athletes were killed and 143 seriously injured while playing collegiate football (Gerdy, 1997), prompting President Theodore Roosevelt to intervene. He called representatives from Harvard, Yale, and Princeton to two White House conferences to discuss the problems. At the request of Chancellor Henry M. MacCracken of New York University, representatives of 13 institutions met in New York City in December 1905 (Smith, 2011). The original intent of this meeting and a follow-up meeting later that month was to resolve issues related to football. However, the result was much more significant. More university administrators shared concerns, and as a result, 62 members founded the Intercollegiate Athletic Association of the United States (IAAUS) to oversee and regulate all college sports. The association was officially constituted on March 31, 1906.

Evolution of College Sport Organizations

The development of the IAAUS represented a pivotal moment in the history of American intercollegiate athletics and marked the beginning of an era in which collegiate sport instituted rules, regulations, supervision, and philosophical direction. Faculty members in physical education departments were hired to coach teams and administer programs.

In 1910, the IAAUS renamed itself the National Collegiate Athletic Association. During its initial years, the NCAA was composed only of faculty members from its affiliate institutions. It was a discussion group and rules-making body. Collegiate sports continued to grow, and more rules committees were formed. The evolution of the NCAA continued, and in 1921, the first national championship was held in track and field. Other sports and more championships were gradually added over the years. By 1973, the membership was divided into three legislative and competitive divisions (Divisions I, II, and III) based on institutional size. Subsequently, Division I members voted to subdivide football into Divisions I-A and I-AA. More recently, Division I football now uses the categories Football Bowl Subdivision (FBS) and Football Championship Subdivision (FCS). As the NCAA has grown in events and membership, a shift in power away from the collection of colleges to the centralized authority of the NCAA has taken place. Today, the NCAA is a large, powerful organization staffed by more than 500 full-time employees and delivering 90 championships in 24 sports across 3 divisions; its National Office is located in Indianapolis (NCAA, 2017f).

Growth of Women's Sport

In the United States, female participation in intercollegiate sport was conspicuously missing in the beginning. Little in the way of formal competition existed for women until 1971, when women physical educators established the Association for Intercollegiate Athletics for Women (AIAW). Several national championships were sponsored, and women's intercollegiate athletics gained momentum, quickly becoming an important component of college athletics. This interest prompted the NCAA to expand its structure to include programming for women just ten years after the AIAW was established. The first NCAA programming for women occurred in 1980 when Divisions II and III took a leadership role by adding ten national championships for women. This historic action prompted an extensive governance plan to be passed in 1981–1982, including 19 additional women's championships, along with services and representation in decision making for administrators of women's athletics.

Historically Black Colleges and Universities

Historically black colleges and universities (HBCUs) are liberal arts institutions that were established before 1964 with the intention of serving the African American community in the United States. Those institutions with large African American student populations but founded after the *Brown v. Board of Education* ruling that outlawed racial segregation are known as "predominantly black," but not "historically black."

Today, 107 HBCUs exist as public and private institutions, including community colleges, four-year institutions, and medical and law schools. Over the years, HBCU graduates have gone on to make names for themselves in all spectrums of society including athletics, where some notable graduates include NFL Most Valuable Player (MVP) Steve McNair (Alcorn State University) and Eddie Robinson (Grambling State University), one of the winningest coaches in college football history (408 wins at one institution). HBCUs are affiliated with both the NCAA Division I and II, and the NAIA. Examples of HBCU institutions with traditions of excellence in college athletics include Morgan State University located in Maryland, Norfolk State University and Hampton University in Virginia, Grambling State University in Louisiana, and Florida A & M in Florida.

Although the name might lead one to believe that only black student-athletes attend HBCUs, today their student populations, while predominantly black, do contain a more representative picture of society. As such, most HBCU athletic mission statements emphasize this diverse aspect to their population, such as the one from Morgan State University in Exhibit 8.1.

Morgan State Bears
www.morganstatebears.com

However, in comparison to more "traditional" colleges and universities, HBCU athletic budgets are much lower. In 2016, only six black schools ranked among the top 200 (out of 351) athletic budgets in Division I (Bolling, 2016). Some small schools, such as Division I FCS Southern University, rely heavily on one or two games to generate the majority of the revenue for their athletic departments, usually an annual game between two schools, or what is termed "a guarantee game," where small schools travel to face national powerhouses. Two examples of guarantee games include Delaware State's game against the University of Michigan or when Bethune-Cookman played the University of Miami. While these games usually guarantee a substantial payday for the small school, it is hard to compete against more resource-rich institutions. Since the economic downturn in 2008, many HBCU institutions have cut programs, left vacant positions unfiled or eliminated them altogether, and slashed team travel budgets (Trahan, 2016).

exhibit   **8.1**   The Mission of Athletics at Morgan State University

Morgan State University Mission Statement

The Morgan State University Department of Intercollegiate Athletics is an integral part of the University that strives to achieve the same standards of excellence within the athletics program that exists in the various academic disciplines at the University. Further, the athletics department embraces the concept that the student-athletes are first and foremost students, possessing individual rights, academic abilities, personal interests and ambitions comparable to those of other members of the general student body. The Morgan State University Athletics Department is committed to the principle and practice of gender equity. This commitment shall be reflected in every aspect of departmental operations. The Athletics Department is committed to abiding by the rules established by the NCAA and the Mid-Eastern Athletics Conference. It acknowledges and upholds the concepts of institutional control and broad based participation within the University community in the development and review of the Athletics policies by the University President, the Athletics Representative and the Student-Athlete Advisory Board. All Athletics booster organizations, alumni and other groups and individuals who represent the University's Athletics interests are expected by the University, the NCAA and MEAC for the governance of its intercollegiate athletics programs.

Source: Morgan State Bears (2017).

GOVERNANCE

The growth, popularity, and subsequent reform of college sport dictated a more formal approach to managing and governing intercollegiate athletics. The NCAA is the largest and oldest organization formed for this purpose, and its history is closely intertwined with the growth of intercollegiate athletics. However, other organizations also govern intercollegiate athletics. In the United States, the NAIA is another umbrella organization of like-minded institutions, often compared in philosophical orientation to NCAA Division II schools. The National Junior College Athletic Association and the National Small College Athletic Association each exist to oversee the athletic programs of junior and small colleges, respectively. Finally, the National Christian College Athletic Association administers intercollegiate competition for Christian schools.

National Collegiate Athletic Association

www

National Collegiate Athletic
Association
www.ncaa.org

The NCAA has global recognition, thanks to television and marketing efforts. It is technically a voluntary association of colleges and universities, run by a President and staffed by about 500 employees. Members of the NCAA consider issues and policies affecting more than one region, thus making them national issues.

Mission

The NCAA is devoted to the expert administration of intercollegiate athletics for its membership. The core purpose of the NCAA is to govern competition in a fair, safe, equitable, and sportsmanlike manner. According to the NCAA (2017g), the goals of the organization are specific to supporting student-athletes with academic services, opportunities and experiences, financial assistance, wellness and insurance, and personal and professional development. The association supplies a governance structure to provide rules and establish consistent policy through which all NCAA member institutions operate. NCAA literature states seven core values that guide its purpose and operations, as presented in Exhibit 8.2.

Membership

The NCAA is comprised of member institutions whose representatives retain voting privileges on setting policy and directing the future of intercollegiate athletics. Currently 1,260 institutions, conferences, and affiliated organizations are members of the NCAA (NCAA, 2017n).

It is important to note that NCAA members are institutions, not individuals. Institutions are afforded membership by virtue of their mission in higher education, along with other membership criteria. All sizes and types of institutions are eligible for membership, as long as they are accredited by the

NCAA Core Values	*exhibit* **8.2**

The Association—through its member institutions, conferences and national office staff—shares a belief in and commitment to:

- The collegiate model of athletics in which students participate as an avocation, balancing their academic, social and athletics experiences.
- The highest levels of integrity and sportsmanship.
- The pursuit of excellence in both academics and athletics.
- The supporting role that intercollegiate athletics plays in the higher education mission and in enhancing the sense of community and strengthening the identity of member institutions.
- An inclusive culture that fosters equitable participation for student-athletes and career opportunities for coaches and administrators from diverse backgrounds.
- Respect for institutional autonomy and philosophical differences.
- Presidential leadership of intercollegiate athletics at the campus, conference and national levels.

Source: NCAA (2017h).

recognized agency within their academic region, offer at least one sport for both men and women in each of the three traditional sport seasons, abide by the rules and regulations set forth by the NCAA (as certified by the CEO), and agree to cooperate fully with NCAA enforcement programs (NCAA, 2017n).

NCAA member institutions belong to one of three divisions labeled Division I, II, or III. The main criteria used for establishing an institution's divisional classification are its size, number of sports offered, financial base and sport-sponsorship minimums, focus of programming, football and basketball scheduling requirements, and availability of athletic grants-in-aid (NCAA, 2017n). Division I (DI) football institutions are further subdivided into I–FBS and I–FCS. DI–FBS programs must meet minimum paid-football attendance criteria. Institutions competing in Division I in sports other than football are categorized simply as Division I. Divided fairly evenly among each division are the 1,098 active institutional members: DI has 347, DII has 309, and DIII has 442 (NCAA, 2017j).

Finally, athletic conferences and affiliate organizations are also members of the NCAA. There are 98 voting athletic conferences such as the Big Ten, Southeastern Conference, the Ivy League, the East Coast Conference, and the New England Collegiate Conference; and 39 affiliated organizations such as the National Association of Collegiate Directors of Athletics (NACDA) and the National Association for College Admissions Counseling (NACAC). Affiliate members must be nonprofit organizations whose function relates to NCAA sport and that involve coaches or university administrators.

Financials

The NCAA is a nonprofit organization, yet it is also a multi-million-dollar enterprise. Given the breadth of focus described above, it requires substantial revenue to fund an incredibly wide-ranging agenda. It is in a healthy financial situation, reporting revenues over expenses of almost $295 million in 2016. Revenues are generated from television rights, championships, royalties, investments, sales and services, and philanthropic contributions. The association's expenses include championships, special events, revenue sharing, association-wide programs, management, and the NCAA Foundation. At the end of 2016, the NCAA held net assets in excess of over $530 million (NCAA, 2017i).

Association-Wide and Division-Specific Structure

As with most other self-governing organizations, the NCAA began and existed for many years with a governance structure allotting one vote to each member institution. At an annual national convention, members debated issues and voted on matters of policy. This organizational structure was reformed on August 1, 1997. In general, the reform provided each division greater autonomy for managing division-specific matters and gave university presidents more involvement in and control of developing legislation. For instance, in Division I the one-vote-per-institution principle was replaced with a system based on conference representation. Rather than every member voting on each issue at an annual convention, a 20-member Board of Directors is charged with managing all legislation, and one elected member from each conference votes on behalf of the conference. Members of the Board of Directors are institutional CEOs or college presidents, a move made, as mentioned above, to ensure more presidential involvement in intercollegiate athletics. In 2014 the Board was expanded to include the student-athlete, Faculty Athletic Representative (FAR), Athletic Director (AD), and female administrator voice. Of course, the Board of Directors is not able to complete all of the Division's business.

DIVISIONAL GOVERNANCE STRUCTURE. Prior to 2008 the Division I Management Council reported to the Board of Directors. However, the Management Council was then replaced with two 31-member councils: the Leadership Council and the Legislative Council. These changes were prompted to increase efficiency and in order to provide more support to the Board of Directors. Today one Division Council exists with a variety of committees that assist with issues of strategy and policy development. The Council is comprised of athletic administrators and faculty athletic representatives, academics from the college faculty appointed to provide their perspective to athletic policy making, and student-athletes.

Committees report to the Council in the following areas with variable membership numbers presented in brackets: Student-Athlete Experience (10), Strategic Vision and Planning (10), Legislative (19), Competition Oversight (19), Men's Basketball Oversight (12), Football Oversight (12), Women's Basketball Oversight (12), and Student-Athlete Advisory (32). In effect, NCAA Division I is organized into three layers within its decision-making structure (see Exhibit 8.3).

Divisions II and III are structured similarly to Division I but have several important distinctions for conducting division-specific business. Each has a Board of Directors made up of institutional CEOs, but the body is called the Division II Presidents Council, not a Board. The Division II Presidents Council includes 16 presidents, while the Division III Presidents Council comprises 18 presidents of institutions belonging to Division III. Both Divisions II and III also have Management Councils (with 27 and 22 members, respectively), but Division III has broadened the representation of this group by adding both institutional CEOs and student-athlete representatives to the athletic administrators and faculty athletic representatives comprising the Division I and II councils. Although Division II and III are structured in a similar way to Division I, one very important distinction remains: legislation in both divisions is considered by the traditional one-school, one-vote method, as opposed to the conference representation used by Division I. Both Divisions II and III have a committee structure to deal with issues specific to their business and sports.

exhibit 8.3 Division I Governance Structure

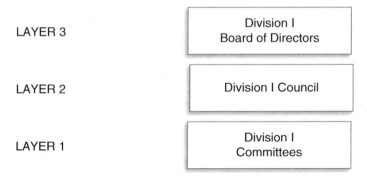

LAYER 3	Division I Board of Directors
LAYER 2	Division I Council
LAYER 1	Division I Committees

ASSOCIATION-WIDE GOVERNANCE STRUCTURE.   As you can see, the NCAA is a large enterprise. Each division has many members and layers of committee structures for managing the business of intercollegiate sport. As with any large conglomerate, however, there is always the need to oversee association-wide issues. This coordinating function falls to the NCAA Board of Governors, comprised of 18 voting members of the Board of Directors and the Presidents Councils of the three divisions (eight from Division I–FBS, two from Division I–FCS, two from Division I, three from Division II, and three from Division III). The NCAA President and Chairs of the Division Management Councils also belong to the Board of Governors as ex-officio (nonvoting) members. The Board of Governors is commissioned to ensure each division operates consistently with the overall principles, policies, and values of the NCAA.

In addition, 11 association-wide committees exist to ensure that the principles, policies, and values of the NCAA on common issues like medical and safety concerns are articulated and communicated. They include Competitive Safeguards and Medical Aspects of Sports, Sportsmanship and Ethical Conduct, Women's Athletics, Honors, Minority Opportunities and Interests, Olympic Sports, Playing Rules, Postgraduate Scholarship, Research, and Walter Byers Scholarship. See Exhibit 8.4 for a summary of the governance structure of the NCAA.

The NCAA has undergone much change during the last couple of decades. Major initiatives in enforcement and governance have occurred since 1981. An agenda of reform and strategy of college presidential involvement in the affairs of the organization, along with a philosophical push to put academics first in the athlete–education dyad was emphasized through changes to rules, governance structures, and institutional change. The

Governance Structure of the NCAA   *exhibit* **8.4**

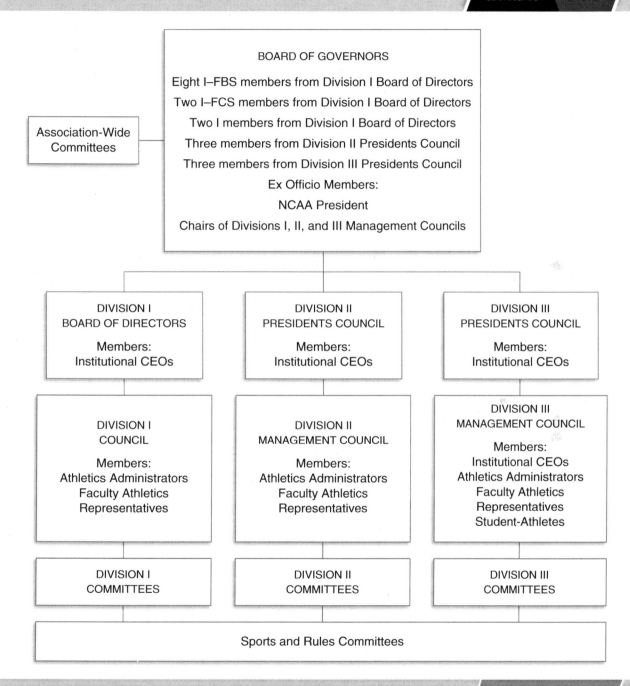

BOARD OF GOVERNORS

Eight I–FBS members from Division I Board of Directors

Two I–FCS members from Division I Board of Directors

Two I members from Division I Board of Directors

Three members from Division II Presidents Council

Three members from Division III Presidents Council

Ex Officio Members:

NCAA President

Chairs of Divisions I, II, and III Management Councils

Association-Wide Committees

DIVISION I BOARD OF DIRECTORS

Members: Institutional CEOs

DIVISION II PRESIDENTS COUNCIL

Members: Institutional CEOs

DIVISION III PRESIDENTS COUNCIL

Members: Institutional CEOs

DIVISION I COUNCIL

Members: Athletics Administrators Faculty Athletics Representatives

DIVISION II MANAGEMENT COUNCIL

Members: Athletics Administrators Faculty Athletics Representatives

DIVISION III MANAGEMENT COUNCIL

Members: Institutional CEOs Athletics Administrators Faculty Athletics Representatives Student-Athletes

DIVISION I COMMITTEES

DIVISION II COMMITTEES

DIVISION III COMMITTEES

Sports and Rules Committees

Source: NCAA (2017n).

NCAA's focus on Academic Progress Rate (APR), for example, is indicative of the action taken to improve graduation rates. Although many argue that the changes have not worked or do not go far enough, that significant changes have been made is evident given the size and complexity of the *NCAA Division Manuals and sport-specific Rule Books*. New rules have evolved governing athlete eligibility and financial aid, cost containment, recruitment, coach salaries, drug testing, championships, women's issues, and student-athlete welfare. Television has contributed to the growth and has publicized such issues as academics and amateurism, expectations put on student-athletes, growth and finance, diversity, and external interventions by government and courts of law. As the organization and its members' goals and values evolve, one area has not faded: problems within the NCAA continue to be visible and critics are more vocal and active than ever before.

On January 17, 2015, the NCAA granted autonomy to five "power" conferences including the ACC (Atlantic Coast Conference), Big Ten, Big 12, Pac-12, and SEC (Southeastern Conference), allowing them to pass legislation through their own voting process (Trahan, 2015). Legislation is then adopted as rules changes by all Division I NCAA member institutions. Legislation may also be implemented by the NCAA, however, by granting autonomy to the power conferences, member schools have more power to control decisions on operation. While the power is passed on, certain rules, particularly those pertaining to maintaining athlete amateurism, are expected to remain unchanged (Trahan, 2015).

National Association of Intercollegiate Athletics

National Association of
Intercollegiate Athletics
www.naia.org

The NAIA is another national association governing intercollegiate athletics in the United States. More than 250 mostly small-size institutions comprise the NAIA, many of which emphasize the link between education and athletics more strongly than revenue generation. Initially formed to regulate intercollegiate basketball, the association was called the National Association of Intercollegiate Basketball (NAIB) until 1952, when the organization changed its name to the NAIA.

Mission

NAIA institutions view athletics as "co-curricular," that is, as part of the overall educational process, something that goes hand in hand with the pursuit of academic goals. They believe involvement in athletics will enrich the student-athlete's college experience, balancing success in both the classroom and on the field of play. The NAIA National Office is the hub of organization and planning for national championships, and it defines the rules, regulations, and structures that govern member institutions. The purpose of the association is presented in Exhibit 8.5.

Purpose of the National Association of Intercollegiate Athletics *exhibit* **8.5**

The purpose of the NAIA is to "promote education and development of students through intercollegiate athletics participation. Member institutions, although varied and diverse, share common commitment to high standards and the principle that athletics serve as an integral part of education".

Source: NAIA (2017b).

Fundamental to the NAIA mission is their Champions of Character initiative. Champions of Character is a training program that attempts to instill and align the core values of integrity, respect, responsibility, sportsmanship, and servant leadership into the behaviors of athletes, coaches, and administrators. The student-athlete Champions of Character orientation program is known as Live 5. It is an interactive program that teaches student-athletes how to apply the NAIA core values to their lives in and outside sport.

WWW

Champions of Character
http://www.naia.org/
ChampionsOfCharacter.
dbml?DB_OEM_ID=27900

Live 5
www.naia.org/ViewArticle.
Dbml?DB_OEM_ID=
27900&ATCLID=205421991

Membership

Like the NCAA, NAIA members are institutions. NAIA membership is rather diverse, with an assorted group of institutions around the United States and a few members from Canada. The NAIA has nearly 250 member colleges and universities in 21 conferences across the United States (NAIA, 2017a). It has two categories of membership: active and associate members (NAIA, 2017d). Active members consist of four-year colleges and universities and upper-level two-year institutions in the United States or Canada that award undergraduate degrees. These institutions must be fully accredited by one of six institutional accrediting bodies from across the United States (such as the Southern Association of Colleges and Schools Commission on Colleges and the New England Association of Schools and Colleges Commission on Institutions of Higher Education), must abide by the constitution and bylaws of the NAIA, must be accepted for membership by the Council of Presidents, and must pay membership fees. Associate members are required to meet the same standards as active members except for full accreditation by one of the six accrediting bodies. These institutions must, however, be committed to the development of a fully accredited baccalaureate (undergraduate) program. Associate members are not eligible for postseason competition, nor do their institutional representatives vote on issues, serve on committees, or participate in national awards programs.

GAIL DENT, *Associate Director of Public and Media Relations,*

NCAA, Indianapolis, IN

I work in Public and Media Relations for the NCAA, answering national and local media inquiries and assisting national office staff and the membership with internal and external messaging opportunities. I work directly with staff in diversity and inclusion, championships, corporate relations, student-athlete leadership development, and with our Hall of Champions museum.

One issue often discussed at the NCAA is health awareness for student-athletes, which can be anything from mental health concerns to concussions in sports. Secondly, I think we'll continue to hear more on the image and likeness topics. Additionally, we will continue to develop and improve policies surrounding academics and getting student-athletes closer to graduation.

One area I continue to work with centers on diversity and inclusion issues. There has been more dialogue in the membership today on complex topics that haven't been discussed broadly in years past. We continue to have discussions and messaging around racial and gender issues to stay abreast of how that impacts our membership and student-athletes. Now we're hearing more discussion around LGBTQ [lesbian, gay, bisexual, trans and queer) issues and how to bridge understanding. The NCAA was one of the first sports organizations to create a transgender policy and the Association has addressed concerns surrounding efforts to create a safe and respectful environment for its fans, student-athletes, and administrators at championships. There is also now more discussion around student-athletes with both learning and physical disabilities. I believe we'll continue to hear about matters happening on campuses and will hold on-going discussions about inclusion and diversity topics more openly in years to come.

Our membership recently restructured at the Division I level in an effort to allow more autonomy or flexibility, which should enhance the student-athlete experience and the overall well-being of our athletes. The new structure also provides student-athletes with more voice, through voting, at the various levels of decision making. Division II and III continue to discuss issues that impact their schools and student-athletes, and are continually working to enhance opportunities for athletes though initiatives like Division II's Life In the Balance. I think one of the key challenges is helping the public and those new to the membership understand that the Association is a diverse body of schools with diverse missions. Our NCAA website at www.ncaa.org has information to help people not only understand the structure, but it also serves as a platform to access current news in an ever-evolving organization.

Helping people understand that the NCAA is an Association focused on academics and athletics in the higher education model is a key mission. The public needs to recognize that many of the decisions in intercollegiate athletics are actually made by committees comprised of athletics and academic administrators. That helps people understand how the policies/rules are made. As a large Association with diverse missions, decisions will impact divisions independently or as a whole. We'll continue to see divisions moving in synch, as well as seeing policy decisions that are best for each specific division. We observe best practices being shared that may lead to policy discussion and future decisions, too. I was pleased to see the membership recommit to diversity hiring and inclusive measures in the Association, and instituting a diversity pledge that was supported by college presidents and chancellors and constituent groups.

The NCAA's work in health education surrounding concussions and the protection of student-athletes will continue. Helping the public understand that intercollegiate athletics is a pathway to opportunities in college and erasing many of the myths about the Association will also be key as we move forward in the future.

Individual institutions become members of one of the NAIA's organized regions and conferences. Issues that impact the overall association or that deal with national championships are deliberated at national meetings or in committee forums.

Financials

The NAIA is a not-for-profit association funded through membership fees, sponsorship, championship revenues, and merchandise sales. It collects fees for running national championships and other special programs and shares net revenues with its membership.

Organizational Structure

While the organization is led by a President & CEO who manages the large NAIA National Office in Kansas City, Missouri, the NAIA is organized to govern its business through a series of councils and committees. The association deliberately places the membership at the top of the organizational chart to emphasize the importance of each institution and its student-athletes for whom programming is organized. Responsive to the membership is the Council of Presidents (COP). Similar to the NCAA, the NAIA relegates control and responsibility of a school's intercollegiate athletic program to the President or CEO of the institution. Each of the 21 Conferences within the NAIA elects one institutional CEO to represent the conference membership on the COP. Several other independent, at-large, or ex officio (nonvoting) Presidents are appointed members based on expertise. An elected Executive Committee, made up of a chair, three other members, and the NAIA administrative head, manages the business of the Council between meetings. The COP employs and supervises the President & CEO of the organization, and has final authority for all fiscal matters, membership applications, and council recommendations. Each member of the Council holds one vote. Exhibit 8.6 illustrates the governance structure of the NAIA.

The NAIA is further subdivided into three major administrative groups: the National Administrative Council, the Council of Faculty Athletics Representatives, and the Council for Student-Athletes.

1. NATIONAL ADMINISTRATIVE COUNCIL (NAC). The NAC is responsible for all sport-related business. Its members are comprised of those individuals at each institution who hold the position of Athletic Director, Sports Information Director, and Coach. An elected President and Vice President, chosen from among the Association Chairs, and a Vice Chair govern it. The purpose of the NAC is to develop rules for national championships and postseason play, and to oversee each of the associations.

exhibit   **8.6**   Governance Structure of the NAIA

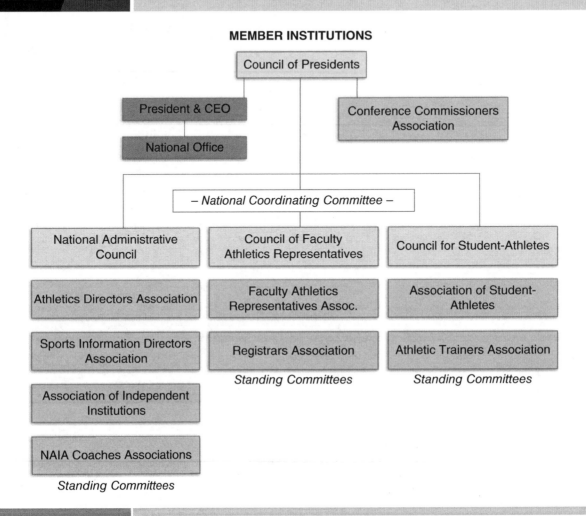

MEMBER INSTITUTIONS

Council of Presidents

President & CEO

National Office

Conference Commissioners Association

– National Coordinating Committee –

National Administrative Council

Council of Faculty Athletics Representatives

Council for Student-Athletes

Athletics Directors Association

Faculty Athletics Representatives Assoc.

Association of Student-Athletes

Sports Information Directors Association

Registrars Association

Athletic Trainers Association

Standing Committees

Standing Committees

Association of Independent Institutions

NAIA Coaches Associations

Standing Committees

Source: NAIA (2017a).

2. **COUNCIL OF FACULTY ATHLETICS REPRESENTATIVES (CFAR).**   This Council oversees, evaluates, and implements NAIA academic standards. It performs this role via interactions with college registrars and faculty athletics representatives. This committee is comprised of faculty members, plus staff liaison members. The CFAR has a mandate for setting operational policies for academic standards within the organization and to liaise with the Registrars' and Faculty Athletics Representatives.

3. **COUNCIL FOR STUDENT-ATHLETES (CSA).**   The CSA promotes the student and academic priorities clearly endorsed by the NAIA. It is made up of administrators and student-athletes who develop policies, services and programming to support the athlete experience. Topics of interest include

the health and safety of student-athletes, and leadership and professional development opportunities.

Committees managing specific elements of NAIA business, such as the Committee on Gender Equity, the Conduct and Ethics Committee, and the National Eligibility Committee, serve each of the preceding three Councils. Each group, along with the COP, is committed to educational athletics and the true spirit of competition as described by five basic principles: (1) respect, (2) integrity, (3) responsibility, (4) servant leadership, and (5) sportsmanship (NAIA, 2017c).

Currently, the NAIA offers 25 national championships. Teams qualify for their championships through regional conferences. The NAIA sponsors a slate of 14 different sports (baseball, basketball, competitive cheer and dance, cross-country, football, golf, indoor track and field, outdoor track and field, soccer, softball, swimming and diving, tennis, volleyball, and wrestling), with competition scheduled for men in 11 and women in

WWW

National Junior College
Athletic Association
www.njcaa.org

United States Collegiate
Athletic Association
www.theuscaa.com

National Christian College
Athletic Association
www.thenccaa.org

Governance Structure of the NJCAA   *exhibit* **8.7**

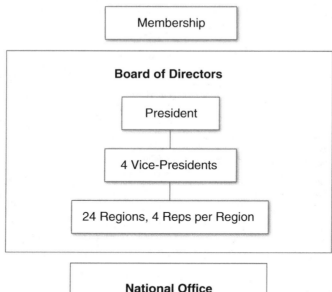

10 sports. The organization has created two divisions for basketball for both men and women, allowing individual schools to select their level of competitive entry.

Other College Athletic Associations in the United States

While the NCAA and NAIA are the largest and best-known associations governing collegiate athletics in the USA, they are not alone. The National

---

exhibit   **8.8**   Governance Structure of the USCAA

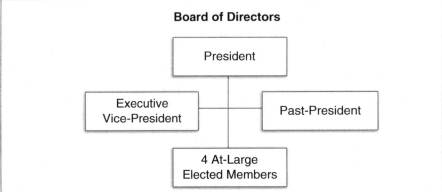

Junior College Athletic Association (NJCAA) was established in 1938 and governs intercollegiate competition for two-year colleges, the United States Collegiate Athletic Association (USCAA) hosts championships for small colleges in nine sports, and the National Christian College Athletic Association (NCCAA) was founded in 1968 to promote intercollegiate sport participation with Christian perspective. These organizations are typically smaller in reach and each have specific missions, memberships, and financials that you can check out on their websites.

The governing structures of the NJCAA, USCAA, and NCCAA are presented in Exhibits 8.7, 8.8 and 8.9.

Governance Structure of the NCCAA   *exhibit* **8.9**

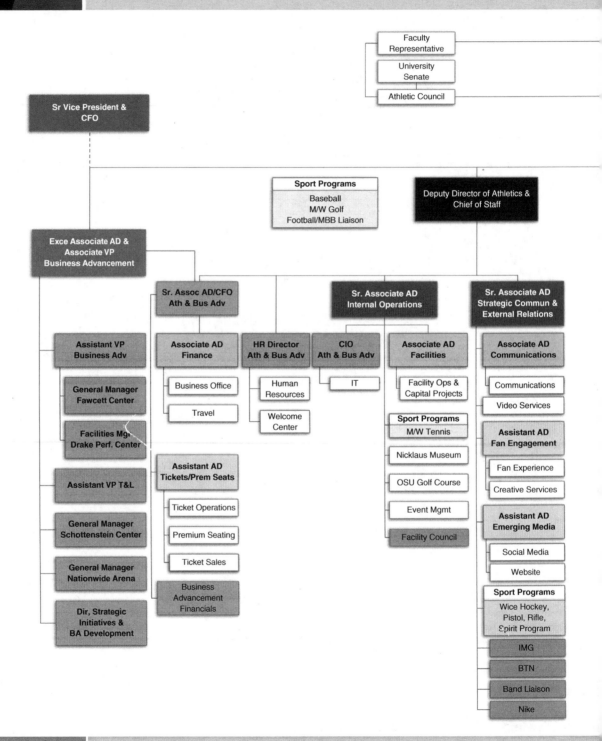

exhibit **8.10**   Organizational Structure of Ohio State University Department of Athletics and Business Advancement

Continued.

exhibit   8.10

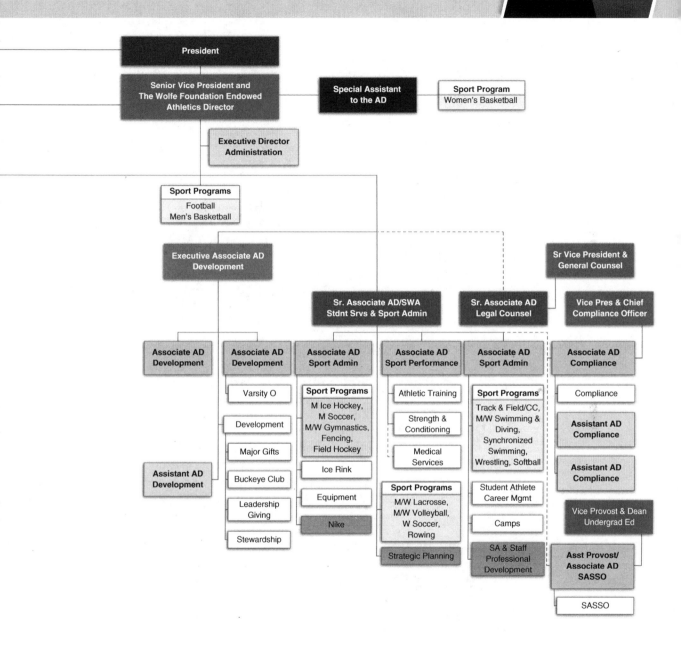

Individual Campus Athletics Management

The organizations discussed above operate on the national level and are comprised of institutional members providing competitive opportunities for their athletes and coaches. A series of rules and regulations, policies, procedures, and bylaws help regulate the competition, focusing on everything from the underlying purpose and philosophy of the competition to how events are operated. Although a great deal of regulatory power exists with the leaders of the national associations and coalitions of larger institutions, the day-to-day responsibility for the intercollegiate athletic program resides on campus in the college Athletic Department.

College athletic departments can be very large or very small, as illustrated in Exhibits 8.10 and 8.11. Larger colleges and universities employ a wide variety of sport professionals to manage, deliver, and supervise intercollegiate athletics: administrators, coaches, trainers, facility and event managers, and faculty representatives all play important roles in the intercollegiate program. Of course, all campus initiatives fall under the auspices of the President's Office. Over the years, the college or university president has had varying degrees of involvement in the athletic program. Today, direct involvement by the college president is more the rule than the exception. University Presidents are directly involved in the NCAA and NAIA, responsible as Board of Governors for strategic direction and financial oversight.

University President

The immense popularity of intercollegiate athletics became apparent early in its history as large crowds gathered to watch games and their outcomes became front-page news. The traditional attitude of college administrators toward student-life initiatives has been supportive but with a hands-off approach. Historically, Presidents have not meddled in Athletic Department business; instead, they hoped for positive results and no scandals. However, the proliferation of highly publicized violations and reported abuses garnered increased presidential interest in intercollegiate athletics. After nearly a decade of highly visible scandals, the Knight Foundation created a Commission on Intercollegiate Athletics (Knight Foundation, 2017). The purpose of the commission was to propose an agenda of reform, outlined in reports originally issued in 1993 (*Keeping Faith with the Student-Athlete*), in 2001 (*A Call to Action: Reconnecting College Sports and Higher Education*), and 2010 (*Restoring the Balance: Dollars, Values and the Future of College Sport*) (Knight Foundation Commission on Intercollegiate Athletics, 2017).

One of the proposals of the Knight Commission was increased presidential control over college athletics. The fear that intercollegiate athletics had become too large, was riddled with unethical behaviors, and was

Organizational Structure Typical of a Small College Athletic Department   *exhibit* **8.11**

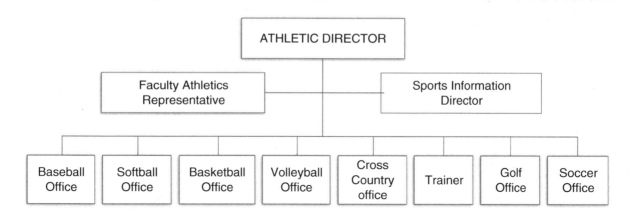

separate from the academic mission of the institution led to the proposal for greater presidential and senior academic management involvement. As a result, the NCAA, for example, holds Presidents accountable for member conduct and requires that they be involved in developing and managing policy through the Board of Directors and the Council of Presidents. In essence, presidential involvement is the result of negativity, corruption, and deceit. However, increased presidential involvement has also resulted from the potential institutional benefits of athletics participation, not the least of which is money. Developing an institutional image of excellence, increasing alumni involvement, and recruiting new students have always been positive goals for university Presidents, but the potential for revenue generation has led to a more serious focus.

Gerdy (1997, p. 9) summarizes the enhanced role of the university president in college athletics:

> This explosion of media attention, coupled with the growing need to market higher education to an increasingly skeptical public, suggests that presidents, and the academic community they represent, take a more active role in managing that exposure. Thus, the heretofore hands-off, keep-me-off-the-front-page approach to managing this powerful university resource no longer serves greater institutional purposes. In short, athletics' visibility and public influence must be looked upon as something not simply to be tolerated but rather harnessed and exploited for larger university gain.

The level of presidential involvement varies from institution to institution. Many Presidents have supported the formation of an Athletic Board and

www

Knight Commission
www.knightcommission.org

the appointment of a Faculty Athletics Representative to help scrutinize policy, direction, and operations of the Athletic Department and advise on athletic activities and issues.

In January 2006 the Summit on the Collegiate Athlete Experience was held, bringing together coaches, journalists, and athletes to discuss the collegiate athlete experience, substance abuse, and recruiting ethics. The results of the summit, along with NCAA statistics regarding rules violations, prompted the Knight Commission to strongly urge college Presidents to support academic reform in college athletics (Knight Foundation Commission on Intercollegiate Athletics, 2017). In 2010 the Knight Commission urged three approaches to reform in intercollegiate athletics (Knight Commission, 2017):

1. Improving transparency through the reporting of assessment measures and accountability metrics.
2. Profiling and rewarding practices that make academic achievement a priority.
3. Treating college athletes as students, not as professionals.

However, according to Robinson (2014, para. 6), "many of the recommended reforms are vague, difficult to implement, or impossible to enforce. It's unlikely that these reforms would make any difference to 'business as usual' in athletics departments" where incentives exist to cheat.

The Athletic Board

The Athletic Board is a committee normally placed at the top of the Athletic Department hierarchy between the Athletic Director (AD) and the college President. Its purpose is to advise the AD and possibly the President and to oversee Athletic Department operations. The Athletic Board is generally composed of a large number of constituents, including faculty, students, alumni, community businesspersons, and university administrators. The group meets regularly each semester to oversee policy development and implementation and to scrutinize budgets. Since the AD is *responsible* to the university President, the Athletic Board in effect serves as part of the checks and balances on Athletic Department operations, a sounding board for the development of new initiatives, and a mechanism for control of operations. The AD is *responsive* to the Athletic Board and works in consultation with it, but usually reports directly to the university President (or indirectly via a Dean or Vice President). The Athletic Board at the University of Kentucky is a committee of the Board of Trustees, comprised of a mixed group of board members who may be community members, students, or faculty and staff. At Arizona State University, the Athletic Board is comprised of students and faculty members. In theory, the Athletic Board wields considerable power; but in reality it is typically relatively powerless, receiving general information and rubber-stamping reports that are peripheral to the major issues facing the unit and its personnel. Even so, perhaps the least powerful position associated with this group, which is sometimes actually marginalized by the Athletic Department, is the Faculty Athletic Representative (FAR).

Faculty Athletic Representative

NCAA Bylaws stipulate that each institution appoint a FAR. The FAR appointee is one of only five institutional representatives authorized to request an NCAA legislative interpretation on behalf of the institution (along with the President, director of athletics, senior woman administrator and compliance coordinator) (NCAA, 2017g). The FAR is appointed by the President and is responsible for ensuring that the operation of the Athletic Department remains within the educational context of the institution. The individual appointed to this position is normally a faculty member, designated to liaise between the Athletic Department and the institution's administration. The FAR also represents the institution in affairs related to academic matters discussed at the NCAA and within the university's member conference. The FAR addresses a variety of topics but typically oversees policy regarding educational priorities of athletes, scheduling and time commitments, graduation rates, academic support programs, policy enforcement, and the appropriate balance between athletics and academics for an institution's student-athletes. The FAR reports to the President and works in concert with the Athletic Board and the AD.

In some cases, this reporting structure can marginalize the FAR, because members of the Athletic Department may construe his or her presence and mandate as intrusive. Since the FAR reports directly to the President, struggles over jurisdiction and perspective between the value of athletics versus the importance of education may occasionally result. Most often, however, the FAR works diligently to reduce such conflict and plays an important contributing role in delivering athletic programming in the higher education setting.

Athletic Director

The AD is the head of the Athletic Department. As leader, the AD is responsible for the unit and must understand the policies, activities, and actions of those working within each department. Recently, in many large athletic departments, the AD's activities have become more externally driven, with fundraising responsibilities, community and alumni relations, and capital building projects now a part of his or her portfolio. Some would even say that the Division I AD is really the CEO of a multi-million-dollar corporation. Ultimately, this individual is responsible for planning, organizing, leading, and evaluating both programs and personnel. Depending on the scope of these external initiatives, an Associate AD (sometimes referred to as an Athletic Coordinator) may manage the day-to-day operations of the unit. In any event, the specific responsibilities of the AD include finance, facilities, medical services, travel, event management, compliance, media, scheduling, marketing, ticket sales, public relations, personnel, communication, risk management, television, and student-athlete services. Effective ADs possess a great deal of business sense, critical-thinking and problem-solving ability, and strong communication skills. They must ensure the Athletic Department's mission coexists effectively with the mandate of higher education. Striving for excellence in two domains means conflicts will certainly arise between athletics and academics. For example, how should the AD respond when a coach develops a schedule requiring a student-athlete to be away from campus for ten days in the middle of the semester? The games may be highly beneficial from a competitive stand-point, but taking a student out of class for this length of time might prove disastrous. The AD must balance academic and athletic goals, in this case by decreasing the length of the trip. Educational concerns must supersede athletic goals, because colleges and universities are first and foremost insti-tutions of higher learning. Without a doubt there are ADs who lose sight of this founding principle in their quest for athletic excellence. Having the management skills to plan and organize is important, but it is perhaps more important that the leader of the Athletic Department effectively promotes the educational priorities of the institution and the personal achievement of the student-athletes. The most important role for the AD is the role of educator. This is also true for coaches, the other main constituent of the Athletic Department.

Coaches

Coaches truly are managers in that they plan, organize, lead, and evalu-ate their teams like small, independent organizations. You might think of the coach as the CEO of the most important component of the Athletic Department, the athletic team. A coach wears many hats in addition to being an educator. In managing and building the athletic program, she establishes liaisons with constituent groups such as student-athletes, stu-dents in general, high school recruits, the media, parents, alumni, Athletic Department administrators and colleagues, sponsors, members of the col-lege community, and professional colleagues. Today's college coaches are skilled in a particular sport and knowledgeable generally about teaching, developing tactics and strategies, communicating, motivating athletes, and building support for their program. They represent an integral compo-nent of the structure of the college Athletic Department because they drive the main business of the organization. Coaches hold a major position of influence and authority. In their highly visible positions, they greatly affect the welfare of their student-athletes and the images of their institutions.

Coaches also can have an important voice in the critical policy areas currently under review within intercollegiate athletics.

CURRENT POLICY AREAS

Many areas within intercollegiate athletics require the development of policy to ensure fairness results from common practices. Countless policy areas are debated in college athletics regardless of the country of origin, division, or affiliation. The sheer numbers of individuals involved with these organizations and the issues evolving from the unique sport environment require a problem-solving, action-oriented culture. The focus on developing new policy and amending old policy helps administrators effectively manage the evolving, dynamic environment of intercollegiate athletics. Let's investigate some recurring and some new governance policy areas facing collegiate athletics today.

Eligibility

Eligibility defines who is allowed to play. In the early days of college sport, concerns arose when an individual not affiliated in any way with the college emerged as the star of the team. If collegiate athletics is about representing one's particular institution, it follows that the members of the team must also be students at the college. *Eligibility*, then, is the global term used to define the rules for entering, in-progress, and transferring student-athletes.

Initial Eligibility

To be eligible to compete in intercollegiate athletics, a high school graduate must possess the required grades in a set of core courses acceptable to the college or university for entrance. Normally, meeting the entrance requirements to a college or university as a full-time student in Canada will enable the student to be an athlete. In the United States, however, the NCAA uses an external body called the NCAA Eligibility Center to process student-athlete eligibility in order to enforce common standards (NCAA, 2017d). Students register with the Eligibility Center (normally after their junior year) by submitting high school transcripts and standardized test scores (such as the Scholastic Aptitude Test [SAT] or American College Test [ACT]). The Eligibility Center then approves an application when an institution requests information about a particular student. Currently, the NCAA Divisions I and II require 16 core courses to be completed satisfactorily along with a minimum standardized test score defined in conjunction with grade point average (GPA). NCAA Division I uses a sliding scale of GPA, SAT, and ACT scores to identify minimum standards of initial eligibility. In Division II, a minimum SAT score of 820 or a sum score of 68 on the ACT is required to compete on an athletic team. The core GPA requirement is a minimum of 2.0 (NCAA, 2017m).

NCAA Initial Eligibility
https://web3.ncaa.org/
ecwr3/

The NAIA (2017e) requires two of the following three items for eligibility: (1) a minimum 2.0 GPA (on a 4.0 scale), (2) graduation in the upper half of the high school graduating class, and (3) a minimum score of 18 on the enhanced ACT or 940 on the SAT. Students who gain admission to a college but have scores below these NCAA or NAIA standards are ineligible to compete for their first full year of attendance (two semesters, three quarters, or the equivalent).

Academic Progress

To maintain eligibility, student-athletes must take and achieve passing grades for a specific number of courses or maintain a specific GPA.

As stated earlier, the NCAA has initiated an academic reform package. In the NCAA, student-athletes must demonstrate steady progress toward graduation: they must be pursuing full-time study, be in good standing, and be making satisfactory progress toward a degree. In addition, the NCAA Division I member institutions must be accountable for the academic success of their student-athletes, and each Division I sports team receives an Academic Progress Rate (APR) score. Essentially, the APR is conceived as a metric developed to track, manage, and enforce accountability for academic achievement by NCAA athletes. One retention point is allotted to an athlete for staying in school and one eligibility point is given an athlete for being academically eligible. The points are added together for each team, divided by the number of points possible, and multiplied by 1,000, yielding the team's APR score. For example, an institution's overall APR requirement of 967 (out of 1,000) approximates a 65 percent Graduation Success Rate. Specific required team APRs are also identified, with football requiring a score of 944, men's basketball 940, and baseball 954. While teams with high APRs receive public recognition from the NCAA, teams that score below 930 can be sanctioned, for example, by receiving reductions in scholarships (NCAA, 2017b). Across a variety of 13 men's and women's sports, 23 teams lost postseason access in 2016–17 (NCAA, 2017b). The APR is a data-driven initiative indicative of the NCAA trend toward utilizing available data in implementing legislation reforms.

Transfer Students

Rules regarding transfer students are an important aspect of intercollegiate athletics' eligibility policy. Transfers to institutions for the sole purpose of playing intercollegiate athletics are discouraged because such moves contradict the philosophy of student first, athlete second. The purpose of attending a college or a university is to get an education, earn a degree, and become a contributing member of society. To promote this philosophy, intercollegiate athletics commonly enforces a transfer rule requiring the transferring student-athlete to refrain from competition for some period of time. The NCAA transfer rule requires a student-athlete to complete one full academic year of residence (two semesters or three quarters) at a certified institution before being declared eligible to compete in men's and women's basketball and same division football. Several Conferences implemented other transfer rule requirements. Coaches also have the ability to block student-athletes from transferring to certain institutions such as in-conference schools or traditional rival institutions. The NAIA requires a 16-week residency period prior to competition after transfer from a four-year institution unless the institution from which the student-athlete transfers provides a no-objection release, in which case immediate play is allowed; it allows a transfer from a two-year institution after filing the appropriate disclosure forms. The small colleges competing in the NJCAA and USCAA, and Christian schools in the NCCAA each enforce transfer rules to declare student-athletes as eligible to compete, some utilizing academic progress and probationary provisions.

Eligibility is a common policy issue in intercollegiate athletics because competing institutions have always valued fairness and a balanced starting point in competition. These are achieved when the respective league-eligibility committees define benchmark standards to guide the agreed-upon concept that collegiate athletics is for full-time college students progressing toward a bona fide diploma or degree. Such eligibility requirements differentiate collegiate athletics from other avenues of amateur and professional sport.

Amateurism

Over the years, intercollegiate athletic administrators have worked hard to ensure college competition is identified as amateur as opposed to professional sport. Many will debate their success, given the requirements placed on student-athletes and the big business nature of college athletics, especially at the NCAA Division I level. According to the NCAA (2017a, paras 1 & 2):

> Amateur competition is a bedrock principle of college athletics and the NCAA. Maintaining amateurism is crucial to preserving an academic environment in which acquiring a quality education is the first priority. The NCAA membership has adopted amateurism rules to ensure the students' priority remains on obtaining a quality educational experience and that all of student-athletes are competing equitably.

In any event, student-athletes are not paid salaries for their services and it is the responsibility of member institutions to validate the amateur status of incoming athletes. With the advent of more global recruiting, this can be challenging. In general, amateurism requirements do not allow for salary or prize money for play or contracts with professional teams (NCAA, 2017a). Their involvement is voluntary and non-contractual, and their primary purpose for attending the institution is educational. Does this ring true? Perhaps not always, and this is the specific reason amateurism is hotly debated by administrators at the institutional, regional, and national levels.

Are college athletes employees? The answer, of course, is "no" in theory and "no" in operation, at least most of the time. College athletics should reflect the tenets of amateurism without any difficulty: competition for the glory of achievement, in a voluntary environment in which no salary is paid. In most cases amateur competition is consistently portrayed in college athletics. However, the competitive nature of NCAA Division I athletics, in which both coaches and athletic administrators push to win games and balance budgets, certainly tests (if not crosses) the line between amateur and professional sport. In this case many critics have complained of a "say . . . do" gap. College athletics is said to be amateur athletics in the context of education, but the demands and the stakes suggest a more professional sport environment to some critics who maintain that colleges should pay athletes for their performance, just as professionals are compensated for the entertainment they provide.

Regardless of the debate, collegiate athletic administrators continue to embrace amateurism and have invoked rules to prohibit professionals from competition. Student-athletes are not paid to compete, but many receive athletic scholarships or grants-in-aid to help offset the costs of a college education. In 2015 the 65 NCAA schools in the Atlantic Coast, Big Ten, Big 12, Pac-12 and Southeastern conferences approved a rule change to allow student-athletes to receive funding apportioned to the cost of attending the institution. The Cost of Attendance rule, since adopted by other Division I schools and conferences, allows schools to provide more dollars for college athletes for elements of attending college that are formally defined by federal guidelines, as established by school financial aid officers. A student's cost of attendance can be adjusted based on individual circumstances such as transportation, childcare needs, and unusual medical expenses (NCAA, 2017c). However, an "athlete turned pro" is prohibited by league policy from returning to college competition in his or her sport. The amateur policy of the NCAA describes many activities that result in an athlete's losing amateur status (NCAA, 2017b):

- playing for pay
- accepting a promise for pay
- signing a contract to play professionally
- prize money above actual and necessary expenses
- competing for a professional team (tryouts, practice, or competition)
- entering into a draft prior to collegiate enrollment
- entering into an agreement with an agent
- benefiting from an agent or prospective agent
- delaying initial full-time enrollment in order to compete in organized sport

Without a doubt, college administrators still believe it is important for college athletes to be students first, competing in amateur athletics as law-abiding, drug-free role models reflective of the entire student body. Policies play a role in fulfilling this mission.

Substance Abuse and Performance Enhancement

Collegiate athletic administrators are united in their opposition to performance-enhancing drugs and other forms of substance abuse by anyone involved in college athletics. Evidence of unequivocal opposition is reflected in policy statements. National and regional associations governing collegiate sport throughout the USA respect the list of banned substances and methods as reported by Olympic, National, and International Federations, along with the Fédération Internationale du Sport Universitaire (FISU), which governs the World University Games held every two years. Policies oppose the use of any banned or restricted substances or methods and the encouragement of such practices by anyone associated with college sport (coaches, administrators, athletic staff, medical practitioners, sport scientists, alumni, boosters, athletes, etc.). The opposition to doping strongly discourages participants from seeking an artificially induced advantage in competition. Student-athletes sign consent forms demonstrating their understanding of drug-testing programs and their willingness to abide by the rules. In the NCAA first-year students must sign forms indicating their willingness to comply with rules prohibiting banned substances.

To establish doping control, policy has been invoked on two levels: education and enforcement. Educational programs have been established by the NCAA and the NAIA and are mandatory for athletes in order to ensure awareness of the rules and the lists of banned substances and methods. Student-athletes are informed through handbooks such as the NAIA myPlaybook, as well as mandatory, online seminars in which a drug education video is shown and verbal explanation of doping-control policy is provided. In addition, the NCAA established unannounced testing programs, which give no notice or short notice. The NAIA announced that testing will be completed at National Championships beginning with the 2017–18 season (Anderson, 2014). Testing is done randomly and, in certain sports such as swimming and track and field, on the basis of finish in a given competition. In the NCAA, a national drug testing program utilizes random drug testing, and a positive test for any banned substance results in loss of eligibility for one calendar year. A second positive test results in permanent loss of eligibility in all sports. Importantly, the NCAA has instituted the "safe harbor" policy, allowing athletes to self-report drug use without fear of losing eligibility.

Policies, procedures, and rules regarding performance enhancement in intercollegiate sport help guide all participants (coaches, athletes, trainers, etc.) in understanding the broader issue of fairness and healthy practices.

William & Mary College safe harbor
www.tribeathletics.com/sports/2017/1/25/safe-harbor-program.aspx?id=790&mobile=skip

NCAA's national drug testing program
www.ncaa.org/health-and-safety/policy/drug-testing

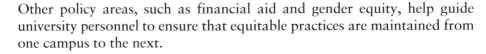

Other policy areas, such as financial aid and gender equity, help guide university personnel to ensure that equitable practices are maintained from one campus to the next.

Financial Aid

Providing athletes with financial aid, commonly known as an athletic scholarship, has been a source of debate within college athletics for decades. NCAA Divisions I and II have set policy providing for awarding a certain number of athletic scholarships, whereas Division III and the NAIA have been more restrictive in their rules. For example, NCAA Division I and II schools sponsor a certain number of athletic scholarships per sport, whereas Division III schools do not offer athletic-based awards. In the United States the source of funding for these awards has not been the most important issue. Rather, intercollegiate governing bodies such as the NCAA have developed policy to ensure fair practices among institutions regarding how much financial aid can be given to a particular athlete (to ensure a distinction from paid professional athletes), to balance awards given to males and females, and to regulate when such an award can be withdrawn. Some questionable practices, such as overpaying or unjustly withdrawing an athletic scholarship, have prompted a focus on these issues. Implementation of the Cost of Attendance policy mentioned earlier in the chapter was a move taken to ensure that athletes are not unfairly treated compared to the regular student body. In 2014, Edward O'Bannon, a former UCLA basketball player, sued the NCAA over their use of athlete images for commercial purposes after the athlete has finished playing. *O'Bannon vs the NCAA* was a class-action lawsuit on behalf of former football and men's basketball players alleging that upon graduation, a former student athlete should be compensated for use of his/her images in productions such as video games. The case went all the way to the Supreme Court which ultimately refused to hear it. One outcome of the case involved a finding that NCAA rules violate anti-trust laws in the United States. This issue is surely to be contested in future.

Fair treatment of athletes and financial aid is an ongoing focus of policy debate. Specifically, the NCAA has long debated the issue of whether student-athletes should be permitted to hold part-time jobs. A large proportion of the student population works part-time to offset the high costs of university tuition and living expenses. Yet, in the past, athlete eligibility rules forbade athletes to hold part-time jobs. The NCAA felt that, considering the demands of the classroom combined with the demands of athletic commitment, a change in policy was necessary. In 2003 the work rule was changed to allow employment on campus to a maximum of $2,000. Currently, a student-athlete is permitted to hold on- or off-campus employment for which monies do not count toward maximum financial aid allowances, provided that compensation is based solely on work performed and does not exceed the going rate for similar service (NCAA, 2017l).

United States Courts for the Ninth Circuit
https://www.ca9.uscourts.gov

Student-athletes must provide information about their employment activity to the Office of Athletics Compliance. Members of the NCAA believe this change is fair, given today's high costs of living, the high cost of attending colleges and universities, and the belief that athletes should be treated more like the rest of the student body. The emergence and evolution of policy regarding gender equity is another good example.

Gender Equity

Virtually every administrative body governing intercollegiate athletics has a policy pertaining to gender equity. In the United States, Title IX is a component of the Education Amendments that came into law in 1972. As you may recall from Chapter 5, Title IX states that "no person in the United States shall, on the basis of sex, be excluded from participation in, be denied the benefits of, or be subjected to discrimination under any education program or activity receiving federal financial assistance" (Title IX, 2017). This law provides the impetus for committee and task force discussions and implementation for change in order to achieve equitable intercollegiate athletic programs for both men and women. The NCAA Gender-Equity Task Force delivered the following policy statement:

> An athletics program can be considered gender equitable when the participants in both the men's and women's sports programs would accept as fair and equitable the overall program of the other gender. No individual should be discriminated against on the basis of gender, institutionally or nationally, in intercollegiate athletics. (NCAA, 2017o, para. 2)

University Presidents and ADs determine specific compliance with Title IX on individual campuses. However, athletes and parents have initiated numerous lawsuits that challenge actual Title IX compliance. Title IX is also being used by males and those involved in smaller, non-revenue-producing sports to challenge practices such as alleged sex discrimination in circumstances where men's sport programs are underfunded or have been dropped. The specific duty to comply with equitable practices rests on individual campuses and must be the joint responsibility of the President, AD, and Athletic Board.

Gender equity has been a long-standing contentious issue in college athletics. The inequities are played out in many different, often systemic, ways. Participation opportunities for men have historically exceeded those for women; many sports, such as football and hockey, existed for men only. The budgets allocated to men's teams and salaries paid to coaches of men's teams are significantly higher than for women's teams. The decision makers in athletic program administration, university central administration, and coaching have predominantly been males. Many more males than females coach women's teams. These and other imbalances in gender that elevate men's sport over women's continue to create issues of inequity that must remain a focus of the reform required in collegiate athletics.

Gambling

Sports gambling is a multi-billion-dollar business. Recent growth, coupled with the expansion of and media hype surrounding college sports, has resulted in a noticeable increase in gambling associated with collegiate sport. The NCAA reports a significant increase over the past decade in the number of cases it processed related to sports wagering. Concern is currently focused on the prevalence of Internet wagering, which is increasingly appealing to college-age students—all you really need to place a bet are a computer or mobile device and a credit card. Administrators and members of the NCAA are concerned about the potential for sports wagering and believe that it threatens the very existence of college sports (NCAA, 2017k). For example, Ellenbogen, et al. (2008) studied over 20,000 NCAA student-athletes, and reported that 62 percent of males and 43 percent of females reported gambling activities, with 13 percent of males engaged in weekly gambling. These authors suggest that:

> Gambling among student athletes represents a multifaceted problem, particularly when examining sport wagering. If students incur significant losses or develop associations with other gamblers, they may be pressured to use or share information conceding collegiate games, or possibly alter their performance to influence the outcomes of games. (p. 249)

The NCAA opposes sports gambling in all its forms, legal and illegal. The zero-tolerance policy adopted by the NCAA prohibits Athletic Department staff and student-athletes from engaging in any form of gambling activities. The policy prohibits gambling on both intercollegiate and professional sports and stipulates that an individual involved in collegiate sport must not knowingly provide information to individuals involved in organized gambling, solicit a bet, accept a bet, or participate in any gambling activity through any method (NCAA, 2017k).

The harshness of the policy results from the NCAA's belief that illegal sports wagering is big business, and big business attracts organized crime. The involvement of impressionable college-age students is a concern. Not only is the welfare of student-athletes jeopardized, the very integrity of sport contests can be undermined. The NCAA (2017k) members believe that sports wagering demeans the competition and competitors alike by sending a message that is contrary to the purposes and meaning of sport. The spirit of competition, not money wagered on an outcome, should drive the effort on the field. The NCAA has responded aggressively to combat the problem and communicate its stance on sport wagering. A media campaign, educational meetings with Final Four participants, web postings, liaison activities with the Federal Bureau of Investigation (FBI) and other law enforcement units, background checks on game officials, signatures by athletes on affidavit forms prior to some championships, public service announcements, and education programs on campuses such as the mandatory "Don't Bet On It" webcast produced by the NCAA—all are active components of the NCAA's sports-wagering education activities (NCAA, 2017k).

The issue of gambling in college sport is not unique to the NCAA. The NAIA also believes gambling undermines the values of NAIA athletics and the organization has a zero-tolerance policy for any form of sports wagering. Administrators and governing bodies have moved quickly to set policy prohibiting any association between gambling and college athletics. Enforcing the rules is the next hurdle.

Social Media

Intercollegiate Athletic Departments and athletes actively use Facebook, Twitter, Instagram, Pinterest, and SnapChat to publicize their activities and their brands. Many Athletic Departments are using social media to increase fan engagement, to interact with fans, to gain their feedback, and to build brand loyalty. Building the fan base by retaining current fans and recruiting new ones is core to using social media technologies today, and Athletic Departments have hired whole units of media directors and graphic designers to effectively communicate their messages. However, a double standard has developed in many Athletic Departments related to social media use by athletes. University Athletic Departments have enacted policies to control and limit an athlete's use of social media, characterizing it as risky to the image and brand of the team. While athletes' social media use will likely be monitored by Athletic Department personnel for content, preventing athletes from using social media is undoubtedly a concern for their personal freedom. Governing bodies such as the NCAA have hesitated to create policy on this issue, likely because of the difficulty inherent to monitoring it and the legal issues associated with doing so. Coaches have voiced concerns within departments because of the potential competitive impact when an athlete announces an injury on Twitter, or a recruit changes her mind about attending a school because of some off-hand, heated comments. This is why many Athletic Departments and teams have created policy for the use of social media. Importantly, athletes need to be trained about the publicity "fishbowl" that is college athletics, where what they do and say is magnified and of interest to millions. Athletes are being coached to use social media minimally and appropriately, and to understand the negative impact it can have for future jobs. Policy that balances the positives and negatives of this issue is required.

Enforcement

Because intercollegiate athletic organizations are collectives of member institutions, legislation is created *by* the members of the organization *for* the members of the organization. Enforcement Services, also called Compliance, is the department that ensures that all institutions are abiding by the rules, thus maintaining the integrity of the rules and fair play among all participants. The intent of enforcement programs is to reduce violations by education, discovery, and the disbursement of appropriate penalties.

College Athletic Departments in the United States are expected to monitor their rules compliance and self-report any violation. In addition, the NCAA has an Enforcement and Infractions staff of approximately ten specialists who work to ensure a level playing field through rules enforcement. The importance of the enforcement policy is underscored by the fact that each NCAA division has a Committee on Infractions (COI), an independent group of lawyers, law school professors, and members of the public who assess penalties for those who break the rules. Unfortunately, this arrangement is frequently perceived as inadequate by members of the NCAA because of the huge workload assumed by only ten people. The inquiry process involves field investigations, formal correspondence of inquiry, the development of a case summary, hearings before the COI, and, if necessary, a ruling regarding the violation and penalty (NCAA, 2017e). An appeal process is also provided, and attempts are made to ensure due process is followed in any investigation.

Enforcement is not accorded as much focus in the NAIA, where self-reporting is virtually the sole means of policing infractions. The organization has a committee to deal with allegations of impropriety, but no full-time enforcement officers. This is primarily a financial issue, given the lack of resources available for full-time enforcement officers. For many sport organizations, funding is problematic, and intercollegiate athletics is no different.

Funding

It seems that every conceivable level of sport has funding woes. Children's sport programs are being dropped, professional sport is losing franchises, and recreational sport is becoming a viable option only for those who are financially well off. Funding, or lack of funding, has also become a major issue for college athletic administrators. Many are surprised that funding is included in the policy issues of intercollegiate athletics. But consider the following three myths: college sports make money, competitive sports fund recreational sports, and no other sports would exist without football. These statements are not accurate most of the time, but they are convenient arguments sometimes used to drive certain status quo decisions (Sperber, 2015). More accurate is that funding is a major concern in intercollegiate athletics on every level (Suggs, 2017). The cost of a Division IA football program is astronomical; the revenues derived, even through television contracts, quickly vanish in the expense column. In addition, the recession of 2008 led to general reductions in university funding generally in the United States that continues to negatively impact budgets across colleges and universities.

Funding pressures for sports programming has been described as the Athletics Arms Race (Leef, 2016; Morales, 2016). College sport programs are in fierce competition which ramps up costly ideas and norms for recruitment, facilities, practice arrangements, and competition. There is a sense that increasing corporatization of cash-strapped American university campuses has resulted in attempts by university administrators to build stadium facilities by imposing higher student fees (Guest, 2015). Alternatively, threats to cancel costly programs due to funding shortages, like the football program at the University of Alabama, Birmingham (Strauss & Schonbrun, 2014), have surfaced at Board of Trustee meetings. To ensure the continuing viability of intercollegiate athletics, the Finance Committees of the NCAA and CIS are defining policies to help curb spending and reduce excess. Although this resulted in rules defining a maximum roster size, the number of games allowed, starting dates, and scheduling efficiencies, authority for creating rules has been downloaded to Conferences more recently, and thus the Athletics Arms Race is alive and well. As such, policy areas will continue to be an important focus for intercollegiate athletic administrators.

SUMMARY

The fall season is here! More than likely, fall conjures up thoughts of cooler weather, bright red and yellow leaves, apple picking, and college football games. For many people, the beginning of the college sports season is synonymous with the new school year. This association indicates the appeal of college athletics, not just for the participants and student body but also for the wider public who attend games and tune in to the mass media. Widespread interest in intercollegiate athletics has resulted in colleges offering a vast array of teams and developing excellent state of the art facilities for participants and spectators on campuses across North America. It has also resulted in the need for college administrators to actively supervise the intercollegiate sport enterprise, its governance, operations, and policy development. From the humble beginning of a crew race between Harvard and Yale in 1852, thousands of competitions among institutions all over the United States and Canada take place today.

To compete with other colleges and universities with similar philosophies and values, institutions become members of governing associations such as the NCAA, the NAIA, and the NJCAA in the United States. Members of these organizations meet to set policy, procedures, rules and regulations, and legislation regulating competitions, and to deal with current issues.

The policies regulating competition are debated from year to year and hinge on the current political and financial environments of the institutions involved. Eligibility seems to be a perennial concern. The preservation of amateurism is also a timeless issue. The issues of performance-enhancing drugs and the implementation of fair practices in providing gender equity have surfaced in more recent decades. Setting policy regarding gambling and enforcement are even newer issues in intercollegiate athletics, whereas financial aid and overall program funding have ignited debate from the beginning.

Intercollegiate athletics and its governance will continue to be hot topics on university campuses, and the governing structures will play an ever-increasing and important role in ensuring a safe and fair environment for competitions between colleges for participants and spectators alike.

caseSTUDY

COLLEGE ATHLETES AND COMMUNITY SERVICE

College Athletic Departments are constantly looking for ways to create a positive public image. One way they can do so is through involving members of the Athletic Department, and particularly student-athletes (SAs), in community service projects.

1. If you were the AD, what might be some approaches your department could use to getting your SAs involved in community service?

    a. Who should choose the activity? SAs? Coaches? The AD? A team of people?

    b. What types of community organizations would make good partners?

    c. How can you get coaches on board to help?

    d. When you or a friend of yours was a SA in high school or college, did you (or they) ever do community service? How was the experience?

    Sometimes coaches use community service projects as punishments for athletes who have broken team rules. The coaching staff for a sport will tell the SA they have to perform a certain number of community service hours in order to make up for their poor behavior. The SA may have no interest whatsoever in really helping the community, just in getting in their hours as mandated.

2. Is requiring someone to do community service an appropriate punishment for breaking team rules? Why or why not?

3. As an alternative, how could the athletes be disciplined?

CHAPTER questions

1. Compare and contrast the organizational structures of the NCAA, the NAIA, and the NJCAA. What is different in these three organizations, and why?

2. How might a policy help an athlete deal with the struggle of balancing requirements and expectations of academics versus athletics? Write a policy encouraging balance between both components of the term *student-athlete*.

3. Suppose you are the AD of a large Division I university with teams competing in the NCAA. It has come to your attention that the men's basketball coach has broken a series of recruiting rules in order to attract a 7-foot center to the team. In the end the coach was unsuccessful in recruiting the athlete, but self-disclosure rules still exist in the NCAA. Using the SLEEPE Principle presented in Chapter 2, analyze the situation to help understand each of the ramifications of your decision. In the end, what will you do?

FOR ADDITIONAL INFORMATION

For more information check out the following resources:

1. NAIA Champions of Character program YouTube video: https://www.youtube.com/watch?v=XM6WvGvJWk4&list=PLYMnW1ercBdXcTe4ZqUMomCYrpNU6AOmD

2. The 25 Worst College Sports Scandals: www.ranker.com/list/college-sports-cheating-scandals/swiperight

3. Student-Athlete Experience: Buckstein, S. (2016). The business and governance of college sport. Practical strategies for thought-leaders in athletics and higher education to improve the overall experience of student-athletes. *Journal of Higher Education Athletics and Innovation*, 1(1), 61–71: http://business.ucf.edu/wp-content/uploads/2016/12/1a.-Journal-Article-The-Business-and-Governance-of-College-Sport-2016.pdf

4. NCAA President Mark Emmert: "Office of the President: On the Mark": www.ncaa.org/about/who-we-are/office-president/office-president-mark

5. Pay for Play in College Sport?: Arguments for: https://www.forbes.com/sites/joshbenjamin/2017/04/04/is-it-time-to-start-paying-college-athletes/#607dab4df71f and against: https://www.wsj.com/articles/lets-not-pay-college-athletes-1459206949

6. Salary Gaps Between Women's and Men's College Coaches: www.localkicks.com/community/news/salary-gap-widens-between-mens-and-womens-coaches

REFERENCES

Anderson, C. (2014). NAIA to implement drug testing and education system starting in 2017. Retrieved from http://doaneline.com/sports/article_9a8653f4-5767-11e5-954d-dbe185becf6f.html

Bolling, L. (2016, March 7). Top 10 revenue-generating HBCU athletic departments. Retrieved from https://msilineup.com/2016/03/07/top-10-revenue-generating-hbcu-athletic-departments/comment-page-1/

Davenport, J. (1985). From crew to commercialism: The paradox of sport in higher education. In D. Chu, J. O. Segrave, & B. J. Becker (Eds.), *Sport and higher education* (pp. 5–16). Champaign, IL: Human Kinetics.

Ellenbogen, S., Jacobs, D., Derevensky, J., Gupta, R., & Paskus, T. S. (2008). Gambling behavior among college student-athletes. *Journal of Applied Sport Psychology, 20,* 349–362.

Gerdy, J. R. (1997). *The successful college athletic program: The new standard.* Phoenix, AZ: Oryx Press.

Guest, A. (2015, January 29). Fighting the great sports myth. Retrieved from http://theallrounder.co/2015/01/29/fighting-the-great-sports-myth/

Knight Foundation. (2017). About. Retrieved from http://knightcommission.org/about

Knight Foundation Commission on Intercollegiate Athletics. (2017). Commission reports. Retrieved from www.knightcommission.org/presidential-control-a-leadership/commission-reports

Leef, G. (2016, September 7). College sports: Isn't it time to de-escalate the arms race? Retrieved from https://www.jamesgmartin.center/2016/09/college-sports-isnt-time-de-escalate-arms-race/

MacGaffey, J. (2013). *Coal dust on your feet: The rise, decline, and restoration of an anthracite mining town.* Lewisburg: Bucknell University Press.

Meyer, J., & Zimbalist, A. (2017). Reforming college sports. The case for a limited and conditional antitrust exemption. Retrieved from http://journals.sagepub.com/doi/abs/10.1177/0003603X16688829?journalCode=abxa

Morales, J. (2016, March 15). The college sports arms race is only getting more extravagant. College AD. Retrieved from http://collegead.com/the-college-sports-arms-race-is-only-getting-more-extravagant-nutrition-centers-indoor-practice/

Morgan State Bears. (2017). Athletics mission statement. Retrieved from www.morganstatebears.com/sports/2003/7/17/mission.aspx

NAIA. (2017a). About the NAIA. Retrieved from www.naia.org/ViewArticle.dbml?DB_OEM_ID=27900&ATCLID=205323019

NAIA. (2017b). A guide for the college bound student athlete. Retrieved from www.playnaia.org/d/NAIA_GuidefortheCollegeBoundStudent.pdf

NAIA. (2017c). Live 5. Retrieved from www.naia.org/ViewArticle.dbml?DB_OEM_ID=27900&ATCLID=205421991

NAIA. (2017d). Membership. Retrieved from www.naia.org/fls/27900/membership/membership.html

NAIA. (2017e). US freshmen eligibility. Retrieved from www.playnaia.org/page/eligibility.php

NCAA. (2017a). Amateurism. Retrieved from www.ncaa.org/amateurism

NCAA. (2017b). APR reports. Retrieved from www.ncaa.org/about/resources/research/division-i-academic-progress-rate-apr

NCAA. (2017c). Cost of attendance q & a. Retrieved from www.ncaa.com/news/ncaa/article/2015-09-03/cost-attendance-qa

NCAA. (2017d). Eligibility center. Retrieved from www.ncaa.org/student-athletes/future/eligibility-center

NCAA. (2017e). Enforcement. Retrieved from www.ncaa.org/enforcement

NCAA. (2017f). NCAA – about us. Retrieved from www.ncaa.org/content-categories/media-center/ncaa-101

NCAA. (2017g). NCAA bylaw 6.1.3. Retrieved from http://farawebsite.org/what-is-an-far/fara-handbook/

NCAA. (2017h). NCAA core values. Retrieved from www.ncaa.org/about/ncaa-core-values

NCAA. (2017i). NCAA financial statements. Retrieved from www.ncaa.org/sites/default/files/2015-16NCAA_FinancialStatement_20170223.pdf

NCAA. (2017j). Our three divisions. Retrieved from www.ncaa.org/about/resources/media-center/ncaa-101/our-three-divisions

NCAA. (2017k). Sports wagering. Retrieved from www.ncaa.org/enforcement/sports-wagering

NCAA. (2017l). Summary of NCAA regulations for athletes. Retrieved from http://fs.ncaa.org/Docs/AMA/compliance_forms/DI/DI%20Summary%20of%20NCAA%20Regulations.pdf

NCAA. (2017m). 2016–17 guide for the college-bound student athlete. Retrieved from www.ncaapublications.com/productdownloads/CBSA17.pdf

NCAA. (2017n). What is the NCAA? Retrieved from www.ncaa.org/about/resources/media-center/ncaa-101/what-ncaa

NCAA. (2017o). Women, gender equity and Title IX. Retrieved from www.ncaa.org/about/resources/inclusion/women-gender-equity-and-title-ix

OSU Department of Athletics. (2017). Department of Athletics & business management at Ohio State University. Retrieved from www.ohiostatebuckeyes.com/ot/organizational-charts.html

Robinson, J. (2014, July 23). I take a look at three reform-minded athletics reports and find a few (very few) good ideas. Retrieved from https://www.jamesgmartin.center/2014/07/i-take-a-look-at-three-reform-minded-athletics-reports-and-find-a-few-very-few-good-ideas/

Rudolph, F. (1990). *The American college and university: A history*. Athens: University of Georgia Press.

Scott, H. A. (1951). *Competitive sports in schools and colleges*. New York: Harper and Brothers.

Shahen, P., & Heron, M. (2015, January 27). Battle continues to save UT men's track & field program. Retrieved from www.wrcbtv.com/story/27954046/UTC-drops-mens-track-and-field-programs

Smith, R. A. (2011). *A history of big-time college athletic reform*. Urbana: University of Illinois Press.

Sperber, M. (2015, March 13). *Five myths about college sports*. Retrieved from https://www.washingtonpost.com/opinions/five-myths-about-college-sports/2015/03/13/d50b1626-c8de-11e4-b2a1-bed1aaea2816_story.html?utm_term=.ac7119433528

Strauss, B., & Schonbrun, Z. (2014, December 3). It's a game of spiraling costs, so a college tosses out football. Retrieved from https://www.nytimes.com/2014/12/03/sports/ncaafootball/uab-cancels-football-program-citing-fiscal-realities.html?_r=0

Suggs, D. W. (2017). Myth: College sports are a cash cow. The America Council on Education. Retrieved from www.acenet.edu/news-room/Pages/Myth-College-Sports-Are-a-Cash-Cow2.aspx

Thomas, K. (2011b, April 25). Gender games. College teams, relying on deception, undermine gender equity. *New York Times*. Retrieved from http://www.nytimes.com/2011/04/26/sports/26titleix.html?pagewanted=all

Thomas, K. (2011b, April 26). Gender games. Colleges teams, relying on deception, undermine Title IX. *New York Times*. Retrieved from www.nytimes.com/2011/04/26/sports/26titleix.html?pagewanted=all

Title IX. (2017). Title IX and Sex Discrimination. Retrieved from www2.ed.gov/about/offices/list/ocr/docs/tix_dis.html

Trahan, K. (2015, January 17). The 4 things to know about the new NCAA's autonomy structure. Retrieved from www.sbnation.com/college-football/2014/8/7/5966849/ncaa-autonomy-power-conferences-voting-rules

Trahan, K. (2016, May 12). Should Grambling State, Southern, and other HBCUs drop out of Division I football? Retrieved from https://sports.vice.com/en_us/article/should-grambling-state-southern-hbcus-drop-division-i-football

Wann, D. L. (2006). Examining the potential causal relationship between sport team identification and psychological well-being. *Journal of Sport Behavior*, 29(1), 79–95.

The Major Games

Mary A. Hums
Joanne C. MacLean

Think of amateur sport as a highway. The highway is a stretch of road spanning informal, recreational opportunities (such as pickup basketball and Sunday afternoon touch football) to elite, multi-event competitions (such as World Championships and the Olympic Games). Lanes are open for participants, coaches, officials, and spectators. Participants can easily enter and exit the highway as their interests and abilities dictate. Events are organized all along the highway, filling specific needs for competition for all age groups and ability levels of the athletes. Along the road amateur sport evolves from recreation into elite competition. Such events exist for a variety of age groups at the local, national, and international levels. And not all athletes are amateur in status, as professional athletes compete in major games in some sports as well. For example, teams compete for National Championships. Athletes are selected to represent their country on national teams competing in the World Championships, World University Games (also called the FISU [Fédération Internationale du Sport Universitaire] Games), and Pan American/Para-Pan American Games. Such competitions lead to the pinnacle event staged every four years—the Olympic and the Paralympic Games (discussed in Chapter 10). The athletes are from high schools and colleges, and from amateur and professional leagues. The purpose of this chapter is to investigate the governance structures of the organizations delivering the major games in elite athletics. Given the scope and the importance of the Olympic and Paralympic Games, the organization and governance of the Olympic and the Paralympic Games will be discussed in separate chapters.

How did other major games come to exist, and how are they organized and governed? This chapter approaches these questions in two ways. First, we discuss the governance of different organizations that provide athletes for major games. Second, we present several major games to illustrate the governance structures of the actual events. Let's look briefly at the evolution and history of the major games.

HISTORY OF THE MAJOR GAMES

Major advances in technology and urbanization led historians to describe the 19th century as "the age of progress" (Riess, 1995). Sport progressed at a phenomenal rate as well: "[T]he international foundation was truly laid for the gigantic proportions of sport today" (Glassford & Redmond, 1988, p. 140). Inventions such as the camera (1826), the railroad (1830), the electric lamp (1881), the motorcar (1885), and the radio (1901) were among the profound technological changes contributing to the evolution of sport (Glassford & Redmond, 1988).

Urbanization was also a major factor in the growth of the sport industry. The city became the site of huge stadiums and other facilities and the focal point for crowds of participants and spectators. Tournaments, festivals, and special events became more commonplace as both leisure time and general affluence increased (Kidd, 1999). Technology, especially that related to easing long-distance transportation, provided the opportunity for both national and international competition. Before long, governments focused on the idea of sport as an alternative to war, whereby political ideologies and national strength could be displayed by winning international sporting competitions (Riordan & Kruger, 1999).

The advancement of political ideology through sport likely occurred around the time Baron Pierre de Coubertin revived the ancient Olympic Games in the late 19th century. Baron de Coubertin's dream was that sport could be used to increase goodwill among nations of the world. He reinstated Olympic competition when, in 1894, officials from 12 countries endorsed a modern cycle of Olympic Games (Glassford & Redmond, 1988).

Baron de Coubertin's Olympic Games were not entirely original. Games in England's Cotswolds and the Highland Games of Scotland were staged in the 19th century. The concept of major games and festivals spread quickly. The Far Eastern Championship Games were organized in 1913 as regional games after the rebirth of the modern Olympic Games. Teams from China, Japan, the Philippines, Thailand, and Malaysia participated (Glassford & Redmond, 1988). Similar games were established in Central America, and teams from Puerto Rico, Cuba, Mexico, and other Latin American countries participated. The first British Empire Games (later renamed the Commonwealth Games) took place in Hamilton, Canada, in 1930. Other countries organized regional games such as State Games and National Championships. In addition, international competitions such as the Asian Games, the Pan American Games, the Goodwill Games, and other special group events developed. For instance, the International Student Games were first held in 1924 (renamed the Universiade in 1959), and in 1960 the first Paralympic Games were held for individuals with physical disabilities. Today, games exist for every age group in virtually every sport. The World Little League Baseball Championships, the America's Cup yachting competition, World Championships for speed skating, and the Deaflympics are examples of major amateur sporting events that dominate today's sporting calendar. Who organizes these events, and how are they operated? Next, we investigate the organizations and governance structures of several major games in amateur sport.

GOVERNANCE

The governance of amateur sport differs in countries around the world. Government focus on policy involving amateur sport via nonprofit and voluntary organizations became more prominent in the latter half of the 20th century (Langlois & Menard, 2013). Even so, the degree to which a government is involved in sport policy differs depending on a nation's social, cultural, and political perspectives. In the United States, sport is intensely popular and a cause for national unity. However, US public policy has historically claimed (some say rhetorically) that sport is independent of government (Chalip & Johnson, 1996). In countries around the world the promotion of national unity and identity are central themes in government involvement in sport-policy development. Some level of government involvement helps shape the policies governing the athletes representing their nations at the major games of amateur athletics.

Governing Structures for Amateur Sport

Three branches of government exist in the United States: the legislative branch is responsible for policy making; the executive branch implements laws and public policies; and the judicial branch interprets the law. Each branch plays an important role in policy development, along with state and local governments. In fact, many state and local governments are influenced by national policies. The policy developed at each level of government has implications for amateur sport. At the national level, laws specific to sport have been enacted; for example, the Amateur Sports Act of 1978 promotes, coordinates, and sets national goals for amateur sport in the United States through the development of national governing bodies (United States Amateur Sports Act, 1978). Another example is the Stevens Amendment of 1998, which changed the Amateur Sports Act so that it became known as the Ted Stevens Olympic and Amateur Sports Act. The new law strengthened athletes' rights, provided procedures for dispute resolution, and incorporated the Paralympic Movement into the Act by updating provisions for athletes with disabilities (US Senate S.2119, 1998). Policies affecting sport might also result from the application of laws not written specifically for sport, such as the Americans with Disabilities Act of 1990, established to prevent discrimination on the basis of disability, or through federal government agencies such as the President's Council on Physical Fitness and Sport, which sets policy on issues related to physical fitness and sport (Americans with Disabilities Act, 1990; Chalip & Johnson, 1996).

www
Ted Stevens Olympic and Amateur Sports Act
https://www.govtrack.us/congress/bills/105/s2119

State and national organizations exist in order to provide rules, regulations, promotion, and competition for specific sports. In the next sections three examples of state and national organizations are presented. First, the Amateur Athletic Union (AAU) is described. It is one of the largest multisport organizations in the United States, incorporating both state and national offices with the mandate to promote and develop amateur opportunities in a variety of sports. Second, the United States Olympic Committee (USOC) is discussed. Unlike most other nations, the US federal government does not have a sports ministry, but rather has given the USOC the exclusive rights to use and authorize the use of Olympic marks in the United States. The USOC works with national sports organizations or governing bodies to set policy and provide leadership for US national teams. Finally, USA Basketball is presented. This is an example of a national sport organization that organizes basketball in the United States by operating in conjunction with 20 affiliate associations. How are these groups organized and how is policy developed?

The Amateur Athletic Union

The AAU is a multisport organization dedicated to promoting and developing amateur sport and physical fitness programs. It was founded in 1888 to establish standards for amateur sport participation (AAU, 2017). In the early days, the AAU represented all amateur sports at International Federation meetings and was responsible for organizing national teams to represent the United States at international competitions, including the Olympic Games. As mentioned earlier, in 1978 the US Senate and the US House of Representatives enacted the Amateur Sports Act, the purpose of which was to coordinate amateur sport throughout the United States. This was done, in part, by establishing individual organizations for the purpose of developing specific sports. The Amateur Sports Act had a profound effect on the mandate of the AAU and caused the organization to refocus its purpose away from representing US teams internationally and toward the development and provision of sports programs for a wider spectrum of participants (AAU, 2017). At this point the AAU introduced the "sports for all, forever" philosophy. Today, the AAU offers a broad spectrum of activities, from baseball to wrestling, with 34 sports in between.

www

Amateur Athletic Union
www.aausports.org

MISSION.   The AAU promotes and delivers amateur sport widely within the United States. It is a network of local chapters that provides programs for children, men, and women in a large number of activities. The breadth of its mandate is illustrated by the inclusiveness of its programming. The mission statement of the AAU is presented in Exhibit 9.1.

MEMBERSHIP.   Athletes, coaches, volunteers, and officials make up the membership of the AAU. The organization has thousands of members (700,000 participants and 150,000 volunteers) and offers programming for both youth and adult participants.

FINANCIALS.   The AAU is a nonprofit organization funded through membership dues and donations. Yearly member dues are modest: Any youth can

---

Mission of the Amateur Athletic Union

exhibit   **9.1**

The mission of the AAU is "to offer amateur sports programs through a volunteer base for all people to have the physical, mental, and moral development of amateur athletes and to promote good sportsmanship and good citizenship."

Source: AAU (2017).

ESPN Wide World of Sports Complex

www.espnwwos.com/

belong for only $14, and the Extended Coverage Membership option (which allows participation in non-AAU licensed events) is only an additional $16. Dues for coaches and adults are only slightly higher. Sponsorships and partnerships are solicited, such as the alliance made between the AAU and Walt Disney World in 1996, which precipitated the relocation of the AAU National Office to Lake Buena Vista, Florida. Each year more than 40 AAU national events are held at the ESPN Wide World of Sports Complex near the Disney Resorts in Florida.

ORGANIZATIONAL STRUCTURE. Fifty-five district offices for associations make up the AAU, each representing either a state (for example, Oklahoma) or a region (for example, New England) of the United States. The AAU is managed by a small Executive Committee, which comprises a group of officers elected by the Congress: the President, First and Second Vice President, Secretary, and Treasurer. Each officer is elected for a four-year term. The Congress is the primary actor for the business of the AAU and is composed of district representatives elected at the local, National Sport Committee, or National Officers levels. The Congress consists of approximately 600 members. The Congress constitutes a 36-member Board of Directors, consisting of designated members and those elected to act on AAU business between meetings of the Congress. National Sport Committees responsible for a particular sport define and direct policy related to that sport. The entire operation is managed by full-time staff members led by the Executive Director. In addition, a host of committees deal with AAU activities such as Finance, Insurance, Youth Sport, Adult Sport, and Law and Legislation. Policy is developed through committees, analyzed and voted on by the Executive Committee, and then voted upon by the Board of Directors at annual national meetings. Much of the policy discussion involves the development of rules, regulations, and hosting guidelines for events. Exhibit 9.2 depicts the organizational structure of the AAU Board of Directors.

Sport Canada

Sport Canada is a branch within the Department of Canadian Heritage of the Canadian federal government. It is an excellent example of how government is involved in amateur sport in many countries of the world, such as Australia and Great Britain, although the United States has no such government department. Sport Canada is responsible for elite sport programming and sport policy development and is dedicated to valuing and strengthening the Canadian sport experience. "Sport Canada provides leadership and funding to help ensure a strong Canadian sport system which enables Canadians to progress from early sport experiences to high performance excellence" (Sport Canada, 2017, para. 2). Sport Canada has three programs of support: (1) the Athlete Assistance Program, that provides funding to athletes to support them during training and competition, (2) the Hosting Program, that provides support for the hosting of Canada

Organizational Structure of the AAU | *exhibit* **9.2**

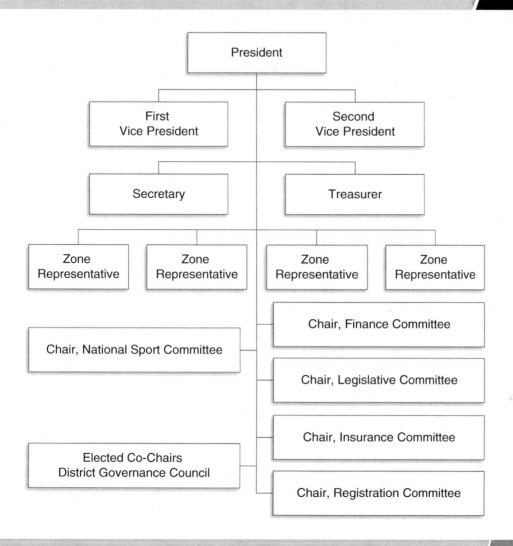

Source: AAU (2017).

Games and international sports events, and (3) the Sport Support Program, which involves funding for developing coaches and athletes' technical abilities at the highest international levels, and promoting and increasing the number of Canadians involved in sport at all levels.

MISSION. The mission of Sport Canada is to promote sport opportunities for all Canadians. The organization coordinates and encourages excellence among Canadian athletes on the world stage and works with a variety of partners, including national sport organizations, coaches, and other levels of government to provide the necessary environment for high-performance

www

Sport Canada
http://canada.pch.gc.ca/
eng/1414151906468

athletes to achieve. Sport Canada's mission also promotes sport as a source of pleasure, personal satisfaction, and a means of achieving good health. Each of these pursuits is captured in the Canadian Sport Policy, a document that originally defined the goals for sport to achieve in Canada by 2012 (Canadian Sport Policy, 2012) and which was subsequently updated and reviewed (Sutcliff Group, 2016). These goals include enhancing participation, excellence, capacity, and interaction of members of the sport community. The mission statement of Sport Canada is presented in Exhibit 9.3.

MEMBERSHIP.   Sport Canada is an umbrella organization that supports the mandate of high-performance sport. As such, it does not have a membership like national or state sport organizations have, but instead is comprised of civil servants of the Canadian federal government. It is important to note that Sport Canada is separate and distinct from Canadian National Sport Organizations (NSOs) and the Canadian Olympic Committee (COC). The NSOs are linked to Sport Canada because they provide some degree of funding in return for compliance with policy and directives as set by Sport Canada. The COC, however, is completely separate from Sport Canada. While consultation and an open chain of communication are encouraged by both organizations, no formal relationship or reporting structure exists.

FINANCIALS.   Sport Canada receives its funding from the Canadian federal government. It then establishes funding priorities and guidelines for the Canadian sport system. Sport Canada finances the following programs (Sport Canada, 2017):

1. Athlete Assistance Program—living and training allowances for athletes
2. Sport Support Program—national team funding; development of coaches and officials; increasing Canadian's sport participation
3. Sport Hosting Program—financial assistance for the hosting of international events (World Championships, World Cups, Qualification Tournaments) in Canada

| *exhibit* | 9.3 | Mission of Sport Canada |

Sport Canada supports the achievement of high performance excellence and the development of the Canadian sport system to strengthen the unique contribution that sport makes to Canadian identity, culture and society.

Source: Sport Canada (2017).

ORGANIZATIONAL STRUCTURE.   Sport Canada is led by a Director General who reports through a Deputy Minister to the Minister of Sport and Persons With Disabilities. The organization is subdivided into program areas including Policy and Planning, Sport Support, Athlete Assistance, Hosting, Canadian Sport Centres, and Business Operations. The areas of sport policy and sport programs are further subdivided to deal with specific areas of focus, for instance, the national sport policy and policies covering Sport For Women and Girls, Doping, Tobacco Sponsorship, Persons With Disabilities, and Aboriginal Peoples Participation in Sport. Within Sport Canada, policy is set regarding eligible forms of funding for athletes, NSO requirements regarding gender and language equity, and intergovernmental strategy and communication. A variety of program managers and sport consultants handle the duties within each subunit of Sport Canada. The organizational structure of Sport Canada is presented in Exhibit 9.4.

Organizational Structure for the Department of Canadian Heritage, Sport Canada Branch / *exhibit* **9.4**

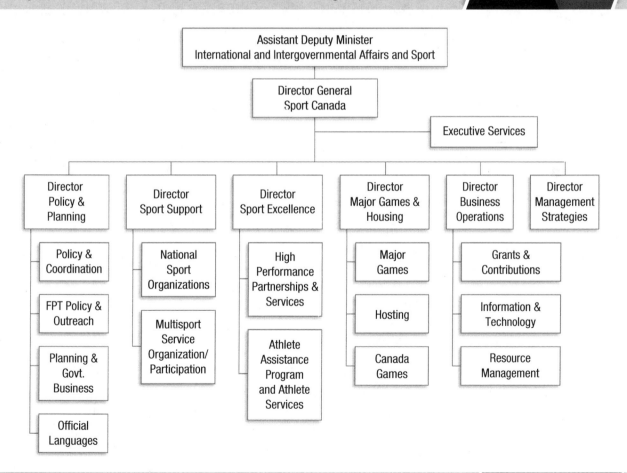

Source: Sport Canada (2012).

USA Basketball
http://web.usabasketball.com

Water Ski Canada
www.waterskicanada.ca/

Hockey Australia
www.hockey.org.au

USA Basketball
www.usab.com

National Sport Governing Bodies

Within each country, one national-level sport organization generally is recognized as the regulatory body for a particular sport. Sometimes these are governmental units, and other times they are freestanding sport organizations. These organizations have names like USA Baseball, Water Ski Canada, or Hockey Australia. Depending on the nation, these organizations are called national governing bodies or national sport organizations. To illustrate the governance structure, USA Basketball is an excellent example.

USA Basketball is the NGB for basketball in the United States. As such, its employees oversee the development of the game of basketball from the grass roots through the elite levels.

MISSION. USA Basketball is the international US representative to the USOC, and acts as the Fédération Internationale de Basketball Association (FIBA) member in the United States (USA Basketball, 2017c). FIBA is the international governing body for basketball. USA Basketball is responsible for selecting, training, and fielding national teams to compete in international FIBA competitions and in the Olympic Games. The association is also responsible for the development, promotion, and coordination of basketball in the United States, and identifies 11 components of its stated organizational purpose to do the following (USA Basketball, 2017a):

1. Develop interest and participation, and take responsibility for basketball in the US.
2. Coordinate between organizations in order to minimize conflicts in scheduling basketball events and practices.
3. Inform athletes about policy.
4. Sanction competitions.
5. Provide participation for amateur athletes.
6. Provide equitable support for both men and women.
7. Encourage and support individuals with disabilities.
8. Provide and coordinate technical, coaching, training, and performance analysis.
9. Encourage, support, and disseminate research in basketball safety and sports medicine.
10. Commit to equal opportunity and fair treatment to job applicants and employees without regard to race, color, religion, sex, national origin, age, physical handicap, sexual orientation or marital status, and actively involve qualified minorities and women to occupy positions at all levels of the Association.

The mission statement of USA Basketball is presented in Exhibit 9.5.

| Mission Statement of USA Basketball | *exhibit* 9.5 |

The purpose of this Association is to act as the national governing body for the sport of basketball in the United States, and in such connection, to be recognized as such by the USOC and to act as the FIBA member in the U.S.

Source: USA Basketball (2017b)

MEMBERSHIP.   There are five membership types at USA Basketball: professional, collegiate, scholastic, youth, and associate. Professional membership includes those organizations delivering a national, professional competitive basketball program, such as the National Basketball Association (NBA) and Women's National Basketball Association (WNBA). Collegiate membership includes national sport organizations delivering basketball in university, college, and collegiate-level programs, like the National Collegiate Athletic Association (NCAA) and National Association of Intercollegiate Athletics (NAIA). The scholastic membership category involves national organizations in school sport, like the National Federation of State High School Associations. Youth membership currently includes only the Amateur Athletic Union, a community-based non-scholastic and non-collegiate sport organization that delivers national basketball programs for youth. Finally, associate memberships include other organizations that conduct significant basketball programs in the United States. Examples of associate members include Athletes in Action, National Basketball Players Association, USA Deaf Sports Federation, and United States Armed Forces. Members are non-voting, except that they have the right to elect or select certain members of the Board of Directors.

FINANCIALS.   USA Basketball is a nonprofit organization. Although member organizations pay annual dues (ranging between $250 and $2,000), the majority of funding is derived from revenues associated with corporate partnerships and sponsorships, television, sales of apparel and souvenirs, hosting rights, and Olympic revenue sharing.

ORGANIZATIONAL STRUCTURE.   USA Basketball members meet at an Annual Assembly of the association. In addition to the memberships defined above, active athletes are eligible for 20 percent of the total Board of Directors voting power and are elected to the Assembly. The USA Basketball Assembly receives reports on the "State of USA Basketball" from the Board of Directors on past and future activities. The Assembly has no rule-making, budgetary, legislative, or other authority, but rather acts in an advisory capacity to the Board of Directors.

USA Basketball is governed by a Board of Directors. The Board is led by the Chairperson, and the immediate Past Chair holds a position in the year immediately following the Olympic Games to ensure continuity. The majority of the board consists of elected members from three categories of directors whose votes each count as two votes: professional from the NBA (three members), collegiate from the NCAA (three members), and active athlete (two members). The National Federation of High Schools appoints one individual, and that person has one vote. The organizational membership directors also have a vote that counts as one. The membership directors include one elected person from each of the following organizations: NBA, National Basketball Development League, WNBA, NCAA, National Junior College Athletic Association (NJCAA), NAIA, National Federation of State High School Associations (NFHS), and AAU. The board meets at least four times per year and has primary responsibility for developing policy and approving actions regarding the competitive basketball programs of the association (USA Basketball, 2017b). The Board of Directors provides leadership for the organization's Executive Director/CEO and professional staff. The Board of Directors includes 11 members, led by an elected Chair, and includes appointed NBA, NCAA, NFHS, Players Associations, athlete representatives, and at-large members. The past USA Basketball Chairperson is an ex-officio member of the Board. Policy is defined by the Board and the Executive Committee and via committee work. Standing

exhibit 9.6 Organizational Structure of USA Basketball

Annual Assembly

Board of Directors

USA Basketball Committees

USA CEO & Staff Members

Source: USA Basketball (2017c).

committees of the association include Constitution and Bylaws, Disabled, Finance, Membership, Officials, and committees defined by the board for specific basketball programs and events. The organizational structure of USA Basketball is presented in Exhibit 9.6.

The governing bodies discussed above are all involved in organizing athletic competitions for elite-level athletes or sending elite athletes to major competitions. State and provincial organizations feed into national governing bodies (NGBs) and NSOs, respectively. NSOs are aided by other organizations such as the AAU, Sport Canada, national coaches associations, and the NCAA via their roles in training elite athletes, coaches, and officials. One component of their collective missions is to enhance the ability of athletes to perform on the world stage at international competitions and major games. Next, we investigate the governance structures of some of the major games of amateur athletics.

Organizations that Manage Major Games in Amateur Sport

Major games are national or international events run as single-sport or multisport championships. International world championships are common to many sports, for example, the FIBA World Basketball Championships and the FIFA Soccer World Cup. Also common are major international multisport games for which participation is restricted by eligibility criteria (such as country of origin, age group, or disability). This includes the Pan American Games, Commonwealth Games, World University Games, Deaflympics, and Special Olympics World Games. How are these major games organized? The next sections will address these multisport competitions.

Fédération Internationale de Basketball Amateur
www.fiba.com

Fédération Internationale de Football Association
www.fifa.com

Pan American Games

The Pan American Games are a celebration of sport, competition, and international friendship for nations of the Americas in the Western Hemisphere (Toronto 2015 Pan Am/Para Pan Am Games, 2015). The Games have run on a strict quadrennial cycle since the first competition in 1951 in Buenos Aires, Argentina, typically scheduled for the summer in the year preceding the Summer Olympic Games.

MISSION.   The Pan American Games are first and foremost an international multisport competition. However, since the event's inception the organizers have sought a broader purpose. Along with sporting competition, the Pan American Games are about friendship, life, culture, and the strength of human spirit (PASO, 2017a). They are also a celebration of the Americas' community and of each country's dedication to their fellow nations making up the Americas. The motto of the Pan American Sports Organization (PASO) incorporates Spanish, Portuguese, English, and French: "America, Espirito, Sport, Fraternite," which translates loosely as "The American spirit of friendship through sports" (PASO, 2017a). The mission statement of the Pan Am Games is presented in Exhibit 9.7.

Pan American Games
http://www.paso-odepa.org/en/pan-american-games

| exhibit | 9.7 | Mission Statement of the Pan American Games |

> The principal objects are the celebration and conduct of the Pan American Games and the promotion, development and protection of sport, as well as the Olympic Movement, in the Americas through its member National Olympic Committees.

Source: PASO (2017b).

MEMBERSHIP.   Athletes from countries in the Americas are eligible to compete in the Pan American Games. This includes North, Central, and South America, as well as Caribbean nations. Currently, 41 nations belong to PASO, divided as follows: 3 North American members, 19 Caribbean members, 7 Central American members, and 12 South American members.

FINANCIALS.   The Pan American Games are a huge undertaking, third in scope after the 2016 Olympic Games and 2015 Asian Games (Toronto 2015 Pan Am/Para Pan Am Games, 2015). Depending upon the extent of facility development required, the budget for the games can be in the millions or even billions of dollars. The majority of the expenses include building or upgrading facilities, organizing the games and festivals, housing the competitors, and hosting dignitaries. While competing nations are responsible for their own travel costs, the host committee covers on-site expenses. A fee is guaranteed to PASO for the hosting rights, and additional revenues are generated from television, sales, sponsorships and advertising, and entry fees. Lima, Peru, is hosting the Pan American Games in 2019. Projecting for inflation, the overall budget for those games is estimated to be approximately C$1.8 billion in 2018. The budget is split almost equally between operating funds and capital development budgets for facility construction. In the case of Lima, there is a need for a total 33 sports venues in different areas of the city, including a stadium for 25,000 people, a coliseum for 12,000 people, a 2.4 km rowing center, a major aquatic center upgrade, and a games village to host 10,000 people (Australian Trade and Investment Commission, 2017).

ORGANIZATIONAL STRUCTURE.   PASO governs the games, awards the hosting rights, and sets the policy and direction for the competition. PASO headquarters is located in Mexico City and is presided over by a President and an Executive Council. Each host country then establishes its own organizing

Organizing Committee of the 2015 Pan Am Games

exhibit   **9.8**

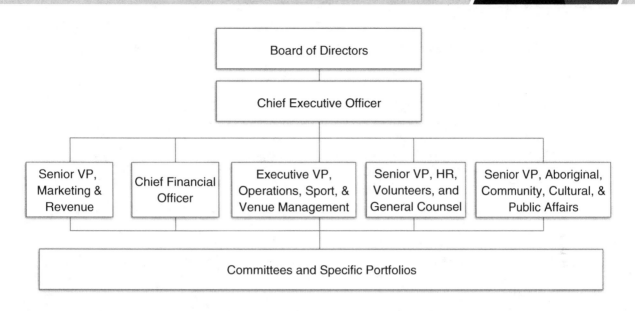

Source: Toronto Organizing Committee (2015).

committee. Normally, the organizing committee is comprised of a Chair or President, Executive or Senior Vice Presidents, Financial leadership, and an extensive number of Organizing Committee members who are assigned portfolios and committees (Toronto 2015 Pan Am/Para Pan Am Games, 2015). An example of the host organizing committee structure for the XVII Pan American Games in Toronto, Canada, which attracted nearly 7,000 athletes in 36 Pan Am and 15 Para Pan Am sports, is presented in Exhibit 9.8. The 2007 Games in Brazil were the first in which the Para Pan American Games for athletes with disabilities were held in conjunction with the events for able-bodied athletes, a practice that quickly became the standard.

Commonwealth Games

The Commonwealth Games are a multisport competition bringing together countries from around the world that are united by history, as opposed to geography (as in the Pan American Games). The Commonwealth Games involve competition among countries that once belonged to the British Empire (see Exhibit 9.9) and for nations and territories that subsequently joined the British Commonwealth after the empire (Dheensaw, 1994). The countries comprising the Commonwealth share a history and acceptance of a common past. The Commonwealth Games continue to bring

www

Commonwealth Games
www.thecgf.com

| exhibit | 9.9 | Competing Countries of the 2018 Commonwealth Games |

AFRICA				
Botswana	Lesotho	Namibia	South Africa	Zambia
Cameroon	Malawi	Nigeria	Swaziland	
Ghana	Mauritius	Seychelles	Tanzania	
Kenya	Mozambique	Sierra Leone	Uganda	

AMERICAS				
Bahamas	Bermuda	Falkland Islands	St. Helena	
Belize	Canada	Guyana		

OCEANIA				
Australia	Kiribati	Niue	Samoa	Tuvalu
Cook Islands	Nauru	Norfolk Islands	Solomon Islands	Vanuatu
Fiji	New Zealand	Papua New Guinea	Tongo	

CARIBBEAN				
Anguilla	Barbados	Grenada	St. Lucia	Trinidad and Tobago
Antigua & Barbuda	British Virgin Islands	Jamaica	St. Vincent & The Grenadines	Turks and Caicos Isles
Bahamas	Cayman Islands	Montserrat		
	Dominica	St. Kitts & Nevis		

EUROPE				
Cyprus	Gibraltar	Isle of Man	Malta	Scotland
England	Guernsey	Jersey	Northern Ireland	Wales

ASIA				
Bangladesh	India	Maldives	Singapore	
Brunei Darussalam	Malaysia	Pakistan	Sri Lanka	

Source: Commonwealth Games Federation (2017a).

athletes and spectators of these nations together every four years for a significant festival of sport.

MISSION. The vision of the Commonwealth Games Federation is "building peaceful, sustainable and prosperous communities globally by inspiring Commonwealth Athletes to drive the impact and ambition of all

| Mission Statement of the Commonwealth Games Federation | *exhibit* 9.10 |

To be an athlete-centred, sport-focused Commonwealth Sports Movement, with integrity, global impact and embraced by communities that accomplishes the following:

- We deliver inspirational and innovative Commonwealth Games and Commonwealth Youth Games, built on friendships and proud heritage, supported by a dynamic Commonwealth Sports Cities Network;
- We nurture and develop one of the best governed and well-managed sports movements in the world;
- We attract and build on public, private and social partnerships that widely benefit Commonwealth athletes, sports and communities;
- We champion, through our brand, Commonwealth athlete, citizen and community engagement in everything we do.

Source: CGF (2017b).

Commonwealth Citizens through Sport" (Commonwealth Games Federation, 2017b, para. 2). The organization seeks to achieve this vision by hosting a world-class multisport event for peoples of Commonwealth nations. The idea of a friendly festival of competition, held on a four-year cycle, is part of their mission statement, presented in Exhibit 9.10.

MEMBERSHIP. Athletes from 71 nations worldwide competed in a variety of individual and team sports at the 2014 Glasgow, Scotland Commonwealth Games. These nations and territories are located in parts of Africa, the Americas, Asia, Caribbean, Europe, and Oceania. Some countries are eligible to compete in both the Pan American and Commonwealth Games, including Canada and many Caribbean countries.

FINANCIALS. The economics of the Commonwealth Games are very similar to the Pan American Games. Revenues are generated through television, sponsorship and advertising, and ticket and merchandise sales. Perhaps more importantly, the games play an economic role and create a legacy for the hosting community; one of the first host committees to embrace this approach was Manchester, England, in 2002. Part of Manchester's platform for hosting was based on the economic impact to be gained for the region. The organizing committee identified the crucial role the Games would play in the continued physical, economic, and social regeneration of Manchester, bringing regional economic benefits. The 2006

Commonwealth Games were also successful in creating a financial legacy for the City of Melbourne, Australia (Tucker, 2006). Surplus revenue of approximately US$22 million was reinvested into the city's and region of Victoria's sport programs: $5.7 million to sport development, $4.86 million to community programs, and $11.44 million to develop community facilities (Government of Victoria, 2012). The 2014 Commonwealth Games hosted by Glasgow, Scotland, also focused on legacy, sustainability, accessibility, and the environment. Forty-six major sponsors enabled the Games to exceed the overall commercial target of roughly $167.62 million (Glasgow 2014, 2014). Gold Coast City, Australia will host the 2018 Commonwealth Games, with a goal to showcase the city and lifestyle of this place of natural beauty. The estimated cost of delivering the Gold Coast Games is $1.51 billion, with funding sources including the Queensland government, Commonwealth government, City of Gold Coast, and other sources such as sponsorship, broadcast rights, ticket sales, licensing and merchandising (Ahead of the Games, 2015).

ORGANIZATIONAL STRUCTURE. The Commonwealth Games Federation (CGF) is the umbrella organization responsible for regulating the competition. It is led by a President and three Vice Presidents, along with an Executive Board. The Executive Board is composed of six elected Regional Vice Presidents (representing Africa, Americas, Asia, Caribbean, Europe, Oceania, and Australia, but not the host region); positions of Legal Advisor and Medical Advisor; and the CGF CEO, currently David Grevemburg, as of this writing (Commonwealth Games Federation, 2017a). The Executive Board and Officers help to set policy enacted by a CGF professional staff led by the CEO.

As with the Pan American Games, the local hosting community develops an organizing committee to deliver the competition. This group forms to bid for the event and, if successful, operates for several years prior to staging the Commonwealth Games. The committee then dissolves in the year after the games, once final financial and operational reports are completed.

World University Games

The World University Games (also called the Universiade or FISU Games) is a sporting and cultural festival held every two years for university-level athletes and governed by FISU, the international university sports federation.

International University
Sports Federation
www.fisu.net

MISSION. Founded in 1949, FISU is responsible for supervising the summer and the winter Universiades, as well as World University Championships in select sports. Universiades bring university-level student-athletes from around the world to different countries to compete in both compulsory (sports contested at each Universiade) and optional sports (as chosen by the host country) (FISU, 2017). For example, the 2017 FISU Summer

Games were in Taipei City, Chinese Taipei. The theme for the Universiade is "Excellence in Mind and Body," implying the infinite value of incorporating educational and cultural aspects of sport competition in the spirit of friendship and sportsmanship for student-athletes around the world. The Taipei City FISU Games include competition in the 14 compulsory sports: artistic gymnastics, athletics (track and field), basketball, diving, fencing, football (soccer), judo, swimming, rhythmic gymnastics, table tennis, taekwondo, tennis, volleyball, and water polo; and seven optional sports: archery, badminton, baseball, golf, roller sports, weightlifting, and wushu (martial arts) (Summer Universiade, 2017). The goal statement of the 2017 Summer Games in Taipei City illustrates the universal purpose of using the games as more than a sporting event, as a city-transforming social movement (Exhibit 9.11).

MEMBERSHIP. FISU is comprised of 170 National University Sports Federations (FISU Today, 2017). One of these is the United States Collegiate Sports Council, which is composed of representatives of the various administrators and support staff of the NCAA, NAIA, and their member institutions. Membership in FISU is divided by countries within the five world continents, Africa (43), America (32), Asia (38), Europe (47), and Oceania (10). National university sports federations gain membership by paying fees and providing proof of eligibility. The Universiades are open to all student-athletes between the ages of 17 and 25 who are eligible to compete in university sport at home and who have not been out of school for more than a year (FISU Today, 2017).

FINANCIALS. FISU is funded through marketing activities, television revenue, organizing and entry fees, and subscriptions (FISU Today, 2017). The

---

Goal Statement of the 29th World University Summer Games in Taipei City, Chinese Taipei: A Better Taipei

exhibit **9.11**

The hosting of the Universiade will boost our international image and forge cooperative links across multiple sectors and cities. The Universiade includes public participation to improve public athleticism and sustainable urban development, transforming our city into a transparent, just, healthy, and safe city as well as sharing her rich cultural elements and the human elements of friendliness and care. Together we shall help create a *Better Taipei*.

Source: Taipei 2017 (2017).

Universiade is run as a multisport festival, bid for by a host country, and run as a business. Revenues are generated in manner similar to the Pan American and the Commonwealth Games, with government funding, corporate sponsorship, television-rights fees, entry fees, and sales making up the largest components of the budget. Summer World University Games are generally one of the largest sporting festivals in the world, in the top three in size with the Olympic Games, involving as many as 174 nations (in Daegu, Korea, in 2003) and 11,785 participants (in Kazan, Russia, in 2013) (FISU Today, 2017). Size alone often dictates the need to develop new facilities to stage the FISU Games.

ORGANIZATIONAL STRUCTURE. FISU is composed of a General Assembly in which each of the 170 member nations is represented. The General Assembly elects an Executive Committee to act on its behalf between meetings of the Assembly. The Executive Committee of FISU is composed of 28 positions and most members are elected for four-year terms. It is led by the President and comprised of a First Vice President, four Vice Presidents, a Treasurer, the First Assessor, 15 Assessors, and 1 delegate for each of the 5 continental associations. This committee meets twice per year and periodically at the call of the President, and is the main policy-making group within FISU. In addition, the host city for the Universiade names an Organizing Committee to plan and manage the staging of the World University Games.

World Games for the Deaf: The Deaflympics

The Deaflympics
www.deaflympics.com

The first International Games for the Deaf (renamed World Games for the Deaf in 1969) were held in 1924 in Paris, France (Carbin, 1996). Just prior to the inaugural games, a group of European men with hearing impairments organized the International Committee of Silent Sports, abbreviated CISS. Today, CISS refers to the International Committee of Sports for the Deaf (CISS, 2017). This organization oversees the World Games for the Deaf (known as the *Deaflympics*) and the Deaf World Championships.

MISSION. The motto of the International Committee of Sports of the Deaf (ICSD) is "Equal Through Sports." The organization brings athletes with hearing impairments together to compete in a range of athletic events, offering them the opportunity to celebrate their achievements and uniqueness as athletes with hearing impairments. The ICSD mission statement is presented in Exhibit 9.12. It stresses the value of competition, equality through sports, and adhering to the ideas of the Olympic Games (ICSD, 2017).

MEMBERSHIP. The CISS has five membership categories: full, provisional, regional confederations, associate, and honorary. Full members are national associations and have voting privileges and participate at the Congress, the governing body of the ICSD. National associations are admitted to the Congress upon review of the report of the Legal

Deaf athletes strive to reach the pinnacle of competition by embracing the motto of PER LUDOS AEQUALITAS (Equality through sports) and adhering to the ideals of Olympics, through more and better athletes with higher standards of excellence, international recognition, increased budget, and efficient and effective organization.

Source: CISS (2017).

Committee, which investigates each applicant's constitution, documents of incorporation, financial reports, and qualifications for membership. Only one national association per country may be admitted as a full member of the ICSD. Currently, the organization has 108 national deaf sports federations as members from around the world. The Deaflympics are organized and run exclusively by members of the deaf community. Only people with hearing impairments are permitted to serve on the ICSD Board of Directors or committees.

FINANCIALS. The ICSD is funded through annual membership fees and levies, along with contributions, donations, sponsorships, and government grants (ICSD, 2017). Local communities bid for the hosting rights of the World Games or sport-specific world championships and generate revenue in support of the event through government funding, corporate sponsorship, sales, and other marketing initiatives.

ORGANIZATIONAL STRUCTURE. Each member has a vote at the Congress. Between congresses, an Executive Committee has the power to deal with the business of the association. The Executive Committee is composed of the President, the Vice President of World Sports, the Vice President of World Youth Sports, two at-large members, and the President of each regional confederation (nonvoting). In a similar fashion to other World Games, the Deaflympics are awarded to a city on the basis of a bid to host the event. An organizing committee, convened to carry out the event, includes a President; Vice President; Secretary; Treasurer; and Chairs for Facilities, Marketing, Sport Operations, Transportation, Special Events, and Media Relations.

Special Olympics World Games

Most people are familiar with Special Olympics. Perhaps you have volunteered at local- or state-level events. But did you know that Special

Olympics also hold major international summer and winter events? The Special Olympics World Games is a multisport festival held every four years in both summer and winter for individuals with all levels of cognitive and developmental disabilities. The Special Olympics and the Paralympic Games are two separate organizations recognized by the IOC. The Special Olympics provides sport opportunities for individuals with cognitive and developmental disabilities, while the Paralympic Games provide sports opportunities for elite athletes with physical disabilities. The Special Olympics World Games take place the year before the Olympic Games, while the Paralympic Games are conducted immediately following the Olympic Games (Special Olympics, 2017).

Special Olympics World Games
www.specialolympics.org

MISSION. The mission of the Special Olympics World Games includes providing an exceptional sporting experience for participants with disabilities from around the world. The motto of the Special Olympics World Summer Games in Abu Dhabi, United Arab Emirates (UAE) in 2019 is "A Vision of Inclusion" which organizers chose because of the inspirational and compelling impact the UAE seeks to create through inclusion for people with intellectual disabilities throughout their country, region, and the world.

The mission statement of the Special Olympics is presented in Exhibit 9.13.

MEMBERSHIP. The Special Olympics World Games have participants rather than members. The 2015 Games in Los Angeles, USA showcased the athletic skills, courage, and dignity of thousands of athletes with cognitive and developmental disabilities from around the world. Approximately 6,500 athletes, 2,000 coaches, 10,000 volunteers, 3,500 event officials, 500,000 spectators, and thousands of families, journalists, and spectators attended the games

---

exhibit **9.13**   Mission of the Special Olympics

> The mission of Special Olympics is to provide year-round sports training and athletic competition in a variety of Olympic-type sports for children and adults with intellectual disabilities. This gives them continuing opportunities to develop physical fitness, demonstrate courage, experience joy and participate in a sharing of gifts, skills and friendship with their families, other Special Olympics athletes and the community.

Source: Special Olympics (2017).

(2015 Special Olympics World Games, 2015). The athletes' oath for the Games was "Let me win, but if I cannot win, let me be brave in the attempt."

FINANCIALS. The host committee of the Special Olympics World Games shoulders a significant endeavor to resource the event, a multi-million-dollar undertaking for facilities, operations, and products and services. The Los Angeles (LA) Games in 2015 had expenses of over $121 million. To deliver the event, sponsorship and corporate partnerships were needed, along with revenue from sales and municipal support. For 2015 the LA organizing committee raised over $115 million in sponsorship money from a dozen major corporate sponsors and over 100 Special Olympics supporters, individuals, trusts, and foundations. Beyond corporate sponsorship, fundraising was initiated through programs such as the Law Enforcement Fun Run, A Very Special Christmas Album, and other special events (2015 Special Olympics, 2015).

ORGANIZATIONAL STRUCTURE. The Special Olympics World Games are managed by a Games Organizing Committee (GOC). The GOC is led by a Chair and is composed of a fairly large number of high-profile community members who act as Directors. The 2015 LA GOC had 49 Directors, and the 2007 Games in Shanghai and the 2011 Games in Athens maintained a large organizational structure and over 20 Directors. The GOCs are incorporated as a company under the name of the Games being organized. The GOC's Board of Directors includes highly experienced individuals from a variety of public and private sector backgrounds. These volunteers, led by a CEO, oversee the activities of paid staff. For the 2015 LA Games, the Board included a Lead Director and Vice Chair, two other Vice Chairs, a Treasurer, Secretary and two Associate Secretaries. Committees such as Security, Quality Management, Transportation, Information Technology, Competitions, Volunteers, among many others, were employed. The 2017 Special Olympic Winter World Games were hosted in Graz, Schladming and Ramsau, Austria, and the 2019 Special Olympic Summer Games will be held in the UAE.

CURRENT POLICY AREAS

Hosting major games as described above is a significant undertaking. Each event requires considerable organizational efforts, large financial support, and thousands of paid and volunteer workers. The organizing committee may plan for three or four years to ensure a safe and effective competition. Some issues organizers will surely deal with are internal to the particular event, such as fundraising and security. Many others are externally imposed, often by the governing international federation and include issues such as doping control and the influences of the media. Other concerns stem from our global society and involve the world's perspective on global conflict, political involvement in sport, and the very definition of *amateurism*. Each of these issues involves current policy areas.

LOU LAURIA, *Chief of Games and Competitions, Special Olympics International*

Washington, DC

In my role as Special Olympics International Chief of Games and Competitions, my primary responsibilities are centered around the Special Olympics World Games and Special Olympics Winter World Games. Our team's responsibilities start from the design and implementation of the bid process and continue through to the evaluating/awarding and delivery of World Games.

We are the lead department in all of the games planning and integration required for the World Games. This includes building the coordination and management framework, as well as the production of technical materials that outline requirements across all major areas (e.g. Sport, Transport, Accommodation, etc.)

Cost is a key issue as many major games are struggling to find bids for their events. In most democratic societies public funds are used to pay for events and major games organizers strong opposition to fund major sporting events. All major games are having to strategically review the scale, scope, and service level of their operations. We have to answer pivotal questions about our event. Can my multisport event continue to exist by requiring a city to host 22 sports, or can we reduce it to 12 core sports and then let the host city select 4 additional sports from a list? Can I reduce the number of venues required? Can we reduce additional requirements, etc.? The flip side of this is that major games must now prove their value across the board from economic impact, which had long been the only real measure, to now including social impact. We are a long way from the boom period where countries rich in natural resources who were seeking to nation build would bid for every event on the calendar.

The second major challenge is making your event relevant to a younger market. You are seeing the innovative International Federations modify or in some cases create new disciplines in their sport. In the 2010 Singapore Youth Olympic Games, the basketball federation FIBA introduced 3 on 3 basketball. A mere ten years later it will be contested as a medal sport at the Tokyo 2020 Olympic Games. Other additions include skateboarding, surfing, and sport climbing, all of which are making their Olympic Games debut in Tokyo in 2020. Part of this youth market challenge is the way the media delivers sport to the public. The old model does not work and many sports have not yet adjusted to the digital world in a meaningful way.

One area that our team is working hard on is identifying cities and regions where the Special Olympics World Games are a good fit. One of our primary goals is to be a good partner to the host city and country. When looking for a host, we consider what cities/countries are investing in social inclusion, health, and education for people with intellectual disabilities. This is where we want to have a dialogue about hosting our event. I want to be assured that after hosting the Special Olympic World Games a city is closer to realizing its strategic objectives. This will leave a sustainable legacy and also place the country's national Special Olympics Program in a stronger position. Our conversation related to government support with a potential host should be broad and include more than the Minister of Sport. It should include health, education, social development, etc. We need to look at public–private partnerships in markets where this model could be successful.

In the Olympic and Paralympic context, where I spent 20 years of my career, the International Federation model was long dominated by European male sports professionals. They occupied a bubble which consisted of the "haves" and "have nots" depending if their sports were on the Olympic Program. They were often slow to react to challenges like doping or appealing to a diverse and youthful market. The decision to award their events where often based on extracting the largest hosting fee possible, as this would help them get re-elected. The focus was not on helping the host develop their sport long term. Many major games owners provided little to no support to their host cities. In some cases this was due to a lack of internal expertise and in other cases a lack of interest once the host agreement was signed.

Major games need to do more to innovate and create their point of differentiation. It is a crowded marketplace with far too many "off the shelf" type sporting events. They need to connect with a new generation of spectators who are looking for something different and often seeking some social value. This is true in the companies they want to work for and the products they purchase.

You are also looking at incredible growth in areas like eSport, and to a lesser degree, Drone Racing. These events did not exist 15 years ago and now universities are offering scholarships for their eSports teams. Ownership and control of major games is also an interesting area. Some organizations such as UEFA [Union of European Football Associations] control key areas of their premier event, the European Football Championships. They install staff within the host nation and manage the planning according to their systems. It will be interesting to see if more events look at some areas in which they need to assume control. It is not, however, a solution that everyone can implement due to resource limitations. This will be an ongoing issue as major games continue to grow around the world.

Sport and International Politics

The association between sport and politics, and the subsequent political maneuvering that might occur through major games, is a policy area of interest to event participants and organizers. Recent issues of the international politics of sport include the advance of political ideologies such as democracy versus communism; capitalism and international relations; religion, gender, and disability sport; sport and terrorism; and international travel bans (Hassan, 2012; Levermore & Budd, 2004; Longman, 2017). Sport has traditionally been used for nation building. It symbolizes the values of success, "of our ways compared to your ways," "of our people over your people." Sport illustrates power, wealth, business might, and general superiority. It has even been used as a show of moral authority and political legitimization (Allison, 2005; Houlihan & Lindsey, 2013).

Political factors have influenced the location of game sites. For instance, international federations have chosen host sites on the basis of generating economic support and facilitating legacy to an underdeveloped part of the world. Boycotting tactics—a nation refusing to send athletes and teams to an event in protest over another country's domestic or foreign policy—have been used as a form of political maneuvering. In this case national policy might directly influence sport policy, and a nation may decide the extent to which sport will be used on the world stage to further other national objectives. The degree to which sport is used to enhance a national political agenda directly affects the political maneuvering associated with major games. Another factor might include the involvement of business and the commercialization of sporting events. Today, the long-term involvement of businesses in sport might actually weaken the ability of a government to manipulate and exploit sport as a means for promoting a diplomatic agenda, as the international sport agenda becomes more and more dominated by big business as opposed to state politics (Allison, 2005).

Financing the Games and Economic Impact

Fundraising and marketing have become increasingly important to hosting major games in amateur athletics (Coates & Wicker, 2017). While several levels of a government might commit to contributing some financial support, such an offering is seen as a component of a larger financial landscape. Therefore, since hosting requires significant resources, particularly when new facilities are required, developing the financial backing to deliver the event is critical for success.

The importance of marketing for a major amateur athletic event is a given (Smith, 2017). While significant positive results can accrue from attracting donor funds and marketing the event (even to the extent that one without the other may well be impossible), other issues arise from marketing and fundraising practices. Members of organizing committees are debating methods of increasing the value of television and sponsorship packages, not to mention the impact of social media. Increased commercialization of amateur sport results in a shift of power and control toward sponsors. Struggles develop as a result of exclusive sponsorship categories. For example, water and isotonic drinks are obviously an important sponsorship category associated with major games. When exclusive sponsorship rights are awarded to one company, the extent of the sponsorship agreement might become a source of problems. Does the sponsorship agreement extend to all other products associated with the company? This becomes an issue because today's multinational conglomerates produce a vast array of products. A balance between the sponsor's needs and the best interests of the games is required. Without fundraising, sponsorship, and marketing, the very existence of major games could be jeopardized, given the significant requirement for operating revenues.

Today's global economy drives both cost and value. On the one hand the hosting of most major games runs in the millions of dollars or euros. The value of selling certain properties associated with major games, such as title sponsorship or television rights, slides on a scale depending on the location and economic factors. Organizers are constantly concerned with keeping costs down and value up. While costs can remain fairly neutral once established, the values of the properties of major games are more difficult to pinpoint. These values depend on many factors, and they change as a result of economic and political factors. For instance, how does the value of television rights for hosting the Pan American Games differ between a host site in North America versus South America? Many factors, such as the number of potential television carriers, the size of target markets, the time of year, competition with other established events, and the ability of the host to attract other corporate partners affect the value of the television package. Of course, the organizing committee enacts policies to drive the value of the contract as high as possible. These policies might suggest the importance of publicity to increase the television audience, scheduling games and events at the best time of day to ensure the highest possible television numbers, and so on.

Broadcasting and sponsorship revenues come with an associated cost. When outside groups buy services or properties, conflict may arise over how the event is run. Policies to define rights and privileges associated with each partnership are critical to successfully hosting major games. For instance, the organizing committee must define a specific television policy that establishes explicit guidelines for how the event will be scheduled, with game-day timelines determined in advance. The policy will also suggest how changes to the timelines can be made, naming the groups or individuals who must be consulted.

Exclusivity is a term used for selling sponsorships that involves dividing the event into sponsorship categories and allowing for each category to be sold only one time, thereby providing one sponsor with "exclusive rights" without competition for its product. For instance, selling soft drink sponsorship exclusively to Pepsi would preclude any sponsorship with Coke or any other soft drink company. It may be difficult to decide which categories of sponsorship should be sold exclusively. Often, the sponsorship policy defines exactly which sales categories will be sold with exclusivity. Preferably, the marketing and sales personnel of the organizing committee will carefully define and communicate this practice to sponsors in advance, thereby lessening the potential for conflict between sponsors, controlling for ambush marketing attempts, and enhancing the sponsors' interest in being associated with the event.

Amateur athletic organizers rely heavily on marketing and sponsorship to deliver an event of the magnitude of FISU or Commonwealth Games. The comments made by Slack (1998) still apply: "in no previous time period have we seen the type of growth in the commercialization of sport that we have seen in the last two decades. Today, sport is big business and big businesses are heavily involved in sport" (p. 1). Such reliance, however, is of concern to event organizers. In a best-case scenario, a major games could run as an entity by itself. Given this is not the case, international federations and major games organizing committees set policy to encourage revenue generation beyond corporate sponsorship and advertising. For example, the Finance Committee of a major games would define sources of funding in order to manage the event. Those sources will be as diverse as possible in order to decrease the threat of reliance on any one funding category. Government funding, television rights, categories of exclusive and nonexclusive sponsors and corporate partners, pure advertising, ticket sales, merchandising, entry fees—all are sought by organizing committees to diversify revenue sources, prevent running an overall deficit, and deflect undue influence and/or control of the games by outside groups.

Finding the resources to deliver the games is an imperative. A highly touted outcome of hosting the games is now commonly referred to as economic impact. Economic impact is defined as the complex measurement of factors associated with hosting the games that leave a legacy for the area in terms of infrastructure and urban renewal, tourism and construction jobs, factors of the economy, and so on. The 2010 Commonwealth Games was reported to have a $4.9 billion impact on India's gross domestic product (GDP) between 2008 and 2012 (Institute of International Trade, n.d.). This was almost three times the GDP for Australia's hosting of the 2006 Games in Melbourne (Institute of International Trade, n.d.).

Global Conflict, Terrorism, and Security

Global conflict and the war on terrorism seem to be constant issues on the world agenda. War, conflict, terrorism, political maneuvering, and alliance building are issues for virtually every government. Terrorism is defined as a politically motivated form of violence, usually employed to overthrow governments (Toohey, 2008). Terrorism, especially since the September 11, 2001, attacks on the United States, continue to have world leaders and the rest of the world on alert.

The changes to daily life associated with a world on alert are manifested in many ways. Citizenship, travel, security, privacy, and global politics each take on heightened meaning. The impact on event management is particularly important. Imagine being the Director of Security for a large international event in this environment. Your task is to ensure the safety of 5,000 competitors from 145 countries and the 400,000 people who will gather to enjoy the competition and related cultural events. This is a monumental task and the focus of extensive debate and policy development. Unfortunately, the issue is not brand new. The tragic hostage crisis in the Olympic Village during the Munich Olympic Games of 1972 resulted in the deaths of 11 Israeli athletes and coaches, 5 Palestinian terrorists, and 1 German police officer. Major games bring global representatives and world media attention. In 1996, Atlanta hosted the Olympic Summer Games and was the site of a terrorist bombing that tragically killed 2 and injured 111 people. Major games are mega-events and represent a primary focus for certain terrorist cells given the media attention focused on the events and publicity gained (Horne & Manzenreiter, 2006). Look no further than the attack at the Boston Marathon. The potential for terrorist action at major games is of real and continued concern for games organizers.

Enacting policy regarding safety at major athletic games involves the collaboration of several levels of administration. Security and law enforcement personnel from local and governmental offices provide the foundation. Sport federations might provide expertise on past experience that proves valuable for future actions. The organizing committee ensures the coordination of all agencies and the implementation of the policy. Other levels within the government of the host country help with coordination. The governments of competing countries may offer assistance and will undoubtedly require assurances of readiness. In the end the policy will define parameters for safe and secure travel, admittance, contact, and conduct of participants, spectators, and affiliates of the major games.

The successful bid by Gold Coast City, Australia, to host the 2018 Commonwealth Games identifies security as a main planning theme.

www

Gold Coast City Bid for the 2018 Commonwealth Games
www.thecgf.com/ games/2018/Gold_Coast_ VOL_1.pdf

Historical evidence of managing security, having the capacity and systems in place to coordinate massive numbers of visitors and venues, and experience in command and control are a consistent requirement of major games hosting. At this event, as with Pan American Games, World University Games, and other events and championships, security is of paramount concern, and significant resources, planning, and collaboration with local and national law enforcement are required.

Performance Enhancement

The use of drugs to enhance performance and influence the outcomes of athletic contests is termed *doping*. Worldwide, sport agencies and federations view doping as cheating and prohibit the use of performance-enhancing drugs (PEDs). Athletic competition is about pitting the natural athleticism and skills of an individual or group against another. Fairness requires each individual or group to compete within a common set of parameters. PEDs are considered detours around the rigors of training and preparation. As such, doping is considered artificial and is thus banned as a means of achieving a competitive edge. In addition, many doping practices are dangerous and in direct opposition to the concept of "healthy mind, healthy body" that is the benefit of sport and physical activity. To combat the issue of doping in sports, national associations such as the United States Anti-Doping Association (USADA), UK Anti-Doping, and the Canadian Centre for Ethics in Sport (CCES) have been organized to work in conjunction with Olympic Committees and the World Anti-Doping Agency (WADA). Policy on doping in sport has been defined in order to

- protect those who play fair
- educate about the dangers and consequences of doping
- research and publish prohibited substances and methods lists
- coordinate anti-doping activities globally
- deter those who might cheat
- apply common sanctions for doping infractions and provide detailed procedures for establishing a breach in the rules (WADA, 2017)

All major games, international federations, and the Olympic Movement have provided a unified approach to setting policy that outlines banned substances and practices, and outlaws anyone contributing to doping in sport. WADA provides for this required unified approach to developing doping-control policy, referred to as the World Anti-Doping Code (WADA, 2017). Testing procedures, penalties, laboratory analyses, results management, protests and appeals, and reinstatement procedures are basic elements of doping-control policy. The ultimate goal of the policy is to create anti-doping rules, set mandatory international standards for banned substances and testing procedures, and model best practices. The issue is

www

United States Anti-Doping Agency
www.usantidoping.org

UK Anti-Doping
http://ukad.org.uk/

Canadian Centre for Ethics in Sport
www.cces.ca

World Anti-Doping Agency
www.wada-ama.org/

defined as a current policy area because it remains a dynamic issue. The use of banned substances and subsequent reports of positive tests remain a common occurrence at major games such as the Commonwealth Games and Pan American Games. For example, a 16-year old Nigerian weight lifter was stripped of her gold medal at the Glasgow 2014 Commonwealth Games after testing positive for two banned substances (Harris, 2014). Eighteen athletes tested positive for a range of banned substances at the 2015 Toronto Pan-Am Games (Harrison, 2015). Testing and strict anti-doping procedures are enacted at all major games by organizing committees. However, the will to win and the stakes for winning on the world stage help promulgate a win-at-any-cost attitude, which results in the development of new performance-enhancing techniques and substances. Thus, policy makers at all national and international levels continue to focus on this issue to curb such behaviors.

SUMMARY

The major games of amateur sport have a rich and diverse history. The Olympic Games are still the world's largest and most prestigious sport festival, but in between Olympic Games many other events are organized and attended by nations worldwide. Major games are organized mostly for amateur competitors, and NGBs and NSOs help initiate and manage the competitors selected to represent their nation. In the United States, the AAU plays a major role in developing and organizing competitive athletics. State and national governing bodies oversee national-level competition and send representatives to international games, set policy and provide funding for teams to compete at world championships.

Major international games include the Pan American Games, the Commonwealth Games, the FISU Games, the Deaflympics, and the Special Olympic World Games. Such events require extensive planning and organizing and are major financial undertakings. Organizing committees spend years preparing and managing many policy areas in an effort to ensure a safe, effective sporting competition. Current policy issues include political maneuvering, funding, security, terrorism and issues of global conflict, and doping control. The stakes are high for participants and organizers, given the enormity of the overall profile, size, and financial commitment involved in major games.

caseSTUDY

MAJOR GAMES IN AMATEUR SPORT

You work for your local area sports commission. You are putting together your strategic plans for the next ten years and have decided to put in a bid for the Pan American Games. You are located in a major metropolitan area with a population of approximately two million residents. Your city has a large university with excellent sport facilities and a college with good outdoor facilities. Your community also has one AAA minor league baseball team; considerable other sports facilities, both private and public; and extensive park areas that could serve as potential venues.

Using the bids created by the communities of Ciudad Bolívar, Venezuela, La Punta San Luis, Argentina, Lima, Peru, and Santiago de Chile, Chile, for the 2019 Pan Am Games that are presented on the Bids for the 2019 Games website for assistance, answer the following questions:

1. Make a list identifying each area of information that will be required, forming an outline of the sections of the bid document.
2. With which governing bodies (local, national, international) will you need to communicate?
3. Exactly which sports will be on the games program, and what is your plan for selecting the venues you would like to use for each sport?
4. Whom will you work with to ensure the security of athletes, coaches, and fans?
5. What local community groups will you actively pursue to assist with your bid, and what will their specific roles be?

CHAPTER questions

1. Choose any two of the major games presented in this chapter. Using the Internet, compare the content of their constitution and bylaws. How are they different or similar?
2. How do major games market their product and entice sponsors? Using the websites of any three major games, review the fundraising practices of the organizing committee. Given the four strategic management practices (presented in Chapter 3) used by sport managers to maximize their potential, assess the degree to which the organizing committees maximize their revenue-generating potential.
3. What is WADA, and why does it exist? Explain WADA's goal. What role do major games organizers play in helping WADA achieve its mission? Within a group of classmates, debate whether WADA is working to ensure that athletes "play true."

FOR ADDITIONAL INFORMATION

For more information check out the following resources:

1. Huffington Post Article: Pan Am Games 2015. This is how much they cost: www.huffingtonpost.ca/2015/11/05/pan-am-games-cost_n_8483828.html
2. The Sport of Globalization. It's a home run: https://writingmerrimack.wordpress.com/2013/10/14/the-sport-of-globalization-its-a-home-run/comment-page-1/
3. You Tube Video: Highlights of the 2015 Deaflympics: https://www.youtube.com/watch?v=QN2cirBumyI
4. Understanding Social Media and Sport: https://www.clearinghouseforsport.gov.au/knowledge_base/organised_sport/sports_administration_and_management/social_media_and_sport
5. The winter Universiade: www.fisu.net/events/winter-universiade
6. Sepp Blatter full interview (BBC).https://www.youtube.com/watch?v=EnywMpFLJdw

REFERENCES

2015 Special Olympics World Games. (2015). World Summer Games Los Angeles. Retrieved from www.specialolympics.org/la2015/

AAU. (2017). About AAU. Retrieved from http://aausports.org/

Ahead of the Games. (2017). Ahead of the games. The inside story on Gold Coast 2018 Commonwealth Games preparations. Retrieved from http://aheadofthegames.embracing2018.com/2015/06/assets-2015/docs/Ahead-of-the-Games.pdf

Allison, L. (2005). The curious role of the USA in world sport. In L. Allison (Ed.), *The global politics of sport: The role of global institutions in sport* (pp. 101–117). London: Routledge.

Americans With Disabilities Act. (1990). ADA of 1990. Retrieved from www.ada.gov/

Australian Trade and Investment Commission (2017). Export markets—Peru. Retrieved from www.austrade.gov.au/Australian/Export/Export-markets/Countries/Peru/Industries

Canadian Sport Policy. (2012). The Canadian sport policy. Retrieved from www.sport.mb.ca/Canadian_Sport_Policy.pdf

Carbin, C. F. (1996). *Deaf heritage in Canada: A distinctive, diverse and enduring culture.* Toronto: McGraw-Hill Ryerson.

Chalip, L., & Johnson, A. (1996). Sport policy in the United States. In L. Chalip, A. Johnson, & L. Stachura (Eds.), *National sport policies: An international handbook* (pp. 404–430). Westport, CT: Greenwood Press.

CISS. (2017). International Committee of Sports for the Deaf. Retrieved from www.ciss.org/

Coates, D., & Wicker, P. (2017). Financial management. In R. Hoye & M. M. Parent (Eds.), *The Sage handbook of sport management* (pp. 117–137). London: Sage.

Commonwealth Games Federation. (2017a). The Commonwealth Games. Retrieved from www.thecgf.com/

Commonwealth Games Federation. (2017b). Transformation 2022. The CGF strategic plan 2015–2022. Retrieved from www.thecgf.com/media/content/CGF-transformation-2022.pdf

Dheensaw, C. (1994). *The Commonwealth Games.* Victoria, BC: Orca.

FISU. (2017). International university sports federation. Retrieved from www.fisu.net/events/summer-universiade#

FISU Today. (2017). FISU today. Retrieved from www.fisu.net/fisu/today

Glasgow 2014. (2014). Glasgow Commonwealth Games. Retrieved from www.glasgow2014.com/media-centre/press-releases/glasgow-2014-says-big-thank-you-xx-commonwealth-games-sponsor-family

Glassford, R. G., & Redmond, G. (1988). Physical education and sport in modern times. In E. F. Zeigler (Ed.), *History of physical education and sport* (pp. 103–171). Champaign, IL: Stipes.

Government of Victoria. (2012). Commonwealth Games Legacy. Retrieved from www.dpcd.vic.gov.au/sport/major-events/commonwealth-games/commonwealth-games-legacy

Harris, R. (2014). 16 year old weight lifter stripped of Commonwealth Games gold after positive doping test. Retrieved from http://news.nationalpost.com/sports/16-year-old-weightlifter-stripped-of-commonwealth-games-gold-after-positive-doping-test

Harrison, D. (2015). 18 Pan-Am Games athletes tested positive for doping: Report. Retrieved from www.cbc.ca/sports/athletes-positive-doping-pan-am-games-1.3220819

Hassan, D. (2012). Sport and terrorism: Two of modern life's most prevalent themes. *International Review for the Sociology of Sport*, 47(3), 263–267.

Horne, J., & Manzenreiter, W. (2006). An introduction to the sociology of sports mega-events. *Sociological Review*, S2, 1–24.

Houlihan, B., & Lindsey, I. (2013). *Sport policy in Britain*. London: Routledge.

ICSD. (2017). About the ICSD. Retrieved from https://www.deaflympics.com/icsd.asp

Institute of International Trade. (n.d.). Commonwealth Games and the economy. Retrieved from www.iitrade.ac.in/km/ibank/Commonwealth%20Games%20and%20the%20Economy.pdf

Kidd, B. (1999). *The struggle for Canadian sport*. Toronto: University of Toronto Press.

Langlois, M.-C., & Menard, M. (2013). Sport Canada and the public policy framework for participation and excellence in sport. Retrieved from www.lop.parl.gc.ca/Content/LOP/ResearchPublications/2013-75-e.htm

Levermore, R., & Budd, A. (2004). *Sport & international relations: An emerging relationship*. London: Routledge.

Longman, J. (2017, January 28). Trump's immigration order could have big impact on sports. *New York Times*. Retrieved from https://www.nytimes.com/2017/01/28/sports/trump-refugee-ban.html?_r=0

Pan Am Sports. (2017a). Pan American Sports Organization. Retrieved from http://www.panamsports.org/

Pan Am Sports. (2017b). PASO constitution. Retrieved from http://www.panamsports.org/constitutions/

Riess, S. A. (1995). *Sport in industrial America 1850–1920*. Wheeling, IL: Harlan Davidson.

Riordan, J., & Kruger, A. (1999). *The international politics of sport in the 20th century*. New York: Routledge.

Slack, T. (1998). Studying the commercialisation of sport: The need for critical analysis. *Sociology of Sport Online*, 1(1), 1–16.

Smith, A.C.T. (2017). Sport marketing. In R. Hoye & M. M. Parent (Eds.), *The Sage handbook of sport management* (pp. 138–159). London: Sage.

Special Olympics. (2017). Special Olympics. Retrieved from www.specialolympics.org/

Sport Canada. (2012). Sport Canada funding programs. Retrieved from https://www.canada.ca/en/canadian-heritage/services/funding-sport.html

Sport Canada. (2017). The role of Sport Canada. Retrieved from http://canada.pch.gc.ca/eng/1414510019083

Summer Universiade. (2017). Taipai sports. Retrieved from http://2017.taipei/ezfiles/0/1000/img/30/FISU_Regulation_for_SU2017.pdf

Sutcliff Group. (2016). Canadian Sport policy formative evaluation and thematic review of physical literacy and LTAD: Final report. Retrieved from http://sirc.ca/sites/default/files/content/docs/CSP_documents/tsgi_pim_formeval_csp_themrev_final_report.pdf

Taipei, 2017. (2017). Purpose, bid history, value of universiade. Retrieved from http://old.2017.gov.taipei/files/11-1000-131.php?Lang=en

Toohey, C. (2008). Terrorism, sport and public policy in the risk society. *Sport in Society: Cultures, Commerce, Media, Politics*, 11, 429–442.

Toronto 2015 Organizing Committee. (2015). Organizing committee. Retrieved from www. toronto2015org/about-us/organizing-committee

Toronto 2015 Pan Am/Para Pan Am Games. (2015). About the Pan Am Games. Retrieved from www.toronto2015.org/about-us/ pan-am-games

Tucker, S. (2006, April 8). Rewards for a city that lifted its game. *Financial Times*, p. 16.

United States Amateur Sports Act. (1978). United States Amateur Sports Act. Retrieved from https://www.govtrack.us/congress/bills/95/s2727

US Senate S.2119 (105th): Olympic and Amateur Sports Act. (1998). Committee clears legislation, nominations. Retrieved from https:// www.govtrack.us/congress/bills/105/s2119/ summary

USA Basketball. (2017a). Constitution. Article 3 purpose. Retrieved from https://www.usab.com/ about/about-usa-basketball/constitution.aspx

USA Basketball. (2017b). Constitution. Articles 7–9. Retrieved from https://www.usab.com/about/ about-usa-basketball/constitution.aspx

USA Basketball. (2017c). Inside USA basketball. Who we are. Retrieved from https://www.usab.com/ about/about-usa-basketball.aspx

Uyoe, I., & Peters, M. (2017). United States Olympic Committee organizational analysis. Retrieved from https://www.slideshare.net/Idorenyin/ usoc-organizational-analysis-57391480

WADA. (2017). What we do. Retrieved from https:// www.wada-ama.org/en/what-we-do

Olympic Sport

Mary A. Hums
Joanne C. MacLean

Imagine what it must be like to strive to be the best in the world in your chosen sport: the years of preparation, the excitement of the competitions, the media attention, the applause of fans, the travel, the agony of defeat, and the thrill of victory. Now imagine the feelings of competing at the Olympic Games, often described by athletes as the adventure of a lifetime. Without doubt, the Olympic Games are the most significant sporting competition in the world, scheduled every four years for both summer and winter events. Athletes at virtually every level dream of one day competing for their nation on the world stage in the Olympic Games. Winning an Olympic Gold Medal holds tremendous meaning worldwide. Not only does it signify world supremacy for the athlete(s) involved, Olympic Gold means instant recognition, fame, financial success, nation building, and legitimization of political ideologies. Olympic Gold Medals are symbolic of success throughout the society the winner represents. No wonder the Olympic Games are held in such high regard and taken so seriously by nations around the world.

Citius, Altius, Fortius ("Faster, Higher, Stronger") is the motto of the modern Olympic Games. The Summer and Winter Olympic Games alternate every two years so that four years (a *quadrennial*) passes in a full cycle. A global audience of half the world's population, nearly 6.9 billion people watched some portion of the 2016 Rio de Janeiro Summer Games and digital consumption of the Games reached new levels with 7.2 billion video views of official contents (IOC Marketing and Broadcast, 2017a). The Sochi 2014 Games enjoyed the most extensive coverage ever produced for the Winter Olympic Games, reaching a record potential audience of 4.4 billion people, with 250 broadcasters and television stations providing coverage in over 220 countries and territories of the world (IOC Marketing and Broadcast, 2017b). The incredible global reach, especially given the popularity of digital consumption, of the Olympic Games makes them more than just a sporting event. They are a media extravaganza, a cultural festival, an international political stage, an economic colossus, and a location for developing friendships. Everyone strives for excellence, from the competing athletes to the host city. The Olympic Games are a showcase, and "Faster, Higher, Stronger" reflects the essence of the event. This chapter looks at the history of the Games, their organization and governance, and the policy issues currently confronting organizers.

HISTORY OF THE OLYMPIC GAMES

The history of the Olympic Games can be divided into two distinct timeframes. The games originated in Ancient Greece, were discontinued for at least 1,500 years, and then were reinstituted in the late 19th century. In the early Olympic Games, the Ancient Greeks competed for the glory of their gods. Much later in history, in the so-called modern era of the Games, the ancient festival was reintroduced and evolved into the event we know today.

The Ancient Olympic Games

Early Greek civilizations loved athletics and assimilated strength and vigor with rhythm, beauty, and music in their style of games and pursuits (Nelson, 2007). The Greeks participated in contests and athletic events like chariot racing, boxing, wrestling, footraces, discus throwing, and archery. The first Olympic Games were held in 776 BCE in Olympia, Greece and were celebrated again every four years until their abolition by the Roman Emperor Theodosius in 393 CE (Young, 2004). The four years between Games were called an *Olympiad*, a system upon which time was calculated in ancient Greek history (Ancient Olympic Games, 2017). Specific events changed over the centuries, but footraces, the pentathlon, boxing, and various types of chariot races were common. The ancient Olympic Games were restricted to free Greek male citizens. It was not until the modern Olympic era that women were included (either as competitors or as spectators) and that people of different nations were allowed to compete.

The Modern Era of the Olympic Games

From 1859 until the actual revival of the Olympic Games in 1896, the idea of reinstituting the festival of the Olympiad was discussed by both Greek nationalist Evagelis Zappas and Englishman William Penny Brookes (Toohey & Veal, 2007). Baron Pierre de Coubertin of Paris visited with Brookes and is the individual now credited with successfully launching the modern Olympic Games. Baron de Coubertin believed strongly in the healthy mind–healthy body connection (de Coubertin, 2000). He envisioned amateur athletes from all around the world competing in a festival of sports similar to those of ancient Greece. In 1894, the Baron presided over a congress held at the Sorbonne in Paris. Representatives from 13 countries attended the meeting, and another 21 wrote to support the concept of reviving the Olympic Games (Toohey & Veal, 2007). The assembled nations unanimously supported the revival of the Greek Olympic festival, to be held every four years, and to which every nation would be invited to send representatives. The modern Olympic Games were reborn in 1896 and were held in Athens, Greece. Two hundred and forty-one athletes (all men) from 14 nations participated in nine sports (43 events) in the first modern Olympiad (IOC, 2017a).

Many traditions taken for granted in the Olympic Games today were born during the early modern Olympic Games, including the opening ceremony and the parade of nations into a stadium; the medal ceremonies and the flag raising of the Gold Medal-winning athlete; housing the participants in an Olympic Village at the site of the Games; and beginning and ending the Games with the lighting and the extinguishing of the Olympic flame, brought to the site from the ancient site in Olympia, Greece. Quickly, the Olympic Games became a world focus, and today young men and women come from all over the world to compete in various sports for the glory of representing their nation. Since the revitalization of the modern Games, the Olympic Games have grown in size and complexity, requiring an increasingly sophisticated international governance structure. Exactly how are the Olympic Games governed, and how is an Olympic Games planned, organized, and managed?

GOVERNANCE

Mention "the Olympic Games" and competition, ceremony, and colors of the world come to mind, along with memories of spectacle and stories of unimaginable achievements. But from a sport management perspective, what makes these Games happen? In reality, an enormous amount of planning and coordination is required, in addition to volumes of policy that set standards for what and how things are done. Three main levels of organizational influence direct the Olympic Games as we know them. First, the Olympic Games are organized through the jurisdiction of the International Olympic Committee (IOC), led by its President, the Session (an annual General Assembly or Annual Meeting), and the Executive Board (similar to an Executive Committee). Bids to host the Olympic Games are made by National Olympic Committees (NOCs) from interested countries. Once a bid has been awarded to a particular country, the responsibility for organizing an Olympic Games falls upon the Organizing Committee for the Olympic Games (OCOG). Each, in turn, contributes significantly to the staging of the Olympic Games.

International Olympic Committee

www
International Olympic
Committee
www.olympic.org

The IOC, founded on June 23, 1894, is a group of officials governing Olympic organization and policy. The members are elected at the Session from the worldwide sport community. The headquarters of the IOC is located in Lausanne, Switzerland, and is a nonprofit organization independent of any government or nation. Having a NOC does not guarantee that a country will be eligible to have an IOC representative. However, an effort is made to ensure that IOC membership represents geographical regions of the world. In addition, while countries that have hosted Olympic competitions are eligible to have two IOC members, some other countries choose not to fill their IOC seat, and they are not required to do so. Some countries have more than two IOC members because those additional members head an International Sports Federation for one of the sports on the program of the Olympic Games. Keep in mind that all IOC members are elected to their positions and serve as representatives to the IOC to promote Olympism. They are not required to reside in the country for which they are a delegate to the IOC.

MISSION.   The roles of IOC members are specific: first, they are expected to serve the Olympic Movement (that is, to promote the tenets of Olympism) by helping to organize and govern policy relative to the staging of the Olympic Games. They are also expected to further the cause and understanding of all things associated with the Olympic Movement in their respective countries. IOC members are not representatives of their *nation* to the IOC. Rather, they are representatives of the *IOC* to their nations. They are expected to care first and foremost about what's best for the Olympic Games and work only on furthering the Olympic Movement as a whole. The fundamental tasks of the IOC include (1) promoting Olympism, (2) celebrating the Olympic Games, (3) leading the Olympic Movement, and (4) supporting and protecting clean (drug-free) athletes (IOC, 2017d). To achieve these goals the IOC has developed a Strategic Roadmap, *Olympic Agenda 2020*, which presents 40 recommendations to safeguard the Olympic Movement and strengthen sport in society.

Key goals of the IOC Olympic Agenda 2020 are presented in Exhibit 10.1.

MEMBERSHIP.   Historically, IOC members were elected by the other members of the committee, a practice that labeled the committee as elitist, incestuous, and existing for the gratification of its members. In the beginning, the committee was an extended group of friends and business associates of the original members, mostly from the upper class of society. Following the corruption allegations associated with the 2002 Salt Lake City Winter

---

Key Goals of the Olympic Agenda 2020   *exhibit* **10.1**

- Changes to Games hosting application procedures
- Reduce costs of bidding for the Games
- Move from a sport-based to an event-based program
- Strengthen non-discrimination of sexual orientation in the Olympic Charter
- Launch an Olympic channel
- Adapt and strengthen the IOC governance principles
- Protection of clean athletes.

Source: IOC (2017d).

IOC Marketing Fact File
https://www.olympic.org/
documents/ioc-marketing-
and-broadcasting

Olympic Games bid, the IOC changed some of its procedures. For instance, the IOC is now composed of 95 members (IOC, 2017c). Members of the IOC are allowed to serve until age 70 (except for members coopted between 1966 and 1999 who may serve to age 80), although some choose to retire earlier. Positions are still elected by the members of the General Assembly, individual members, active Olympic athletes elected by their peers at the Olympic Games, members from International Federations (IFs) and NOCs. Restrictions limit the numbers of a particular group being from the same country or Federation.

FINANCIALS. The IOC generates extensive revenues through its ownership of the rights to the Olympic Games and associated marks and terminology. These include the Olympic symbol, consisting of the five interlocking Olympic rings, and the Olympic motto, anthem, flag, and the Olympic flame and torch. Permission to use these symbols is granted to the host organizing committee, and NOCs are permitted to use the rings in developing their own national Olympic symbol. (In the United States, a special statute requires the United States Olympic Committee's (USOC) consent to all commercial uses of Olympic-related marks and terminology.) Countries hoping to host the Olympic Games guarantee a percentage of the money they will raise to the IOC in return for the rights to host. The size of the IOC's share became an issue after the 1984 Summer Olympic Games in Los Angeles. These games generated a surplus of $225 million. The IOC was unsuccessful in getting a share of the revenue, but it intensified its resolve to get a fair share of Olympic revenues from future hosting rights and acted to establish its own sources of income through marketing the Olympic symbols, with amazing success (Senn, 1999). According to the IOC (2017d), revenues are generated through Broadcasting (47 percent), TOP (The Olympic Partner) Sponsorship Program (45 percent), Ticketing (5 percent), and Licensing (3 percent). The IOC manages broadcast and sponsorship programs and the OCOGs manage domestic sponsorships, ticketing and licensing within the host country, under the direction of the IOC. To give you an idea of the economic scope of the IOC, its total revenue for the 2013–16 quadrennium was US$5.6 billion, an increase of 6.2 percent over the London Olympiad (Olympic Marketing Overview, 2016).

ORGANIZATIONAL STRUCTURE. Three components are central to IOC governance and the development of policy: the Session, the Executive Board, and the Office of the President.

1. *The Session.* The Session, comparable to a General Assembly, is a regularly scheduled meeting of all IOC members. The purpose of the Session is to adopt or modify policy relating to the Olympic Charter. The Olympic Charter, the official governing document of the Olympic

Movement, includes the purpose and description of the ideals of Olympic participation, along with the rules and regulations for Olympic events, membership in and recognition by the IOC (IOC, 2017e). The Olympic Charter provides the framework for governing the organization and operation of the Olympic Movement and stipulates conditions for hosting the Olympic Games. Elections for accepting new IOC members are also held during the Session. Meetings are held annually unless unusual circumstances dictate the calling of a special meeting.

The Session is also responsible for two other vital tasks—choosing the host cities for upcoming Games and approving the sports that will be competed in as part of the Olympic Programme for upcoming Games.

2. *The Executive Board.* The Executive Board is a smaller subset of the Session and is responsible for the management and overall direction of the IOC between meetings of the Session. It was first conceived by Baron de Coubertin in order to share the responsibility for directing the IOC and to prepare for an orderly succession of leadership (Senn, 1999). Executive Board membership (Exhibit 10.2) includes 15 positions: the President, four Vice Presidents, and ten additional members elected by the Session. Each Executive Board member's term of office is a minimum of four years, with the exception of the President, who is elected to an eight-year term. The board meets regularly, at the call of the President or at the request of a

---

Executive Board of the IOC   *exhibit* **10.2**

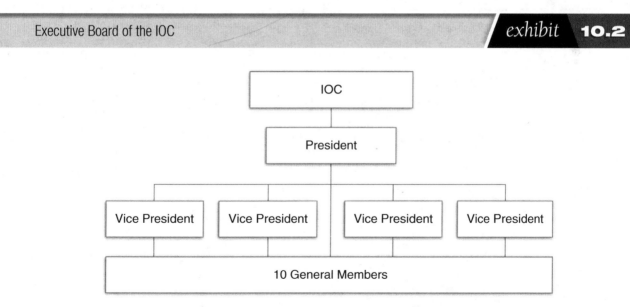

Source: IOC (2017c).

majority of its members. The Executive Board of the IOC has the following specific responsibilities (IOC, 2017c):

- ensures that the Olympic Charter is observed and promoted
- administers the IOC and appoints the Director General, who oversees the daily business affairs of the IOC
- manages IOC finances and financial reporting
- formulates bylaw or rule changes for implementation by the General Assembly
- approves the organizational chart and internal operations of the IOC
- makes recommendations for elections
- establishes the agenda for all IOC meetings
- enacts all regulations for the proper organization of the Olympic Games
- maintains the records of the IOC
- creates and allocates IOC honorary distinctions

3. *The Office of the President.* The President of the IOC is elected from members of the Session. It is a critical position with power and responsibility for directing the general course of the IOC. The President is the official spokesperson of the IOC and presides over the Executive Board. It is the President's role to convene the Executive Board and lead the business of the IOC. The term of office is initially eight years, and the incumbent President may be reelected for one subsequent four-year term. In the modern era, the Olympic Games has had only eight Presidents (see Exhibit 10.3).

The officers of the IOC do not actually organize the Olympic Games. Rather, the IOC works with the groups responsible for Olympic sport and hosting activities within individual nations, NOCs, and OCOGs.

National Olympic Committees

NOCs control operations and policy relative to the Olympic Games for a particular country, as well as oversee the delegation sent to represent a nation at the Olympic Games. With rare exceptions, only athletes certified by an NOC are permitted to compete at the Olympic Games. The NOC is required to check participant eligibility rules as defined by Olympic, International Sport Federation, and NOC policies. NOCs have been described as "the basic building blocks in the structure of the Olympic Games" (Senn, 1999, p. 11).

If a nation is interested in hosting an Olympic Games, the NOC is responsible for choosing one city to go forward to the IOC for consideration. The NOC selects that city no later than nine years in advance of the Games. For example, in 2015 the USOC chose the city of Los Angeles as the bid city for the 2024 Summer Olympic Games. The NOC makes

| Presidents of the IOC | | *exhibit* **10.3** |

President	Country of Origin	Years of Service
Dimitrius Vikelas	Greece	1894–1896
Pierre de Coubertin	France	1896–1925
Henri Baillet-Latour	Belgium	1925–1942
J. Sigfrid Edstrom	Sweden	1942–1946 (acting) 1946–1952
Avery Brundage	United States	1952–1972
Lord Killanin	Ireland	1972–1980
Juan Antonio Samaranch	Spain	1980–2001
Jacques Rogge	Belgium	2001–2013
Thomas Bach	Germany	2013–

Source: Olympic Museum (2017).

this choice nine years in advance because the IOC makes its final selection seven years in advance of the Games. However, in 2017 the IOC made history by selecting two Summer Games hosts at the same Session in Lima, Peru. Both the 2024 and 2028 Summer Olympic Games hosts were elected, with Paris, France, unanimously elected to host the 2024 Games and Los Angeles, USA, unanimously elected to host the 2028 Summer Games. The IOC described this historic approach as a tripartite agreement, bringing stability to the Olympic Movement by announcing to the athletes of the world Olympic host cities well in advance.

United States Olympic Committee

The USOC is a federally chartered nonprofit organization which governs, manages, promotes, and liaises within and outside the United States for all activities of the Olympic, Paralympic, and Pan American Games. As mentioned in Chapter 9, in 1978 the US Congress passed the Amateur Sports Act, which was amended in 1998 and is now called the Ted Stevens Olympic and Amateur Sports Act. The amended law includes activities associated with the Paralympic Games and addresses athletes' rights and other matters. The law specifically mandates the USOC to govern all American activities for those three major games. Pursuant to the federal government act, the USOC has the exclusive right to use the Olympic symbols, marks,

United States Olympic Committee
www.teamusa.org

images, and terminology in the US. Further, it has the power to authorize the use of the Olympic marks with sport governing bodies sending athletes to represent the USA at competitions and to act as a coordinating body for Olympic sport within the country. The USOC is composed of a group of individuals and organizations whose common goals are athletic excellence and achievement on the world stage and promoting nation building through the achievement of athletes.

Although more than a century old at the time, the year 2003 represented a historic time for the USOC. In 2002, the USOC's President was forced to resign because of misstatements on her resume. In 2003, the organization was confronted with allegations of violations of its Code of Ethics by its CEO, and infighting between the CEO and the President of the organization. The good name of the USOC was tarnished, and the image of the association was at an all-time low. The US Congress even voiced concern: three Senators requested an independent commission be appointed to investigate the practices of the organization and recommend change. In addition, the USOC appointed a Governance and Ethics Task Force to recommend a course of action for changing the practices, mandate, and expectations of the USOC. The sizes of the Board of Directors and Executive Committee were particularly criticized, along with the breadth of the USOC's all-encompassing mandate, which extends very broadly beyond training athletes, building facilities, and designing equipment.

The independent commission and the USOC Governance and Ethics Task Force focused their recommendations on these three major issues (Sandomir, 2003):

1. narrowing the USOC mandate to focus on training athletes for national and international competition related to the Olympic and Paralympic Games
2. ensuring ethical, responsible, and transparent business and financial practices
3. creating a workable governance structure that better defines the responsibility of volunteers and professional staff and that reduces and changes the numbers and constituents involved in decision making

They recommended that (1) the mission, goals, and objectives of the organization be focused to ensure that the ideals of the Olympic Games be preserved and reflected in practice and conduct; (2) the governance structure of the USOC be clearly redefined concerning responsibilities, authority, and accountability; (3) the overall governance structure of the USOC be streamlined and downsized; and (4) that ethical policy and compliance with ethical policy be instituted (US Senate Report, 2003). As a result of both Chicago and New York City's inability to garner necessary support in bids to host the Olympic Games and a perceived frosty relationship between the USOC and the IOC, the Board of Directors formed an Independent Advisory Committee in 2009 to review the governance structure of the

USOC (USOC Report, 2010). The results of the Committee's work included drastic changes to the governance of the USOC, including refining its mission, board of directors' size and composition, election procedures, and role of the Chairman, Board, CEO, and Assembly.

MISSION. The USOC mission connects to the themes and the meanings of the Olympic Games as outlined by the IOC. The mission statement speaks to the ideals of Olympism, the promotion of ethical conduct, and peace between nations achieved through sport competitions. The USOC hopes to drive national unity and pride within the United States through the accomplishments of US athletes in competition with their peers from other countries. The USOC mission statement is presented in Exhibit 10.4.

MEMBERSHIP. Members of the USOC are properly qualified organizations who have the authority for managing athletes attending Olympic, Paralympic, and Pan American Games, or those that widely promote the participation and engagement in amateur sport in the US. A number of requirements of membership are set out in the USOC bylaws and membership remains fairly static year after year. There are 39 US National Sport Governing Body' members of the USOC along with members in the following categories: community-based multisport organizations, education-based multisport organizations, armed forces organizations, recognized sport organizations, and other sport organizations. Organizations that are strictly commercial or political are not eligible for membership. The power to elect members to the USOC resides with its Board of Directors (USOC Bylaws, 2017).

FINANCIALS. The USOC has the use and authority to authorize the use of the Olympic marks within the United States. It licenses that right to sponsors, thereby generating significant revenues in support of its mission. The organization's main sources of revenues are television broadcast rights, sponsorship and philanthropy in the form of major gifts, and sales through its online store. Further, significant revenue comes to the USOC from the IOC.

Mission of the United States Olympic Committee | *exhibit* 10.4

To support US Olympic and Paralympic athletes in achieving sustained competitive excellence while demonstrating the values of the Olympic Movement, thereby inspiring all Americans.

Source: USOC (2017e).

These revenues are largely the result of lucrative television and sponsorship deals from the Olympic Games. In 2014 the USOC had revenues in excess of $270 million (Fischer, 2015).

The organization has extensive reach in the corporate world, with a corporate partnership and advertising program contributing high yearly revenues. In addition, the USOC established a trust fund after the successful Los Angeles Olympic Games in 1984 as an endowment for Olympic sports. The trust fund is called the United States Olympic Foundation and operates as a separate not-for-profit corporation. Although the initial endowment of $111 million must remain intact according to the terms of the trust, it generates an annual grant that has varied by year between 5 percent and 10 percent (or just under $9 million) to the USOC for the promotion of Olympic-related sports in the United States. In 2013 the US Olympic and Paralympic Foundation was established, through which $28.3 million in philanthropic support was contributed in 2015 (USOC, 2015). Through all revenue sources, the USOC reported contributing $51.4 million to national sport governing bodies (NSGBs) and other sport organizations, and $25 million directly to national level athletes for grants, medical benefits, gold medals, and tuition assistance (USOC, 2015).

ORGANIZATIONAL STRUCTURE. The USOC employs almost 400 staff members and relies heavily on the expertise of its volunteer leadership (USOC, 2017b). Volunteers involved with the USOC include some of the most influential leaders in both sport and business from around the United States. The organization is structured such that an appointed group of officers form the Board of Directors and various other committees, which provide direction to the staff, who implement policy (see Exhibit 10.5).

Officers. Two of the most important leaders of the USOC are the Chair of the Board of Directors (an elected volunteer) and the CEO (a paid employee). Both fulfill leadership roles in establishing USOC policy and are the principal spokespersons for the organization. The CEO is also responsible for day-to-day operations, strategic policy initiatives and directions, and management of the professional staff (USOC, 2017d). Day-to-day operations are lead by the USOC Executive Team, an additional group of 13 professional administrators in addition to the CEO. Each officer is responsible for specific portfolios such as, for example, Sport Performance, Marketing, Security, Finance, or Human Resources (USOC, 2017d).

Board of Directors. The task force investigating USOC reform began working on a new leadership structure for the organization in February 2003. The organization was viewed as being too large and overly bureaucratic. To overcome these issues, the Task Force recommended that the Board of Directors be reduced in size (from 125 members to 11, which has since been amended to 16), the numbers of standing committees be reduced, the Executive Committee be eliminated from the governance structure, delineation of roles and responsibilities be enacted, and a US Olympic Assembly be created. Like many other sport organizations, a

Organizational Structure of the USOC   *exhibit* **10.5**

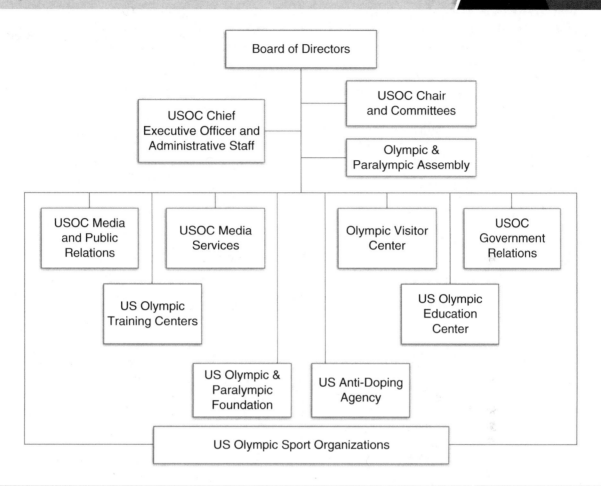

Source: USOC (2017c).

two-tiered governance structure is used to manage USOC affairs. The Board of Directors has the ultimate authority and responsibility for the finances, policy development, election of officers, and activities of the USOC. The Board has the authority to amend the constitution and bylaws of the USOC, admit and terminate members, and receive and review reports from committees and members. The Board of Directors meets four times each year. (See Exhibit 10.6 for a list of the 2017 Board of Directors, included to show their diverse backgrounds.)

Olympic and Paralympic Assembly. The Olympic and Paralympic Assembly is held once per year, and is an event where all constituent groups of the USOC gather to discuss the achievements of the organization and communicate to the Board of Directors. According to the USOC

WWW

USOC Board of Directors
https://www.teamusa.org/
About-the-USOC/Inside-
the-USOC/Leadership/
Board-of-Directors

WWW

USOC Bylaws
www.teamusa.org/
Footer/Legal/Governance-
Documents

exhibit 10.6   Membership of the 2013 USOC Board of Directors, Reflecting Diverse Backgrounds

Name	Position	Distinguished Background
Larry Probst	Chairman, IOC member	Chairman, Electronic Arts
Anita DeFrantz	Director, IOC member	Olympian, President of Kids in Sports
Angela Ruggiero	Director, IOC member	Olympian, Entrepreneur
Robert Bach	Director	Business Executive, Microsoft
James Benson	Director	Business Executive, Financial Services
Nina Kemppel	Director	Olympian, Entrepreneur
Susanne Lyons	Director	Business Executive
Dave Ogrean	Director	Executive Director, USA Hockey
Bill Marolt	Director	VP, International Ski Federation
Cheri Blauwet	Director	Paralympian, Sports Medicine Doctor
Daniel Doctoroff	Director	Lawyer & Business Executive
Steve Mesler	Director	Olympian, Entrepreneur
Whitney Ping	Director	Olympian, Business Executive
Kevin White	Director	Athletic Director, Duke University
Robert Wood	Director	Business Executive, Chemical Co.
Scott Blackmun	Ex Officio Director	CEO, USOC

Source: USOC (2017a).

Bylaws (2017), the purpose of the Olympic and Paralympic Assembly is to facilitate communication among the Board and USOC members and constituent groups, and the Advisory Committees of the USOC. Information on USOC organizational and financial performance, preparations for the Olympic, Pan American, and Paralympic Games, and actions taken are presented and discussed. Although input is sought, the Olympic Assembly does not conduct or perform any governance functions (USOC Bylaws, 2017).

Other committees. Five additional councils or committees deal with specific USOC areas of importance, interest, and concern. These are the (1) Athletes' Advisory Council, (2) National Governing Body Council, (3) Multi-Sport Organization Council, (4) Paralympic Advisory Committee, and (5) Working Groups, formed for shorter periods of time (six months) to address specific issues. Working groups on Safe Training Environments, Diversity and Inclusion, and Athlete Career, Education and Life Skills have recently made recommendations to the USOC as well.

Organizing Committees for the Olympic Games

OCOGs are another vital component of the Olympic structure. An OCOG is formed within a community after it has successfully won the bid to host the Olympic and Paralympic Games. (As part of the bid process, the host city is responsible for staging both the Olympic and Paralympic Games.) The work for the OCOG begins many years (perhaps 10 to 14) in advance of the actual event. The predecessor to this committee prepares the bid and plans for all aspects of hosting. With the support of the host country's NOC, the bid is submitted to the IOC and judged on many criteria. If the bid is unsuccessful, the bid committee finalizes its affairs and dissolves. The bid committee that is awarded the hosting rights becomes an OCOG and continues and intensifies planning. Some examples of successful OCOG bids are the Tokyo 2020 (Japan) Organizing Committee which is organizing the 2020 Summer Games, and the Beijing (China) Organizing Committee for the Winter Olympic Games in 2022.

Given that the summer and winter Olympic Games occur in a different location each four years, OCOGs are developed to manage one event at a time. As mentioned in the discussion on NOCs, bids for hosting the Games are made well in advance of the event to allow for facility development and proper event planning. Developing a bid is a process that takes years from idea to plan to concept. The IOC typically has awarded the Games to a host city seven years in advance of the Games (IOC, 2017b). On a historic day, however, the IOC empowered itself to award the 2024 and 2028 Sumer Games simultaneously. The two cities involved are Los Angeles and Paris. This would mean the 2014 Games would be awarded 7 years out and the 2028 Games would be awarded 11 years out. This is a major shift in traditional IOC policy (Ford, 2017). Although the bid is presented to the IOC by a city interested in hosting, the OCOG must demonstrate the support of various levels of government and the NOC. The process is so competitive that few cities receive the IOC's support after their first application. Once the application to bid is supported, the OCOG will move into action to prepare for the Games and will stay active for about a year after the event to finalize all financial accounting, resolve on-going legal issues, and file final reports. In total, members of the OCOG are likely to be involved in some stage of bidding, planning, executing, or reporting for 10 to 12 years. At any given time, four OCOGs (two for the Winter Games and two for the Summer Games) are in some stage of this process. Many OCOG employees come from the host city, while some sport and event managers travel the world with the Olympic Games, moving from position to position as specialists in some capacity with the organizing committees.

MISSION. The mission of an OCOG clearly reflects the ideals of the Olympic Movement: to be the best, to host the best, to show the world the best Olympic Games ever. When the President of the IOC speaks at the Olympic closing ceremonies, the local organizers listen carefully. They want to hear something to the effect of "This was the best Olympic Games ever," which is the goal of every OCOG. An example mission statement of the Vancouver, Canada Winter Games OCOG is presented in Exhibit 10.7.

www
USOC Working Groups
www.teamusa.org/About-the-USOC/Inside-the-USOC/Leadership/Working-Groups

www
Tokyo 2020
https://tokyo2020.jp/en/

Beijing 2022 Organizing Committee for the Olympic Games
www.beijing2022.cn/en/

exhibit   **10.7**   Example mission of an Olympic Games Organizing Committee: VANOC, Vancouver-Whistler 2010 Winter Olympic Games

> To touch the soul of the nation and inspire the world by creating and delivering an extraordinary Olympic and Paralympic experience with lasting legacies.

Source: Vancouver (2010).

MEMBERSHIP AND ORGANIZATIONAL STRUCTURE.   OCOG members include both paid professional staff and volunteers. The OCOG is usually led by a volunteer President and Board of Directors, and a staff CEO. The OCOG is then subdivided into areas of responsibility such as finance, facility development, sports, technical liaison, marketing and sponsorship, volunteers, security, ticket sales, merchandising, television, doping control, and so forth.

Each of the governing structures presented above plays a role in setting or enforcing policy for the Olympic Games. The IOC is charged with this mandate, and the NOCs and OCOGs help enact it. Policy is often under scrutiny, depending upon the prevailing issues of the day. For example, the 1999 scandal associated with IOC members accepting bribes from the Salt Lake City Organizing Committee resulted in a focus on procedures for choosing the host city. The presence of doping, as illustrated by positive drug tests at virtually every recent Olympic Games, continues to focus attention on testing procedures. The threat of terrorism has resulted in heightened security measures and the scrutiny of security procedures. The participation of the Refugee Olympic Team at the Rio 2016 Summer Games served to highlight the magnitude of the worldwide refugee crisis. These and other current policy issues are discussed below.

FINANCIALS.   The Olympic Games are run like a business. The goal is to have surplus funds available after the Games in order to leave a legacy for the next host city and country. An inordinate amount of money goes into hosting, and it is raised through government grants and funding, television rights, corporate sponsorship and advertising, licensing and sale of merchandise, ticket sales, and other marketing and special event functions. For example, the total costs associated with hosting the Olympic Winter Games in Sochi, Russia, was about $51 billion, the costliest Olympic Games in history (Ahmed & Leahy, 2016). It's also worth noting that the hosting of an Olympic Games has the potential for tremendous positive financial impact for the host city generally referred to as economic impact. Economic impact is defined as additional expenditures in a geographical area, such as spectators coming to an event who stay in a hotel, eat in restaurants, buy tickets to events, travel, and make purchases. It includes expenditures made by organizers of the event as well. Consider the jobs involved in building new facilities and community infrastructure. The British government issued a report, although with some skepticism from economists, indicating that the UK economy saw a £9.9 billion boost in trade and investment from hosting the 2012 London Olympic and Paralympic Games (BBC News, 2013). The question of short-term financial gains from tourism and job creation is often offset, however, by enormous levels of long-term debt incurred from cost of facility construction (Zimbalist, 2016).

CURRENT POLICY AREAS

Baron Pierre de Coubertin envisioned the modern Olympic Games as the focus of the world spotlight, and he purposely kept the four-year time span between Games so the spotlight would continue to burn bright long into the future. Given the continued interest and prestige of the Games today, de Coubertin and his collaborators would be well pleased. Every so often during the interlude between Olympic Games the media focuses on an issue related to international sport and ultimately the Olympic Games. These areas of intense interest and speculation are a good starting point for discussing current Olympic policy issues.

Choosing a Host City

Imagine this: the President of the IOC moves toward the microphone, paper in hand, to announce the successful bid for hosting the next Summer Olympic Games. You and other members of the Organizing Committee sit in the audience of the capacity-crowd press conference, thinking back over the last seven years of work spent on the bid: hundreds of meetings; millions of dollars or euros raised and a good sum spent; victory upon victory in convincing citizens, city workers, and government officials of the value of bringing the Olympic Games home; visits by Olympic and IOC members; a massive enterprise coordinated. Yet, you still have not won the bid to host the Olympic Games. The President of the IOC announces, "And the winner is . . . ."

At the press conference to award the bid to host the Olympic Games, the stakes are immense because of the time and money invested as well as the potential for gain in achieving the bid. It is a city's chance to gain the world spotlight. Given this situation, it is easy to understand why the IOC procedures for awarding the bid to host are considered an important area for policy development. The policy must stipulate exactly how the decision will be made, what criteria will be used, and what the timeline will be. In this case, a policy provides a framework for the bidding committee. What is important to the IOC in terms of staging the Olympic Games? Who will make the decision, and when will the decision be made? How can we position our bid to be held in the best possible regard by members of the IOC?

The IOC has established a set of themes to guide this process. The selection criteria themes upon which Olympic bids are judged have a dual purpose. They define the content of the bid and also provide a framework for members of the IOC who will vote on the bids. Policy to guide IOC voting members in deciding the successful bid has long been a topic of discussion that has come under intense criticism. Rumors of IOC members accepting bribes of money, trips, gifts, and promises had been debated for years, but the December 1998 scandal that erupted as a result of alleged bribes associated with the 2002 Salt Lake City Olympic bid resulted in a thorough scrutiny and revision of the policy mandating the conduct of IOC members. In the past, the IOC did not condone IOC Bid Selection Committee members accepting gifts, but it also did little to monitor the policy. In effect, it produced a scenario where it appeared that the votes of IOC members had to be secured through bribes in order to win the bid. Organizing committees spent considerable time, money, and thought on planning how to best influence members of the IOC. However, the public outcry resulting from the Salt Lake City corruption allegations resulted in the IOC sanctioning those involved. Investigators discovered that the Salt Lake City Bid Committee paid hundreds of thousands of dollars in cash, gifts, travel, and medical aid to IOC members. In the end, four IOC violators resigned, six were expelled, and ten received official warnings by the IOC President. The IOC Vice President at the time, Canadian Richard Pound, was tasked with investigating the bribery scandal and developing policies to "modernize" IOC procedures. His report released in 1999 mandated that specific election procedures be used for selecting the host city, that visits by IOC members to candidate cities be abolished, and that more accountable and transparent procedures involving the media be implemented.

In addition to the changes implemented in 1999, the election procedure was revised in 2006 to consist of three phases:

1. the *Applicant City phase*, which includes applicant cities completing a comprehensive questionnaire about their bid intentions regarding motivation to host, venues, transportation, etc.;
2. the *Candidature phase*, in which five candidate cities respond to a new 250-page questionnaire covering topics like media operations, marketing, athlete's village, financial management, etc., followed by a comprehensive evaluation of the bid by the IOC Evaluations Commission over four days of on-site visit; and
3. the *Selection phase*, during which reports are created outlining strengths, weaknesses, and recommendations regarding bids, and IOC members vote at a General Assembly meeting by secret ballot. In the first round of voting, if no city receives a majority of votes, the city receiving the fewest votes is dropped from the ballot, and subsequent rounds of voting continue until a winner is identified.

Today, candidature processes continue to evolve as the costs of hosting the Games continue to rise and fewer cities bid to host. The process is very similar to the above: ten years prior to the Games the IOC invites NOCs to declare interest and bidding, and runs individual workshops for interested cities. Cities put forward by NOCs engage Stage 1: Vision, Games Concept, and Strategy; followed by Stage 2: Governance, Legal and Venue Funding; followed by Stage 3: Games Delivery, Experience and Venue Legacy. Report submissions occur at intervals during the three-year process and cities participate in observation of any Olympic Games which take place during this time. Candidate cities are then visited by the IOC Evaluation Commission and Reports are shared with IOC members and IFs prior to Final Candidate City presentations and election of the host city by IOC members at the Session. In the wake of the Rio 2016 Summer Games, human rights activists around the world are calling out the IOC to include more focused human rights policy in candidate bids and the importance of enforcing human rights (Gibson, 2016). Rio illustrated the large numbers of families who were relocated against their wills for Games facility construction and ensuing major clashes with police.

www
IOC From Candidate to Host City
https://www.olympic.org/host-city-election

The Rising Costs of Hosting the Olympic Games (Corporate Sponsorship and Media Rights)

Financing an Olympic Games may be the biggest issue facing an OCOG (Ahmed & Leahy, 2016). Without sponsors and revenue from television and other media rights, the Olympic Games would not exist in their current form given the size and complexity of the sport spectacular. Some countries rely on their government for funding, others get funding from public sources such as lottery returns, and many will raise money privately through corporate sponsorship. The United Kingdom and Brazil relied heavily on revenues raised from corporate partnerships for hosting the 2012 London and 2016 Rio Summer Games.

The Rio, Brazil, 2016 Summer Olympic Games were the richest in 120 years of Olympic history (Chapman, 2016). The television industry paid more $4 billion to screen the Olympic Games 19-day competition and 11 global sponsors (Coca-Cola, Atos, Bridgestone, Dow, GE, McDonalds, Omega, Panasonic, P&G, Samsung, and Visa) paid as much as a half billion dollars, with local companies such as America Movil ($320 million) and Banco Bradesco ($320 million) also contributing huge sums (Chapman, 2016).

Costs now present a major issue for the IOC because the costs of delivering the Games continues to rise exponentially and of course depend upon building the required new infrastructure. For instance, here are the approximate final operating budgets and total costs in millions of US dollars for hosting some past Summer Olympic Games: Tokyo 1964—$72/$72; Moscow 1980—$231/$1,350; Atlanta 1996—$1,800/$2,000;

MEREDITH MILLER, *Sport Performance,*

USOC, Colorado Springs, CO

I work for the United States Olympic Committee. Specifically I work in the USOC's Sport Performance department. The main goal of our department is to help US Athletes reach the Olympic podium. I spent the last two and a half years working on the logistics side of this operation. It is my job to set things up for Team USA to ensure athletes only need to worry about performing on the field of play. At the 2016 Rio Olympic Games I managed the USOC's High Performance Training Center (HPTC). The HPTCs are facilities we set up in host cities that ideally mirror the US Olympic Training Centers. The Centers are intended to provide our athletes with a competitive advantage. Two of the more important policy issues confronting sport managers working in Olympic Sport today include Safe Sport—ensuring a culture of safety, and the issue of ethics.

Our organizational policies are created by the USOC's Board of Directors and implemented by staff. Therefore, I am not particularly involved in creating policy. I do have to ensure that set policies are implemented and followed. One example is in regards to background checks as they relate to facility access at the Olympic Games. There are specific set policies on who can access the US High Performance Training Centers and what these users must do before becoming accredited at one of these facilities. Since I am in charge of running these Training Centers, I have to work with the National Governing Bodies, hired staff, volunteers, and various other groups to ensure that we identify all users early enough to complete the set requirements. It can be difficult to manage, especially when working in foreign countries. That being said, it is very important that this policy is followed.

There are positives and negatives to the current governance structure of Olympic Sport. One positive trait of the USOC's governance structure is that it has a small Board of Directors. Having a small team allows it to be nimble and more effective than Boards of the past which had over 100 members. The smaller board is also mostly made up of business professionals who have extensive business experience. On the negative side, the IOC and many IFs have large Executive Committees. These committees often have a great deal of power to make decisions. For example, the IOC's Executive Committee votes on which cities will be put forward to the IOC's General Assembly for a vote on hosting future Olympic Games. Many would argue that this is not the best group to make these important decisions.

Possible amendments to the Ted Stevens Olympic and Amateur Sports Act could pose future challenges to policy development in Olympic Sport in the US. The proposed amendments are in regards to Safe Sport. An amendment to the Act would likely yield necessary policy changes, particularly at the National Governing Body level. Significant policy changes can be challenging to implement even when they are for the best.

The host city bidding process poses a challenge for the future of the Olympic Movement. It is no secret that there have been issues around awarding various events to host cities. These publicly known issues vary from corruption and bribes to bankrupting cities to building new and expensive facilities that will be underutilized after the awarded event takes place. The International Olympic Committee and its numerous International Federations need to address these issues and begin to refine is process for how it awards events. The processes they put in place must be ethical and justifiable.

Beijing 2008—$44,000/$44,000 (Campbell, 2016; Hodgkinson, 2007; Pravda Report, 2008). Where do the billions of dollars come from? For the 2012 London Olympic Games, the British government spent $14.61 billion in public funds to build the Olympic Park in a run-down neighborhood of London and to provide security for the Games. The London

OGOG spent another $2 billion to stage the Games (sponsorships, ticket sales, merchandise sales, IOC contribution) (Weir, 2012).

The IOC has acknowledged rising costs in its strategic plan Olympic Agenda 2020 (IOC, 2017d). The report presents 40 strategic recommendations meant to strengthen the Olympic Movement. Two key areas addressed involve a change to the bidding process such that candidate cities can submit a project that better fits the long-term needs of its city and reducing the costs for bidding to host the Games. These initiatives are the result of the IOC receiving fewer bids to host (there were only two candidates to host the 2022 Winter Games), and of potential host cities (Rome and Budapest for 2024) withdrawing due to the costs of competitive bids (Goldblatt, 2016). To better manage costs and maximize sponsorship and broadcast revenues, the IOC has developed extensive sponsorship policy. However, sponsorship is a complicated area. The stakes are high because of the potential for revenue generation. The issue is complicated because of the need to define exactly who owns the rights to the various Olympic symbols. Three layers of organizations have an interest or a right to sponsorship associated with the Olympic Games: the IOC, the NOC, and the OCOG.

The IOC has a written policy to define who has the right to market and sell which sponsorships. Beyond outlining who has the right to which properties, Olympic sponsorship policy is intended to set guidelines for the practices of the different levels of governance. For example, are title sponsorships allowed? Could the Olympic Games be called the Coke Olympic Games? Obviously, that practice is not allowed by the IOC. However, defining the limits of acceptance regarding sponsors is a hot topic for debate.

Of all the sponsorship, advertising, and marketing opportunities available at the Olympic Games, no property for potential revenue generation is larger than television. In the aftermath of the 1984 Los Angeles Olympic Games, when huge profits were realized from hosting, the IOC began intense scrutiny of its own funding portfolio. It focused first on hosting guarantees and revenue-sharing methods and second on the revenues to be generated from selling television broadcast rights. The IOC decided to retain the right to negotiate television contracts and to share the revenues among the IOC, NOCs, OGOCs, and International Sport Federations. The Rio 2016 Summer Games television rights were sold for $4 billion (Chapman, 2016). It is easy, given this tremendous potential revenue stream, to understand the importance of the policy issue regarding who owns the television rights. The IOC has acted to retain the rights of negotiation and dispersal of television revenues. Its purpose included control, consistency, and ensuring value. By setting policy ensuring central control of this important negotiation, the IOC has ensured the potential for developing consistent, long-term contracts of the highest possible value. Of course, OCOGs would prefer to hold the rights themselves, and they can be expected to push for further debate on this issue. In addition, in the

United States, the USOC takes the position, and the IOC recognizes, that the Ted Stevens Olympic and Amateur Sports Act grants it certain rights to participate in and to share in the proceeds of the US television-rights broadcast negotiations.

New Olympic Sports

The size of the Olympic festival has been a topic of ongoing debate. The masses of visitors and spectators at the Sydney 2000 Olympic Games resulted in further scrutiny and policy development by the IOC, and the concern is revisited with each Olympic hosting. The issue of the number of competitors and sports has been added to the debate. Of course, many ISFs lobby intensely to have their sports included in the Olympic Games. How many sports should the Olympic Games include? How many competitors are too many? How can the IOC balance the interest in Olympic competition and its mandate to provide opportunities for nations all around the world (206 NOCs), with the management issues that arise from competitions that are simply too large? Should every nation be permitted to send Olympic participants in all sports, even though the individuals may not meet world standards?

The IOC has developed policy to define exactly which sports will compete in the Olympic Games and how to add new sports. Currently there are 41 Summer and 15 Winter Games sports with over 400 events (Olympic Charter, 2015). Within the Olympic Charter, policy is written to define the following:

- Olympic sports
- disciplines (different events within sports)
- events (competitions resulting in medals; summer—310, winter—100)
- criteria for admitting each sport
- approximate numbers of athletes (summer—10,500, winter—2,900), coaches/support personnel (summer—5,000, winter—2,000)

Often, the IOC will name an addition to the sport program at a particular Olympic Games in accordance with the wishes of the OCOG. As you might imagine, a significant amount of lobbying occurs in an attempt to have a sport recognized for Olympic competition. Policy is required to define the criteria, procedure, and timing of decisions relative to the sports program of an Olympic Games. Recent debates involved whether to drop wrestling, synchronized swimming, and baseball and softball from the Olympic program and to add roller sports, sports climbing, rugby, and golf, among other events (Mahoney, 2014). The discussions revolved around spectator interest, worldwide participation in these sports, and the number of competitors in the Games. In another example, snowboarding was added to the Winter Olympic Games program to attract young viewers and thereby boost television ratings and sponsorship revenues. Defining which sports will be offered at Olympic Games is the responsibility of the Olympic Programme Commission. This committee is charged with reviewing and analyzing the program of sports and defining the permissible number of athletes in each Olympic sport, with a focus on events delivered. It is also responsible for developing recommendations on the principles and structure of the Olympic program. Members of the commission vote on adding or removing sports from the program with a simple majority of votes required to add or remove events from the Olympic program. The 2020 Tokyo Summer Games will include five new sports: baseball/softball (returning after not having been included in the 2012 and 2016 Games), karate, sport climbing, surfing, and skateboarding. The Olympic Programme Commission makes recommendations to the IOC Executive Board and presents reports to the IOC Session.

www

Olympic Program Commission
https://www.olympic.org/olympic-programme-commission

Politics at the Olympic Games

The originators of the Olympic Games sought to avert governmental interference by forming the IOC as a group independent of the funding requirements, politics, and power of a particular nation's government. In reality, however, it has been impossible to keep politics out of the Olympic Games. The IOC is a very political organization in which alliances are regularly formed to enact some vision or goal. Even more so, political involvement in the Olympic Games occurs as a result of the gains possible for a national government and its ruling ideology. The Olympic Games have a diverse following of people around the world, and governments naturally try to exploit the Games for their own purpose. In this way, the Olympic Games provide an avenue to unite people, to develop a national consciousness, and to provide ammunition to suggest that "our ways" are better than "your ways." Governments have used sport to send political messages to another country by sending a team to compete prior to an Olympic Games. For example, when the US table tennis team went to China in the early 1970s (the so-called "Ping-Pong Diplomacy"), it signaled a renewed interest in discussing foreign policy between the two nations. There are many other examples of political motives driving decisions associated with athletic competitions. Take the country of Taiwan, for example. When Taiwan competes at the Olympic and Paralympic Games, the athletes must compete under the country name "Chinese Taipei" and are not allowed to display their country's flag or play their country's anthem. This is due to the influence China exerts on the international political and sport stage.

For the 2016 Rio Summer Olympic Games, the IOC established the Refugee Olympic team. Ten athletes with refugee status were chosen to compete under the Olympic flag in order to raise awareness of the magnitude of the worldwide refugee crisis. The UN Refugee Agency estimates that more than 65 million people are refugees or displaced people, forced from their homes by war, famine, and natural or civilization-created disasters (Jones, 2016). The IOC, NOCs, IF and the UN Refugee Agency worked to identify Olympic level athletes with refugee status. Ten were selected from a larger pool of almost 1,000, and are supported by funding, coaches, and medical staff provided by the IOC. These athletes have no home, no team, and no national anthem. They come from Syria, South Sudan, Ethiopia, and the Congo. The IOCs efforts to include refugee athletes makes a political statement, sending a signal of hope to all refugees of the world of the human capacity to overcome tragedy and contribute to society (Jones, 2016).

The political ramifications of the Olympic Games are most certainly an issue for policy definition, whether the political issues are related to the internal workings of the IOC or external to the governments of the participating nations. Each group will set policies to manage their own interests and perspectives. Perhaps organizing committees and their sponsors engage in political maneuvering. Or perhaps all parties are worried about the dangers of terrorist violence, the embarrassment of positive tests for performance-enhancing drugs, legal injunctions over team membership, or the authority of International Sport Federations. One thing is for sure: policies to deal with issues of power and politics in the Olympic Games will be necessary into the foreseeable future. As Senn (1999) put it almost two decades ago, "Those who refuse to recognize the politics of the Games put themselves at the mercy of the people and organizations who actively participate in the political competition" (p. 296).

SUMMARY

The Olympic Games are the pinnacle of world sporting events. Even professional athletes dream of winning an Olympic Gold Medal. Participating at an Olympic Games is described as an experience of a lifetime, and athletic careers are routinely described in terms of Olympic Medals won and number of Games attended.

All things Olympic are governed by the IOC, an elected group of Olympic enthusiasts charged with overseeing Olympic events and promoting the Olympic Charter. Policies of the Olympic Charter are developed by IOC committees and approved by the Session of the IOC, which meets at least once per year. National Olympic Committees control operations and policy for Olympic participation within the country and are responsible for choosing between possible cities interested in bidding to host the Olympic Games. Host cities create Organizing Committees for the Olympic Games well in advance of hosting to build facilities and plan for hosting athletes and visitors. There are many issues related to hosting, involving bidding for the Games, rising costs of hosting, the number of Olympic sports, the size of the Games, and political maneuvering.

case STUDY

OLYMPIC SPORTS

You are lucky enough to be involved with putting together the Olympic bid for the Summer Olympic Games in 2032. You have a choice of the following cities: Boston, Central Florida, Dallas, Denver, Philadelphia, San Antonio, Seattle, and St Louis.

For your choice of cities, you have been asked to help assemble the bid documents for six of the required IOC bid themes:

1. Choose a city.
2. Research the bid themes that are required components of the Olympic bid.
3. For your choice of city, explain as thoroughly as possible what information will go into the sections you are writing. You may need to do some Internet research to learn more about the specific city. Explain why your bid information is worthy of IOC support.
4. What procedures might you implement to ensure that all procedures and actions detailed in the bid document meet the highest legal and ethical standards?

CHAPTER questions

1. Compile a chart that depicts the levels of all organizations involved in delivering Olympic sport. Because the IOC has supreme authority, put it at the top of the chart and work down to state sport organizations.
2. Does television have a positive or negative effect on the Olympic Games? Make a list of both positive and negative effects before making your final decision.
3. How do sports become Olympic events? Review the list of current Olympic sports. Are they popular and interesting? Are there any sports that might be replaced? If so, which ones, and what would replace them? What rationale would you provide the IOC for adding or dropping a sport? Discuss your ideas as a whole class activity.
4. Consider the costs of hosting an Olympic Games. Using a search engine such as Google Research, compare the predicted costs of hosting identified in Sochi's 2014 or Rio's 2016 bid to actual costs involved in hosting. If there was a change in predicted versus actual costs, where did it come from?

FOR ADDITIONAL INFORMATION

For more information check out the following resources:

1. Olympic Games Bids website: www.gamesbids.com
2. The tradition and meaning of the Olympic rings: http://www.olympics.mu/meaning-olympic-rings.html
3. Olympic Games Costs and Finances: https://www.factretriever.com/Olympic Games-costs-facts
4. The Youth Olympic Games, YouTube: https://www.youtube.com/user/YouthOlympics
5. Policy regarding use of logos at the Olympic Games: http://inside.fei.org/system/files/Rule%2050%20-%20Guidelines%20regarding%20Authorised%20Identications%20-%20Rio%202016.pdf
6. Lomong, L., & Tabb, M. (2016). *Running for my life: One lost boy's journey from the killing fields of Sudan to the Olympic Games*. Nashville, TN: Thomas Nelson.

REFERENCES

Ahmed, M., & Leahy, J. (2016). Rio 2016: The high price of Olympic glory. Retrieved from https://www.ft.com/content/594d2320-5326-11e6-9664-e0bdc13c3bef

Ancient Olympic Games. (2017). Frequently asked questions about the ancient Olympic Games. Retrieved from http://www.perseus.tufts.edu/Olympics/faq1.html

BBC News. (2013). London 2012 Olympic Games 'have boosted UK economy by £9.9bn.' Retrieved from www.bbc.com/news/uk-23370270

Campbell, J. (2016, September 25). Costs to host Olympic Games skyrockets. Retrieved from http://abcnews.go.com/US/story?id=95650&page=1

Chapman, B. (2016). Rio 2016: The richest Games in 120 years of Olympic history. Retrieved from www.independent.co.uk/news/business/analysis-and-features/rio-2016-olympic-games-richest-ever-usain-bolt-mo-farah-a7171811.html

de Coubertin, P. (2000). *Olympism: Selected writings*. Ed., Norbert Muller. Lausanne: IOC.

Fischer, B. (2015). USOC costs rising along with revenue. Retrieved from www.sportsbusinessdaily.com/Journal/Issues/2015/05/25/Olympics/USOC-finances.aspx

Ford, B. (2017, July 11). IOC vote moves Los Angeles, Paris closer to 2024, 2028 Games. Retrieved from www.espn.com/olympics/story/_/id/19962445/ioc-empowers-award-2024-2028-summer-game-simultaneously

Gibson, O. (2016). Olympic Games 2016. How Rio missed the gold medal for human rights. *The Guardian*. Retrieved from https://www.theguardian.com/sport/2016/aug/02/olympic-games-2016-rio-human-rights

Goldblatt, D. (2016, July 26). It wasn't always so expensive to host the Olympic Games. Here's what changed. *Time*. Retrieved from http://time.com/4421865/OlympicGames-cost-history/

Hodgkinson, M. (2007, February 8). London 2012 must learn from the £1bn Sydney hangover. *The Telegraph*. Retrieved from http://www.telegraph.co.uk/sport/Olympics/2307426/London-2012-must-learn-from-the-1bn-Sydney-hangover.html

IOC. (2017a). Athens 1896. Retrieved from https://www.olympic.org/athens-1896

IOC. (2017b). From candidate to host city. Retrieved from https://www.olympic.org/host-city-election

IOC. (2017c). IOC executive board. Retrieved from https://www.olympic.org/executive-board

IOC. (2017d). Olympic Agenda 2020. Retrieved from https://www.olympic.org/olympic-agenda-2020

IOC. (2017e). What we do. Retrieved from https://www.olympic.org/the-ioc/what-we-do

IOC Marketing and Broadcast. (2017a). 04—Rio 2016 Olympic Games. Retrieved from https://www.olympic.org/documents/ioc-marketing-and-broadcasting

IOC Marketing and Broadcast. (2017b). 05—Sochi 2014 Winter Olympic Games. Retrieved from https://www.olympic.org/documents/ioc-marketing-and-broadcasting

Jones, I. (2016). Refugee Olympic athletes deliver message of hope for displaced people. Retrieved from https://www.olympic.org/news/refugee-olympic-athletes-deliver-message-of-hope-for-displaced-people

Mahoney, J. (2014, December 8). Six Olympic sports that may be in danger of being dropped. *The Globe and Mail*. Retrieved from www.theglobeandmail.com/sports/OlympicGames/six-olympic-sports-that-may-be-in-danger-of-being-dropped/article21993578/

Nelson, M. (2007). The first Olympic Games. In G. P. Schaus & D. P. Wenn (Eds.), *Onward to the Olympic Games*. (pp. 47–68). Kitchener, ON: Wilfrid Laurier University Press.

Olympic Charter. (2015). By-law to rule 45. Sports Programme. Retrieved from https://stillmed.olympic.org/Documents/olympic_charter_en.pdf

Olympic Marketing Overview. (2016). IOC marketing report—Rio, 2016. Retrieved from http://touchline.digipage.net/iocmarketing/reportrio2016/1-1

Olympic Museum. (2017). Presidents of the IOC since 1894. Retrieved from http://olympic-museum.de/president/pres_ioc.html

Pravda Report. (2008, June 8). Beijing Olympic Games to cost China 44 billion dollars. Retrieved from www.pravdareport.com/sports/games/06-08-2008/106003-beijing_OlympicGames-0/

Sandomir, R. (2003, April 13). Olympics: Drastic U.S.O.C. revision proposed. *New York Times*. Retrieved from www.nytimes.com/2003/04/13/sports/OlympicGames-drastic-usoc-revision-proposed.html

Schaffer, K., & Smith, S. (2000). *The Olympic Games at the millennium*. London: Rutgers Press.

Senn, A. E. (1999). *Power, politics, and the Olympic Games*. Champaign, IL: Human Kinetics.

Toohey, K., & Veal, A. J. (2007). *The Olympic Games: A social science perspective* (2nd ed.). Cambridge, MA: Cabi.

USOC. (2015). 2015 Annual report. Retrieved from http://2015annualreport.teamusa.org/

USOC. (2017a). Board of directors. Retrieved from www.teamusa.org/About-the-USOC/Inside-the-USOC/Leadership/Board-of-Directors

USOC. (2017b). Careers. Retrieved from www.teamusa.org/Careers

USOC. (2017c). Governance documents. Retrieved from www.teamusa.org/Footer/Legal/Governance-Documentscc

USOC. (2017d). Leadership. Retrieved from www.teamusa.org/About-the-USOC/Inside-the-USOC/Leadership

USOC. (2017e). Mission and culture. Retrieved from www.teamusa.org/careers/mission-and-culture

USOC Bylaws (2017). Governance documents. Retrieved from https://www.teamusa.org/Footer/Legal/Governance-Documents

USOC Report. (2010). Report of the USOC independent advisory committee on governance. Retrieved from https://www.google.ca/search?q=usoc+governance+and+ethics+task+force&rlz=1C1AVNG_enCA632CA632&oq=usoc+&aqs=chrome.0.69i59l3j69i57j0l2.3043j0j7&sourceid=chrome&ie=UTF-8#

US Senate Report (2003). US Olympic Committee reform Act of 2003. Retrieved from https://books.google.ca/books?id=oStJ-OnsJ7AC&pg=RA4-PA4&lpg=RA4-PA4&dq=usoc+governance+and+ethics+task+force&source=bl&ots=EywVRK9_kE&sig=hRQ9uQrD5ECyFQh43gqIUQ8mR6M&hl=en&sa=X&ved=0ahUKEwjs6r7f4OXTAhVny1QKHXHvD6QQ6AEIPTAF#v=onepage&q=usoc%20governance%20and%20ethics%20task%20force&f=false

Vancouver. (2010). Staging the Olympic winter games knowledge report. Retrieved from https://stillmed.olympic.org/Documents/Reports/Official%20Past%20Games%20Reports/Winter/EN/Staging-the-Games.pdf

Weir, K. (2012, March 8). Factbox. How the Olympic Games are funded. Retrieved from http://uk.reuters.com/article/uk-Olympic-Games-funding-idUKBRE8270TY20120308

Young, D. C. (2004). *A brief history of the Olympic Games*. New Jersey: Wiley-Blackwell.

Zimbalist, A. (2016). *Circus maximus: The economic gamble behind hosting the Olympic Games and the World Cup*. Washington, DC: Brookings Institution Press.

Paralympic Sport

Mary A. Hums
Joanne C. MacLean

When we hear the word *athlete*, certain images come to mind. We envision people who are strong and fast, can throw or run great distances, shoot three pointers, or ski downhill at incredible speed. When we read about athletes running the 100 meters in just under 11 seconds, high jumping more than 6 feet (1.97 meters), or lifting

600 pounds (272 kilograms), we know they most certainly are elite athletes. All these *are* accomplishments of elite athletes—elite athletes with physical disabilities who competed in the Paralympic Games, an event that draws thousands of elite athletes with disabilities from more than 140 nations every four years, enjoys millions of corporate sponsorship dollars, lights up social media, and includes worldwide media coverage that reaches more than 3 billion fans. Who are these athletes, and what are the Paralympic Games?

DEFINING DISABILITY SPORT

The term *disability sport* may bring to mind the image of a Special Olympian. However, that is not the only form of sport for individuals with disabilities. DePauw and Gavron (2005) define *disability sport* as "sport designed for or specifically practiced by athletes with disabilities" (p. 8). People who participate in the Special Olympics are typically living with cognitive or developmental disabilities. This chapter does not deal with that form of participation. For the purposes of this chapter, the focus will be on highly competitive, international, elite-level disability sport for people with specific physical disabilities, specifically, the Paralympic Games.

PARALYMPIC ATHLETES

The Paralympic Games showcase elite-level athletes with disabilities. Incorporating the same ideology as the Olympic Games in celebrating the accomplishments of elite international athletes, the Paralympic Games take place two weeks after the Olympic Games conclude. Competitions occur in the same cities and venues, and are staged by the same organizing committee. When a host city is awarded the Olympic Games, the Paralympic Games are an obligatory part of the host city bid process.

The motto of the Paralympic Games is "Spirit in Motion." This motto represents the vision of the International Paralympic Committee (IPC), which is "to enable Paralympic athletes to achieve sporting excellence and excite the world." The sports on the official Paralympic Games Programme are presented in Exhibit 11.1. Not all disability types are eligible to compete in the Paralympic Games. The athletes who compete in the Paralympic Games have a range of disabilities, including visual impairments, cerebral palsy, amputations, spinal cord injuries, and on a very limited basis, athletes with intellectual disabilities. Note that athletes with hearing impairments do not compete in the Paralympic Games. They compete in separate World Games and other competitions for the deaf, including the Deaflympics. Athletes with cognitive disabilities such as Down syndrome also do not compete in the Paralympic Games. The Special Olympics were established to provide opportunities for people with cognitive and developmental disabilities. The mission of Special Olympics includes skill development and social interaction, not the development of international elite-level athletes.

Paralympic Games Programme for PyeongChang 2018		
Alpine Skiing	Cross-Country Skiing	Wheelchair Curling
Biathlon	Ice Sledge Hockey	Snowboard
Paralympic Games Programme for the 2020 Tokyo Summer Games		
Archery	Goalball	Tae Kwon Do
Athletics	Judo	Triathlon
Badminton	Powerlifting	Volleyball (Sitting)
Boccia	Rowing	Wheelchair Basketball
Canoe	Shooting	Wheelchair Fencing
Cycling	Swimming	Wheelchair Rugby
Equestrian	Table Tennis	Wheelchair Tennis
Football 5-a-side		

HISTORY OF THE PARALYMPIC GAMES

Sport for people with disabilities existed for many years before the founding of the Paralympic Games and began to grow after World War II, when sport was used to rehabilitate the many injured military and civilian persons. In 1944, Sir Ludwig Guttmann opened the Spinal Injuries Center at Stoke Mandeville Hospital in England and incorporated sport as an integral part of the rehabilitation process (IPC, n.d.b). On July 28, 1948, the first Stoke Mandeville Wheelchair Games were held and athletes competed in archery competitions. The date was significant because it corresponded to the Opening Ceremonies for the Summer Olympic Games in London that same day. Disability sport soon expanded beyond athletes who used wheelchairs. The International Sport Organization for the Disabled (ISOD) was formed in 1964. The ISOD brought together athletes with disabilities such as visual impairments, cerebral palsy, and amputees. Additional sport organizations for people with disabilities formed as well, such as the Cerebral Palsy International Sport and Recreation Association (CPISRA) and the International Blind Sports Association (IBSA), organized in 1978 and 1980, respectively. To help these and other sport organizations for athletes with disabilities coordinate their activities, the IPC was founded in 1989 in Düsseldorf, Germany. The IPC remains today the only multidisability international sport organization in the world recognized by the IOC (IPC, n.d.a).

The summer Paralympic Games began with the 1960 in Rome, Italy. The first Winter Paralympic Games were held in 1976 in Sweden. The first Paralympic Games under the direct management of the IPC were the Winter Paralympic Games in Lillehammer in 1994. As the statistics show, the Paralympic Games are showing steady growth in the number of both athletes and nation members participating. The 2008 Paralympic Summer Games in Beijing, China, had 3,951 athletes from 146 nations; 4,237 athletes from 164 countries competed at the London 2012 Paralympic Games; and 4,328 athletes from 159 countries plus two Independent Paralympic Athletes competed in the 2016 Summer Games in Rio de Janeiro, Brazil.

GOVERNANCE

Just as with the Olympic Movement, the Paralympic Movement and the Paralympic Games fit into a complex set of governance structures. A number of governing bodies are involved with Paralympic Sport, including the IPC, National Paralympic Committees (NPCs), and International Federations (IFs).

International Paralympic Committee

International Paralympic Committee
www.paralympic.org

The IPC, the supreme authority of the Paralympic Movement, is the international representative organization of elite sports for athletes with disabilities. The IPC organizes, supervises, and coordinates the Paralympic Games and other multidisability competitions at the elite sports level, of which the most important are the regional and world championships.

CPISRA
www.cpisra.org

IBSA
www.ibsa.es

INAS-FID
www.inas.org/

IWAS
www.iwasf.com/iwasf/

VISION/MISSION. The IPC has a vision statement and a mission statement. (See Exhibits 11.2 and 11.3.) The vision statement for the IPC contains an overall picture of IPC philosophy (IPC, n.d.a). Its mission statement is more detailed, including statements that could also be seen as goals for the organization. This mission statement is longer than mission statements for some sport organizations, but it provides a detailed picture of what the IPC does and strives for.

MEMBERSHIP. The members of the IPC include the International Organizations of Sport for the Disabled (IOSDs), the NPCs, the International Paralympic Sport Federations (IPSFs), and regional/continental Paralympic organizations.
    The IOSDs are as follows:

CPISRA	Cerebral Palsy International Sport and Recreation Association
IBSA	International Blind Sport Federation
INAS-FID	International Association for Sport for Para-Athletes with an Intellectual Disability
IWAS	International Wheelchair and Amputee Sports Federation

Vision Statement of the IPC

exhibit **11.2**

- The Vision To enable Paralympic athletes to achieve sporting excellence and inspire and excite the world
- Enable Creating conditions for athlete empowerment
- Para-athletes The primary focus from initiation to elite level
- Achieve Sporting excellence is the goal of a sport centered organisation
- Inspire & Excite Touch the heart of all people for a more equitable society

Source: IPC (n.d.a).

Mission Statement of the IPC

exhibit **11.3**

- To guarantee and supervise the organization of successful Paralympic Games
- To ensure the growth and strength of the Paralympic Movement through the development of National Paralympic Committees in all countries and the support to the activities of all IPC member organizations.
- To promote and contribute to the development of sport opportunities and competitions, from initiation to elite level, for Paralympic athletes as the foundation of elite Paralympic sport
- To develop opportunities for female athletes and athletes with a severe disability in sport at all levels and in all structures
- To support and encourage educational, cultural, research and scientific activities that contribute to the development and promotion of the Paralympic Movement
- To seek the continuous global promotion and media coverage of the Paralympic Movement, its vision of inspiration and excitement through sport, its ideals and activities
- To promote the self-governance of each Paralympic sport either as an integral part of the International sport movement for able-bodied athletes, or as an independent sport organization, whilst at all times safeguarding and preserving its own identity
- To ensure that in sport practiced within the Paralympic Movement the spirit of fair play prevails, violence is banned, the health risk of the athletes is managed and fundamental ethical principles are upheld
- To contribute to the creation of a drug-free sport environment for all Paralympic athletes in conjunction with the World Anti-Doping Agency (WADA)
- To promote Paralympic sport without discrimination for political, religious, economic, disability, gender, sexual orientation, or race reasons
- To ensure the means necessary to support the future growth of the Paralympic Movement

Source: IPC (2011b).

Asian Paralympic Committee
www.asianparalympic.org

European Paralympic Committee
www.europaralympic.org

Oceania Paralympic Committee
www.oceaniaparalympic.org/

In addition to these international sport organizations, NPCs or National Contact Agencies from different nations are also full members of the IPC. Currently, approximately 170 NPCs are members of the IPC. Four regional organizations (the African Paralympic Committee, the African Sports Confederation for the Disabled [ASCOD], the European Paralympic Committee [EPC], and the Oceania Paralympic Committee) and two regional committees—the Americas Paralympic Committee and the Asian Paralympic Committee—are also members. These full members have voting rights at the IPC's General Assembly. In addition to the above-mentioned full members, the IPSFs have voting and speaking rights at the IPC's General Assembly. Besides being the supreme authority for the supervision and organization of the Paralympic Games, the IPC also fulfills an important role as the international federation for several sports.

FINANCIALS. Approximately 50 percent of IPC funding comes from the Paralympic Games revenues (IPC, n.d.e). "The IPC grants all the related marketing rights to the local Games Organizing Committees in exchange for a fixed rights fee" (IPC, n.d.e, para. 1). Income used by organizing committees to operate the Games themselves is derived from a combination of government support, Olympic support, and sponsorship deals. Currently, the IPC has six worldwide partners: VISA, Otto Bock, Atos, Panasonic, Toyota, and Samsung. In addition, Allianz SE is an international sponsor (IPC, n.d.d). Other companies sign on to be sponsors of a specific Games, for example, British Airways and Sainsbury's during the 2012 Summer Games in London, or Bradesco or Correios for the 2016 Rio Games. Finally, the Agitos Foundation was established to help support specific sport and athlete development projects.

ORGANIZATIONAL STRUCTURE. The structure of the IPC consists of the General Assembly, the Governing Board, Management Team, and a number of Standing Committees. Exhibit 11.4 illustrates the general structure of the IPC.

The General Assembly is the governance body for the IPC and its highest authority. The General Assembly is the biannual assembly of the IPC members and decides on any matters relevant to the IPC (IPC, n.d.c). Members of the General Assembly meet at least once every two years to discuss and vote on policy matters of concern to the Paralympic Games. At the General Assembly, each full member has one vote. The 14-person Governing Board members include a President, Vice President, ten Members-at-Large, one Athlete Representative, and one CEO ex-officio member. The General Assembly is responsible for the following:

- Elect the President, the Vice President, ten Members at Large
- Consider and approve the IPC's budget and the IPC membership fee policy

IPC Organizational Chart   *exhibit*   **11.4**

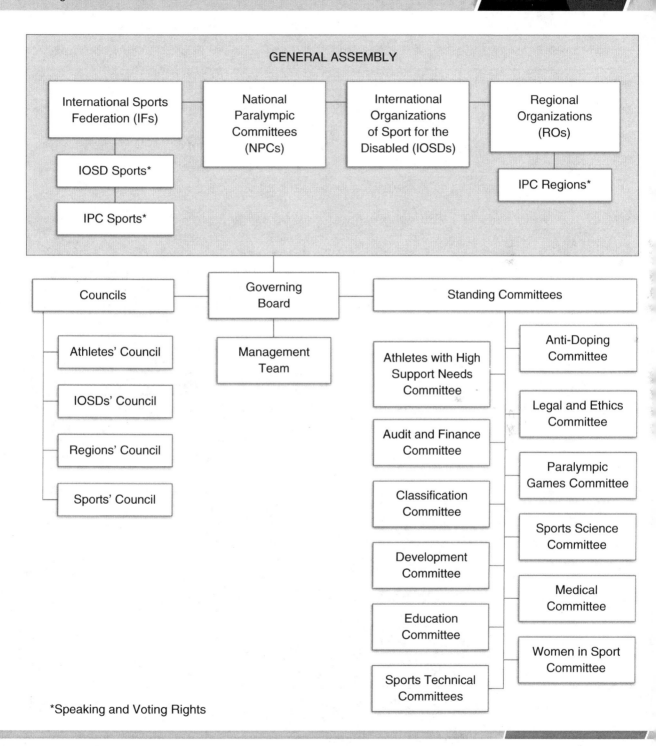

- Consider and approve the policy and procedures for nomination and election of Governing Board members
- Consider motions from members and through the Governing Board from Standing Committees
- Hear and receive the reports of the Governing Board and CEO
- Approve and admit full members in the IPC
- Consider and approve the financial reports and audited accounts and thereby discharge the Bodies of the Organization
- Consider and approve the bylaws outlining the Members' rights and obligations
- Approve amendments to the IPC constitution

The Governing Board is primarily responsible for the implementation of policies and directions set by the General Assembly. Additionally, the Governing Board provides recommendations on membership to the General Assembly, including motions received from members. It is also responsible for approving budgets and auditing accounts, IPC Rules and Regulations, membership of IPC Committees and the Paralympic Games (IPC, n.d.c).

The IPC Management Team "consists of the professional staff working under the direction of the CEO" (IPC, n.d.c, para. 2). These are the paid sport managers who work at IPC Headquarters. The Headquarters for the IPC has been located in Bonn, Germany, since 1999. Approximately 50 paid Executive Staff members work at the Headquarters, including the CEO, who oversees numerous departments including Sport Information Technology; Protocol, Hospitality and Events; Development; Administration, Finance and Corporate Services; Media and Communications; Marketing and Commercial; Medical and Scientific; Membership Engagement; and Paralympic Games (IPC, n.d.c). In addition, specific sports fall under here including World Para Swimming, World Para Powerlifting, World Shooting Para Sports, World Para Dance Sports, IPC Snow Sports, and World Para Ice Hockey. Managing the Paralympic Games is as complex as managing any large multisport event and sport managers need to be aware of the social, technological, economic, ethical, political, legal, and educational aspects of running this growing global event (Hums & Wolff, 2017).

National Paralympic Committees

Every nation participating in the Paralympic Games must have an NPC or, if an NPC has not yet been established, a National Contact Agency. In terms of sport governance, "NPCs undertake the coordination within the respective country or territory and are responsible for relations and communications with the IPC" (IPC, 2011, Rights and Obligations of IPC Members section).

portraits + perspectives

CHERI BLAUWETT, *MD*

Chairperson, International Paralympic Committee Medical Commission

I currently serve as Chairperson of the IPC Medical Committee. The Committee is comprised of eight professionals from various world regions. The Committee's ultimate goal is setting policy and organizational structure that best protects the health of the athlete.

One major policy issue facing the Paralympic Movement is professionalization of the classification system. Currently, most classifiers serve in a volunteer capacity which leads to a less-consistent approach and also, at times, difficulty with standardization. Some people are even advocating for all classification to be moved outside of the IPC and put into the hands of an external, independent organization (akin to our anti-doping system). A second issue involves anti-doping and our global context. As of late, there has been a discrepancy between the Olympic and Paralympic response to aggregious cases of doping, which has created political tensions that then translate into many other areas related to the Olympic/Paralympic relationship.

For several years, the Medical Commission has been involved in developing policy to deter the practice of "boosting"—the intentional induction of autonomic dysreflexia for performance enhancement. Beginning in 2008, the Committee developed a screening process to be carried out in major international competition, which involves random blood pressure checks just prior to athletes entering the field of play.

The Paralympic Movement has experienced extraordinary growth over the past 20 years, creating both challenges as well as exceptional opportunities. By far and away the most positive aspect of our current governance structure is that it fosters the involvement of leaders who are truly passionate about Paralympic sport. Most of the negatives are due to the fact that the Paralympic Movement is still quite young and is evolving out of a grassroots model to one that is increasingly professional. For example, as it currently stands, elections of the IPC Board of Governors take place every four years, however the whole Board is up for re-election at that time, meaning that in theory, there is the potential (although unlikely) that the whole Board would turn over at once. This can and should likely evolve into a structure in which Board members finish their terms in a staggered fashion.

As the Paralympic Movement moves forward, one future challenge its leaders face is the ongoing tension between the goals of (a) maintaining the passion and grassroots feeling of the Movement and (b) professionalization of the Movement—which inevitably may lead to change and a less "personal" feel. A second challenge deals with sport governance. Currently the IPC serves as both an international federation (for several "IPC sports") as well as a major event organizer. This is very different from the IOC, and can at times create "role confusion."

In the United States, the USOC acts as the NPC and is constitutionally obligated to do so by the Amateur Sports Act. This is very unusual, as most nations have a separate NPC. For example, in Canada the Canadian Paralympic Committee is responsible for the Paralympic Movement, Australia has the Australian Paralympic Committee, and Greece has the Hellenic Paralympic Committee. In 2001, the USOC established US Paralympics, a division of the USOC, to manage Paralympic sport. The mission statement of US Paralympics reads as follows: "To support U.S. Olympic and Paralympic athletes in achieving sustained competitive excellence while demonstrating the values of the Olympic Movement, thereby inspiring all Americans" (USOC, 2017, para. 3).

Canadian Paralympic Committee
www.paralympic.ca

Australian Paralympic Committee
www.paralympic.org.au

Hellenic Paralympic Committee
www.paralympic.org/npc/greece

US Paralympics
https://www.teamusa.org/US-Paralympics

US Paralympics and the appropriate NGB help prepare and select the athletes who will represent the United States at the Paralympic Games. It works to meet the urgent need to provide opportunities for people with disabilities, including an increasing number of military veterans, to participate in sport. Offering programs from the grassroots (Paralympic sports clubs) to the elite level (Gateway to Gold), US Paralympics works to improve the lives of people with disabilities through sport (USOC, 2017).

International Federations

IFs serve as the representatives of sports that compete under the IPC's governance. The IPC recognizes the 14 IFs that hold jurisdiction over Paralympic sports. In addition, the IPC, "serves as the IF for nine sports that compete within the Paralympic umbrella as of 2015: alpine skiing, athletics, biathlon, cross-country skiing, ice sledge hockey, powerlifting, shooting, swimming, and wheelchair dance" (Hums & Pate, 2018).

CURRENT POLICY AREAS

Like any major international sport entity, the Paralympic Movement faces a wide variety of issues for which it must formulate policies. Because of the Movement's global nature, many of these policy issues are complex and many have strong ethical components (Hums, 2006). To illustrate some of these issues, the three strategic goals presented in Exhibit 11.5 from the 2015–18 IPC Strategic Plan will serve as a starting point for this section (IPC, 2015). This Strategic Plan illustrates how a sport governing body identifies and addresses important issues. Selected strategic priorities for each of the goals clearly outline the most important current issues facing the Paralympic Movement today.

Although some of these goals represent issues mainly directed inward to the organization, forces external to the IPC also raise important questions for sport managers in the Paralympic Movement. Many of these result in ethical dilemmas as well (Hums, 2006, 2007). One of these external forces is attitudes toward people with disabilities. As the IPC attempts to develop more competitions for athletes with significant disabilities, some of those in the media or sponsors may not consider these competitors to be athletes or to "look like" athletes, making it difficult for the IPC to be more inclusive. Another external factor is the economy. Companies with limited sponsorship budgets may decide that sponsoring athletes with disabilities is not essential to their business plans. Thus, the IPC may have fewer resources and will need to make decisions on how to distribute its limited resources fairly.

Changing Technologies

Advances in technology have an impact on sport every day, whether through introduction of a new golf club, lighter football shoes, or improved

Strategic Goal #1: Consolidate the Paralympic Games as a premier sporting event

Strategic priorities:

Further enhance the appeal of the Paralympic Games by ensuring a balanced yet attractive sports programme with high-quality and easily understood competition.

Promote the value of the Paralympic Games by maximising legacy and social impact opportunities as well as by harnessing commercial potential.

Use the Rio 2016, PyeongChang 2018 and Tokyo 2020 Games to further improve the global reach of the Paralympic Games.

Leverage existing Paralympic Games know-how and the positive relations with the IOC, IFs and NPCs to strengthen the effectiveness of work with OCOGs.

Strategic Goal #2: Empower Para-athletes and support the development of para-sports

Strategic priorities:

Ensure resources exist to improve access and opportunities in para-sport through the continued development of athlete pathways, from the grassroots level to Paralympic success.

Provide robust sport-specific classification, supported by policies, procedures and evidence, as a prerequisite for fair and easily understood competition.

Support para-athletes in reaching their full potential during their sporting career and beyond, as they transition to life after sport.

Ensure that sports in the Paralympic Movement are practiced in a manner that protects the health of para-athletes, addresses their needs and respects fair play and ethics.

Strategic Goal #3: Improve the recognition and value of the Paralympic brand

Strategic priorities:

Develop and implement a long-term brand vision that ensures greater understanding, consistent usage, exposure, recognition and affinity across the world, in particular within key territories.

Develop and implement a strategy to increase the quality, profile, recognition and awareness of para-sport, its main events and leading para-athletes 365 days a year.

Source: IPC (2015).

athletic turf. The impact of technology is felt deeply in the Paralympic Games, as prosthetics and wheelchairs become lighter and stronger and athletes become faster. New technologies were at the forefront at the Rio 2016 Paralympic Games in the following ways (Knowles, 2016):

- the running blade and sports knee
- high-tech swim caps

- carbon body fit
- BMW's wind tunnel bikes
- indoor bike training
- altitude chamber and anti-gravity treadmill
- 3D printed prosthetics
- trick bike bits
- new improved boccia kit

How technology affects sport presents larger questions for sport managers. Just because new equipment can be manufactured that improves performance, does that mean the equipment should be allowed in competition? For example, just because a company can manufacture a golf ball that can fly 500 meters does not necessarily mean golf governing bodies must sanction the ball for use in competition. In making such decisions, sport governing bodies need to assess three factors: (1) safety, (2) ability of people to access or acquire the equipment, and (3) fairness. First and foremost, sport equipment must be safe for the athletes using the equipment and for the other athletes competing in the same game or event. Second, governing bodies must assess whether the cost of the new equipment is excessive, thereby eliminating the possibility for athletes, particularly those from developing countries, to acquire it. Finally, there is the basic question of fairness. Does using certain equipment provide one athlete an unfair advantage over the competition?

Lack of Competitive Depth

Another issue facing the Paralympic Movement is the lack of competitive depth in several sports, but particularly in athletics (track & field) (Bloom, 2015). This often results in athletes from different classifications having to compete against each other in the same event when they should be racing in separate events. An athlete with a lower classification may be placed in a race with competitors s/he should not be on the track at the same time. This obviously disadvantages the lower classification athlete, who stands no chance to win the event, even though s/he may set a new record for the proper classification. Not only is this issue challenging for the athletes, it can also cause confusion for fans who wonder why a certain athlete finishes so far off the pace.

As Bloom (2015) points out, there is no simple solution. The situation does suggest, however, that more effort needs to be made to increase opportunities for athletes at the grassroots level to further develop. Of course, in many countries this is difficult due to cultural perceptions about people with disabilities (Forber-Pratt, 2012). As Dr Forber-Pratt points out, "In some nations or environments, there are often stigmas surrounding disability that commonly prevent individuals with disabilities from full participation in society, let alone sport. Sport can, however, be used as a catalyst for social change" (para. 4). While the presence of this stigma is often the case in developing nations, the same can be said of the ableism (discrimination against people with disabilities) that exists in the developed world as well.

Integration of Athletes with Disabilities into Able-Bodied Sport

This complex policy area is one in which the solutions are evolving differently in different parts of the world. The extent to which athletes with disabilities have been integrated into able-bodied sport can be measured by the following organizational components: (1) governance, (2) media and information distribution, (3) management, (4) funding and sponsorship, (5) awareness and education, (6) events and programs, (7) awards and recognition, (8) philosophy, and (9) advocacy (Hums, Legg, & Wolff, 2003; Hums, Moorman, & Wolff, 2009; Wolff, 2000). Each of these components can be examined as presented in Exhibit 11.6.

Nine Organizational Component Model for Analyzing the Integration of Athletes with Disabilities — *exhibit* **11.6**

1. *Governance:* Examine how organizational policies and procedures deal with athletes with disabilities.

2. *Media and Information:* Look at representation of athletes with disabilities in organizational publications or media guides.

3. *Management:* Examine the number of persons with disabilities working in management positions or sitting on governing boards.

4. *Funding and Sponsorship:* Determine from the budget how much money raised by the organization is going to support athletes with disabilities.

5. *Awareness and Education:* Consider how informed and knowledgeable people within the organization are about disability sport.

6. *Events and Programs:* Determine the number of competitive opportunities the organization provides for athletes with disabilities.

7. *Awards and Recognitions:* Evaluate how the organization publicly recognizes the accomplishments of its athletes with disabilities.

8. *Philosophy:* Review the organization's mission statement and determine how athletes with disabilities are reflected in it.

9. *Advocacy:* Determine whether a sport organization is actively promoting sport for people with disabilities via special programming.

How can these components relate to policy development within a sport organization? For media and information distribution, sport organizations can make sure athletes with disabilities are presented on a consistent basis in social media and in press releases. Under management, sport organizations could establish hiring procedures creating opportunities for people with disabilities to be represented in the pool of candidates for open management positions. Under events and programs, sport organizations could establish participation categories for athletes with disabilities, just as there are categories of participation for men and women. For funding, sport organizations could establish funding opportunities specifically for athletes with disabilities so when organizational representatives meet with potential donors, disability sport is part of the conversation. These examples show how criteria for inclusion can influence organizational policy making, and they also provide a solid framework for assessing the status of athletes and people with disabilities within sport organizations.

Organizations that embrace diversity are acting as socially responsible partners in society. Including athletes with disabilities into the management structure of sport organizations increases the size of the networks involved and allows for more voices at the table.

The Wounded Warriors

US Olympic Committee Paralympic Military & Veteran Programs
https://www.teamusa.org/
US-Paralympics/Resources/
Military

Given the reality of war and conflict around the world, a growing number of wounded soldiers and civilians are seeking ways to reclaim their lives as best they can. One way people feel more fully alive after having been injured is through sport and physical activity. One program that supports wounded servicemen and servicewomen is the US Olympic Committee Paralympic Military Program. The program

> uses Paralympic sport opportunities to support wounded, ill and injured American service members and veterans, including those with amputations, traumatic brain injuries and visual impairments. Through camps and clinics held year-round across the country, service members and veterans are introduced to Paralympic sport techniques and opportunities, including local and regional competitions, and are also connected to ongoing Paralympic sport programs in their communities including those provided by Paralympic Sport Clubs. (USOC, 2017, para. 1)

At the 2012 London Paralympic Games, Team USA featured 20 military athletes as US Paralympic Team members (USOC, 2012). Team US at the Rio 2016 Paralympic Games included 35 military athletes (US Paralympics, 2016). It is interesting to see how the Paralympic Movement has come full circle. The first Stoke-Mandeville games were held to help wounded World War II veterans, and today we see the benefits of sport for wounded veterans from the wars and occupations in Iraq and Afghanistan. The spirit of those first Games lives on today.

SUMMARY

The Paralympic Games motto is "Spirit in Motion." The Games are an ever-growing, international, multidisability, multisport competition. Attracting thousands of athletes from numerous nations, the Games showcase the best elite athletes with disabilities. As a sport property, the Games are gaining the interest of corporations eager to connect with millions of consumers around the world. The governing structure of the Paralympic Games parallels that of the Olympic Games in many ways; both are large multisport international events. Just as women and racial and ethnic minorities have contributed to diversifying the sport industry, so too are people with disabilities making an impact. This large part of the sport industry is often overlooked in spite of its size and importance, and sport managers are advised to keep an eye on the growth and development in this area.

The Paralympic Games, as a growing competition, must deal with evolving policy issues and refocused strategic goals. The question of inclusion of athletes with disabilities into able-bodied sport will continue to be an ongoing debate, and Oscar Pistorius's Olympic Games debut brought this discussion to the forefront. As the Games grow, pressure will increase to maximize corporate sponsorship opportunities. It is an exciting time for the Paralympic Games, given their future growth potential.

case STUDY

SPORT FOR INDIVIDUALS WITH DISABILITIES

You are working with USA Hockey, the NGB for ice hockey in the United States. Recently, the USOC has asked you to consider the inclusion of the Paralympic men's ice sledge hockey team into USA Hockey. At the 2014 Sochi Paralympic Games, the US men's team brought home the Gold Medal, defeating Russia in the sold-out exciting final game.

The ultimate goal after making this assessment is to integrate the activities of the Paralympic sledge hockey team within USA Hockey. What types of events or activities for the Paralympic sledge hockey team could USA Hockey sponsor? What types of publicity could it provide? In other words, what are some concrete strategies USA Hockey could use to help sledge hockey grow and prosper? How should you go about starting your task?

1. The best place to start is to use the nine-component model designed by Hums, Legg, and Wolff (2003); Hums, Moorman, and Wolff (2009); and Wolff (2000) and presented in Exhibit 11.8. Using each component, show how USA Hockey could incorporate the ice sledge hockey team into its organization.

2. Think of other sport organizations that could assist you in your tasks, such as the NHL, Hockey Canada, or any other sport organization that could potentially be working with hockey players with disabilities.

3. Some people would argue that athletes with disabilities should retain a separate identity from able-bodied athletes and compete only with other athletes with disabilities. Do you agree or disagree, and why? What benefits do disability sport and athletes with disabilities offer to able-bodied sport organizations?

CHAPTER questions

1. The IPC is considering expanding the Summer and Winter Games by one sport each. Which sports would you choose to add, and why?

2. The US Paralympic men's soccer team is playing a series of exhibition matches against the Brazilian Paralympic men's soccer team. Your college or university has been awarded one of the matches. Develop a series of marketing strategies to promote the event. What community groups and sponsors will you want to involve?

3. What are some specific strategies the IPC could use to increase sport participation by athletes with disabilities who live in developing nations?

4. A number of Paralympic athletes are talented enough to compete in the Olympic Games. For example, at the Rio 2016 Paralympic Games, four 1500 meter runners recorded times faster than the Gold Medal winner in that event in the Olympic Games. Natalia Partyka of Poland competed in both Games in table tennis. What are your thoughts on Paralympic athletes competing in the Olympic Games? What effect could competing in the Olympic Games possibly have on the Paralympic Games, where they also compete? Where do you weigh in on the role technology plays in Paralympians performances?

FOR ADDITIONAL INFORMATION

1. Youtube: We're the Superhumans: Rio Paralympics 2016 Trailer: https://www.youtube.com/watch?v=IocLkk3aYlk&t=40s

2. Paralympic Athlete Biographies, Interviews, and Medalists: https://www.paralympic.org/athletes

3. Paralympian Hannah Cockroft Accuses Sportswear Giants of Discrimination: Steinberg, J. (2016, September 6). *The Guardian*. https://www.theguardian.com/sport/2016/sep/06/hannah-cockroft-paralympics-nike-adidas-discrimination

4. International Organisations of Sport for the Disabled: https://www. paralympic.org/the-ipc/international-organization-for-the-disabled
5. Putin: IPC has "Humiliated Itself" with Russian Paralympic ban decision: http://edition.cnn.com/2016/08/25/sport/vladimir-putin-paralympics-ipc/index.html
6. The History of the International Paralympic Committee: www. insidethegames.biz/history/paralympics/the-ipc

REFERENCES

Block, M. E. (1999). Did we jump on the wrong bandwagon? Making general physical education placement work. *Palaestra*, 15(3), 30–36.

Bloom, B. (2015, October 28). Paralympic athletics has a major problem that is easy to see and hard to solve: a complete lack of depth. *The Telegraph*. Retrieved from www.telegraph. co.uk/sport/othersports/athletics/11959963/ Paralympic-athletics-has-a-major-problem-that-is-easy-to-see-and-hard-to-solve-a-complete-lack-of-depth.html

DePauw, K., & Gavron, S. (2005). *Disability and sport* (2nd ed.). Champaign, IL: Human Kinetics.

Forber-Pratt, A. (2012, August 22). The challenges and responsibilities of para-athletes. Retrieved from https://www.sportanddev.org/en/article/ news/challenges-and-responsibilities-para-athletes

Hums, M. A. (2006, July). Ethical issues facing the Paralympic Movement. Paper presented at the International Olympic Academy Educator's Session, Olympia, Greece.

Hums, M. A. (2007). Ethical issues of changing classification systems. *Proceedings of the II Conferencia Internacional sobre Deporte Adaptado*, Malaga, Spain.

Hums, M. A., & Pate, J. R. (in-press). The International Paralympic committee as a governing body. In I. Brittain & I. Beacom (Eds.), *The Palgrave handbook of Paralympic studies*. London: Palgrave.

Hums, M. A., & Wolff, E. A. (2017). Managing Paralympic sport organisations: The STEEPLE framework. In S. Darcy, S. Frawley, & D. Adair (Eds.), *Managing the Paralympics* (pp. 155–174). London: Palgrave.

Hums, M. A., Legg, D., & Wolff, E. A. (2003, June). Examining opportunities for athletes with disabilities within the International Olympic Committee. Paper presented at the Annual Conference of the North American Society for Sport Management, Ithaca, NY.

Hums, M. A., Moorman, A. M., & Wolff, E. A. (2009). Emerging disability rights in sport: Sport as a human right for persons with disabilities and the 2006 Convention on the Rights of Persons with Disabilities. *Cambrian Law Review*, 40, 36–48.

IPC. (n.d.a). About us. Retrieved from www. paralympic.org/TheIPC/HWA/AboutUs

IPC. (n.d.b). History of the Movement. Retrieved from www.paralympic.org/TheIPC/HWA/ HistoryoftheMovement

IPC. (n.d.c). IPC management team. Retrieved from https://www.paralympic.org/the-ipc/ management-team

IPC. (n.d.d). Partnerships. Retrieved from www. paralympic.org/TheIPC/HWD/Partnerships

IPC. (n.d.e). The IPC: How we do it. Retrieved from www.paralympic.org/TheIPC/HWD/Funding

IPC. (2010). *International Paralympic Committee strategic plan 2011–2014*. Bonn, Germany: Author.

IPC. (2011). Handbook. Retrieved from www. paralympic.org/TheIPC/HWA/Handbook

IPC. (2015). *Strategic plan 2015–2018: Strategic outlook for the International Paralympic Committee*. Bonn, Germany: Author.

Knowles, K. (2016). 9 awesome technologies at the 2016 Paralympics. Retrieved from https://www. thememo.com/2016/09/05/rio-paralympics-2016-technology-rio-paralympics-tech-sports-2016/

USOC. (2012). Military athletes. Retrieved from https://www.teamusa.org/US-Paralympics/Resources/Military/Military-Athletes

USOC. (2017). About US Paralympics. Retrieved from www.teamusa.org/us-paralympics/about

US Paralympics. (2016, August 27). Twenty-two athletes added to Paralympic team. Retrieved from http://www.teamusa.org/News/2016/August/27/22-Athletes-Added-To-US-Paralympic-Team

Wolff, E. A. (2000). Inclusion and integration of soccer opportunities for players with disabilities within the United States Soccer Federation: Strategies and recommendations. Senior Honors Thesis, Brown University.

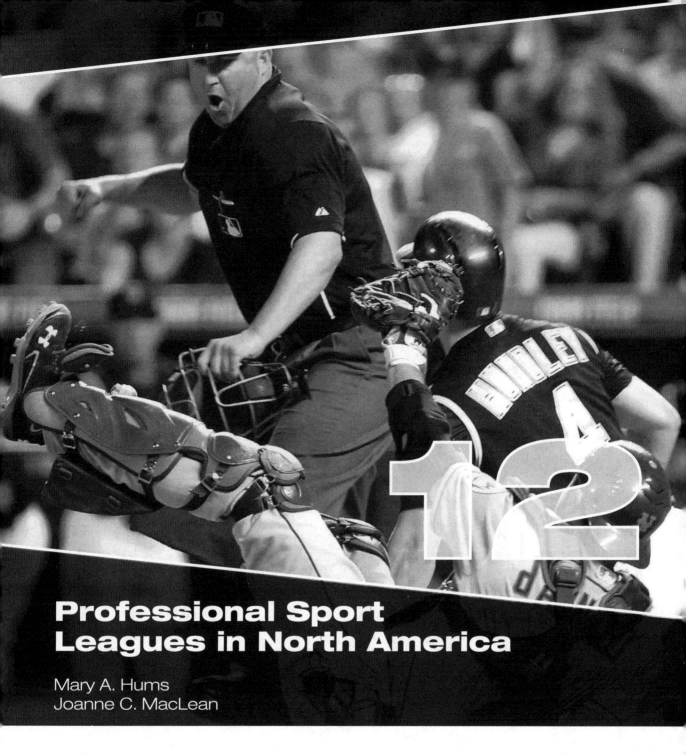

Professional Sport
Leagues in North America

Mary A. Hums
Joanne C. MacLean

Many people dream of hitting a home run in the bottom of the ninth inning to win the World
Series, making the game-winning shot at the buzzer in the National Basketball Association
(NBA) Finals, throwing a touchdown pass to a wide-open receiver in the Super Bowl, or
scoring the game-winning goal in the final game of the Stanley Cup. In North America we

have grown up watching these exciting moments at the stadium, streamed online, on TV, or through highlights on ESPN or TSN. All these spectacular plays belong to the most visible of all our sport industry segments—professional sport. Yet most of us have warning track power at best, shoot the occasional air ball, are unable to throw a true spiral, and cannot even skate backward. The odds against making it as a professional athlete in the Big Four—Major League Baseball (MLB), the NBA, the National Football League (NFL), and the National Hockey League (NHL)—are astronomical, but these athletes' games would not happen and their exploits would remain relatively unknown if not for the sport managers (Masteralexis, Barr, & Hums, 2015; Teamworkonline, 2016). Without these men and women working tirelessly behind the scenes, there would be no season tickets for sale, no sponsorships available, no games broadcast on TV, no T-shirts emblazoned with logos, no social media to follow, and no new high-tech stadiums to visit.

Professional sport in North America takes many forms. We think first of the Big Four. Professional sport also takes place in other forms: tours or organized series, such as we see in professional golf with the Professional Golfers' Association (PGA), Ladies Professional Golf Association (LPGA), and the Champions Tour; or in motor sports with the NASCAR Xfinity Series and the Camping World Truck Series. These tours and series will be addressed in Chapter 13. Other professional leagues exist as well, including the Women's National Basketball Association (WNBA) and Major League Soccer (MLS), and we should not overlook the current popularity of UFC—Ultimate Fighting Championship. There are also minor league sports, particularly baseball, hockey, and basketball. Other sports also have professional competition, such as the Professional Bull Riders (PBR), Professional Bowlers Association (PBA), and Bass Anglers Sportsman Society (BASS). We cannot overlook the growing popularity of eSports as well.

How are these professional sports organized? Who are the people delivering the product to the public? Who are the power players and groups governing these sports? This chapter focuses on the governance structures of professional sport leagues in North America. The authors recognize there are a wide variety of these leagues in North America, but the main focus of the chapter is on the traditional Big Four. Chapter 13 addresses the governance of individual sports, and Chapter 14 explains the governance structures of professional sport outside of North America.

HISTORY AND DEVELOPMENT OF PROFESSIONAL SPORT

While a comprehensive history of the development of professional sport in North America is beyond the scope of this book, it is important to note key dates for certain events in the histories of each of the

Big Four; for example, when the leagues took the form they have today. It is also important to note governance issues, such as when rival leagues formed to compete with existing leagues.

Major League Baseball

MLB has the longest history of any professional sport in North America. The first professional club, the Cincinnati Red Stockings, was founded in 1869. The first professional sports league was baseball's National League, established in 1876, followed by the American League in 1901. The signing of the National Agreement between the National League and the American League in 1903 established much of the basic governance structure for MLB (Scully, 1989). Early on, the players formed a number of rival leagues such as the Players' League and the Federal League. Players objected to management's strict rules, such as the reserve system that "reserved" a player to his club and prohibited other clubs from negotiating with him, thus controlling players' salaries. While these leagues presented brief challenges to professional baseball's structure, all eventually failed (Abrams, 1998). As you will discover, this long-standing unchallenged status is quite different from the history of the other Big Four leagues.

Currently, MLB has 30 teams. The American League has 15 (five in the East, five in the Central, and five in the West Division). The National League has 15 (five in the East, five in the Central, and five in the West Division).

Major League Baseball
www.mlb.com

National Football League

The first professional football league, the American Professional Football Association, was established in 1920. It changed its name to the National Football League in 1922 (NFL, 2013). The NFL has experienced a long history of rival leagues, dating all the way back to its first inter-league battle in 1926 with the American Football League (AFL) (Quirk & Fort, 1992). Different forms of the AFL emerged and challenged the NFL, and finally in 1966 the leagues signed an agreement establishing an inter-league championship, and full amalgamation began in 1970. This event marked the first time that TV income played a critical role in the survival of a rival league, because the AFL had an existing TV contract that by 1969 gave each team approximately $900,000 (Quirk & Fort, 1992). Since then, the NFL has been challenged by the World Football League (WFL) in 1974–75, the United States Football League (USFL) in 1983–85, and the Xtreme Football League (XFL) in 2001.

Currently, the NFL has 32 teams with two conferences, the American Football Conference (AFC) and the National Football Conference (NFC). The AFC North, AFC South, AFC East, and AFC West each have four teams, as do the NFC North, NFC South, NFC East, and NFC West.

National Football League
www.nfl.com

National Basketball
Association
www.nba.com

National Basketball Association

The first professional basketball league was established in 1924 as the American Basketball League. It disbanded in 1947, and another league emerged, the Basketball Association of America (BAA) (Quirk & Fort, 1992). At the same time a league called the National Basketball League (NBL) was also in existence. By 1949 the BAA absorbed the remaining NBL teams, and the organization renamed itself the National Basketball Association (NBA, 2017). In 1967, the rival American Basketball Association (ABA) formed, which had sufficient financial backing and talent to pose a threat to the NBA. In 1976, however, an agreement was reached between the two leagues, resulting in four franchises from the ABA—Denver, Indiana, New York, and San Antonio—moving to the NBA (Quirk & Fort, 1992). No rival leagues have attempted to compete with the NBA since then.

Currently, the NBA has 30 teams in two conferences. The Eastern Conference has five teams each in the Atlantic, Central, and Southeast Divisions. The Western Conference has five teams each in the Northwest, Pacific, and Southwest Divisions.

National Hockey League
www.nhl.com

National Hockey League

The NHL started in 1917 with four teams located in Canada—Toronto, Ottawa, and two teams in Montreal. The league expanded to the United States in 1924 (Quirk & Fort, 1992). The NHL faced its biggest challenge from rival leagues from the World Hockey Association (WHA), a league that began in 1972. The WHA attempted to establish itself in medium-size Canadian markets without NHL franchises as well as in major United States cities in direct competition with existing NHL teams. After a seven-year war with the NHL, four remaining franchises—Winnipeg, Quebec, Edmonton, and Hartford—moved to the NHL in 1979 (Quirk & Fort, 1992).

Currently, the NHL has 30 teams in two conferences. The Eastern Conference has eight teams each in the Atlantic and Metropolitan Divisions. The Western Conference has seven teams each in the Central and Pacific Divisions.

GOVERNANCE

Each professional sport league has various levels of governance structures. The governance structures exist at the league level and the front-office level. The league level includes the league offices and the Office of the Commissioner, which constitute the structures on the management side of professional sport. The players' side is governed by Players Associations. Although the governance structures of the various leagues are not identical, they share common components. According to Gladden and Sutton (2011, p. 125), these components are:

1. a league Commissioner
2. a Board of Governors or a committee composed of team owners
3. a central administrative unit that negotiates contracts and agreements on behalf of the league and assumes responsibility for scheduling, licensing, record keeping, financial management, discipline and fines, revenue sharing payments, marketing and promotional activities, developing and managing special events, and other functions such as coordinating publicity and advertising on behalf of the teams as a whole

In addition to these components, governance issues are also dealt with at the team level. We will briefly examine each of these components.

Commissioner's Office

Major professional sports leagues are led by a Commissioner. The first Commissioner in professional sport was Kenesaw Mountain Landis, who became Major League Baseball Commissioner in 1921 (Abrams, 1998). As Commissioner, he ruled with an iron fist, basing his decisions on his interpretation of what was in the game's best interest. Although the original concept of a Commissioner's role was modeled on Landis, commissioners in different sports did not follow his lead completely (Masteralexis, 2015). Some would argue, however, that NFL Commissioner Roger Goodell "has acted with more power than any other Commissioner in U.S. sports history" (McCann, 2012, para. 8).

The Commissioner is in some ways an employee of the owners, because the owners have the power to hire and terminate him or her. However, in other ways the Commissioner is the owners' boss, having disciplinary power over them (Wong, 2002).

The Office of the Commissioner is typically created and defined within a league's collective bargaining agreement (CBA) and its constitution and bylaws (Pacifici, 2014). The role of the Commissioner in professional sport has evolved over time, but some of the basic powers of the office have remained throughout the years in different sports. In general, the discretionary powers of the Commissioner include (Yasser et al., 2003, p. 381):

- approval of player contracts
- resolution of disputes between players and clubs
- resolution of disputes between clubs
- resolution of disputes between players or clubs and the league
- disciplinary matters involving owners, clubs, players, and other personnel
- rule-making authority

The power to act in the best interest of a sport has carried over from Landis' days, and according to Renicker (2016, p. 1051):

The power of professional sports commissioners to determine what is in the "best interests" of their respective sport is a significant aspect of sports today, and can be traced back to 1921, when the federal courts authorized then-Commissioner Kenesaw Mountain Landis to act with a broad range of discretion in protecting the "best interests" of baseball. This precedent set in motion a long history of commissioners using the "best interests" of the game power to accomplish various goals, and most recently has been used to discipline players for alleged misconduct.

As Wharton (2011) notes, however, "the scope of the commissioner's power—as it has developed over the years—varies from sport to sport. The NHL does not have a 'best interests' clause as baseball does, a league spokesman said. The NFL and NBA do" (para. 12). The Professional Baseball Agreement (MLB, 2008, pp. 1–2) contains the following language:

Sec. 2. The functions of the Commissioner shall include:

(b) To investigate, either upon complaint or upon the Commissioner's own initiative, any act, transaction or practice charged, alleged or suspected to be not in the best interests of the national game of Baseball, with authority to summon persons and to order the production of documents, and, in case of refusal to appear or produce, to impose and enforce penalties as are hereinafter provided . . . (a) a reprimand; (b) deprivation of a Major League Club of representation in Major League Meetings; (c) suspension or removal of any owner, officer or employee of a Major League Club; (d) temporary or permanent ineligibility of a player; (e) a fine, not to exceed $2,000,000 in the case of a Major League Club, not to exceed $500,000 in the case of an owner, officer or employee, and in an amount consistent with the then-current Basic Agreement with the Major League Baseball Players Association, in the case of a player.

While these basic duties remain relatively unchanged, the office itself has changed. "The modern commissioner must have expertise in TV contracts, labor relations, player health, handling Congress, handling lawsuits, criminal law, public relations, finding new revenues in new media and, as ever, owner relations. That last one might be the trickiest" (Allen & Brady, 2014, para. 6). Gary Bettman, NHL Commissioner as of this writing had the following to say about how the office duties have evolved (aquoted in Allen & Brady, 2014, para. 16):

- "For better or worse, the world seems more litigious," he says. "That is something you have to manage. And being a lawyer certainly helps."
- "You need to be facile and adaptable with respect to the changes in media that are happening at breathtaking speed," he says. "You have to be on top of the industry."
- "And finally you have to be prepared to look at A.) new business opportunities, such as international and the shrinking of the

world and B.) changing old business into new businesses, such as how you distribute your licensed products," he says. "Retail in a brick-and-mortar building used to be the only way for fans to go, and now you can get anything on the Internet in 24 hours."

Commissioners' actions often go unnoticed by the public, as they are handled internal to the league. However, some notable exceptions include MLB Commissioner Bart Giamatti's banning Pete Rose from baseball for life for gambling, NFL Commissioner Roger Goodell's actions related to the New England Patriots' "Deflate-gate" case, and NBA Commissioner Adam Silver's multi-million-dollar fine and lifetime ban imposed on Donald Sterling for racist remarks. As evidenced in this section, the Commissioner's Office exercises its regulatory power in professional sports leagues through decisions concerning fines, suspensions, and disciplinary actions. Some regulatory power also rests at the league level and with the Players Associations.

Board of Governors or Owners Committee

Despite a wide range of powers, the Commissioner is not necessarily the final decision maker in issues involving governance of professional sport leagues. Although the Commissioner is very influential, the owners still have the ultimate say in policy development (Robinson, Lizandra, & Vail, 2001). We have all read about the annual league owners' meetings, where policies, rules, and business decisions concerning league operations are addressed. Each league has a committee structure made up of owners who ultimately make decisions on matters concerning franchise relocation, league expansion or contraction, playing facility issues, collective bargaining rules and rule changes, and revenue sharing (Sharp, Moorman, & Claussen, 2010). This committee also represents management in labor negotiations with players (Robinson et al., 2001). As an example, for the NFL (2017c, para. 7),

> The Executive Committee includes one representative—an owner or top officer—from each of the league's 32 clubs. Any change in game rules, league policy or club ownership or other modification to the game must be approved by at least three-fourths of the committee. Without consensus, nothing will pass.

At this level policy making often takes place within the frameworks of each league's constitution and bylaws. In professional sport this level is where the power lies on the management side. As we will see shortly, the players' side has a governance structure as well. Although policy making occurs at this level, daily league operations occur at another league-wide governance level. Each league has a league office employing paid sport managers to handle these tasks.

Central Administrative Unit: League Office

As mentioned earlier, this governance level deals with league-wide operations. A unique aspect of professional sport, as opposed to other businesses, is that the teams must simultaneously compete and cooperate (Mullin, Hardy, & Sutton, 2014). League offices schedule games, hire and train officials, discipline players, market and license logoed merchandise, and negotiate broadcast contracts (Sharp et al., 2010). League offices are usually organized by function, with a range of different departments. For example, the NBA League Office includes the following departments: Commissioner's Office, Basketball Operations, Communications, Content, Digital Media, Facilities and Administration, Finance, Global Media Distribution, Global Partnerships, Global Strategy, Information Technology, International Regional Offices, Legal, Marketing, Media Operations and Technology, NBA Development League, People and Culture, Referee Operations, Security, Social Responsibility and Player Programs, Team Marketing and Business Operations, and WNBA (NBA Media Ventures, 2016).

Individual Team Level

The day-to-day operations of a professional sports franchise take place on the individual team level. The two major groups that are responsible for daily operations—the owners and the front-office staff—are discussed in the following sections.

Owners

What drives the people who own major professional sport franchises? Today's owners are multibillionaires, many of whom are members of the Forbes 400 richest individuals in the nation. Some of the more recognizable team owners are Microsoft's Paul Allen (Seattle Seahawks), former NBA superstar Michael Jordan (Charlotte Bobcats), music mogul Jay-Z (Brooklyn Nets), and entrepreneur Mark Cuban (Dallas Mavericks). What motivates a person with money to purchase a professional sports franchise? Reasons include the excitement of being involved in professional sport and the publicity and spotlight that accompany owning a team, especially a winning team. But do not be fooled—these individuals did not accumulate wealth without keeping a sharp eye on the bottom line. According to Quirk and Fort (1999), "As important as winning is to them, it might well be a matter of ego and personal pride that they manage to do this while pocketing a good profit at the same time" (p. 97). Owners also know that in the long run, few franchises have ever been sold for less than their purchase price, basically ensuring future long-term capital gains.

While some owners, such as Cuban, want to be closely involved with the daily operations of their franchises, for the most part the owners leave those daily chores to the people who work in the front offices. The owners' place in the policy-making process lies mainly at the league level, as discussed earlier. Some owners may impose policies on their front-office staff and players, but that is not necessarily the norm. For example, Steven Bisciotti, owner of the NFL's Baltimore Ravens, refused to silence Brendon Ayanbadejo in his support for same-sex marriage in Maryland, despite being asked to do so by a state legislator.

Front-Office Staff

The front office is the place where the day-to-day operational and business decisions are made for the individual professional sports franchise. Similar to league offices, the front-office staff are usually departmentalized by function. A typical NBA front office will have Vice Presidents who head departments such as Basketball Operations, Sports Media Relations, Marketing, Operations, Finance, Corporate Partnerships, Ticket Operations and Strategic Planning, Human Resources, Player Personnel, Player Programs, Retail Business and Development, Mobile Strategy and Innovation, and General Counsel (NBA Media Ventures, 2017).

Let's compare that to an NFL franchise. The Minnesota Vikings front office includes the following departments: Player Personnel/Football Administration, Equipment, Medical, Operations/Facilities, Dining, Player Development/Legal, Video, Security, Sales and Marketing, Partnerships Activation and Special Projects, Corporate Partnerships, Corporate Development and Guest Relations, Corporate Strategy, Tickets and Sales Analytics, Accounting and Finance, Community Relations, Public Relations, Human Resources, and Information Technology (Minnesota Vikings, 2016). As students who may want to potentially work in pro sport, you can see there are a wide variety of opportunities for internships and careers. The entities and governance levels described so far in this chapter all deal with the management side of professional sport. However, governance structures also exist on the players' side of professional sport. These organizations, the players' unions, are commonly referred to as *Players Associations*.

Players Associations

Each of the Big Four professional leagues has what is known as a Players Association. These Players Associations, or PAs as they are sometimes called, are the players' unions. Professional baseball has the longest history of labor organization of all the professional sports. A player named John Montgomery Ward led the earliest unionization efforts; he founded the first players' union in 1885 and the Players League in 1890 (Abrams, 1998). Baseball players saw themselves as skilled tradespeople, similar to those workers who filled the factories of that era. Professional baseball witnessed these and other failed attempts at unionization until the Major League Baseball Players Association (MLBPA) was established in 1953.

www

Major League Baseball Players Association
www.mlbplayers.com

National Hockey League Players Association
www.nhlpa.com

National Basketball Players Association
www.nbpa.com

National Football League Players Association
https://www.nflpa.com

SHELLEY VOLPENHEIN, *Manager of Season Ticket Sales and Retention,*

Cincinnati Reds, Cincinnati, OH

I am a Manager of Season Ticket Sales and Retention for the Cincinnati Reds. I am in charge of planning and executing our strategic plan to retain, grow and acquire current and new Season Ticket Members. I recruit, hire, train, and develop Client Service Representatives (CSRs). I am also in charge of the Season Ticket Membership renewal campaigns with a team of five CSRs. We address customer issues to ensure effective and long-term solutions. We also planned and implemented 25+ special events as part of a new Season Ticket Membership service platform to effectively build and measure relationships with our Season Ticket Members.

As a manager of selling and retaining Season Ticket Memberships we are always creating and developing new policies to better serve our loyal consumers. We don't sell wins and losses, but we have the opportunity to provide once in a lifetime experiences, enhance business relationships, and create memories that last for generations. We maintain consistent and exemplary customer service from the sales process through the game day experience (Reds Way). From the Sales and/or Service representative setting up your Season Ticket Membership purchase to the parking attendant accepting your parking pass on Opening Day to the person cleaning up the soft drink you spilled on yourself in the middle of the concourse, all of the staff representing our brand must provide the same level of superior customer service. We are all a team working together.

We shifted from being a Season Ticket Holder to making the Season Ticket Membership a year-round experience and service plan for our most loyal consumers. Being a Season Ticket Member is more than just having Season Tickets.

Our Client Service Representatives are committed to building relationships through superior service. We serve our community and enhance our fans' experiences and memories. We strive for customer intimacy: knowing and understanding our fans on multiple levels. In order to obtain a better understanding and anticipate our customers' needs and wants we communicate with and service our customers year-round (not just during baseball season).

In 2016 we re-branded the way exclusive benefits were awarded to our Season Ticket Holders by creating a membership concept to offer customizable benefits and continuing year-round service. Prior to 2016, Season Ticket Holders were awarded benefits based on the number of games in their plan (Full Season/Half Season/20 Games). We selected the "best" benefits and offered these items/events to our Season Ticket Holders and then to people who had purchased the most games. Through survey data we found that our idea of the "best" benefits didn't always fit the needs of our customers as assigned. As a result, we implemented a commercial innovation concept that marketed season tickets in a new and unique way. We rolled out a new Season Ticket Membership Benefit platform providing a clear and transparent benefit list to fans that they may choose from.

Additionally, myself and my team of CSRs are constantly creating and developing new members only access policies and experiences to enhance the Season Ticket Membership experience. Being a Season Ticket Member is more than just having Season Tickets. We send out surveys after every special event to gather feedback from our members and suggestions for improvement. We also communicate with our counterparts at other teams to see what benefits/experiences/rewards work well for them.

The Season Ticket Membership platform has been very successful for our members who have engaged in the program. Our survey data indicates our members enjoy the flexibility and variety of options available to them.

Future challenges to policy development in Professional Sport include continuing to create and develop fresh and new members-only access and experiences each year to enhance the Season Ticket Membership experience. Also, acquiring new Season Ticket Membership business will be critical moving forward. Securing advance commitment from individuals and businesses to 20/40/80 games per year on a Season Ticket Membership purchase will help provide financial stability and a solid fanbase for the team into the future.

To ensure that the rights of NBA players are protected and that every conceivable measure is taken to assist players in maximizing their opportunities and achieving their goals, both on and off the court.

Source: NBPA (n.d.).

In 1966, former United Steelworkers employee Marvin Miller became its first Executive Director (Pessah, 2016). Miller negotiated the players' first collective bargaining agreement in 1968. The National Hockey League Players Association (NHLPA) began in 1967 when player representatives from the original six clubs met, adopted a constitution, and elected a president (NHLPA, 2017). In 1954, NBA All Star Bob Cousy began organizing the players, ultimately forming the National Basketball Players Association (NBPA) (NBPA, 2016). The NFL players' efforts were first organized in 1956, when a group of NFL players authorized a man named Creighton Miller and the newly formed National Football League Players Association (NFLPA) to represent them (NFLPA, 2014).

MISSION STATEMENTS.   Each PA has its own mission statement. The mission statement of the NBPA is presented in Exhibit 12.1. This mission statement clarifies that the number-one priority of any PA is its members—the players—and protecting their rights.

PAs share the common goals of representing players in matters related to wages, hours, working conditions, and players' rights. They help players with any type of dispute or problem they may have with management. They also deal with insurance benefits, retirement, and charitable opportunities, just as non-sport labor unions do. The NFLPA, for example, is a member of the American Federation of Labor–Congress of Industrial Organizations (AFL-CIO), a major non-sport union representing workers from a variety of industries.

MEMBERSHIP.   The membership of any PA may include more than just active players. MLBPA membership includes all players, managers, coaches, and trainers holding a signed contract with MLB (MLBPA, n.d.a). For basketball, the NBPA represents players while the National Basketball Coaches Association (NBCA) is the labor union that represents NBA coaches (NBCA, 2016).

FINANCIALS.   PAs rely on two primary sources of revenues. The first is individual membership dues. For example, in the MLBPA in 2012, the players' dues were set at $70 per day during the season (MLBPA, n.d.a). The second revenue source is each association's licensing division. For example, National Football League Players Incorporated, which is known as NFL PLAYERS, is the for-profit licensing, marketing, sponsorship, and content development subsidiary of the NFL Players Association (NFLPA, 2011). Created in 1994, its mission is "taking the helmets off" the players and marketing them as personalities as well as professional athletes.

ORGANIZATIONAL STRUCTURE.   PAs share relatively common governance structures, with Player Representatives, an Executive Board, and an Executive Committee. However, ultimate power rests with the players themselves. Every year each team elects, by secret ballot, a Player Representative (called a "Player Rep") and an Alternate Player Representative to serve on a Board of Player Representatives (for the NFL) or on an Executive Board (for MLB and the NHL). Player Reps generally serve one-year terms and act as liaisons between the union and the team members. According to the NFLPA, the Player Reps serve the following roles in addition to serving on the Board of Representatives (NFL Players, 2014, para. 2):

- collect membership dues or check-off cards from their teammates
- help teammates with grievances and fine appeals
- collect group licensing authorizations from other team members
- act as spokesmen for the organization on their team and in their local communities
- bring important issues to the full Board for action

These Boards of Player Reps select the members of an Executive Committee. For the NBPA the Executive Committee consists of nine players, and for the NHLPA the Executive Committee consists of seven players, one of whom holds the title of President.

PAs also employ full-time sport managers to staff their offices. The staff members of the MLBPA have titles such as Director of Communications; Executive Director; Director, Player Operations; Chief Financial Officer; Counsel; Director of Licensing and Business Development; Chief Operating Officer; Digital Media Director; Director of Player Services; and Director, Players Trust (MLBPA, n.d.b). The NBPA is divided into numerous offices including the Executive Director's Office, Senior Management, Finance, Strategy Engagement and Development, Digital, Brand Communications, Legal, Operations, Sports & Medicine, Marketing, Player Programs, Career Development, Off the Court, Player Wellness, Human Resources & Benefits, and Security & Logistics (NBPA, 2018). Currently, the offices for the MLBPA, NBPA, and NFLPA are located in New York City, while the offices for the NHLPA are housed in Toronto.

CURRENT POLICY AREAS

As with any segment of the sport industry, professional sport has a myriad of policy areas to discuss. Among these are use of social media, reaching the millennial audience, criminal activity by players, player and coach misconduct, player safety, and responding to athlete activism.

Use of Social Media in Professional Sport

The use of social media in sport by athletes, coaches, and front-office staff has exploded in the past few years. From Facebook to Twitter to Instagram to the next form of social media that doesn't even exist yet, fans and the media cannot get enough instantaneous information about their favorite teams or athletes. How are teams using social media to engage fans? According to Greenhalgh and Greenwell (2012), six distinct categories of tweets exist: interactivity, diversion, information sharing, content, fanship, and promotional. For example, the Cleveland Indians, dubbed one of MLB's and pro sports most Twitter-friendly teams, opened the first social media-only space in professional sport in their home stadium, Progressive Field (Olensky, 2012). As another example, the Boston Celtics launched a Facebook application called 3-Point Play, which fans have received enthusiastically (Stringer, 2012).

Athletes are also jumping on the social media bandwagon. Hambrick et al. (2010) examined Twitter usage by 101 professional athletes from NBA/WNBA, MLB/Minor League Baseball (MiLB), NFL, NHL, MLS, golf, auto racing, and other sports. The athletes used the social networking site primarily to interact with other Twitter users (34 percent of the time) and discuss non-sports topics (28 percent), while using the site less frequently to talk about sports (15 percent) and promote their sponsors or endorse products (5 percent). With such a small percentage of time devoted to promoting their sponsors, more opportunities exist for athletes to use Twitter for promotional purposes as part of their sponsor/endorsement contracts.

Of course, the downside to social media is the lack of control by the front office. Interactivity gives athletes the chance to connect with their fans, but the open nature of Twitter can cause problems, such as athletes revealing too much about themselves or their teams. Players may wish to express their opinions and air out their grievances against their teammates, coaching staff, opponents, and the league itself. Hence, sport organizations have established policies that provide some parameters for social media use. Here is a synopsis of the social media policies for the Big Four:

MAJOR LEAGUE BASEBALL: In order to illustrate what goes into a social media policy, we will use MLB as an example. Exhibit 12.1 contains the direct language of MLB's social media policy.

exhibit   **12.2**   Major League Baseball Social Media Policy

SOCIAL MEDIA POLICY

Major League Players

Definitions:

Covered Individuals – All Players who are represented by the Major League Baseball Players Association.

Social Media – Any form of online or interactive media, including, but not limited to profiles, commentary, writings, photographs, images, logos, and audio or video files posted on outlets including but not limited to Facebook, MySpace, Twitter, blogs, podcasts, message boards and websites.

Content – All material posted on Social Media, including links to other websites.

MLB Entity – Any entity affiliated with Major League Baseball, including the 30 Major League Clubs, Minor League Clubs, the Office of the Commissioner, MLB Enterprises, MLB Properties, MLB Productions, MLB Advanced Media, MLB Media Holdings, MLBInternational, MLB Online Services, Major League Baseball Scouting Bureau, and the MLB Network.

Prohibited Conduct:

In addition to the prohibition on the use of electronic equipment during the period beginning thirty minutes prior to a game and ending upon the conclusion of a game that is contained in Baseball Operations Bulletin A-2, Players may not engage in the following conduct with respect to the use of Social Media:

1. Displaying or transmitting Content via Social Media that reasonably could be construed as an official public communication of any MLB Entity without obtaining proper authorization.
2. Using an MLB Entity's logo, mark, or written, photographic, video or audio property without obtaining proper authorization.
3. Linking to the website of any MLB Entity on any Social Media outlet without obtaining proper authorization.
4. Displaying or transmitting Content that contains confidential or proprietary information of any MLB Entity or its employees or agents, including, for example, financial information, medical information, strategic information, etc.
5. Displaying or transmitting Content that reasonably could be construed as condoning the use of any substance prohibited by Major League Baseball's Joint Drug Prevention and Treatment Program.
6. Displaying or transmitting Content that questions the impartiality of or otherwise denigrates a Major League umpire.
7. Displaying or transmitting Content that is derogatory or insensitive to individuals based on race, color, ancestry, sex, sexual orientation, national origin, age, disability, or religion, including, but not limited to, slurs, jokes, stereotypes or other inappropriate remarks.
8. Displaying or transmitting Content that constitutes harassment of an individual or group of individuals, or threatens or advocates the use of violence against an individual or group of individuals.
9. Displaying or transmitting Content that contains obscene or sexually explicit language, images, or acts.
10. Displaying or transmitting Content that violates applicable local, state or federal law or regulations.

Enforcement:

A Player who violates this policy may be subject to discipline for just cause by either his Club or the Commissioner in accordance with Article XII of the Basic Agreement.

Source: MLB. (2012).

NATIONAL BASKETBALL ASSOCIATION: Use of cell phones and other electronic devices is banned during games. This period is defined as 45 minutes before tipoff until after media obligations have been completed. Players can use social media during pregame media access. The NBA recently released some guidelines on use of social media meant to reign in some exchanges taking place by players. The memo included three bullet points specifying what would be considered inappropriate material for team social media accounts (McMahon, 2017, paras. 8–10):

- Disparage, belittle, or embarrass an individual opponent or game official
- Mimic or impersonate an opponent or game official in a negative manner
- Criticize officiating or the NBA officiating program.

The memo continued:

In addition, teams should never disparagingly or negatively refer to an opponent's or game official's personal life, family, race, color, ethnicity, national origin, religion, sexual orientation or any other status or characteristic protected by law . . . Teams are also prohibited from using social media to highlight or encourage player altercations, flagrant fouls or hard physical contact between players, or to condone or make light of violence in any way or form.

Teams may use social media for fun and lighthearted banter that does not reflect poorly on any team, player, other team or League personnel, or the League as a whole. However, such activity cannot become inappropriate or offensive. As such, we encourage teams to properly and extensively train their social media staff members to ensure that they know what kind of postings are appropriate and what kind are not.

NATIONAL FOOTBALL LEAGUE: Here is the language for social media use for the NFL (Shore, 2012, para. 5):

- The use of social media by NFL game officials and officiating department personnel is prohibited at any time.
- League policy allows for the use of social media or networking sites (including Twitter and Facebook) by players, coaches and football operations personnel up to 90 minutes before kickoff and after the game following media interviews.
- The use of these sites by these individuals is not permitted during the game, including halftime.
- No updates are permitted to be posted by the individual himself or anyone representing him during this prohibited time on his personal Twitter, Facebook or any other social media account.

NATIONAL HOCKEY LEAGUE: The NHL policy contains the following restrictions (Wyshynski, 2011, paras. 8–9):

> Use of social media by Hockey Operations personnel is prohibited on game day (including all preseason, regular season and playoff games but excluding All-Star events or other exhibitions) beginning at 11 a.m. on the day of the game and ending after postgame media obligations.
>
> Use of social media by Players scheduled to play in a particular game (including all preseason, regular season and playoff games, but excluding All-Star events or other exhibitions) is prohibited beginning two hours prior to the opening faceoff and ending upon cessation of postgame media obligations.
>
> Non-compliance with the preceding sentence may result in fines.

The fact is that social media is here to stay. Teams and athletes need to recognize the potential public relations and monetary values of utilizing social media to expand and engage their fan base as well as the drawbacks involved with its use.

Engaging the Millennial Fan

According to Cobb (2015, para. 4), "To win today, sports brands must 'fish where the millennials are' and adhere to these four trends in digital media consumption: social, mobile, video and personal."

Some sport organizations are beginning to respond to this notion. For example, for the 2016–2017 season the NBA Developmental League (NBDL) made the decision to go where the millennial audience would be found and are streaming most games on Facebook Live. In addition, the NBA and its players are active on Facebook, Twitter, and Instagram and their presence discusses not just on the court achievement but the style of the players as well.

> "Young basketball stars today are ingrained in culture and fashions and life in a way that the stars from other sports here are not," said Darren Rovell, who covers the business of sports for ESPN. "People talk about Russell Westbrook's glasses and Dwyane Wade's shoes. When you look at the numbers in terms of most Twitter and Instagram followers, the NBA blows other sports away." (Ferdman, 2015, para. 6)

Other leagues are taking steps to engage millennial fans, but the NBA is the clear leader as of this writing. The NFL recently signed a deal with Twitter to livestream its Thursday Night Football games. MLB has done the same, and has begun streaming one game every Friday night on Facebook during the 2017 season.

A second challenge is how to "align the changing needs and interests of the millennial population with the features offered to create the facility of the future, so that arenas and stadiums continue to be a place that younger fans want to go to and experience" (*Sports Business Journal*, 2016, para. 9). Leagues are working to upgrade their connectivity at stadiums so fans can more easily use league apps and also share their in-game experience on social media. The Broncos, Patriots, and 49ers are all providing free Wi-Fi to all stadium attendees (Deen, 2016). "According to Nielsen Sports 360 research, 81% of Millennials use their mobile device as part of a live sporting event experience, compared with 38% of adults 55+" (Sports Business News, 2017, para. 3). Millennials thrive on being personally connected so league officials hope these strategies will help make this set of fans feel a part of the league experience.

Criminal Activity by Players

Unfortunately, professional athletes' names are linked to run-ins with the law almost daily. The stories of current and former NFL players Johnny Manziel, Greg Hardy, Josh Brown, and Darrell Revis, MLB's Aroldis Chapman, and the NBA's Draymond Green are all too familiar to sports fans in North America. According to Gaines (2016), 321 NFL players were arrested between the end of the 2009 season and September 2016.

Dealing with off-the-field incidents is difficult from the league perspective. First, the incidents are widely covered in the media. Second, taking punitive action may give the appearance of guilt even if the legal system has not yet passed judgment on an accused athlete. Third, if a team or league controls information about an incident, it is often accused of covering up information. Finally, the issue of how the PA will react to punishing players for off-the-field incidents remains. In 1997, the NFL introduced a new violent-crime policy to deter criminal behavior by its players (Wong, 2002). The Personal Conduct Policy for NFL Players includes this statement (NFL, 2015, p. 1):

> It is a privilege to be part of the National Football League
>
> Everyone who is part of the league must refrain from "conduct detrimental to the integrity of and public confidence in" the NFL. This includes owners, coaches, players, other team employees, game officials, and employees of the league office, NFL Films, NFL Network,or any other NFL business.
>
> Conduct by anyone in the league that is illegal, violent, dangerous, or irresponsible puts innocent victims at risk, damages the reputation of others in the game, and undercuts public respect and support for the NFL. We must endeavor at all times to be people of high character; we must show respect for others inside and outside our workplace; and we must strive to conduct ourselves in ways that favorably reflect on ourselves, our teams, the communities we represent, and the NFL.

The policy further defines *prohibited conduct* as including, but not limited to (NFL, 2015, p. 2):

www

Conduct Policy for NFL Players

https://nflpaweb.blob.core. windows.net/media/Default/ PDFs/Active%20Players/ PersonalConductPolicy2015. pdf

Actual or threatened physical violence against another person, including dating violence, domestic violence, child abuse, and other forms of family violence;

Assault and/or battery including sexual assault or other sex offenses;

Violent or threatening behavior toward another employee or a third party in any workplace setting;

Stalking, harassment, or similar forms of intimidation;

Illegal possession of a gun or other weapon (such as explosives, toxic substances, and the like), or possession of a gun or other weapon in any workplace setting;

Illegal possession, use, or distribution of alcohol or drugs;

Possession, use, or distribution of steroids or other performance-enhancing substances;

Crimes involving cruelty to animals as defined by state or federal law;

Crimes of dishonesty such as blackmail, extortion, fraud, money laundering, or racketeering;

Theft-related crimes such as burglary, robbery, or larceny;

Disorderly conduct;

Crimes against law enforcement, such as obstruction, resisting arrest, or harming a police officer or other law enforcement officer;

Conduct that poses a genuine danger to the safety and wellbeing of another person; and

Conduct that undermines or puts at risk the integrity of the NFL, NFL clubs, or NFL personnel.

Players convicted of criminal activity are subject to discipline as determined by the Commissioner, including possible fines and suspensions (NFLPA, 2015). Players always have the right to appeal any sanctions.

Responding to allegations of player misconduct is a delicate area for sport managers, and one where the SLEEPE Principle is very important in deciding on a course of action, because the decisions have social, legal, ethical, economic, and political ramifications. Athletes are role models, and criminal activities, like issues involving drugs and violence, reflect negatively on the players or the leagues. Thus, codes of conduct are necessary.

Player and Coach Misconduct

The NFL faced a significant on-the-field scandal with the "Bounty Gate" allegations and punishment of the New Orleans Saints. Everyone recognizes football is a violent contact sport, but in the eyes of many, players on the New Orleans Saints crossed the line. According to the Sporting News (2012, para. 2), "The program included 'bounty' payments for 'knock-outs' and 'cart-offs,' plays on which an opposing player was forced to leave the game. At times, the bounties even targeted specific players by name." Commissioner Goodell stepped in and handed out punishments and suspensions not only to players, but to the front office as well.

> [Head Coach Sean] Payton (one season), general manager Mickey Loomis (eight games) and assistant head coach Joe Vitt (six games) were punished for not doing enough to stop the bounty system after repeated NFL warnings. The Saints also were fined $500,000 and stripped of 2012 and 2013 second-round draft choices. (Marvez, 2012, para. 25)

It is important to note how the Commissioner chose to sanction not just players, but also the coaching staff and the front office. This should serve as a signal to sport managers that they are ethically responsible for the actions of their employees. The days of owners actually sanctioning this type of player misconduct may be nearing an end. Bounty Gate was followed more recently by the infamous "De-Flate Gate," whereby the New England Patriots were accused of deflating game balls so that quarterback Tom Brady could grip them better. Brady was initially suspended for four games, and the resulting legal challenges continued between Brady and the league. Ultimately, Brady served a four regular season game suspension.

Actions by coaches that affect the integrity of the game have also been in the news. The New England Patriots were at the center of a storm over stealing signals from other teams, resulting in monetary fines and loss of draft picks. MLB's Toronto Blue Jays, the Cleveland Indians, and the Boston Red Sox have also been accused of stealing signs and tipping batters off about pitches. Former Miami Marlins Manager Ozzie Guillion angered many in the team's community with statements about Fidel Castro, prompting team ownership to suspend him for five games. These types of activities negatively impact the integrity of each sport. Of course, no one is naïve enough to believe coaches will not do everything possible to help their teams win. However, it is up to the sport managers in each organization to set the tone for ethical behavior from the top down.

Player Safety

Player safety is an issue that came to the forefront particularly with the concerns over concussions in the NFL. The NFL's webpage states that the league is committed to protecting all players and helping create a safer playing environment in other sports as well (NFL, 2017a). Over the years, the NFL has instituted numerous safety related rules. Within the past five years, rules have been out in place dealing with chop blocks, horse collar tackles, defenseless players, and peel back blocks. Perhaps the most hotly debated of the new rules, however, were the ones making it "illegal for a runner or tackler to initiate forcible contact by delivering a blow with the top or crown of his helmet against an opponent when both players are clearly outside the tackle box" (NFL, 2017b).

The NBA instituted safety rules that established a larger area that must be clear underneath the baskets and also set limits on the number of photographers along the baseline (Freeman, 2014). MLB has established new safety rules as well, starting with banning home plate collisions (Buster Posey Rule) and then later the league banned players sliding into second from kicking, shoving, or throwing their bodies into an oncoming infielder (Chase Utley Rule). As you can imagine, players are not always supportive of some of these changes, as they change the nature of the game they have played all their lives, and of course the players associations have weighed in on their appropriate implementation. Professional leagues recognize the importance of keeping their stars healthy and on the field.

Responding to Athlete Activism

From the days of the great Muhammad Ali, through the iconic stance of Tommy Smith and John Carlos with raised fists on the Olympic medal stand, to most recently, Colin Kaepernick's choosing not to stand for the national anthem, brave athletes have spoken up in support of just causes in the face of public backlash. Since 2012, these activist athletes have provided new ways to engage in social issues, forcing responses from their professional organizations. For instance, in 2012 LeBron James and the rest of the Miami Heat players posted a team photo on James' Twitter page with the hashtags #WeAreTrayvonMartin and #WeWantJustice. The photo was in response to the death of an unarmed Black teenager, Trayvon Martin, just a few miles away from the Miami organization. The Heat front office issued a statement in support of the athletes stating, "We support our players and join them in hoping that their images and our logo can be part of the national dialogue and can help in our nation's healing" (Lawrence, 2012, para. 12). The Heat organization was supportive of their players and allowed them to wear their logo and team name to help promote positive social change. In a similar instance, the St Louis Rams responded to the St Louis County Police Department after activism by their players. In 2014, five Rams' players came out for introductions in a "Hands up, Don't shoot" gesture protesting the police shooting of Black teen Michael Brown. The St Louis County Police Department, in response to the demonstration, demanded an apology from the players and the St Louis Rams organization. The Rams front office stated they respected the concerns the police department raised, but would neither apologize, nor force their players to apologize (Yan, 2014). The Rams organization actively supported their players when an external source wanted them silenced. Some organizations, however, do not condone their athletes engaging in activism during their games or matches. Take, for instance, the case of Megan Rapinoe kneeling during the US national anthem in support of Colin Kaepernick. Rapinoe knelt during the national anthem of a Seattle Reign's soccer match in the National Women's Soccer League. Three days later, the Reign's next opponent, the Washington Spirit, played the national anthem before the players took the field. The Spirit ownership made this change to prevent Rapinoe from "hijacking our organization's event to draw attention to what is ultimately a personal—albeit worthy—cause" (Diaz, 2016, para. 3). The policy change by the Spirit was unpopular, as Spirit fans, including the supporter group for the Spirit, chanted "Let Her Kneel." The truth is that professional sport organizations in the United States are still learning how to respond to athlete activism. Some, like the Heat and the Rams, are supportive of their athlete's right to free speech and actions. Others, like the Washington Spirit, attempt to silence their athletes in an effort to keep them from being a distraction.

SUMMARY

Professional sport in North America takes many forms. Most prominent are the Big Four—MLB, the NBA, the NFL, and the NHL. These major sport organizations have different governance levels, including Commissioners, league offices, and individual franchise levels on the management side, and PAs on the players' side. The policy issues facing managers in the professional sport industry segment are numerous and become more complex when athletes belong to a players' union, so both sides must be cognizant of their respective collective bargaining agreements when developing policy and deciding on governance issues.

case STUDY

NORTH AMERICAN PROFESSIONAL SPORT

It is obvious that engaging the millennial fan is a priority for sport managers in professional sport. You have been hired as the Social Media Director for the Chicago Fire Major League Soccer (MLS) team. Arguably, the MLS fan base is slightly different than the fan bases for any of the Big Four leagues. You were hired because of your social media experience with a minor league baseball team and having interned at your university's Athletic Department while in school.

1. What strategies used by Big Four teams might you be able to adjust and use with an MLS franchise?
2. What strategies used by minor league baseball teams might you be able to adjust and use with an MLS franchise?
3. How would your strategies be different because of differences in the MLS fan base?
4. How will you work with the MLS' Director of Social Media to maximize your team's outreach to millennials?

CHAPTER questions

1. Which of the Big Four do you consider to be the model example of a professional sport league? Why?

2. You have been hired to work in the Marketing Department of an NBA franchise. In your position, how will you interact with the various governance levels in the NBA, both directly and indirectly?

3. Who are the Commissioners of each of the Big Four, and what are their employment backgrounds? Which do you consider to be the most powerful, and why? If you could write a letter to one Commissioner and give that Commissioner three suggestions to improve that league's operation, which league would you choose, and what suggestions would you offer?

FOR ADDITIONAL INFORMATION

1. YouTube: What's it like to spend a life in professional baseball? Roland Hermond interview: https://www.youtube.com/watch?v=BangNQCj6GI

2. I n Sport Governance, Silver Takes the Gold: Bostic, R. (2014, June 10). *Forbes*: https://www.forbes.com/sites/raphaelbostic/2014/06/10/in-sports-governance-silver-takes-the-gold/

3. Three Governance Lessons Learned from the NFL: Finn, L. (2015, February 10). Linkedin: https://www.linkedin.com/pulse/three-governance-lessons-learned-from-nfl-laura-finn-laurajfinn-

4. US Lacrosse Governance: US Lacrosse. (n.d). Board and Committees: https://www.uslacrosse.org/about-us-lacrosse/board-committees

5. National Pro Fastpitch League: www.profastpitch.com

6. Philadelphia Eagles Organizational Structure: www.philadelphiaeagles.com/team/staff.html

REFERENCES

Abrams, R. I. (1998). *Legal bases: Baseball and the law*. Philadelphia: Temple University Press.

Allen, K., & Brady, E. (2014). A commissioner's job description changes over time. *USA Today*. Retrieved from https://www.usatoday.com/story/sports/mlb/2014/08/13/commissioner-bud-selig-adam-silver-roger-goodell-gary-bettman/14016343/

Cobb, S. (2015, Aug. 24–30). How teams, leagues can program for the millennial fan.

Sports Business Journal. Retrieved from www.sportsbusinessdaily.com/Journal/Issues/2015/08/24/Opinion/Steve-Cobb.aspx

Deen, A. (2016). How the NFL is developing brand loyalty with millennials. Retrieved from https://www.fridgemagazine.com/nfl-developing-brand-loyalty-millennials/

Diaz, H. (2016, September 7). NWSL's Washington Spirit reschedule the national anthem to prevent Megan Rapinoe from protesting. Retrieved from https://www.sbnation.com/2016/9/7/12842910/nwsls-washington-spirit-reschedule-the-national-anthem-to-prevent-megan-rapinoe-from-protesting

Ferdman, R. A. (2015, April 6). What the NBA gets that other sports leagues don't. *Washington Post*. Retrieved from https://www.washingtonpost.com/news/wonk/wp/2015/04/06/what-the-nba-gets-that-the-other-big-sports-leagues-dont/?utm_term=.58456af1d6a4

Freeman, E. (2014, August 26). NBA will institute new baseline safety rules, which have been a long time coming. Retrieved from https://sports.yahoo.com/blogs/nba-ball-dont-lie/nba-will-institute-new-baseline-safety-rules--which-have-been-a-long-time-coming-004102107.html

Gaines, C. (2016, September 20). There have been 321 NFL players arrested since 2010. *Business Insider*. Retrieved from www.businessinsider.com/nfl-players-arrested-2010-2016-9

Gladden, J., & Sutton, W. A. (2011). Professional sport. In P. M. Pedersen, J. B. Parks, J. Quarterman, & L. Thibault (Eds.), *Contemporary sport management* (4th ed., pp. 122–141). Champaign, IL: Human Kinetics.

Greenhalgh, G., & Greenwell, T. C. (2012, June). What did they say? Content analysis of professional team tweets. Presented at the 2012 annual conference of the North American Society for Sport Management, Seattle, WA.

Hambrick, M. E., Simmons, J. M., Greenhalgh, G. P., & Greenwell, T. C. (2010). Understanding professional athletes' use of Twitter: A content analysis of athlete tweets. *International Journal of Sport Communication*, 3, 454–471.

Lawrence, M. (2012, March 24). NY Knicks' Amar'e Stoudemire, Heat's LeBron James, Dwyane Wade show support for Trayvon Martin after tragic shooting. *New York Daily News*. Retrieved from www.nydailynews.com/sports/basketball/knicks/ny-knicks-amar-stoudemire-heat-lebron-james-dwyane-wade-show-support-trayvon-martin-tragic-shooting-article-1.1050095

Marvez, M. (2012, May 3). NFL suspends four players in New Orleans Saints bounty scandal. Retrieved from http://msn.foxsports.com/nfl/story/jonathan-vilma-scott-fujita-anthony-hargrove-will-smith-suspended-in-new-orleans-saints-bounty-scandal-050212

Masteralexis, L. P. (2015). Professional sport. In L. P. Masteralexis, C. A. Barr, & M. A. Hums (Eds.), *Principles and practice of sport management* (5th ed., pp. 231–264). Burlington, MA: Jones & Bartlett.

Masteralexis, L. P., Barr, C. A., & Hums, M.A. (2015). *Principles and practice of sport management* (5th ed.). Burlington, MA: Jones & Bartlett.

McCann, M. (2012, May 17). Why *Vilma v. Goodell* is so much more than a defamation lawsuit. *Sports Illustrated*. Retrieved from https://www.si.com/more-sports/2012/05/17/vilma-goodellsuit

McMahon, T. (2017, Feb. 11). NBA memo: Rules prohibit mocking opponents on social media. Retrieved from www.espn.com/nba/story/_/id/18655666/nba-memo-urges-teams-follow-social-media-rules-wake-chandler-parsons-cj-mccollum-twitter-war

Minnesota Vikings. (2016). Front office. Retrieved from www.vikings.com/team/front-office.html

MLB. (2008). *Major League Constitution*. New York: Author.

MLB. (2012). Memorandum. Retrieved from www.baseball-almanac.com/downloads/mlb_social_media_policy.pdf

MLBPA. (n.d.a). Frequently asked questions. Retrieved from www.nmnathletics.com/ViewArticle.dbml?&DB_OEM_ID=34000&ATCLID=211044889#membership

MLBPA. (n.d.b). Press room. Retrieved from www.mlbplayers.com/ViewArticle.dbml?DB_OEM_ID=34000&ATCLID=211075201

Mullin, B. J., Hardy, S., & Sutton, W. A. (2014). *Sport marketing* (4th ed.). Champaign, IL: Human Kinetics.

NBA. (2017). Season review: 1949–50. Retrieved from www.nba.com/history/seasonreviews/1949-50/index.html

NBA Media Ventures. (2016). NBA career opportunities. Retrieved from http://careers.nba.com/

NBA Media Ventures. (2017). Heat group directory. Retrieved from www.nba.com/heat/contact/directory_list.html

NBCA. (2016). About the National Basketball Coaches Association. Retrieved from http://nbacoaches.com/about/

NBPA. (2018). Departments. Retrieved from https://nbpa.com/leadership/

NBPA. (2016). About & history. Retrieved from https://nbpa.com/about/

NFL. (2013). NFL chronology of professional football. Retrieved from http://static.nfl.com/static/content/public/image/history/pdfs/History/2013/353-372-Chronology.pdf

NFL. (2015). National Football League personal conduct policy 2015. Retrieved from https://nflpaweb.blob.core.windows.net/media/Default/PDFs/Active%20Players/PersonalConductPolicy2015.pdf

NFL. (2017a). Health and safety. Retrieved from http://operations.nfl.com/football-ops/nfl-ops-honoring-the-game/health-safety/

NFL. (2017b). Health and safety rule changes. Retrieved from http://operations.nfl.com/football-ops/nfl-ops-honoring-the-game/health-safety-rules-changes/

NFL. (2017c). League governance. Retrieved from https://operations.nfl.com/football-ops/league-governance/

NFLPA. (2014). History. Retrieved from https://www.nflpa.com/about/history

NFL Players. (2014). About NFLPA. Retrieved from https://www.nflpa.com/players

NHLPA. (2017). What we do. Retrieved from https://www.nhlpa.com/the-pa/what-we-do

Olensky, S. (2012, April 21). Cleveland Indians offer social media suite. Retrieved from http://espn.go.com/blog/playbook/fandom/post/_/id/133/cleveland-indians-offer-social-media-suite

Pacifici, A. (2014). Scope and authority of sports leagues disciplinary power: Bounty and beyond. *Berkeley Journal of Entertainment and Sports Law*, 3(1), 93–115. Retrieved from http://scholarship.law.berkeley.edu/cgi/viewcontent.cgi?article=1041&context=bjesl

Pessah, J. (2016). *The Game: Inside the secret world of Major League Baseball's power brokers.* New York: Little, Brown & Company.

Quirk, J., & Fort, R. (1992). *Pay dirt: The business of professional team sports.* Princeton, NJ: Princeton University Press.

Quirk, J., & Fort, R. (1999). *Hard ball: The abuse of power in pro team sports.* Princeton, NJ: Princeton University Press.

Renicker, C. (2016). A comparative analysis of the NFL's disciplinary structure: The Commissioner's power and players' rights. *Fordham Intellectual Property, Media and Entertainment Law Journal*, 26(4), 1051–1113. Retrieved from http://ir.lawnet.fordham.edu/cgi/viewcontent.cgi?article=1636&context=iplj

Robinson, M. J., Lizandra, M., & Vail, S. (2001). Sport governance. In B. L. Parkhouse (Ed.), *The management of sport: Its foundation and application* (3rd ed., pp. 237–269). Boston: McGraw-Hill.

Scully, G. W. (1989). *The business of Major League Baseball.* Chicago, IL: University of Chicago Press.

Sharp, L. A., Moorman, A. M., & Claussen, C. L. (2010). *Sport law: A managerial approach* (2nd ed.). Scottsdale, AZ: Holcomb Hathaway.

Shore, J. (2012, Sept. 25). What are the NFL rules for social media? Retrieved from http://mashable.com/2012/09/25/nfl-social-media-rules/#LW6Fiidr_sqp

Sporting News. (2012). NFL statement on Saints 'bounty-gate' punishment. Retrieved from http://aol.sportingnews.com/nfl/story/2012-03-21/new-orleans-saints-sean-payton-gregg-williams-suspended

Sports Business Journal. (2016). What is the biggest challenge facing the sport industry overall? Retrieved from www.sportsbusinessdaily.com/Journal/Issues/2016/04/18/Power-Players/Challenges.aspx

Sports Business News. (2017, July 7). Millennial baseball fans pair watching with mobile activities. Retrieved from http://sportsbusinessnews.com/content/millennial-baseball-fans-pair-watching-mobile-activities

Stringer, P. (2012, Feb. 27). Moving beyond like: How one team monetized Facebook base. Retrieved from www.sportsbusinessdaily.com/Journal/Issues/2012/02/27/Opinion/Peter-Stringer.aspx

Teamworkonline. (2016). Home page. Retrieved from www.teamworkonline.com/

Wharton, D. (2011). Commissioners walk a fine line. *Los Angeles Times.* Retrieved from http://articles.latimes.com/2011/may/15/sports/la-sp-0515-commissioner-power-20110515

Wong, G. M. (2002). *Essentials of sport law* (3rd ed.). Westport, CT: Praeger.

Wyshynski, G. (2011, Sept. 15). Inside the NHL's new social media policy for players. Retrieved from https://sports.yahoo.com/nhl/blog/puck_daddy/post/inside-the-nhls-new-social-media-policy-for-players?urn=nhl,wp12624

Yan, H. (2014, December 2). St. Louis County police, Rams spar over reported apology. Retrieved from www.cnn.com/2014/12/02/us/ferguson-nfl-st-louis-rams/index.html

Yasser, R., McCurdy, J., Goplerud, P., & Weston, M. A. (2003). *Sports law: Cases and materials* (5th ed.). Cincinnati, OH: Anderson Publishing.

Professional Individual Sports

Marion E. Hambrick
Sun J. Kang

The previous chapter focused on the governance of North American professional team sports. As mentioned in that chapter, not all professional sports are team sports. Individual sports also have a professional component. The governance of these sports' competitions differs from the governance of professional team sports and leagues. For example, individual sports such as professional golf require athletes to complete extensive qualifying requirements before they can compete in select events. Other individual sports such as professional tennis place a heightened focus on grassroots development, similar to national governing bodies (NGBs) in the Olympic Movement. Overall, individual sport organizations develop and focus their rules and structures based on individual athletes' needs rather than on a team.

Each year in the United States alone, an estimated 29 million people play golf (Statistic Brain Research Institute, 2016) and over 17.9 million people play tennis (Tennis Industry Association, 2017a). These numbers reflect participation on the recreational level, but as we all know, professionals compete internationally in organized pro tours in both sports. Governing bodies such as the US Golf Association and the US Tennis Association play integral roles in the governance and growth of these sports. Automobile racing such as NASCAR (National Association for Stock Car Auto Racing) represents another individual professional sport. Speedways dot the countryside, ranging from small town tracks like the Salem Speedway in Salem, Indiana, or Dixie Speedway in Woodstock, Georgia, to superspeedways like Talledega in Alabama or Daytona in Florida, which accommodate over 100,000 spectators.

Internationally, individual sports are also on the rise, and their governing bodies operate differently depending on the nature of sport. For instance, Surf Australia is supported by the Australian Sports Commission and Australian Olympic Committee. Similar to the United States, the purpose of Australia's involvement with such non-mainstream sports is to facilitate grassroots development and to promote individual lifestyle sports rather than focusing solely on popularity of the sport.

Although there are many differences between these professional sports and professional leagues and teams, one aspect remains the same—the need for governing structures to establish rules, regulations, and policies. This chapter examines golf, tennis, automobile racing, and surfing and each sport's history, governance structure, and current policy issues.

PROFESSIONAL GOLF

Four major organizations are involved in the governance of golf: the United States Golf Association (USGA), the Professional Golfers' Association of America (PGA), the PGA TOUR, and the Ladies Professional Golf Association (LPGA). Although all four work closely together, they have different purposes (see Exhibit 13.1). The USGA oversees the regulations and rules of golf and equipment standards. The PGA and LPGA serve professional golfers, and the PGA TOUR organizes national tour events.

Professional Golf Organization Responsibilities in the United States   *exhibit*   **13.1**

USGA

Establishes Rules of Golf

Determines equipment standards

Sets handicap and course rating systems

Sponsors turf management research

Operates 13 national championships

PGA

Focuses on professional instruction and golf management

Operates 4 major championships:

- Ryder Cup
- PGA Championship
- PGA Grand Slam of Golf
- Senior PGA Championship

Sponsors a juniors golf program

PGA TOUR

Focuses on professional play

Hosts 47 events for 3 tours:

- PGA TOUR
- Champions Tour
- Nationwide Tour

LPGA

LPGA Teaching and Club Professionals (T&CP)

- Focuses on female golf instruction

LPGA Tour

- Focuses on female professional play
- Operates 30 tournaments

Operates the Symetra Tour with 16 events

Sponsors a juniors golf program

USGA

History

The USGA, formally known as the Amateur Golf Association of the United States, is a nonprofit organization established in 1894 as the central body of golf in the United States.

Governance

MISSION. The USGA is dedicated to serving "the best interests of the game for the continued enjoyment of those who love and play it" and strives to promote and conserve "the true spirit of the game of golf as embodied in its ancient and honorable tradition" (USGA, 2017c, para. 1). The USGA oversees the Rules of Golf (revised every four years) and amateur status, ensures golf equipment complies with current rules, manages the Course Handicap and Course Rating Systems, and offers research-based turf management expertise (USGA, 2017d). Currently, the organization also hosts 13 national championships, including three open championships (US Open, US Women's Open, and US Senior Open) and ten amateur championships each year.

At the international level, the Royal and Ancient Golf Club of St Andrews was founded in Scotland in 1754 to serve the United Kingdom and other countries. Until recently, this organization oversaw all the golfers and tours around the world except those in the United States. In 2004, a major reorganization took place that formed a separate entity called the R&A, which is independent from the Royal and Ancient Golf Club of St Andrews, to take over joint administration of the rules of golf with the USGA. The R&A is responsible for administering the rules of golf for over 30 million golfers in 128 countries in Europe, Africa, Asia-Pacific, and the Americas, while the R&A and USGA jointly develop and issue the rules of golf for the United States and Mexico. Additionally, the R&A organizes the Open Championship (British Open) as well as other amateur and junior events sanctioned by golf governing bodies around the world.

MEMBERSHIP. As of 2017 the USGA listed membership as over 700,000, with 8,000 member clubs. USGA membership is open to both amateur and professional golfers—in essence, to anyone interested in playing golf. Golf clubs, public and private, can also be members of the USGA. In fact, USGA member club representatives control over 10,600 golf courses nationwide, and more than 680 golf clubs hold qualifying rounds for USGA or state golf championships. Finally, USGA membership includes approximately 130 men's and women's state and regional golf associations that provide services to millions of golfers across the United States (USGA, 2017a).

FINANCIALS. The USGA's main sources of revenue are generated from championships and broadcast rights. In 2015 the USGA received over

$64 million from the US Open, the US Women's Open, the US Senior Open, ten national amateur championships, team championships, and international matches (USGA, 2016b). The 2016 prize fund was $10 million for the US Open, $4.5 million for the US Women's Open, and $3.75 million for the US Senior Open (USGA, 2016a). Additional revenues come from USGA membership fees, corporate sponsorships, merchandise licensing, green section services (turf grass management), and equipment testing. From the revenues generated, the USGA spends a large portion of its earnings supporting grassroots level development programs such as The First Tee; LPGA–USGA Girls Golf; Drive, Chip & Putt Championship; and PGA Junior League Golf. The USGA also provides financial support for the Special Olympics, which hosts the Special Olympics Golf National Invitational Tournament annually (USGA, 2017b).

ORGANIZATIONAL STRUCTURE.   The leadership of the USGA is organized as shown in Exhibit 13.2.

PGA of America and PGA TOUR

History

The PGA of America was founded in 1916 in New York City with 35 charter members. These golf professionals and amateurs believed the formation of a golf association would improve golf equipment sales. The inaugural PGA Championship was held from October 10 through October 14 that

---

Organization of the USGA Leadership   *exhibit* **13.2**

EXECUTIVE COMMITTEE

A 15-member volunteer group serves as the Association's executive policy-making board.

SENIOR LEADERSHIP TEAM

The senior management team directs and oversees the Association's day-to-day operations.

WOMEN'S COMMITTEE

The 14-member committee that helps conduct the USGA's women's championships.

Source: USGA (2017d).

same year at Siwanoy Country Club in Bronxville, New York, and the organizers awarded the winning trophy and $2,580 in prize earnings to James M. Barnes, who defeated Jock Huthinson 1-up in match play. In 1917 the USGA extended privileges to the PGA, and allowed the organization to choose golf club Whitemarsh Valley Country Club in Pennsylvania to host the US Open (PGA, 2017a). With the continuous support of professional golfers, the PGA published the first issue of the *Professional Golfer of America* in 1920. The close relationship between the PGA and the USGA flourished when the USGA adopted the PGA's suggestion to host the US Open annually in June. They also worked together in adopting the new steel iron club technology, and the USGA legalized the PGA line of irons in 1926. The two organizations still maintain this relationship today as PGA and PGA TOUR golfers compete under the rules and guidelines established by the USGA (PGA, 2017a).

www

Professional Golfers'
Association of America
(PGA)
www.pga.com/home

PGA TOUR
www.pgatour.com

As an individual sport, professional golf is divided into two distinct organizations: the PGA and the PGA TOUR. The PGA serves male and female professional instructors, players, and local clubs, while the PGA TOUR is the tournament division organizing men's professional golf tours in North America. In 1968 the PGA TOUR separated from the PGA to operate the Tournament Players Division. Although the separation was considered risky at the time, it seemed inevitable due to the two distinct groups of professional golfers involved in the sport (PGA, 2017b). One group of golf professionals includes players who compete regularly on national tours (e.g., Bubba Watson, USA; Rory McIlroy, Ireland; Ryo Ishikawa, Japan; Adam Scott, Australia), while the second group represents professional golfers operating or teaching golf at local country clubs and golf facilities. The separation became necessary to better serve golf professionals with different needs. For example, players on national tours are trained toward perfecting the game of golf and mastering the skills necessary to win tour events. In comparison, teaching professionals are trained to help amateur golfers learn and better understand the fundamentals and mechanics of the golf swing and other elements of the game. Some golf professionals are also trained to operate, maintain, and design golf courses.

Since making this distinction, the PGA and the PGA TOUR organize and operate separate major tournaments. The PGA operates four major golf championships: the Ryder Cup, the PGA Championship, the PGA Grand Slam of Golf, and the Senior PGA Championship (PGA, 2017b), and the PGA TOUR hosts 47 annual events for three tours: the PGA Tour for qualified professionals, the Champions Tour for players 50 and over, and the Nationwide Tour for professionals who have not qualified for the Tour card or are not on the PGA TOUR (PGA TOUR, 2017b). An athlete who demonstrates top performance in the Nationwide Tour may compete in the PGA TOUR the following year. In fact, Phil Mickelson and Tiger Woods competed in the Nationwide Tour prior to joining the PGA TOUR. When players turn 50, they are eligible to compete in either the PGA TOUR or the Champions Tour. Details of the tour qualifications are discussed in the membership section.

Governance

MISSION. The mission of the PGA is "to establish and elevate the standards of the profession and to grow interest and participation in the game of golf" (PGA, 2017f, para. 1), while the PGA TOUR's mission is to "To entertain and inspire our fans, deliver substantial value to our partners, create outlets for volunteers to give back, generate significant charitable and economic impact in the communities where we play, grow the game of golf and provide financial opportunities for PGA TOUR players" (PGA TOUR, 2017a, para. 1). As stated earlier, the PGA and PGA TOUR both serve professional golfers with distinctively different purposes. The PGA provides services and support for teaching professionals, while the PGA TOUR only serves professional athletes who play for the national tours.

MEMBERSHIP. The PGA is currently comprised of 28,000 qualified men and women professionals teaching and managing the game of golf in its 41 PGA sections (PGA, 2017a). The PGA of America membership license features 31 different categories depending on the type of qualification each professional has earned as shown in Exhibit 13.3 (PGA, 2017b).

Conversely, PGA TOUR membership is exclusive to professional golfers who have earned a PGA TOUR card by finishing in the top 25 of the PGA Qualifying Tournament (Q-School), finishing in the top 25 on the Nationwide money list for a year, or winning three Nationwide Tour tournaments in a season. Players receiving exemptions to the above qualifications include former major champions, former multiple tournament winners, and those listed in the top 50 in lifetime career earnings or listed numbers 126 to 150 on the money list the previous year. To participate in the qualifying tournament as an amateur, players must have a handicap index of two or under (The Thomson Tide, 2010).

FINANCIALS. The PGA organizes and operates four major championships, which represent the organization's main source of revenue. In 2015 the PGA generated over $114 million from these championships, which included revenues from spectator ticket sales, PGA merchandise sales, and sponsorships (see Exhibit 13.4). Spectator attendance is limited at each tournament based on each golf course's capacity, yet 24,000 spectators visited the PGA Championship each day during the tournament in 2015. The estimated economic impact exceeded $100 million at Valhalla Golf Club (KY) in 2014 and $102.1 million at Oak Hill Country Club (NY) in 2013 (Heitner, 2015). The PGA also has negotiated sponsorship revenues. Additional revenues derive from business development, member dues, golf course operations, and other investments (PGA, 2017c).

Similar to the PGA of America, the PGA TOUR generates revenues from tournament operations, sponsorships, licenses, merchandise sales, membership dues, and network media rights deals. The PGA TOUR signed a media rights deal with CBS and NBC, an agreement that will end in 2021, exhibit **13.3**   PGA of America Member Classifications

Member Classification	Apprentice Classification	Description
A-1	B-1	Head Professional at a PGA Recognized Golf Course
A-2	B-2	Head Professional at a PGA Recognized Golf Range
A-3	Not Applicable	Exempt PGA TOUR, Champions Tour, Nationwide Tour, LPGA Tour and Futures Tour Players
A-4	B-4	Director of Golf at PGA Recognized Golf Facilities
A-5	Not Applicable	Past Presidents of the Association
A-6	B-6	Golf Instructor at a PGA Recognized Facility
A-7	B-7	Head Professional at a PGA Recognized Facility Under Construction
A-8	B-8	Assistant Golf Professional at a PGA Recognized Facility
A-9	B-9	Employed in Professional Positions in Management, Development, Ownership Operation and/or Financing of Facilities
A-10	B-10	Golf Clinician
A-11	B-11	Golf Administrator
A-12	B-12	College or University Golf Coach
A-13	B-13	General Manager
A-14	B-14	Director of Instruction at a PGA Recognized Facility
A-15	B-15	Ownership or Management of a Retail Golf Facility
A-16	B-16	Golf Course Architect
A-17	B-17	Golf Course Superintendent
A-18	B-18	Golf Media
A-19	B-19	Golf Manufacturer Management
A-20	B-20	Golf Manufacturer Sales Representative
A-21	B-21	Tournament Coordinator/Director for Organizations, Businesses or Associations
A-22	B-22	Rules Official
A-23	B-23	Club Fitting/Club Repair
A-24	Not Applicable	Employed within the golf industry and not eligible for another Active classification
HM	Not Applicable	Honorary Member
IN	Not Applicable	Not eligible for classification as Active, Life Member or Retired Member
LM/LMM	Not Applicable	Not eligible for classification as Active Member and who have held a minimum of 20 years in an Active Classification (whether continous or not)
LMA/LMMA	Not Applicable	Not eligible for classification as Active Member and who have held a minimum of 20 years in an Active Classification (whether continuous or not)
MP	Not Applicable	Master Professional
RM	Not Applicable	Members who are fully retired (cannot be working in either a golf or non-golf position) and who have achieved a combined 65 years of age and Active membership and who are not eligible for Life Member
F	Not Applicable	Failure to meet the requirements of the Professional Development Program

Source: PGA (2017b).

The PGA of America Statement of Activities

exhibit **13.4**

THE PROFESSIONAL GOLFERS' ASSOCIATION OF AMERICA
COMBINED Statements OF CHANGES IN UNRESTRICTED NET ASSETS
YEARS ENDED JUNE 30, 2015 AND 2014 (000'S OMITTED)

	2015			2014		
	Revenue	Expense	Increase (Decrease)	Revenue	Expense	Increase (Decrease)
Revenue Producing Activities						
Championships	$ 114,045	$ 74,927	$ 39,118	$ 94,128	$ 55,652	$ 38,476
Business development	19,154	6,019	13,135	12,800	5,156	7,644
Member dues	2,398	112	2,286	2,411	582	1,829
Golf course operations	16,345	20,961	(4,616)	15,599	20,811	(5,212)
Total revenue producing activities	151,942	102,019		124,938	82,201	
Unrestricted net assets available for support			49,923			42,737
General and Administrative Costs						
Corporate services	63	23,926	(23,863)	–	14,511	(14,511)
Marketing and communications	87	18,779	(18,692)	4	22,936	(22,932)
Income tax provision	2	1,220	(1,218)	–	1,901	(1,901)
Board, officers, past presidents	–	2,058	(2,058)	–	1,517	(1,517)
Depreciation	–	1,024	(1,024)	–	1,175	(1,175)
Impairment of long lived assets	–	4,164	(4,164)	–	–	–
Total general and administrative costs	152	51,171		4	42,040	
Unrestricted net assets available for program support	152,094	153,190	(1,096)	124,942	124,241	701
Program Activities						
Education	8,590	7,145	1,445	9,422	7,507	1,915
Awards	1	519	(518)	–	682	(682)
Member benefit programs	8,977	7,744	1,233	10,367	8,709	1,658
Membership meetings	–	1,968	(1,968)	–	2,220	(2,220)
Membership program administration	952	1,029	(77)	1,303	1,115	188
Member communications	100	393	(293)	119	429	(310)
Employment services	50	1,450	(1,400)	38	1,885	(1,847)
Section affairs	743	9,020	(8,277)	893	7,331	(6,438)
Member championships	4,272	4,899	(627)	4,389	5,069	(680)
Amateur tournaments	621	924	(303)	577	919	(342)
Player development	950	4,346	(3,396)	740	5,433	(4,693)
PGA REACH	3,952	3,191	761	874	1,432	(558)
Total program activities	29,208	42,628		28,722	42,731	
	$ 181,302	$ 195,818		$ 153,664	$ 166,972	
Decrease in net assets before investments			$(14,516)			$ (13,308)
Investment income	2,394	917	1,477	26,939	605	26,334
(Decrease)increase in unrestricted net assets			$(13,039)			$ 13,026

and an exclusive cable television agreement with the Golf Channel (PGA Tour, 2017b). Sponsorship revenues come from major corporate partners, and the organization has negotiated merchandise license contracts with many major golf brands including adidas, Calloway Golf, Cutter & Buck, Footjoy, Nike Golf, and Oakley (PGA TOUR, 2017c). PGA TOUR expenses take the form of prize money, salary and benefits, and tournament operations. As a major part of its mission, PGA TOUR events have donated more than $2.3 billion to help over 2,000 charities and countless individuals (PGA Tour, 2016).

ORGANIZATIONAL STRUCTURE. The PGA's national office Board of Directors is elected by the organization's Board Members. The members serve a minimum of one year as an officer, and become eligible for re-election and re-appointment after their first term. The national office also has a President, Vice President, Secretary, Honorary President, and 17 Directors who establish association policies. The Directors include representatives from each of the PGA's 14 districts, two independent directors, and a member of the PGA TOUR. Each section of the PGA in the United States also elects its own board members to serve members nationwide (PGA, 2017e). The CEO of the PGA guides its business decisions (PGA, 2017d).

The PGA TOUR is a tax-exempt membership organization with multiple Executive Officers including Chief Operating and also Chief Financial Officers. There are also Executive Vice Presidents for Global Media, Legal Issues, International Affairs and Human Resources (Executive Committee, n.d.).

Ladies Professional Golf
Association (LPGA)
www.lpga.com

LPGA

History

To meet the needs of female golfers, the Ladies Professional Golf Association (LPGA) was founded in 1950 by 14 pioneering women seeking to create a full professional tour. Over the years, the LPGA has developed 14 US tournaments featuring players from 29 different countries. Similar to the PGA and the PGA TOUR, in 1959 the LPGA established the LPGA Teaching division, called the LPGA Teaching and Club Professionals (LPGA T&CP), and the LPGA Tour to serve two types of golf professionals. In 1980 the LPGA also created Duramed Futures Tour (currently known as the Symetra Tour) to assist players at the developmental level. The creation of the event proved successful: more than 500 players have moved on to the LPGA Tour over the years (LPGA, n.d.a). To strengthen the grassroots development of women's golf, the LPGA Foundation in 1991 started to support junior golf programs. The LPGA and USGA also jointly created the LPGA–USGA Girls to increase their grassroots developmental program. The LPGA has earned the distinction of being "one of the longest-running women's professional sports associations in the world" (LPGA, n.d.a, para. 1).

Governance

MISSION. The LPGA's mission is to "be a recognized worldwide leader in the world of sport by providing women the opportunity to pursue their dreams through the game of golf" (LPGA, n.d.d, para. 1). The organization's values include Leadership, Passion, Giving, and Approachability following the acronyms of the organization. Separate from the PGA and PGA TOUR, the LPGA specifically focuses on serving all professional female golfers around the world, including teaching professionals and professional athletes on tour. The LPGA, PGA, and PGA TOUR have different missions and visions, yet the three organizations strive to improve the game of golf and increase the numbers of individuals watching and playing the sport.

MEMBERSHIP. The LPGA represents the ultimate governing body for female golf professionals. For female tour professionals, the organization administers an annual qualifying school (Q-School) and operates the Symetra Tour, providing privileges for top finishers to join the LPGA Tour the following year.

For teaching and club professional (T&CP) members, the qualification and certification process is similar to PGA members. One major difference between the LPGA and PGA is the type of licenses available to their respective members. Whereas the PGA provides 31 different membership categories, the LPGA only provides two membership types (class A and B) for teaching and operation. Female professionals who wish to obtain specialty licenses, for example as a college or university golf coach or golf course superintendent, must achieve certification through the PGA. In 2017 the LPGA served approximately 510 tour professional members and 1,500 LPGA T&CP members (LPGA, n.d.a).

FINANCIALS. Similar to the PGA and PGA TOUR, the LPGA generates revenues from sponsorships, golf facility management, licenses, merchandise sales, membership dues, tournament operations, and network media rights deals. The prize money for 2016 increased to $63 million (LPGA, n.d.c). In total, the tour will feature 34 events with more than 410 hours of television coverage. The LPGA also receives sponsorship revenues from numerous major marketing partners (LPGA, n.d.b).

ORGANIZATIONAL STRUCTURE. As a nonprofit organization, the LPGA is under the guidance of a Commissioner. The LPGA executive team also contains a Chief Financial Officer, Chief Marketing Officer, and General Counsel. The Board of Directors is composed of six independent directors, including the LPGA Player Directors (Player Executive Committee) and the National President of the LPGA Teaching and Club Professionals (LPGA, n.d.a). Similar to the PGA TOUR, LPGA officials make decisions on player eligibility, suspension, and disqualification while adhering to the USGA golf rules. However, the LPGA is only affiliated with the Legends Tour for female professionals aged 45 and older (LPGA, n.d.a).

BILL OAKES, *Tournament Director, ATP World Tour,*

Winston-Salem, NC

I am a tournament director on the ATP World Tour, the governing body of men's professional tennis. I oversee and manage the Winston-Salem Open, which features 48 Men's Professional Tennis Players in the Singles draw and is held the week prior to the US Open. My duties include overall responsibilities for budget, staff management, operations, governing body relationships, sponsors, tickets, and media relations.

I serve as the Chairperson of the ATP World Tour 250 Executive Committee, which works with the 40 worldwide 250 level tournaments on the ATP World Tour. We are dealing with aggregating our media rights to provide them in one package, as one of the many issues that we are addressing. This is a very difficult issue because dealing with forty different events in 25 countries with different desires and contract terms is very challenging.

An important policy issue confronting my sport sector today is the ability to keep professional tennis relevant within the changing world demographic. Tennis is considered by some as stuffy, and has resisted change for decades. The ability to attract younger fans could mean major changes to how the game is played, and that is difficult for some groups to overcome. Other important issues facing tennis are financial aspects as well as the changing media landscape which presents an opportunity but also a challenge in how we understand and capitalize on new media such as Over the Top, live streaming, or other avenues to distribute our product.

The ATP is owned 50 percent by the players and 50 percent by the tournaments. This arrangement leads to inherent problems and can prevent the tour from making positive changes. The tournaments may only be interested in maximizing profits while the players may only be interested in maximizing prize money. These two areas are very different. Future challenges in policy development in individual professional sport include profit distribution and resolving issues surrounding the aging tennis demographic.

CURRENT POLICY AREAS

The professional golf industry faces potential challenges and growth opportunities in several key areas: Olympic qualifiers, retaining corporate sponsors, and attracting younger audiences.

Olympic Qualification System

Golf returned to the Olympic Games at the 2016 Rio Olympic Games for the first time since 1904. The qualification system decided on by the International Olympic Committee (IOC) and the International Golf Federation (IGF) limited the field to 60 players over 72 holes of stroke play for the men's and women's competitions. Among the 60 players, 59 athletes must qualify through the Olympic Golf Rankings (OGR) and one spot is reserved for a host country athlete. Regardless of player ranking, no more than four players are allowed to compete from one country. Each of the five continents of the Olympic Movement is guaranteed at least one athlete in the women's and men's competitions. The men's OGR recognizes most of the golf tours such as the PGA TOUR, European TOUR, PGA Tour of Australasia, Japan Golf Tour, Asian Tour, PGA TOUR Canada, and other major PGA-sanctioned tournaments. The women's OGR also recognizes official tournaments such as Ladies Professional Golf Association, Ladies European Tour, China Ladies Professional Golf Association, and most other LPGA-sanctioned tournaments. In each tournament, players accumulate points to determine their world ranking (IGF, 2016).

Due to the limitation of four athletes per country, however, some of the biggest names in golf did not compete. A variety of countries were represented, but not all of the best players around the world were included under the current format. Unlike other sports that allow players to compete through qualifying stages, golf adopted qualifying criteria similar to tennis. Compared to the US Open that usually accommodates 156 players, however, the 60-player limitation poses quite a challenge for athletes who wish to compete in the Olympic Games. Others have also criticized the single format event (stroke play), which only offers six medals in total, as it also limits players' ability to compete in various golf events (Greenstein, 2016). The criticism is valid as some countries determine funding based on medal potentials.

PGA TOUR Media Rights

The PGA TOUR's deal with CBS and NBC is contracted through 2021, but the Tour is allowed to open the contract in 2018 in order to modify or consider early termination of the exclusive media rights deal. The Golf Channel deal is through 2021 without an option to modify. As the Tour approaches the 2018 mark, it can consider FOX, ESPN, or Turner as alternative options. Another possible option includes the PGA TOUR owning its own channel dedicated to its tournaments or creating a new golf channel deal with an existing regional sports network. In addition, the Tour's alliance with the LPGA will become a factor when deciding whether to host its own channel. The revenue generated through media rights represents a significant portion of PGA TOUR's overall funding. Therefore, it is critical for the Tour to consider its option in the upcoming years, as it will impact the purse money for all players involved in the PGA.

Attracting Younger Audiences

Professional golf traditionally has appealed to older adults. Yet industry leaders recognize the need to expand beyond the core fan base and attract younger viewers, who may develop a lifelong appreciation for the sport (Starr, 2012). PGA TOUR events such as the Masters now provide interactive websites and mobile apps for spectators. Beginning in 2010 the Masters tournament took an innovative approach by offering a live webcast, interactive leaderboard, video of the entire course, video highlights, overview of the pairings, and player information on the official website and mobile app. These features provided spectators with additional

Masters Tournament
Facebook Page
https://www.facebook.com/
TheMasters/

information and content. For example, the interactive leaderboard gave users a choice between the traditional view of plus and minus overall score and a player's hole-by-hole score, simply by pressing the player's name. This function also provided player biographies, highlights, and live video during the Masters week. Furthermore, the Masters' official Facebook page (over 476,000 likes for the event) and players on Twitter (providing event updates to their millions of followers) helped promote the event. The combined effort to promote the event through the interactive website, mobile apps, and social media attracted a larger fan base, including spectators from younger demographic groups (Starr, 2012). The PGA TOUR's charitable arm also offers special events catering to young adults as a way to introduce potential fans to the sport.

In addition, the PGA TOUR partnered with Avis car rental company in order to launch the PGA TOUR Fantasy Games in 2015 and attract fantasy sport fans who are younger, educated, and have higher household incomes (FSTA, 2015). The Tour fantasy game is organized differently from the PGA TOUR in that it allows fantasy players to customize schedules where they create their own leagues and teams. This fantasy golf game is integrated with ShotLink statistics provided by the Tour official site. Focusing on younger players, the PGA TOUR can extend its reach and create a positive long-term industry outlook through fantasy sports.

UNITED STATES TENNIS ASSOCIATION (USTA)

History

The United States Tennis Association began in 1881 as the United States National Lawn Tennis Association (USNLTA), and later shortened its name to the United States Lawn Tennis Association (USLTA) in 1920 and finally to the USTA in 1975 (USTA, 2017i). The governing body's original goals were to provide standardized playing rules while growing the sport. The organization and its sanctioned events evolved quickly as the doors opened to international players in 1886 and to women in 1889. Other changes over time included the Mixed Doubles Championships in 1892, the National Clay Court Championships in 1910, and the US Open in 1968 (USTA, 2017i). Women received greater recognition in the 1970s when the USTA sanctioned the Virginia Slims Women's tour and offered equal prize money to female and male competitors at the US Open (USTA, 2017i). The governing body also sought to attract new adult and junior players by offering more activities at local parks and recreational facilities and introducing new programs such as the National Junior Tennis League in 1969 and Senior League Tennis in 1991. USTA membership grew to 250,000 in 1984 and doubled to 500,000 by 1993 (USTA, 2017i). Capitalizing on the sport's increasing popularity, the governing body opened the $285 million Billie Jean King National Tennis Center (NTC) in New York City's Flushing Meadows Corona Park in 1995 (USTA, 2017i).

Today, the USTA serves as the governing body for tennis in the United States, and promotes tennis from the grassroots to the professional levels with three divisions: Community Tennis, Player Development, and Professional Tennis (USTA, 2017a). Holding the title of the largest tennis organization in the world, the USTA includes over 700,000 individual members and over 7,800 organizational members. The Community Tennis division emphasizes the USTA's national grassroots efforts. Programs in this division include the USTA League, which offers tennis opportunities for 300,000 adult league members (USTA, 2017h), and the USTA Jr Team Tennis, which serves children and young adults participating in tournaments and other activities (USTA, 2017c). The Player Development division provides coaching services and facilities for the nation's best junior players (ages 18 and younger) to fill the pipeline of top tennis performers from the United States (USTA, 2017e). Finally, the Professional Tennis division arguably represents the most visible part of the USTA, as it hosts the US Open and other tennis tournaments leading up to the Grand Slam tournaments (the Australian Open, the French Open, Wimbledon, and the US Open). This arm of the USTA also assists in forming teams for the Olympic and Paralympic Games as well as the Davis Cup and Fed Cup, the premier international tennis team events for men and women, respectively. USTA leaders believe this division helps attract new players to the sport, as professional tennis increases fan exposure through television viewing and event attendance (USTA, 2017a).

Governance

MISSION. According to its Constitution and By-Laws, the purposes of the USTA (n.d, p. 84) are:

to promote the development of tennis as a means of healthful recreation and physical fitness

to establish and maintain rules of play and high standards of amateurism and good sportsmanship

to foster national and international amateur tennis tournaments and competitions

to encourage, sanction and conduct tennis tournaments and competitions open to athletes without regard to race, creed, color or national origin and under the best conditions possible so as to effectively promote the game of tennis with the general public

to generally encourage through tennis the development of health, character and responsible citizenship and

to carry on other similar activities permitted to be carried on by such a not-for-profit corporation

The governing body strives to increase the number and diversity of people watching and participating in the sport from the grassroots to the professional levels and uses numerous financial resources to help achieve its mission.

MEMBERSHIP. As stated earlier, membership fees represent an important revenue source for the USTA, and the association received $17 million in related revenues in 2015 (USTA, 2016a). The governing body offers a variety of memberships for individuals and organizations. Individuals can take advantage of adult, junior, and family memberships, while organizations can obtain community tennis association, club, school, park and recreation department, or other USTA memberships (USTA, 2017b). The governing body takes pride in its memberships and programs, noting that it uses revenues from membership dues and other sources to invest in community outreach activities such as improving public tennis courts and providing scholarships and athletic equipment to those in need. Individual members receive access to tournaments and leagues, and organization members receive benefits such as resources to conduct community tennis development workshops and host USTA sanctioned tournaments (USTA, 2017d).

FINANCIALS. In 2015 the USTA generated $360 million in revenues, an 8 percent increase from the previous year, with the US Open representing the USTA's primary revenue source (USTA, 2016b). Held in Queens, New York, the annual Grand Slam event takes place in late summer and attracts top players from around the world. Spectator numbers rival the Indianapolis 500 with over 691,000 people attending in 2015, an attendance record (US Open, 2016), and many more watching at home and online (Nagle, 2015). The USTA earned $292 million for the 2015 event, or 81 percent of the organization's total annual revenues (USTA, 2016b). ESPN secured exclusive rights to the US Open television broadcasts and online coverage. This media deal will last from 2015 to 2025, and the cable network will pay the USTA $70 million annually for this exclusivity. The partnership marks a shift away from the organization's longstanding television broadcast relationship of 47 years with CBS (Tennis Industry Association, 2017b). Most of the governing body's remaining revenues come from Tour events, membership fees, and tennis facility programs (USTA, 2016b) and these revenues help offset organizational expenses. In 2015 the USTA spent almost $140 million on the US Open. Other large cost categories included $86 million for the Community Tennis division, $30 million for USA Team and Tour events, and $22 million for administrative and support services (USTA, 2016b). See Exhibit 13.5.

ORGANIZATIONAL STRUCTURE. This nonprofit organization boasts a base membership of 700,000 individual members located in 17 regions around the United States and is run by a mixture of volunteer Executive Board Members, paid full-time staff, and other volunteers (USTA, 2017f). There is a Chair of the Board, CEO, and President of the USTA. Other executive leaders at the national headquarters in White Plains, New York, include the

United States Tennis Association Incorporated and Affiliates

exhibit 13.5

United States Tennis Association Incorporated and Affiliates

Consolidated Statements of Revenues and Expenses (dollars in thousands)

Years ended December 31,	2015	2014
Operating Revenues:		
US Open	$291,910	$264,309
USA team events	736	2,932
Tour events (Note 8)	29,292	26,830
Membership	16,848	15,600
NTC tennis facility programs (other than US Open)	3,835	4,375
Community tennis sponsorships	2,616	2,586
Investment return allocated to operations (Note 4)	7,050	6,960
Barter received	6,204	7,398
Other	1,437	1,656
Total Operating Revenues	359,928	332,646
Operating Expenses:		
Program services:		
US Open:		
Direct expenses	99,178	92,057
Depreciation, pledge and debt interest expense (Notes 5,6 and 11)	41,208	28,607
USA team events	3,301	5,491
Tour events (including depreciation) (Note 8)	27,038	23,765
Membership	11,338	10,579
NTC tennis facility programs (including depreciation and debt interest)	10,824	12,138
Community tennis:		
Grants to independent regional associations	47,072	45,861
Other community tennis programs	38,915	36,697
Player development	18,079	16,562
Pro circuit and officials	7,429	7,229
Barter used	6,204	7,398
Other program services	8,463	8,118
Total Program Services	319,049	294,502
Administrative and supporting services (including depreciation and taxes)	21,893	22,277
Total Operating Expenses	340,942	316,779
Excess of Operating Revenues Over Operating Expenses	18,986	15,867
Nonoperating Other (Loss) Income and Deductions:		
Investment return, net of amounts allocated to operations (Note 4)	(10,627)	(145)
Net loss on interest rate swap (Note 7)	–	(139)
Net gain on sale of investment in tennis tournaments (Note 8)	959	–
Equity in earnings of unconsolidated investees (Note 8)	–	92
Early extinguishment of debt (Note 7)	–	(5,460)
Total Nonoperating Other (Loss) Income and Deductions	(9,668)	(5,652)
Excess of Revenues Over Expenses	$ 9,318	S 10,215

Source: USTA (2016b).

Executive Director and Chief Operating Officer, Chief Financial Officer, Chief Marketing Officer, Chief Administrative Officer and Legal Counsel, Chief Information Officer, and Chief Medical Officer (USTA, 2017f). The USTA has three divisions, Community Tennis, Player Development, and Professional Tennis (see Exhibit 13.6), which also have leadership teams to manage their various initiatives and programs. Additionally, each regional section has its own association, and 50 state associations operate alongside the regional sections and the national headquarters. Whether regional, district, or state, the associations are nonprofit organizations run separately with their own boards of directors and staff members. The associations receive support from the Community Tennis Associations, which help the associations provide programs and initiatives to their respective members (USTA, 2017a).

At the international level, the International Tennis Federation (ITF) is the governing body for the sport. It regulates the game and controls major international events, including the Davis Cup and Fed Cup. The ITF has over 200 national tennis organizations as affiliates. Globally, the families of the ITF include the Confederation Africaine de Tennis (CAT), Asian Tennis Federation (ATF), Central American & Caribbean Tennis Confederation (COTECC), Confederación Sudamericana de Tenis (COSAT), Oceania Tennis Federation (OTF), and Tennis Canada. As opposed to the United States, other countries around the world belong to their country's tennis association as well as the regional tennis federations. Tennis Europe comprises 50 European member nations, making it the largest regional association of the ITF. Similar to the USTA, Tennis Europe organizes events that are independent from the ITF and executes tasks delegated by the ITF.

---

exhibit **13.6**   Divisions of the USTA

USTA		
Community Tennis Division	**Player Development Division**	**Professional Tennis Division**
Focuses on grassroots efforts through the USTA League and USTA Jr Team Tennis	Provides coaching services and facilities for the best junior players	Focuses on professional play by hosting the US Open and other tournaments leading to the Grand Slam tournaments

Source: USTA (2017a).

Current Policy Areas

Despite its successes, professional tennis faces ever changing and sometimes challenging policy issues. At an annual tennis industry forum held in 2016, several issues were identified and discussed. These included attracting younger audiences and using technology effectively (Vach, 2016). In addition, questions have arisen about the use of performance-enhancing drugs in the sport (Steinberger, 2016).

Attracting Younger Audiences

As is the case for the golf associations, the USTA faces the challenge of getting young people involved in the sport at an early age in order to ensure the organization and sport's continued popularity and growth. The USTA introduced the 10 and Under Tennis program at the grassroots level to spur interest in the sport among a younger audience. With this program, children use smaller racquets with foam or low-compression balls and play on smaller courts with lower nets. The changes were introduced after tennis analysts observed the challenges children face when playing on regulation courts with adult-sized equipment. Oversized nets and racquets might cause younger players to quickly become discouraged and lose interest in the sport. Conversely, smaller-sized equipment and courts allow them to experience more success sooner and potentially sustain their participation through childhood and beyond. The initiative started in 2012 and attracted younger players to the sport. Yet the initiative also generated controversy among tennis traditionalists, who questioned the research behind the program. The USTA continues to support and promote the movement despite some opposition (Pilon & Lehren, 2014).

The USTA also wants to attract more millennial players and is using social media and on-campus campaigns to increase exposure to the sport. These efforts include using Facebook and Twitter with the hashtag #TOC-Nationals to highlight the collegiate national championship. Beyond this annual event, the USTA is promoting tennis as a sport for club and recreational players on campuses across the nation. Nearly 670 colleges and universities and over 40,000 students take part in this initiative (Vach, 2016). These efforts may help to address tennis industry concerns about the need to attract more Generation Y and Z children and young adults, respectively, to the sport (Vach, 2016). The USTA believes increasing the levels of participation among these demographic groups will prove important—sustaining the sport and the USTA's membership base, which are factors critical to the organization's financial success as older players age and discontinue their participation.

Using Technology Effectively

Coupled with the need to attract younger players, the USTA recognizes the importance of leveraging technology to its fullest (Vach, 2016).

USTA Facebook page
https://www.facebook.
com/USTA/

USTA Twitter feed
https://twitter.com/usta

USTA YouTube channel
https://www.youtube.com/
user/tennis

Part of those efforts includes using social media as discussed above. The USTA has Facebook, Twitter, and YouTube pages. The Facebook page has almost 140,000 likes, the Twitter feed has over 225,000 followers, and the YouTube channel has over 8,000 subscribers. These social media platforms allow the USTA to connect with users beyond its website, television broadcasts, and other outlets. Additionally, the organization expects to benefit from its relationship with ESPN, which will promote coverage of the US Open on ESPN and ESPN2 as well as the WatchESPN app, which users can access through their smartphones, televisions, computers, tablets, and other devices. ESPN noted that online viewership of the US Open has increased, particularly among males aged 18–34, a key age demographic for the USTA (Nagle, 2015). Lastly the industry has experienced growth in online product sales. Tennis industry leaders have emphasized the importance of continuing to pursue opportunities in this area in order to increase tennis product sales and general sport consumption within the industry (Vach, 2016).

Performance-Enhancing Drugs in Tennis

ITF Anti Doping Program
http://www.itftennis.com/
antidoping/home.aspx

Technology usage and reaching younger audiences represent positive opportunities for the USTA. The organization and the larger tennis industry also must contend with negative press related to performance-enhancing drug usage in the sport. In June 2016, one of the sport's biggest stars, Maria Sharapova, received a two-year ban from the ITF after testing positive for meldonium usage. This ban means Sharapova, one of the most accomplished and highest-paid athletes in the sport, will be missing from the sport until 2018, barring a successful appeal to the Court of Arbitration for Sport (Meyers & Rothenberg, 2016). The ITF also updated its Tennis Anti-Doping Program, in particular Article 13.3, which addresses the public disclosure of rules violations and bans. Previously, when tennis professionals previously received bans, these may or may not have been announced to the public. The "silent bans" have now been eliminated in order to increase transparency and to emphasize the ITF's desire to improve the sport's reputation (Axson, 2016).

NASCAR

History

The National Association for Stock Car Auto Racing (NASCAR) is the sanctioning body for North American stock-car automobile racing and is the largest such organization in the United States. NASCAR began in 1948 when Bill France, Sr, along with race car drivers, racetrack owners, and racing enthusiasts, met in Daytona Beach, Florida, to form a new racing series (History Channel, 2017). The sport's popularity increased rapidly through the 1930s and 1940s, and France and others wanted to develop an organized structure to capitalize on that surging interest. During their 1948 meeting, the group settled on an organizational structure and declared France the organization's first Chief Executive Officer (Clarke, 2008). The first race sanctioned by NASCAR took place on February 15, 1948, and a Cup Series was introduced for the 1949 season. Changes occurred quickly in the 1950s and 1960s as more drivers gravitated to the sport. New racetracks emerged to accommodate the rising demand. The tracks were built not just in the South, where a large portion of NASCAR fans resided, but farther north in Michigan, Delaware, and Pennsylvania as the fan base spread (NASCAR, 2015).

The 1970s ushered in additional changes, as Bill France, Sr, relinquished the helm to his son, Bill France, Jr, who led the organization until 2003. In 1971, tobacco company R.J. Reynolds became the title sponsor of NASCAR's premier racing series, and the name changed from the Grand National Series to the Winston Cup Series (Clarke, 2008). A strong corporate presence continued into the 1980s and 1990s, and NASCAR witnessed a significant increase in corporate sponsorships and advertising as other companies followed suit and initiated sponsorships with racetracks and drivers. In 2003, NASCAR moved from long-time title sponsor R.J. Reynolds to a sponsorship with the telecommunications industry's Nextel Corporation. When Nextel and Sprint merged, the Nextel Cup became the Sprint Cup (Clarke, 2008).

NASCAR
www.nascar.com

Beyond corporate sponsorships, NASCAR also experienced an expanded television presence. The organization entered a television partnership with FOX, NBC, and TNT in the 1990s. The contract proved a boon for all parties, as television viewership continued to grow, particularly for the Daytona 500, whose viewership increased by 48 percent from 1993 to 2002. Racetrack owners reported a corresponding growth in attendance, as their facilities often hold from 100,000 to 200,000 fans—rivaling attendance at the National Football League's annual Super Bowl (Amato, Peters, & Shao, 2005). Fans flocked to races, and attendance grew by 80 percent from 1993 to 1998. A large portion of this growth was attributed to the Sprint Cup Series, which witnessed a 57 percent increase during the same time period. The organization also created an online presence, introducing NASCAR.com in 1995, to reach fans before, during, and after the events (NASCAR, 2015).

Governance

MISSION. While NASCAR's mission statement was not publicly available, one can surmise that organization wishes to provide the safest and most exciting motor sports events possible. Headquartered in Daytona Beach, Florida, NASCAR serves as the sanctioning body for the Sprint Cup Series as well as the XFINITY Series, Camping World Truck Series, and other smaller series such as K&N Pro Series, Canadian Tire Series, Toyota Series, Whelen Euro Series, Whelen Modified Tour, Whelen Southern Modified

Tour, and Whelen All-American Series at racetracks across the United States, Canada, Mexico, and Europe (NASCAR, 2015). The Sprint Cup Series is undoubtedly NASCAR's most popular, but the organization also promotes other regional and local events. For example, the Whelen All-American Series represents a training ground for local drivers aspiring to one day compete at the sport's highest levels, and drivers can win local track, state, and national titles for their performances. Other series such as the Canadian Tire Series help develop talent at tracks across North America. As drivers improve on the local and regional circuits, they may seek greater opportunities with the Camping World Truck Series, XFINITY Series, and eventually the Sprint Cup Series (NASCAR, 2015).

MEMBERSHIP.   As a privately owned, family-run organization, NASCAR tries to consistently provide a lifestyle sports product, a goal that helped the company grow from a regional diversion into an international sports giant. Part of NASCAR's original success derived from its consistency through strict management controls. The governing body establishes guidelines for its owners, drivers, and support personnel both on and off the racetrack. In 2016, NASCAR announced an historic overhaul to the governance and membership structure for its premier racing series. First, a charter system was established, whereby 36 racing teams will receive automatic entry into the racing season's Sprint Cup events. Next, the weekly race field was reduced from 43 to 40 spots. The charter members will assume 36 spots and four spots are available for non-charter members each week. Finally, each race charter has a nine-year life, and the 36 charter owners have the opportunity to sell their charter once every five years (Jensen, 2016). These developments marked a notable change from the previous structure, which gave race teams one-year contracts and required them to qualify for the weekly races based on times.

In addition to these changes, NASCAR created a Team Owner Council, affording team owners more involvement in the sanctioning body's decision-making processes and greater opportunities for revenue sharing. These benefits include allowing the chartered racing teams to sell their charters as noted above. Proponents of the new system believe benefits will include more stable revenue streams for race teams, as they will now have guaranteed entry into races throughout the season. The race teams can also capitalize on the potential long-term worth of their respective charters, assuming they increase in value over time. (Early estimates suggest a charter could sell for an amount between $5 and $10 million [Smith, 2016].) NASCAR also established new sanctioning agreements with its racetracks. These five-year contracts will give the racing sites greater stability as well with guaranteed revenue streams lasting the length of their respective contracts (Jensen, 2016).

FINANCIALS.   As a privately held company, NASCAR is not required to disclose its complete financial statements to the public. NASCAR receives sizeable revenues through its television contracts. In 2013, NASCAR signed ten-year agreements with NBC and FOX, and will receive a combined $8.2 billion in revenues from the two broadcast networks during this time. The negotiated amount represents a 46 percent increase over the contracts NASCAR previously signed with ABC, ESPN, FOX, SPEED, and TNT (Smith, 2015).

Coupled with media rights, sponsorships represent an important revenue source for the governing body. Research indicated 70 percent of NASCAR fans would purchase products from corporations sponsoring drivers and races, and 40 percent said they would switch brands if a competing company became a sponsor (Amato, Peters, & Shao, 2005). NASCAR is the self-proclaimed leader in brand loyalty among all North American sports and is one of the most internationally recognized sport brands (NASCAR, 2017). Corporate sponsors have often recognized the value of associating with NASCAR, and the organization has reaped the benefits of this interest. NASCAR signed a naming rights contract with Comcast's XFINITY, the title sponsor of its second biggest race series. The rights were previously held by Nationwide, and NASCAR will receive $20 million per year for a total of ten years starting in 2015 (Smith, 2015). NASCAR also will announce a new sponsorship deal for its Sprint Cup Series. Sprint, the telecommunications company, held the title sponsorship for the premier racing series from 2004 to 2016, paying NASCAR an estimated $50 to $75 million each year for these rights. Industry analysts have predicted the sponsorship amount could increase to $100 million annually—or $1 billion over a ten-year period—with a new sponsor. International consumer product companies such as Coca-Cola, Goodyear, and LG have entertained title sponsorship pitches from NASCAR, but ultimately Monster Energy became the title sponsor for the 2017 NASCAR Cup Series (Heitner, 2016; Monster Energy 2017).

Racecar owners and drivers also benefit from sponsorship agreements. A team's primary sponsor determines the racecar's logos and color schemes, and drivers in the premier racing series receive up to 75 percent of their revenues from these sponsorships (Boudway, 2016). Yet securing sponsors has become increasingly harder for race teams since the 2008–09 recession. Many view the charter system as a way to lure sponsors back to NASCAR with guaranteed race entries for the charter teams. The previous system left sponsors and race teams unsure of whether their racecars would gain entry from week to week, much less year to year. Race teams now expect that sponsors will have a greater level of comfort with signing longer-term contracts under the new system, as they will have guaranteed entries for longer periods of time (Boudway, 2016). In addition to racecar sponsorships, drivers receive purse earnings, depending on where they finish in each race. The Daytona 500 pays over $1.6 million to the winner, while other races may pay as little as $167,000 (FOX Sports, 2015). These earnings, sponsorships, and other endorsements are used to defray team costs—as much as $25 million per year—for pit crews, race cars, travel, and related expenses (Boudway, 2016).

ORGANIZATIONAL STRUCTURE. In 2003, Bill France Jr's son, Brian France, became just the third NASCAR Chairman of the Board and Chief Executive Officer (Clarke, 2008). Reporting to him are two Vice Chairmen, an Executive Vice President and Chief Racing Officer, General Counsel, Senior Vice President and Chief Marketing Officer, Vice President of Analytics and Insights, and finally a Vice President for Partnership Marketing (The Official Board, n.d). The governing body has placed a heightened emphasis on safety and innovation, working to ensure the safety of drivers, pit crew, and spectators at sanctioned events. The organization issues specific guidelines and safety measures regarding modifications racecar owners and mechanics are allowed to make on their vehicles. NASCAR officials monitor alterations closely and quickly issue citations to drivers and owners running afoul of the rules (Clarke, 2008).

Current Policy Areas

NASCAR leaders are constantly focused on innovation and ways to improve their products and organization. Currently, they face challenges in three key areas: addressing declining attendance, reaching different demographics, and increasing diversity on and off the racetrack.

Declining Attendance

The number of people attending NASCAR events is declining—in stark contrast to the increases in revenues generated through its television broadcast rights and title sponsorships. For example, the 2016 attendance at the Indianapolis Motor Speedway race was approximately 50,000 spectators, a record low for this racetrack, which can hold up to 250,000 fans (USA Today, 2016). Industry analysts attribute these attendance figures to a number of factors, including continued challenges associated with the 2008–09 recession and its effects on employment rates, gas prices, and travel costs. Other factors include the aging and in some case retirements of popular NASCAR drivers; more NASCAR fans using social media, apps, and the organization's website to track the sport in lieu of attending events; and shifting interests of younger sports fans in general (USA Today, 2016). Television viewership has also decreased. NASCAR experienced its greatest number of viewers in 2005 with 9.2 million fans tuning in each week. The viewership numbers have since declined to around 5.3 million per race, with the sharpest declines occurring from 2010 to 2014 (Wolfe, 2015). Given its newest television broadcast and sponsorship contracts, NASCAR must work to ensure it can deliver fans to its business partners.

Reaching Different Demographics

Beyond racetrack attendance and TV viewership, NASCAR fanship has also decreased from approximately 115 million fans in 2004 to 98 million in 2015, a decline of 15 percent. No other professional sport in recent history has experienced a similar decline (Mickle, 2015). NASCAR fans are trending older with a mean of 48 years of age, one of the oldest fan bases in professional sports. Only 14 percent of NASCAR fans fall within the 34 and younger category. This age group compares to 45 percent for the NBA, 37 percent for the NHL, and 29 percent for the NFL, respectively (Holodny, 2016). Industry analysts have noted the sport's ongoing difficulties in appealing to a younger demographic while retaining its older, more traditional fan base. In efforts to reach younger fans, NASCAR has employed greater use of social media and has reported increases in fan engagement operationalized as retweets, likes, and shares. The organization has also experienced growth in the number of website users (Gluck, 2016). Focusing on different channels for different audiences could help NASCAR balance its reach with current fans and potentially attract new fans.

Increasing Diversity On and Off the Racetrack

Part of NASCAR's attempt to reach different audiences includes focusing on increased diversity among its racecar drivers, employees, and fans. NASCAR has traditionally been viewed as a sport catering to white fans from rural areas. As such, the demographics for fans of color have either stagnated or decreased over time. Thirty-four percent of African Americans view themselves as NASCAR fans, a number that has held constant. Thirty-two percent of Latinos perceive themselves as NASCAR fans, and this number has declined from a high of 43 percent (Mickle, 2015). Some have attributed these numbers to the Confederate flag, which traditionally has been flown by fans at NASCAR events. NASCAR recognizes the controversy surrounding the flag and its usage. The organization has asked fans to refrain from bringing Confederate flags, but has not issued an official ban on them at events. Instead, NASCAR has focused on other actions to increase the diversity of its fans, with particular focus on African American and Latino attendees. These include the Drive for Diversity to spur greater fan attendance and participation by minority racecar drivers and pit crews (Mickle, 2015).

INTERNATIONAL SPORT: SURFING AUSTRALIA

HISTORY.   Surfing Australia (SA) was formed in 1963 and represents one of the 97 member countries of the International Surfing Association (ISA). SA was established to support the development of surfing in Australia. The structure of SA supports the growth of surfing as a sport as well as a life pursuit for younger generations. SA is recognized by the Australian Sport Commission and the Australian Olympic Committee, and the organization is also a member of the Water Safety Council of Australia (Surfing Australia, 2015).

MISSION. Unlike the individual sports in the US, international individual sports are governed differently depending on each country's governance structure and sports governing bodies. The mission of SA is "to create a healthier and happier Australia through surfing" (Surfing Australia, 2017, para. 6). The core values of SA are: (a) Real—we live the surfing lifestyle and we share the stoke; (b) Progressive—we embrace change and value new ideas; (c) Trustworthy—we deliver on our word and exceed expectations; and (d) Respectful—we appreciate the history, culture, and traditions of surfing (Surfing Australia, 2017).

MEMBERSHIP. The SA surfboard riders belong to a club that teaches and encourages skills needed to pursue a competitive career. Currently 239 clubs are available in Australia for all levels of surfers to join, and these clubs include a combined 17,723 members. Depending on their respective levels, riders join clubs that are dedicated to all age groups at all levels or clubs that are more exclusively designated for professional riders (Surfing Australia, 2015).

FINANCIALS. Unlike the individual governing bodies in the US, SA utilizes the digital media platform mySURF.tv as a primary source of communication rather than securing media rights with major broadcast outlets. Thus, media rights deals are not the biggest contributor to SA's financials. The SA's funds are driven by partnership sponsors and the Australian Sports Commission (ASC). The ASC is a statutory authority within the Australian Government's Department of Health. In 2014–15, the Australian government invested a total of AU$120 million and AIS allocated $20 million to help fund all sports in Australia (Surfing Australia, 2015). The SA secured $571,000 in funding in order to support individual clubs and national events and to develop strategic partnership with sponsors. In detail, the SA generated over $2.6 million from sponsorship and events alone in 2015 (AUsport, 2015).

Current Policy Areas

At the 2020 Summer Games in Tokyo, Japan, surfing will make its Olympic debut. This decision resulted from efforts made by the ISA and President Fernando Aguerre to include five new sports for the 2020 Olympic Games. A total of 40 athletes (20 men and 20 women) will compete in the Games. With a strong history deeply rooted in sport development, SA is hoping to gain global recognition and win Olympic medals (Pierson, 2016). However, adding surfing to this mega-event poses challenges for the organizers. These include venue locations and weather in order to provide an ideal environment for board riders. The IOC and ISA are still discussing the issue of the venue and possibility of artificially made waves as well as the financials associated with the event. In order to prevent host nations from having to invest in new technologies to create waves, the IOC is carefully reviewing its options regarding the logistics of holding surfing events during the Games (Weisberg, 2016). The outcome of the decision will be announced as the 2020 Olympic Games get closer.

SUMMARY

Many individual sports share some governance elements with sports that operate as leagues. For example, both have commissioners, boards of directors, and owners. The governing bodies for individual and league sports are responsible for setting rules and regulations, developing policies, and responding to current issues. Membership in the organizations is well defined. One aspect that is different, particularly with golf and tennis, is the emphasis on grassroots development of the sport. For these sports, the professional aspect is just one part of what governing bodies attend to. Cultivating grassroots participation is also of the utmost importance in order to identify and train the next generation of elite athletes. In this way, these sport organizations resemble National Governing Bodies in the Olympic Movement, which stress both elite athlete development and grassroots participation.

A major difference between individual sports and league sports is the absence of unions and collective bargaining agreements. Also, the qualifying process differs markedly from the drafting process for league sports. From a spectator's perspective, team sports usually create a sense of community by encouraging spectators to be fans of a team. In individual sports, spectators often focus on a specific event (e.g., the Masters, Wimbledon) rather than a single player. Furthermore, individual sports might include senior tours or senior events promoting longevity in the careers of their individual athletes. It is important to recognize organizations that work with individual sports and realize sport governance in professional sport is not just about the Big Four.

case STUDY

FUTURE CHALLENGES FOR NASCAR

Industry analysts believe NASCAR faces a number of challenges. These include declining attendance and viewership numbers. The organization has traditionally benefited from a loyal fan base that has long supported its drivers and sponsors. But the demographic makeup of these supporters has skewed towards an older and less diverse audience. NASCAR has attempted to improve its diversity in different ways. The Drive for Diversity initiative was created to attract more females and people of color to the sport. NASCAR also has placed greater emphasis on its website and social media platforms such as Facebook and Twitter to reach younger audiences. However, challenges related to diversity and perceptions of the sport as one targeted towards older fans persist.

Given the high level of competition among sports to capture and retain an audience, NASCAR must work to address these challenges and grow its fan base. A study addressed the limited interest among younger sports fans in regards to NASCAR (Goldsmith & Walker, 2015). The researchers conducted an experiment whereby they asked sports fans, in this case, college students, to participate in a NASCAR fantasy league in order to determine whether playing this fantasy sport would increase students' interests in NASCAR over time. The results revealed fan interest did increase, as the students became more engaged in the racecar drivers and events. The researchers concluded that NASCAR should identify ways to connect with younger audiences and that fantasy sports could serve as a potential conduit.

NASCAR has signed a sizeable television contract with NBC and FOX, and wants to ensure it delivers viewers week in and week out to its broadcast partners. NASCAR also wants to provide the same assurances to the incoming title sponsor of its premier race series, which could invest up to $1 billion for these sponsorship rights. However, the organization faces a delicate balance in attracting new fans without alienating its older and loyal fan base in the pursuit of younger and more diverse audiences.

1. What can NASCAR do to improve its attendance and viewership numbers? In addition to increases in numbers, what can the organization do to increase the diversity of its fan base?

2. How can the organization leverage its new television contracts, sponsorships, and/or charter system to attract and retain fans?

3. What social media efforts and other technologies and opportunities (e.g., fantasy sports, apps) can the organization use to increase interest in the sport?

4. What detailed plan would you recommend NASCAR develop and execute in order to address these challenges?

CHAPTER questions

1. The USTA has three important divisions but limited funds to support them. As the USTA leader, which division would you emphasize and why? What are the advantages and disadvantages of highlighting one division versus another?

2. NASCAR has transitioned to a charter system to give racecar owners more governance and revenue sharing opportunities. What are the advantages and disadvantages of this charter system for the teams and NASCAR?

3. Professional tennis, golf, and stock car racing rely heavily upon sponsorship revenues. In challenging economic times, how can the three sports ensure ongoing support from sponsors? What alternatives can they pursue in the event of sponsorship declines?

FOR ADDITIONAL INFORMATION

For more information check out the following resources:

1. Youtube: The King of NASCAR is back!: https://www.youtube.com/watch?v=pLtj9ymeCKk
2. USTA Florida, USPTA Florida Growing Tennis Together: Gill, C. (2017, June 8). USTA Florida, USPTA Florida growing tennis together. USTA: https://www.ustaflorida.com/usta-florida-uspta-florida-growing-tennis-together/
3. USGA Rules Changes: Everil, B. (2017, June 14). USGA makes changes to prevent rules issues. PGA Tour: www.pgatour.com/news/2017/06/14/usga-makes-changes-prevent-rules-issues.html
4. Golf Diversity and Inclusion Report: Cooper, M. W. (2015). Golf diversity & inclusion report. World Golf Foundation: www.golf2020.com/media/61532/golf_diversity___inclusion_report_2015.pdf
5. Condoleeza Rice on Golf Diversity: Kerr-Dineen, L. (2016, June 6). Condoleeza Rice on diversity: 'Golf needs to look more like America'. *USA Today Sports*: http://ftw.usatoday.com/2016/06/condoleezza-rice-lpga-tour-golf-diversity
6. Billie Jean King Leadership Initiative: www.bjkli.org

REFERENCES

Amato, C. H., Peters, C. L. O., & Shao. A. T. (2005). An exploratory investigation into NASCAR fan culture. *Sport Marketing Quarterly*, 14, 71–83.

AUSport. (2015). The turning point case study. Retrieved from www.ausport.gov.au/__data/assets/pdf_file/0006/580911/P_and_SS_34122_Surfing_Case_Study_AUG15.pdf

Axson, S. (2016, August 23). ITF amends text in Tennis Anti-Doping Program, will publicly announce bans. Sports Illustrated. Retrieved from www.si.com/tennis/2016/08/23/itf-amendment-tennis-anti-doping-program

Boudway, I. (2016, February 24). What NASCAR learned from the NFL. Bloomberg Businessweek. Retrieved from www.bloomberg.com/news/articles/2016-02-24/what-nascar-learned-from-the-nfl

Clarke, L. (2008). *One helluva ride: How NASCAR swept the nation*. New York: Villard Books.

Executive Committee. (n.d.). Retrieved from http://svrns8web1.pgatourhq.com/Tour/WebTemplate/ElectronicMediaGuide.nsf/vwWebFS/41A07CB2137FC25C852576880069F90C?openDocument

FOX Sports. (2015, October 3). Least to most: The prize money for every Sprint Cup race winner in '15. Retrieved from www.foxsports.com/nascar/photos/sprint-cup-series-prize-money-dale-earnhardt-jr-joey-logano-matt-kenseth-kevin-harvick-100315

FSTA. (2015). Industry demographics. Retrieved from http://fsta.org/research/industry-demographics/

Gluck, J. (2016, July 2). NASCAR looks beyond declining attendance, TV ratings. *USA Today*. Retrieved from www.usatoday.com/story/sports/nascar/2016/07/01/nascar-declining-attendance-tv-ratings-fans-social-media/86573130/

Goldsmith, A., & Walker, M. (2015). The NASCAR experience: Examining the influence of fantasy sport participation on 'non-fans'. *Sport Management Review*, 18 (2), 231–243.

Greenstein, T. (2016, August 15). How to make Olympic golf even better in 2020. *Chicago Tribune*. Retrieved from www.chicagotribune.com/sports/columnists/ct-golf-future-olympics-spt-0816-20160815-column.html

Heitner, D. (2015, August 10). Golf's final major: Impact of the 2015 PGA Championship. *Forbes*. Retrieved from https://www.forbes.com/sites/darrenheitner/2015/08/10/golfs-final-major-impact-of-the-2015-pga-championship/#6326b8ef139e

Heitner, D. (2016, July 18). How much money will NASCAR get from Sprint's replacement? *Forbes*. Retrieved from www.forbes.com/sites/darrenheitner/2016/07/18/will-nascar-get-100-million-per-year-from-sprints-replacement/#66668ac7210e

History Channel. (2017). This day in history. Retrieved from www.history.com/this-day-in-history/nascar-founded

Holodny, E. (2016, March 9). NASCAR got crushed by the recession and is still struggling to get back on its feet. *Business Insider*. Retrieved from www.businessinsider.com/nascar-still-struggling-after-recession-2016-3

IGF. (2016). Qualification system: Games of the XXXI Olympiad-Rio 2016. Retrieved from http://d2aygmo1xd84v8.cloudfront.net/igfgolf/wp-content/uploads/sites/49/2015/11/2015-11-Rio-2016-Qualification-System-FINAL-Golf-EN.pdf

Jensen, T. (2016, February 9). NASCAR formalizes details of revolutionary charter system. FOX Sports. Retrieved from www.foxsports.com/nascar/story/nascar-charter-system-sprint-cup-series-brian-france-joe-gibbs-racing-daytona-500-020916

LPGA. (n.d.a). About the LPGA. Retrieved from www.lpga.com/about-lpga

LPGA. (n.d.b). Directory of marketing partners. Retrieved from www.lpga.com/corporate/ladies-golf/directory-of-marketing-partners.aspx

LPGA. (n.d.c). 2016 LPGA Schedule announcement. Retrieved from www.lpga.com/news/2016-lpga-schedule-announcement

LPGA. (n.d.d). Vision, mission, values. Retrieved from www.lpga.com/tcp/vision-mission-values

Meyers, N. J., & Rothenberg, B. (2016, June 8). Maria Sharapova is suspended from tennis for two years. *New York Times*. Retrieved from www.nytimes.com/2016/06/09/sports/tennis/maria-sharapova-doping-suspension.html

Mickle, T. (2015, June 26). Confederate flag at NASCAR earns a caution. *The Wall Street Journal*. Retrieved from www.wsj.com/articles/nascar-stance-earns-a-yellow-flag-1435359227

Monster Energy. (2017). Kyle Busch: Monster Energy All-Star Race MVP. Retrieved from https://nascar.monsterenergy.com/

Nagle, D. (2015, September 15). ESPNTennis & US Open: Most-viewed in four years; WatchESPN viewership up 4X+. Retrieved from http://espnmediazone.com/us/press-releases/2015/09/espntennis-us-open-most-viewed-in-four-years-watchespn-viewership-up-4x/

NASCAR. (2015, February 10). About NASCAR. Retrieved from www.nascar.com/en_us/news-media/articles/about-nascar.html

NASCAR. (2017). Sponsorship. Retrieved from www.nascar.com/sponsorship

PGA. (2015). Membership. Retrieved from https://www.pga.org/sites/default/files/assets/library/Membership/2014-2015-pga-signedfinancialstmt.pdf

PGA. (2017a). History. Retrieved from www.pga.com/pga-america/ history

PGA. (2017b). Member classifications. Retrieved from www.pga.com/pga-america/pga-information/pga-america-member-classifications

PGA. (2017c). Partners. Retrieved from www.pga.com/pga-america/partners

PGA. (2017d). Peter Bevacqua, PGA of America leaders. Retrieved from www.pga.com/pga-america/pga-information/peter-bevacqua-pga-america-leaders-1

PGA. (2017e). PGA Board of Directors. Retrieved from https://www.pga.org/articles/pga-board-directors

PGA. (2017f). The experts in the game and business of golf. Retrieved from https://www.pga.org/articles/purpose-pgaorg

PGA TOUR. (2016). PGA TOUR and its tournaments set record for charitable giving. Retrieved from http://together.pgatour.com/stories/2016/03/pga-tour-charity-total.html

PGA TOUR. (2017a). About PGA TOUR. Retrieved from www.pgatour.com/company/aboutus.html

PGA TOUR. (2017b). PGA Tour signs 9-year extension with networks. Retrieved from www.pga.com/news/pga-tour/pga-tour-signs-9-year-extension-networks

PGA TOUR. (2017c). PGA TOUR 2012 official retail licensees. Retrieved from http://mediaguide.pgatourhq.com/Tour/WebTemplate/ElectronicMediaGuide.nsf/vwMainDisplay/6528340F25E91CA88525761D0058C528?openDocument

Pierson, D. (2016). 10 things you should know about surfing in the Olympics. Retrieved from www.surfline.com/surf-news/the-decision-has-been-made---surfing-will-be-at-tokyo-2020---heres-whats-been-confirmed-so-far-10-things-you-s_140542/

Pilon, M., & Lehren, A. W. (2014, September 10). Modified training for children stirs new debates. *New York Times*. Retrieved from www.nytimes.com/2014/09/11/sports/tennis/modified-training-for-children-stirs-new-debates.html

Smith, C. (2015, February 18). How NASCAR plans to turn its survival story into a decade of success. *Forbes*. Retrieved from www.forbes.com/sites/chrissmith/2015/02/18/how-nascar-plans-to-turn-its-survival-story-into-a-decade-of-success/#33a5425d2ceb

Smith, C. (2016, February 17). NASCAR's most valuable teams grow even richer with new charter system. *Forbes*. Retrieved from www.forbes.com/sites/chrissmith/2016/02/17/nascars-most-valuable-teams-grow-even-richer-with-new-charter-system/#79d388e21ec8

Starr, R. (2012, April 30). Marketers use creativity, technology to reach new golf audience.

Sports Business Journal. Retrieved from www.sportsbusinessdaily.com/Journal/Issues/2012/04/30/Opinion/From-the-Field-of-Marketing.aspx

Statistic Brain Research Institute (2016). Golf player demographic statistics. Retrieved from www.statisticbrain.com/golf-player-demographic-statistics/

Steinberger, M. (2016, January 20). Tennis could have a much bigger problem than match-fixing. Vanity Fair. Retrieved from www.vanityfair.com/news/2016/01/tennis-match-fixing

Surfing Australia. (2015). Annual report, 2015. Retrieved from https://d30ei0jhgxjdue.cloudfront.net/uploads/ckeditor/attachment_file/data/452/uploads_2F1447372471780-wmale3d6143rf6r-e2e2f621daa1ef1f244a49c5d710e6c4_2F44229_Surfing%2BAustralia%2BAnnual%2BReport%2B2015_LOW.pdf

Surfing Australia. (2017). About Surfing Australia. Retrieved from https://www.surfingaustralia.com/p/about-sa

The Official Board. (n.d). NASCAR. Retrieved from https://www.theofficialboard.com/org-chart/nascar

Tennis Industry Association. (2017a). Tennis participation in the US grows to 17.9 million players. Retrieved from www.tennisindustry.org/cms/index.cfm/news/tennis-participation-in-the-us-grows-to-179-million-players/

Tennis Industry Association. (2017b). USTA, ESPN sign TV deal for US Open and Open Series starting in 2015. Retrieved from www.tennisindustry.org/cms/index.cfm/news/usta-espn-sign-tv-deal-for-us-open-open-series-starting-in-2015/

The Thomson Tide. (2010). Q School primer: Answers to key questions. Retrieved from www.thompsontide.com/2010/10/q-school-primer-answers-to-key.html

US Open. (2016). Event guide. Retrieved from www.usopen.org/en_US/event_guide/year_by_year.html

USA Today. (2016, July 25). Five reasons for empty seats. Retrieved from www.indystar.com/story/sports/motor/2016/07/25/5-reasons-nascars-empty-seats/87534784/

USGA. (2016a). Final results and prize money. Retrieved from www.usga.org/custom-search.html#q=2016%20purse&type=all&startIndex=1

USGA. (2016b). 2011 Annual report. Retrieved from http://data.usga.org/final_annual_report/

USGA. (2017a). Club membership overview. Retrieved from www.usga.org/content/usga/home-page/member-clubs/club-membership-overview.html

USGA. (2017b). Community. Retrieved from www.usga.org/serving-the-game/health-of-the-game/community.html

USGA. (2017c). Mission statement. Retrieved from www.usga.org/content/usga/home-page/about.html

USGA. (2017d). USGA primary functions. Retrieved from https://www.usgashop.com/pages/FAQ

USTA. (n.d.). USTA constitution, by-laws, and diversity and inclusion statement. Retrieved from https://www.usta.com/content/dam/usta/pdfs/20170406_Constitution,%20Bylaws%20and%20Diversity%20Statement.pdf

USTA. (2016a). *Consolidated financial statements years ended December 31, 2015 and 2014.* White Plains, NY: Author.

USTA. (2016b). Consolidated financial statements years ended December 31, 2015 and 2014. Retrieved from https://s3.amazonaws.com/ustaassets/assets/1/15/01_121514-association_final_signed.pdf

USTA. (2017a). How the USTA works for you. Retrieved from www.usta.com/About-USTA/Organization/Organization/

USTA. (2017b). Individual memberships. Retrieved from http://membership.usta.com/section/Individual-Family-Memberships/101.uts

USTA. (2017c). Junior Team Tennis. Retrieved from https://www.usta.com/Youth-Tennis/Team-Tennis/?intloc=headernavsub

USTA. (2017d). Organizational memberships. Retrieved from http://membership.usta.com/section/Organizational-Memberships/122.uts

USTA. (2017e). Player development. Retrieved from www.playerdevelopment.usta.com/

USTA. (2017f). Staff management team. Retrieved from https://www.usta.com/en/home/about-usta/usta-leadership.html

USTA. (2017g). Tennis on Campus. Retrieved from https://www.usta.com/en/home/play/programs-for-everyone/national/about-tennis-on-campus.html

USTA. (2017h). USTA League. Retrieved from http://tennislink.usta.com/Leagues/Common/Default.aspx

USTA. (2017i). USTA key dates. Retrieved from https://www.usta.com/en/home/about-usta/usta-history/national/usta-history.html

Vach, R. (2016, March 23). Blog: Tennis "State of the Industry" forum takeaways. Retrieved from https://www.ustaflorida.com/blog-tennis-state-industry-forum-takeaways/

Weisberg, Z. (2016, June 2). *Surfing in the* 2020 Olympics: Absolutely everything we know. Retrieved from www.theinertia.com/surf/surfing-in-the-2020-olympics-absolutely-everything-we-know/#modal-close

Wolfe, A. (2015, June 26). Brian France tries to broaden NASCAR's appeal. *Wall Street Journal.* Retrieved from www.wsj.com/articles/brian-france-tries-to-broaden-nascars-appeal-1435340325

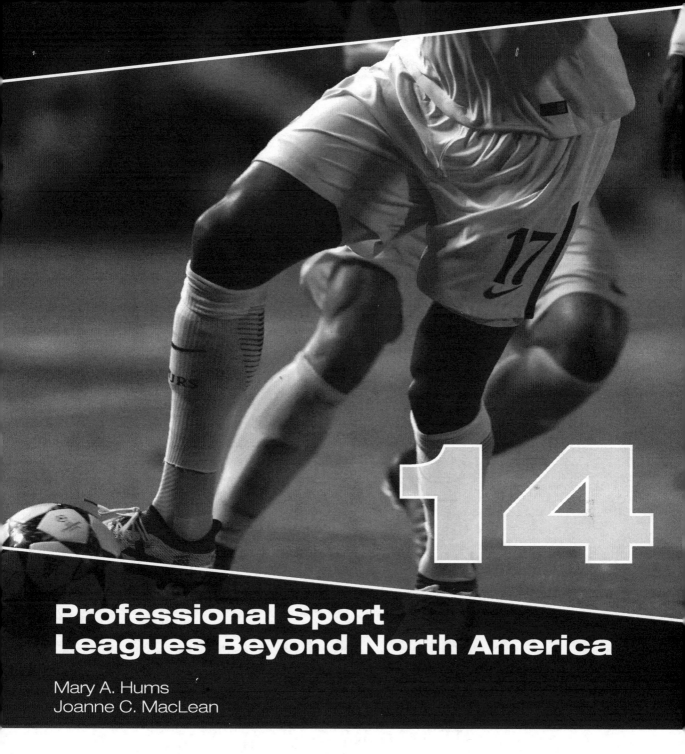

Professional Sport Leagues Beyond North America

Mary A. Hums
Joanne C. MacLean

When you think of professional sport, the first leagues that come to mind are often the National Basket Ball Association (NBA), the National Football League (NFL), the National Hockey League (NHL), and Major League Baseball (MLB). However, in many parts of the world, the topics of discussion are very different. Perhaps a debate rages over upcoming football matches involving FC Barcelona or Real Madrid, the ongoing rivalry between Liverpool and Manchester United, or whether anyone can catch Sebastian Vettel in the next Formula 1 Grand Prix. If you are wondering what these examples refer to, then welcome to the exciting world of professional sport beyond North America, where *football* means *soccer*, basketball has a few different rules, motor sports does not mean NASCAR, and baseball is often completely unknown!

The goal of this chapter is to introduce you to some of the basics of the structures of professional sport outside of North America. As such, we will touch on some of the differences that exist, as well as some similarities. The chapter will primarily use football (soccer) as examples, but remember that many other types of professional leagues and sports exist internationally. Basketball has its EuroLeague and many countries have their own national level leagues. Sports such as cricket, rugby, hockey, and team handball dominate in other countries, and there are motorsports such as Formula One. And women's sports are also alive and well internationally and we will introduce some of those leagues in this chapter, too. Hopefully this chapter will spark an interest for you to enroll in an Internationals Sport class or to take advantage of the growing opportunities to do a Study Abroad experience during your time as a student. Even better, you might actually figure out a way to work or live in another country and learn another language at some point in your life. That would be the best outcome of all since you would get a chance to personally experience our global sport industry.

THE GLOBAL NATURE OF SPORT

As just mentioned, the sport industry is truly global in nature. Similar to other global products, such as Coca-Cola or McDonald's, sport transcends borders. The North American way of organizing and managing sport is not the only—and certainly not always the best way—to organize sport. Sport managers working in an international environment must learn to be respectful of local cultures, norms, and expertise. According to Pitts and Zhang (2016, p. 8):

> Differences in such areas as culture, religion, tradition, politics, law, policy and regulation, communication, language, technology and environment in global, national, regional, and local communities make this task a very challenging one . . . Sport management professionals responsible for making the strategic, cultural, political, and economic decisions for sport organizations must be prepared for the challenges of the new sport landscape.

The only way to truly be successful in today's international sport marketplace to is to actively engage in the global sport industry by reaching out to build bridges with international partners. Sport managers who fail to do so are setting their organizations up to fall behind the competition. According to Germany's Chancellor Angela Merkel, "Whoever believes the problems of this world can be solved by isolationism and protectionism is making a tremendous error" (Collinson, 2017, para. 9). Working together across international differences builds a stronger sport industry for everyone.

This chapter introduces the basics of selected international sport leagues and events. For the most part, people in North America have a relatively narrow view of professional sport—the Big Four, NASCAR, golf, and tennis. Hopefully, this chapter will expand your horizons to professional sport around the world.

SELECTED DIFFERENCES IN PROFESSIONAL SPORT

The governance of professional sport internationally is very different from that in North America. We will highlight three of these governance related themes here: (1) relationships to other sport governing bodies, (2), promotion and relegation, and (3) player movement systems.

Relationships to Other Governing Bodies

Relationships among several levels of sport governing bodies are involved. Specifically, leagues are tied to the National Governing Body (NGB) for the sport in each nation, the International Federation (IF) for each particular sport, and sometimes to a regional governing body. For example, the Premier League in England has ties to the Football Association of England (FA), the Union of European Football Associations (UEFA), and FIFA (Fédération Internationale de Football Association) (Premier League, 2017a).

Promotion and Relegation

Another striking difference between professional leagues in North America and Europe is the system of promotion and relegation used in European leagues (Hums & Svensson, in press; Szymanski & Valetti, 2003). Briefly, this system operates as follows:

> While there are several ways in which this scheme can operate, the most commonly used format is one where the worst performing teams in a league during the season, measured by the number of points won (a measure that is close to win percentage) are demoted to an immediately junior league to be replaced by the best performing teams in that league. (Szymanski, 2006, p. 685)

Here is an example from a hypothetical league setup. Let's say at the end of the 2018–19 season, the final standings looked like this:

A League	B League
Rapid Wein	St Polten
Red Bull Salzburg	Austria Wein
Rheindorf Altach	Kroatische Geresdorf
Sturm Graz	Salzburg
SV Mattersburg	SV Innsbruck
Wolfsberger AC	SV Burgenland
SV Reid	Nikitsch

Using promotion and relegation, at the start of the 2019–20 season, the league membership would look like this:

A League	B League
Rapid Wein	Wolfsberger AC
Red Bull Salzburg	SV Reid
Rheindorf Altach	Kroatische Geresdorf
Sturm Graz	Salzburg
SV Mattersburg	SV Innsbruck
St. Polten	SV Burgenland
Austria Wein	Nikitsch

As you can see, the bottom teams from the A League were relegated to the B League, while the top teams in the B League were promoted to the A League. League membership can fluctuate from season to season under this system. Also, as opposed to North American leagues where the bottom teams might want to have that lower position to ensure a high draft pick, there is incentive to avoid being relegated to a lower league.

As a useful comparison, what might this system look like if applied to Major League Baseball? Let's say that in a given year the team with the worst record in the National League was the San Diego Padres, and the team with the worst record in the America League was the Minnesota Twins. Next, let's say the team with the best record in the AAA-level International League was the Louisville Bats, and the team with the best record in the AAA-level Pacific Coast League was the Nashville Sounds. Applying the European scheme, the Bats would be promoted to the National League, while the Sounds would be promoted to the American League. Consequently, the Twins would be relegated to the Pacific Coast League, and the Padres would be relegated to the International League. "That sounds crazy," you say. "What about stadiums and season tickets and corporate sponsorships?" Although you may wonder how it could possibly work, promotion and relegation is a common practice in professional sport leagues outside of North America and has worked successfully for many years. Of course, as sport is structured currently, this could not apply to the NFL or even the NBA as they often primarily use college sport as the "minor leagues" to develop talent.

Player Movement Systems

In North American leagues, players are routinely traded, reassigned, released, or perhaps put on waivers. The player transaction system is collectively bargained between players associations and management, and federal and state labor laws are also involved. Deals are made involving players, players to be named later, future draft choices, and cash. Player movement systems are somewhat different when we look at professional sport outside of North America. In particular, we need to briefly touch on what is known as the transfer system. The system itself is quite complex (just like the complicated waiver systems in MLB), so the purpose here is just to make you aware of some of the basics.

Here in North America, children begin their sporting careers at rec leagues. The talented ones then move up through high school or Amateur Athletic Union (AAU) sport, and then to college, and a small fraction of them will make it to the professional level. In Europe, children will start their sporting careers playing for a local club. These clubs will have teams for various age levels and abilities, and will develop the talented players as they mature. Once these players become recognized for their talent, other higher level clubs will be interested in signing them, and the players will transfer their rights to a new club. In simple terms:

> Here's how a basic transfer works. Club 1 has a player. Club 2 wants a player. Club 2 and Club 1 thrash out an agreeable price, the player and Club 2 thrash out some agreeable wages, and then the transfer happens—the player's registration is transferred from Club 1 to Club 2, and he signs a new contract—and all parties are happy.
>
> (Thomas, 2014)

Of course, the process is not always this simple and sometimes will takes weeks and months to hammer out.

What about the transfer fee—how is that set? There is no exact formula for this, but here are the basic elements that factor in (Poli, Ravenel, & Besson, 2016):

> A first group of indicators concerns the characteristics of players such as age, position, length of contract remaining, and the residual book value. The latter variable is calculated from the transfer fee amount paid by the employer club, divided according to the percentage of years of contract since the signature.

A second group of indicators takes into account the players' performances, notably in terms of the amount of time played in the different club competitions (domestic leagues, cups) or, eventually, in national teams. Recent performances are given more weight than previous ones.

The last family of indicators refers to the level of the leagues where the footballers played their matches, as well as to the results obtained by the employer clubs. The level of the national team represented is also taken into account.

Once the transfer fee is set, it will include payment to the new club and payment to the player who then gives a cut to his agent. Just as a point of reference, transfer fees have been skyrocketing of late with players such as Cristiano Ronaldo, Gareth Bale, and Luis Suarez all seeing their transfer fees top US$100 million.

Another player transaction that takes place in leagues outside of North America is a loan deal. This more frequently takes pace with a younger player where the team who owns him would like to see him get the playing time he can't with his current club. The player could be loaned to a lower division team, a team in another country, and even occasionally another team in the same league. This gives his owning club the opportunity to observe the player and for the player to gain experience (Explaining Soccer, 2009). When a player is loaned, the team who actually owns the player typically pays his salary, although sometimes the salary is shared by both clubs. This is all determined by the negotiated loan deal. This is certainly something we are not accustomed to in North America. Could you imagine your favorite new young Golden State Warrior being loaned to the Clippers for a while to get more playing time?

Now that we have illustrated a few significant differences in policies in pro sport outside North America, let's have a look at a successful European football league—the English Premier League—and see how its governance structure operate.

FOOTBALL: PREMIER LEAGUE

www

Premier League
www.premierleague.com

Fédération Internationale de Football Association
www.fifa.com

Asian Football Confederation
http://www.the-afc.com

Confederation of African Football
www.cafonline.com

As an organized sport, football has been around for an extremely long time. Football played as a professional sport has a shorter past, however. In this section, we briefly trace the history of the Premier League; then we focus more directly on league operations and governance.

Before discussing specific leagues, let's look at the overall governance of international football. The IF for football, FIFA, is the international governing body for the game. FIFA consists of six regional organizations, including the Asian Football Confederation (AFC); the Confédération Africaine de Football (CAF); the Confederation of North, Central American and Caribbean Association Football (CONCACAF); the Confederación Sudamericana de Fútbol (CONMEBOL); the Oceania

Football Confederation (OFC); and UEFA. Within these regions, every nation has its own FIFA-recognized national football governing body, such as the US Soccer Federation, Canadian Soccer Association, Hellenic Football Federation in Greece, and the Deutscher-Fussball Bund in Germany. Professional football leagues within specific nations must belong to their FIFA-recognized national football governing body to be eligible to advance in international play. For example, in the United States, Major League Soccer (MLS) belongs to the US Soccer Federation. The US Soccer Federation, in turn, is a member of CONCACAF, which is the regional division of FIFA that includes North America. Because of this arrangement, MLS, or any FIFA-recognized professional football league in any nation, must follow the rules and regulations set forth by FIFA. Although the leagues have their own individual league governance systems for daily operation, they must follow many basic policies handed down from FIFA on issues such as drug use, match scheduling, and player transfers. Let's turn now to an example of what is widely considered the world's most successful international league—the English Premier League (EPL).

History

In the late 1980s, English football was in need of restructuring. A 1985 fire at a match at Bradford City Valley's Parade Grounds cost 56 lives when flames engulfed the wooden stadium (Conn, 2010). Around this same time, a number of violent incidents involving fans occurred. The game's image was in tatters, and it also suffered from a lack of financial investment. Establishing itself as a business entity separate from the nation's FA allowed the FA Premier League to negotiate its own television and sponsorship contracts, sources of income that have helped the league transition to its current success. The FA Premier League opening season took place in 1992–93 with 22 clubs (Premier League, 2017b). The league attracts players and fans from all over the world and is a successful business entity. In 2007, it changed its name to simply Premier League.

Governance

How is the EPL, with its independently operating clubs, governed? According to the Premier League (2017a, paras. 1–7), the flowing levels of governance exist:

> Each individual club is independent, working within the rules of football, as defined by the Premier League, The FA, UEFA and FIFA, as well being subject to English and European law.

> Each of the 20 clubs are a Shareholder in the Premier League. Consultation is at the heart of the Premier League and Shareholder meetings are the ultimate decision-making forum for Premier League policy and are held at regular intervals during the course of the season.

Confederation of North, Central American and Caribbean Association Football
www.concacaf.com

Confederación Sudamericana de Fútbol
www.conmebol.com

WWW

Oceania Football Confederation
www.oceaniafootball.com

Union of European Football Associations
www.uefa.com

US Soccer Federation
www.ussoccer.com

Canadian Soccer Association
www.canadasoccer.com

Major League Soccer
www.mlssoccer.com

The Premier League AGM [Annual General Meeting] takes place at the close of each season, at which time the relegated clubs transfer their shares to the clubs promoted into the Premier League from the Football League Championship.

Clubs have the opportunity to propose new rules or amendments at the Shareholder meeting. Each Member Club is entitled to one vote and all rule changes and major commercial contracts require the support of at least a two-thirds vote, or 14 clubs, to be agreed.

The Premier League Rule Book serves as a contract between the League, the Member Clubs and one another, defining the structure and running of the competition.

From this description, you can see that the EPL has an annual general assembly which is referred to as the AGM. This is the same as the General Assembly the International Olympic Committee (IOC) holds or the National Collegiate Athletic Association's (NCAA) annual convention. There is also a governing document called the Premier League Rule Book. This would be analogous to the IOC's Olympic Charter or the NCAA's division manuals.

MISSION.   Rather than calling it a mission statement, the Premier League follows the Chairmen's Charter found in Exhibit 14.1. You can see how the language in this Charter equates to a mission statement.

MEMBERSHIP.   The members of the privately owned EPL are the teams themselves. The Premier League is owned by 20 shareholders—the member clubs (e.g., Arsenal, Leicester, Man United, Newcastle, and 16 others). Nations large and small around the world have professional football leagues with clubs as the members. Some of the most notable, in addition to the Premier League in England, include the J. League in Japan, the Bundesliga in Germany, La Liga in Spain, Serie A in Italy, and MLS in the United States. This is in addition to multination leagues, such as the UEFA Champions League. These are all the top-level leagues in their respective countries. Lower level leagues exist as well. Different from the way MLB is organized, however, with designated minor league affiliates, these lower level league teams are not directly tied to teams at the highest level league. They are separate clubs. For example, the German Budesliga has 18 different clubs. The 2. Bundesliga also has 18 clubs operating independently from the Bundesliga teams. In Japan there is the J2 League and Spain has the Segunda Division, also known as La Liga 2.

FINANCIALS.   The sources of revenues for the EPL is similar to those in North America; they include merchandising programs, broadcast revenues, and corporate sponsorships, in addition to ticket sales. The following major corporations have official status with the Premier League:

Premier League Chairmen's Charter

exhibit   **14.1**

Season 2016/17

Foreword

The Chairmen's Charter is a statement of our commitment and aim to run Premier League football to the highest possible standards in a professional manner and with the utmost integrity.

With that aim we, the Chairmen of the Clubs in membership of the Premier League, are determined:

- To conduct our respective Club's dealings with the utmost good faith and honesty.
- At all times to maintain a Rule book which is comprehensive, relevant and up-to-date.
- To adopt disciplinary procedures which are professional, fair and objective.
- To submit to penalties which are fair and realistic.
- To secure the monitoring of and compliance with the Rules at all times.

The Charter The Chairmen's Charter sets out our commitment to run Premier League football to the highest possible standards and with integrity. We will ensure that our Clubs:

- Behave with the utmost good faith and honesty to each other, do not unjustly criticise or disparage one another and maintain confidences.
- Will comply with the laws of the game and take all reasonable steps to ensure that the Manager, his staff and Players accept and observe the authority and decisions of Match Officials at all times.
- Follow Premier League and FA Rules not only to the letter but also to their spirit, and will ensure that our Clubs and Officials are fully aware of such rules and that we have effective procedures to implement the same.
- Will respect the contractual obligations and responsibilities of each other's employees and not seek to breach these or to make illegal approaches.
- Will discharge their financial responsibilities and obligations to each other promptly and fully and not seek to avoid them.
- Will seek to resolve differences between each other without recourse to law.

Source: Premier League. (2016).

Lead Partner	EA Sports
Official Bank	Barclays
Official Snack Partner	Cadbury
Official Beer	Carling
Official Ball	Nike
Official Time Keeper	TagHeuer
Official Licensee	SportingiD
Official Licensee	Topps

The Premier League distributes broadcast and central income to its individual clubs to help support clubs to develop and acquire talented players, build and improve stadiums, and support communities (Premier League, 2017c). The value of the 2016–17 payouts to the 20 individual clubs totaled in excess of £2.3 billion (approximately US$2.9 billion). Each club received the same amounts in the categories overseas TV, central commercial, and equal share. Facility fees and merit payments differed by club. Chelsea (£150 million) received the highest amounts, while Sunderland (£93 million) was at the bottom of the payment plan.

WOMEN'S PROFESSIONAL SPORTS

Women's professional sport has been represented on the international stage for years. Basketball, football (soccer), tennis, golf, volleyball, and more are played on the professional level across the world, with athletes competing not only in their home countries, but internationally, finding the most competitive events and tournaments in which to participate. With sponsorships, lucrative contracts, and international acclaim available, women's sport at the international level continues to increase in popularity and opportunity.

The highest level of professional basketball for women in Europe, the EuroLeague, began its inaugural season in 1958 (FIBA, 2017). EuroLeague is followed in succession by the next most competitive professional basketball league, EuroCup, with MZRKL (Međunarodna ženska regionalna košarkaška liga), BWBL (Baltic Women's Basketball League), EEWBL (Eastern European Women's Basketball League), and CEWL (Central European Women's League) to follow (Eurobasket, 2017). For women's basketball, FIBA oversees both the EuroLeague and the EuroCup tiers, bringing the annual champions together for the SuperCup championship (FIBA, 2017).

The draw for American female athletes to enhance or subsidize their incomes by playing a season internationally has increased significantly in the past few decades, as the best and highest paid level of the sport is often played in Europe, Russia, or China. The UEFA Women's Champions League made headlines in 2017 when it drew US national team members Carli Lloyd and Alex Morgan to Manchester City's Academy Stadium in a head-to-head match as they represented their respective professional clubs (Evans, 2017). All-time WNBA leading scorer, Diana Taurasi, opted to sit out the 2015 WNBA season and solely play for her club in Russia, as they were paying her approximately 15 times more than her WNBA salary, approximately $1.5 million (Mumcu, 2015). Brittany Griner of the Phoenix Mercury made $61,800 base salary in the fourth year of her initial contract with the team, but made almost $1 million while playing for her EuroLeague team in Russia, UMMC Ekaterinburg (Metcalfe, 2017). However, depending on the sport and if a professional North American league is offered, American women often voluntarily take the pay cut in order to compete in the United States instead, prioritizing location over compensation. Former WNBA Most Valuable Player and 2016 Olympian, Elena Delle Donne, plays strictly in the WNBA, losing out on potential earnings in the seven-figure range, but by choosing not to play year-round could potentially elongate her career (Berkman, 2015).

The organizational structure of women's professional sport in Europe operates in many different ways, with some corporations representing a number of sport entities, most often including soccer and basketball for both men and women. For instance, Polish EuroLeague club CCC Polkowice sponsors not only a women's basketball team, but a professional women's mountain biking team (CCC Polkowice, 2017b). The organization employs a three-person Board of Directors, six Members of Honor, and is very active in the community with a youth group initiative (CCC Polkowice, 2017a). Some professional teams, on the contrary, are solely sponsored by a wealthy individual (Fagan, 2016).

ESPORTS

Another emerging trend beyond North America are eSports. The term, added to the dictionary in 2015, means competitive video game tournaments, especially among professional gamers (Chalk, 2015). eSports' growth over the past five years has been astounding, rising exponentially in a short timespan. In 2014, eSports revenue was $194 million. In 2016, the number rose to $493 million (Newzoo, 2016). The media rights, merchandise, ticket sales, advertising, sponsorships, and game publisher fees are estimated to reach $1.48 billion in the year 2020 (Warman, 2017). The revenues and industry value are increasing because more and more viewers are tuning in to see this new phenomenon. In 2015, an estimated 235 million viewers tuned in to watch eSports. Today, almost 400 million eSports fans watch their favorite eSport America. While the majority of fans are from the Asia-Pacific region (51 percent), Europe (18 percent) and North America (13 percent) provide a substantial amount of viewers (Warman, 2017). Interestingly, despite having only 13 percent of the viewers, the North American eSports market produced the most revenue, amassing $257 million in 2017 (mostly from sponsorships).

What exactly is eSport, though? As mentioned before, eSports are simply competitive video games. The biggest eSports include: League of Legends, Dota 2, Counter Strike: Global Offensive, Call of Duty, Hearthstone, Rocket League, and FIFA. eSports come in all shapes and sizes. League of Legends and Dota 2 are MOBAs (multi-player online battle arenas) where eSports control a character and work as a team to defeat the other team's base. Counter Strike: Global Offensive and Call of Duty are first person shooters. The goal is to defeat the entire team, capture the flag, or secure an objective using modern or futuristic weapons. Hearthstone is a unique eSport as it is a card game. Finally, Rocket League and FIFA are the popular sport video games based on soccer. As you can see, most eSports have nothing to do with sports, but contain more of a fantasy element. But, why are eSports considered sports by many? The parallels between eSports and physical sports provide that link: individuals practice 8 to 14 hours per day to be the best at their respective sport and they engage coaches, teammates, sport psychologists, leagues, tournaments, rules, prize pools, contracts, and many more along the way.

It is impossible to explain the governance structure for each individual eSports, as there are so many unique games. Instead, let's take a case study using eSports' most popular game, League of Legends, to examine the governance structure. League of Legends is a MOBA where teams of five play against one another. Each player picks his/her unique champion to command during the game. The goal of the game is to destroy the other team's turrets and, ultimately, destroy their base. League of Legends was created and released by a company called Riot Games in 2009 (Kollar, 2016). By 2011, Riot Games realized it had a great game to play *and* watch. The company announced a "Season One" for competitive League of Legends. The success of their first competitive season, roughly 100,000 concurrent viewers for the championship matches, lead Riot Games to think about investing into this idea of eSports. Instead of Riot Games letting other tournament organizers run competitive League of Legends tournaments, Riot Games decided to create an eSport division of their organization. That is right, Riot Games not only created video games, but they ran eSport events. The strictly video game company was going to add a division to their organization that included: event operations, broadcasting, sponsorships, merchandising, policy development and enforcement, and other areas we commonly associate with physical sport.

The gamble paid off as the league has grown in multiple ways. League of Legends has multiple leagues in North America, Europe, South Korea, China, Taiwan, South America, and Oceania. Each league has between eight and ten teams that play in two splits: Spring and Summer. Riot Games provides teams with money for a minimal salary for each player (although teams can pay more than the minimum), salary for coaches, and operations for the teams. Many of the teams, including the big names like Cloud9 and Team Solo Mid, have gaming houses where the players live and practice during their seasons. In between the Spring and Summer splits, Riot hosts international tournaments and All-Star games between the regions for fun. The best three teams over the Spring and Summer splits get to go to the World Championships against the other regions to see who is the best in a group stage and tournament stage (similar to the World Cup). The 2016 League of Legends World Championship had 14.7 million concurrent viewers (remember when it was only 100,000 in season one?) and 43 million unique viewers. In terms of money, $6.7 million dollars were given to the teams ($3 million from fans, $2.1 million for them original prize pool, and $1.6 million from icons the average player could buy for their favorite team). In addition, there were 23 broadcasts in 18 languages, and over 370 hours of live eSports were viewed across the globe (Bradmore & Magus, 2016).

Some of the major issues in eSports include: doping policies and gambling. Doping by the players is a major issue. While energy drinks like RedBull are common in eSports, the use of Adderall is problematic. Adderall is a drug prescribed to individuals with attention deficit hyperactivity disorder (ADHD) that provides improved focus, alertness, and working memory. The drug can dangerously increase the heart rate and blood pressure of an individual abusing the drug (Loria, 2016). eSports organizers have to balance the abuse of the drug by those who do not have ADHD with those who need the drug to combat their diagnosed ADHD. Another issue in eSports is the presence of gambling. Esports were born and increased in popularity because of the Internet, where anyone can access betting and gambling. The Gambling Commission, a departmental public body of the United Kingdom responsible for supervising and regulating gambling, has contacted over 100 unlicensed online gambling sites since 2014. The major concern is the opportunity for young people, the main viewers of eSports, to have easy access to gambling before the age of 18 via the Internet (Gerrard, 2017).

CURRENT POLICY AREAS

Just as with professional sport in North America, international professional sport faces a broad range of policy issues. These issues include fighting racism in football, security issues, and the potential impact of Brexit.

Racism in Football

Unforgivable as it is as we begin to approach the mid-21st century, racism is as rampant in many parts of the world as it is in the United States. The past years have seen a continuing number of incidents involving racist behavior on the part of football fans. Unfortunately, racism is still quite alive in some sectors of European football. Partizan Belgrade's Brazilian midfielder Everton Luiz left the field in tears at the end of a 2017 Serbian championship match between Partizan and Rad, after racist remarks from Rad's supporters. Every time he touched the ball, a group of supporters of Rad Belgrade monkey-screamed (Kerr-Dineen, 2017). Ghanian Sulley Muntari endured similar treatment in a match in Italy (Harris, 2017). The examples are all too easy to list. Sport managers need to step up to fight against this onslaught of ignorant behavior and continue to educate the public with messages until the racist behaviors at sporting events end.

So what have sport organizations done to deal with this issue? At the 2010 World Cup in South Africa, the "Say No to Racism" message was expressed often and visibly. FIFA dedicated all four of the quarter finals to spreading the word against racism. Players and officials held banners on the field reading "Say No to Racism" before these games, and team captains read pre-match pledges against racism. In addition, all the stadiums where

www

Football Against Racism in Europe
www.farenet.org

Unite Against Racism
www.uefa.com/
multimediafiles/download/
uefa/keytopics/448328_
download.pdf

matches were played were equipped with a racism monitoring system using trained security personnel (FIFA, 2011).

UEFA (2017, para. 6) has chosen to take a stand through its Unite Against Racism program:

> The No to Racism message aims to increase public awareness of intolerance and discrimination in football, as well as developing ideas and strategies on how to fight them. On the club competition matchday dedicated to the campaign, team captains wear No to Racism armbands, anti-racism messages are played over clubs' public address systems and a video containing player testimonials backing the campaign is shown in stadiums. A No to Racism pennant is also prominently on show, held by players. At the start of every match, "No to Racism" banners are prominently displayed on the pitch.

What specific steps can sport managers take? In 2006, UEFA (2006, p. 18) offered the following ten-point program for football associations and clubs which is still useful today:

1. Issue a statement saying that racism or any other kind of discrimination will not be tolerated, spelling out the action that will be taken against those who engage in racist chanting. The statement should be printed in all match programmes and displayed permanently and prominently around the ground.
2. Make public address announcements condemning racist chanting at matches.
3. Make it a condition for season ticket holders that they do not take part in racist abuse.
4. Take action to prevent the sale of racist literature inside and around the ground.
5. Take disciplinary action against players who engage in racial abuse.
6. Contact other associations or clubs to make sure they understand the association's or club's policy on racism.
7. Encourage a common strategy between stewards and police for dealing with racist abuse.
8. Remove all racist graffiti from the ground as a matter of urgency.
9. Adopt an equal opportunities' policy in relation to employment and service provision.
10. Work with all other groups and agencies, such as the players' union, supporters, schools, voluntary organisations, youth clubs, sponsors, local authorities, local businesses and the police, to develop proactive programmes and make progress to raise awareness of campaigning to eliminate racial abuse and discrimination.

FIFA has just recently given referees the authority to stop a match if they deem racist activity is taking place. On the eve of the Confederations

Cup qualifiers for FIFA's 2018 World Cup in Russia, referees now have the option to abandon a match in the face of abusive racist behavior by fans. In addition, FIFA released the following statement (Collins, 2017, para. 3):

> FIFA is reinforcing its fight against discrimination in football with the introduction of a new anti-discrimination monitoring system for the 2018 FIFA World Cup™ qualifiers. The system includes the deployment of Anti-Discrimination Match Observers to monitor and report issues of discrimination at the games. It will be coordinated by FIFA and implemented in collaboration with the Fare network, an organisation with long experience in the fight against discrimination in football and the deployment of match observers.

Ethical issues facing sport managers have been woven throughout this text. On this particular topic, sport managers have the opportunity to step up and do the right in taking steps to combat racism. Sport has the power to inform, the power to empower, the power to transform (Hums & Wolff, 2014). Sport managers have the opportunity to use their platforms in sport to help fight the international scourge of racism.

Security Issues

Similar to what we see in North America, security at major sporting events is a priority for sport managers in international settings as well. For example, Bayern Munich established tighter security measures at the beginning of its 2016–17 season. Now banned from stadiums are items including bottles, thermos flasks, and liquids. Handbags and backpacks—larger than A4 size—are also not allowed in their home stadium, Allianz Arena (Lovell, 2016). Bundesliga officials routinely review security measures. Since the 2016 attack in Paris, where explosions took place outside the Stade de France, coupled with the Berlin Christmas market attack, officials have been even more mindful, and Germany's stadiums are considered among the safest in the world (Deutsche Welle, 2016).

Other sport organizations have taken note of the need for increased security measures as well. After the 2017 attack at the Manchester Arena after an Ariana Grande concert, the International Cricket Council (ICC) reviewed security policies for its ICC Championship Trophy (AS.com, 2017). Top sporting officials and security officials decided to ramp up security for the "El Classico" match between Real Madrid and Barcelona after the Paris attacks (Reuters, 2017).

The international security agency INTERPOL established a ten-year plan called Project Stadia that was designed to help sport managers of major sporting events manage the security challenges associated with those events (INTERPOL, 2016). Relying on the best practices of locations which have successfully hosted events, INTERPOL makes this information available to sport managers hosting events. Project Stadia includes expert groups, security observations, and debriefing programs, training, conferences, and a stadia knowledge management system. This stadia knowledge management system includes (INTERPOL, 2016, p. 2):

> The learning accrued from the range of activities described above is consolidated and shared among all INTERPOL member countries via a state-of-the-art web-based knowledge management system with two components:
>
> - A comprehensive knowledge repository of good practices in all aspects of sporting event security, which all member countries can contribute to and benefit from;
> - An online collaborative platform where experts in the field can share, discuss, analyse and publish information on the evolving aspects of major sporting event security.

Sport managers will need to continue to be cooperative with local, national, and international agencies in their best attempt to keep their patrons, workers, and athletes as safe as possible. Vigilance is of the essence.

The Potential Impact of Brexit

As of this writing, the vote in the United Kingdom known worldwide as Brexit is still playing out. The issue of interest in this chapter is the potential impact of Brexit on the international sport business sector. Two big question marks remain: the affect on transfer fees and also on work permits (Aarons, 2016). Officials of the Premier League acknowledge the unknowns that face the sport and yet they hope the League's long-standing domestic success will lessen the impact of the vote on the sport industry. For example, according to attorney Paul Shapiro:

> British football clubs may find themselves only able to sign foreign players over the age of 18 as, outside the EU/EEA [European Union/European Economic Area], they would no longer be able to benefit from the exception under the current FIFA regulations given for transfers involving 16 and 17 year old footballers within the EU/EEA . . . If EU law ceases to apply in the UK, the organisers of sports competitions may be able to more effectively restrict the number of foreign players that feature in matchday squads as they could potentially include EU nationals and Kolpak players within any foreign player quota. (quoted in Aarons, 2016, paras. 16–17)

Some experts believe that football will respond by relaxing some of its current work permit rules. "I would be surprised if those work permit rules were not recalibrated," said Professor Raymond Boyle, from the University of Glasgow. The sports industry expert added: "Countries such as Switzerland simply make their own rules. My sense is that elite commercial sport will always have the clout to influence rules so that they benefit" (quoted in Slater, 2016, paras. 31–32).

Regardless of how this all plays out, the fallout from the vote once again reinforces the fact that sport and politics of world events are intertwined. No matter how much we may want to keep politics out of sport, in this day and age, there is no separating the two. The impact of Brexit will be an ongoing saga and sport managers must be continually informed as to the latest developments.

SUMMARY

The world of international professional sport is complex. The interrelationships among professional leagues, IFs, regional federations, and NGBs are unlike any in North America. The promotion and relegation system does not operate in major North American leagues, although it would be interesting to see how that could play out. The player transfer system in European soccer is a completely different mechanism than that used in North America. Despite these differences, similarities exist, particularly when it comes to player movement between teams and corporate sponsorship concerns. Professional sport beyond North America includes more than just the traditional leagues, and has seen rapid growth in the expanding eSports market. Women's sports have a place in the international sportscape as well, with some leagues being lucrative to lure the top female athletes away from North American leagues such as the WNBA. Finally, sport managers working in this international realm need to be aware of and make proactive decisions in terms of fighting racism in football, security issues, and the potential impact of Brexit. What is important to realize after reading is chapter is how global a product sport really is and how many opportunities exist beyond North American shores.

case STUDY

PROFESSIONAL SPORT BEYOND NORTH AMERICA

The time for you to start planning your internship is quickly approaching. After reading this book (especially this chapter), you realize opportunities exist for you to pursue internships in nations outside of North America. The opportunities include professional sports, national sport organizations, IFs, and major games and events.

1. List a number of nations you would like to live in or visit.
2. List a number of international organizations, sports, or events you would consider for an internship.
3. How can you find out more detailed information about these international sport organizations?

4. Ask if any of your classmates have either visited or lived in other parts of the world. What questions would you like to ask them about their experiences? Did they attend any sporting events? If so, what was the fan experience like compared to games here in North America?

5. Have you ever attended a sporting event in another country? If so, what was the fan experience like compared to games here in North America?

6. What are three specific industry experiences an international internship could offer you that a domestic internship could not?

7. How do you see the global face of the sport industry changing in the next ten years?

CHAPTER questions

1. Choose another professional sport league outside of North America and research its history, mission, membership, financials, and governance structure.

2. Choose a nation outside of North America. Research the different professional sport opportunities available in that nation.

3. In addition to the governance structures described in this chapter, some nations also have a governmental agency that oversees all sports, including professional sport, in that nation. Sometimes this agency is named the Ministry of Sport. If such a structure were created in the United States, who should serve on it, and how should it be organized?

4. What are your thoughts on promotion and relegation being used in North American professional leagues? MLB? MLS?

FOR ADDITIONAL INFORMATION

1. How FIFA Works: FIFA. (2017). How FIFA works: www.fifa.com/governance/how-fifa-works/index.html

2. Youtube: International Sports Convention's Sports Integrity and Governance: https://www.youtube.com/watch?v=ciV1UZGHtHw

3. EuroLeague 2016–17 Bylaws: Turkish Airlines Euroleague. (2016). 2016–2017 Turkish Airlines EuroLeague bylaws: www.euroleague.net/rs/7d48dq8t934dpg99/84bd1f8d-134d-42a0-a8ee-cd688d29aaa2/fff/filename/2016-17-euroleague-bylaws-book-19-october-2016.pdf

4. eSport Governing Body: Lynch, A. (2016, May 13). Esports' newest governing body wants to be the FIFA of video games. *FoxSports*:

www.foxsports.com/buzzer/story/esports-wesa-governing-body-counter-strike-global-offensive-cs-go-league-of-legends-051316

5. FIFA Stadium Safety and Security Regulations: FIFA. (2017). FIFA stadium safety and security regulations: https://www.fifa.com/mm/document/tournament/competition/51/53/98/safetyregulations_e.pdf

6. RealMadrid Basketball: RealMadrid. (2017). Baloncesto: www.realmadrid.com/baloncesto

REFERENCES

Aarons, E. (2016, June 24). Brexit vote: What does it mean for professional sport in the UK? *The Guardian*. Retrieved from https://www.theguardian.com/uk-news/2016/jun/24/brexit-vote-what-does-it-mean-professional-sport-eu

AS.com. (2017). ICC to review security measures for Champions Trophy after Manchester terror strike. Retrieved from http://en.as.com/en/2017/05/25/football/1495741401_007459.html

Berkman, S. (2015, July 24). Elena Delle Donne emerges as face of the WNBA. *New York Times*. Retrieved from https://www.nytimes.com/2015/07/25/sports/basketball/elena-delle-donne-emerges-as-face-of-the-wnba.html

Bradmore & Magus (2016, December 6). 2016 League of Legends World Championships by the numbers. Retrieved from www.lolesports.com/en_US/articles/2016-league-legends-world-championship-numbers

CCC Polkowice. (2017a). Klub. Retrieved from http://kosz.mkspolkowice.pl/klub.html

CCC Polkowice. (2017b). Main website. Retrieved from http://mkspolkowice.pl

Chalk, A. (2015, May 8). "Esports" is now officially in the dictionary. Retrieved from www.pcgamer.com/esports-is-now-officially-in-the-dictionary/

CNN. (2012). Croatia faces fresh Euro 2012 racism probe. Retrieved from http://edition.cnn.com/2012/06/20/sport/football/euro-2012-croatia-racism-new/index.html

Collins, P. (2017, June 16). FIFA will allow referees to end matches threatened by racial tension. Retrieved from https://sports.good.is/articles/fifa-referees-racism

Collinson, S. (2017, July 4). The world looks past Donald Trump. Retrieved from www.cnn.com/2017/07/04/politics/world-looks-past-donald-trump/index.html

Conn, D. (2010, May 11). Bradford remembered: The unheeded warnings that led to tragedy. *The Guardian*. Retrieved from www.guardian.co.uk/football/david-conn-inside-sport-blog/2010/may/12/bradford-fire-david-conn

Deutsche Welle. (2016). Berlin attack forces reassessment of security at Bundesliga games. Retrieved from www.dw.com/en/berlin-attack-forces-reassessment-of-security-at-bundesliga-games/a-36843910

Eurobasket. (2017). The complete history of European clubs competitions. Retrieved from www.eurobasket.com/othercups.asp

Evans, S. (2017, April 23). Europe becomes a new destination for American women soccer stars. *Reuters*. Retrieved from www.reuters.com/article/us-soccer-women-europe-americans-idUSKBN17Q043

Explaining soccer. (2009). In soccer, what is a transfer and how does it work? Retrieved from http://explainingsoccer.typepad.com/explaining-soccer/2009/07/in-soccer-what-is-a-transfer-and-how-does-it-work.html

Fagan, K. (2016, May 5). Lost and found in Russia. ESPNw. Retrieved from www.espn.com/espn/feature/story/_/page/espnw-russia160505/brittney-griner-diana-taurasi-opted-play-russia-money-escape-spotlight

FIBA. (2017). SuperCup women. Retrieved from www.fiba.com/supercup-women

Gerrard, B. (2017, May 13). From gaming to gambling: The rising risk of esports. Retrieved from www.telegraph.co.uk/business/2017/05/13/gaming-gambling-rising-risk-esports/

Harris, R. (2017, March 4). Racism scars European soccer with sanctions still often weak. Retrieved from https://www.apnews.com/e6ab521552b64a399f79a223d8006e5e/Racism-scars-European-soccer-with-sanctions-still-often-weak

Hums, M. A., & Svensson, P. (in press). International sport. In L. P. Masteralexis, C. A. Barr, & M. A. Hums, *Principles and practice of sport management* (6th ed.). Burlington, MA: Jones & Bartlett Publishers.

Hums, M. A., & Wolff, E. A. (2014, April 3). Power of sport to inform, empower, and transform. *Huffington Post*. Retrieved from www.huffingtonpost.com/dr-mary-hums/power-of-sport-to-inform-_b_5075282.html?utm_hp_ref=sports&ir=Sports

INTERPOL. (2016). *Project stadia*. Lyon, France: Author.

Kerr-Dineen, L. (2017. Feb. 20). Soccer player left the field in tears after suffering horrific racial abuse. *USA Today*. Retrieved from http://ftw.usatoday.com/2017/02/this-soccer-player-left-field-in-tears-after-horrific-monkey-chants-now-hes-speaking-out-against-racist-abuse

Kollar, P. (2016, September 13). The past, present and future of League of Legends studio Riot Games. Retrieved from https://www.polygon.com/2016/9/13/12891656/the-past-present-and-future-of-league-of-legends-studio-riot-games

Loria, K. (2016, January 15). Some competitive video gamers are abusing drugs to get an edge. *Business Insider*. Retrieved from www.businessinsider.com/esports-doping-scandal-investigated-by-espns-otl-2016-1

Lovell, M. (2016, August 24). Bayern Munich tighten security ahead of new Bundesliga season. Retrieved from www.espnfc.us/bayern-munich/story/2936379/bayern-munich-tighten-security-ahead-of-new-bundesliga-season

Metcalfe, J. (2017, March 12). Phoenix Mercury, Brittney Griner reach multi-year contract agreement. AZCentral. Retrieved from www.azcentral.com/story/sports/wnba/mercury/2017/03/12/phoenix-mercury-brittney-griner-reach-multi-year-contract-agreement/99052300/

Mumcu, C. (2015, August 31). Overseas opportunities could be a boon for WNBA, players. *Sports Business Journal*. Retrieved from www.sportsbusinessdaily.com/Journal/Issues/2015/08/31/Opinion/Ceyda-Mumcu.aspx

Newzoo. (2016, August 31). Esports revenues for 206 adjusted upward to $493M. Retrieved from https://newzoo.com/insights/articles/esports-revenues-2016-adjusted-upward-493m/

Pitts, B. G., & Zhang, J. J. (2016). Introduction: The WASM foundation stone. In B. G. Pitts & J. J. Zhang (Eds.), *Global sport management: Contemporary issues and inquiries* (pp. 3–18). London: Routledge.

Poli, R., Ravenel, L. & Besson, R. (2016). Transfer values and probabilities: The CIES Football Observatory approach. Retrieved from www.football-observatory.com/IMG/sites/mr/mr16/en/

Premier League. (2016). *Premier League handbook*. London: Author.

Premier League. (2017a). About us. Retrieved from www.premierleague.com/en-gb/about/who-we-are.html

Premier League. (2017b, June 10). Premier League history. Retrieved from https://www.premierleague.com/news/59001

Premier League. (2017c, June 1). Premier League value of central payments to clubs. Retrieved from https://www.premierleague.com/news/405400

Reuters. (2017, June 25). Stiff security measures in place for El Classico. Retrieved from http://gulfnews.com/sport/football/la-liga/stiff-security-measures-in-place-for-el-clasico-1.1622828

Slater, M. (2016, March 31). EU referendum: Brexit could have "big effect" on football. Retrieved from www.bbc.com/sport/football/35919247

Szymanski, S. (2006). The promotion and relegation system. In W. Andreff & S. Szymanski (Eds.), *Handbook on the economics of sport* (pp. 685–688). London: Edward Elgar.

Szymanski, S., & Valetti, T. (2003). Promotion and relegation in sporting contests. Retrieved from https://pennstatelaw.psu.edu/_file/Szymanski%20Valetti%20promotion%20relegation.pdf

Thomas, A. (2014, July 28). The European soccer transfer market explained. Retrieved from https://www.sbnation.com/soccer/2014/7/28/5923187/transfer-window-soccer-europe-explained

UEFA. (2006). Tackling racism in club football: A guide for clubs. Retrieved from www.uefa.com/MultimediaFiles/Download/uefa/KeyTopics/448328_DOWNLOAD.pdf

UEFA. (2017). No to racism. Retrieved from www.uefa.org/social-responsibility/respect/no-to-racism/index.html

Warman, P. (2017, February 14). Esports revenues will reach $696 million this year and grow to $1.5 billion by 2020 as brand investment doubles. Retrieved from https://newzoo.com/insights/articles/esports-revenues-will-reach-696-million-in-2017/

The Future of
Sport Governance

Mary A. Hums
Joanne C. MacLean

What will sport governance look like in the future? In this chapter, the authors go back and visit each chapter in the textbook and discuss topics that sport managers in these industry segments may face going forward. This chapter takes a crystal-ball approach to predicting potential future governance and policy initiatives discussed in each of the sport industry chapters in this book. Change within organizations is presented, in order to understand the importance of planned change, pressures for change, goals of planned change, and procedures for organizational change. An operational change process is presented. Issues related to competitive opportunities for disabled high school athletes, harnessing new forms of financial and human resources in amateur community sport, outsourcing facility management in campus recreation, pay from outside sources for college athletes, security and safety at major games, including the Olympic, Paralympics, and professional events, and the future growth of women's professional sports are discussed, along with other potential changes in sport governance. This chapter provides a brief list of these topics, but hopefully the chapter will help generate discussion about where the industry, and the people who manage it, will be in the years to come.

A future without change would be pretty bleak. Imagine if everything always stayed the same—the same people, same events, same physical layout, same schedule. Consider a professional basketball franchise: what if the rosters and schedules never changed, the competition was always the same, the team's social media sites were static, and the arena was never upgraded? For fans, this scenario would be boring and lack energy, and over time it simply would be no fun. While an unchanging situation can be problematic, the exact opposite—rapid or unplanned change—can be equally difficult. Rapid change can be unsettling, creating confusion and uncertainty. Suppose the roster of the basketball team was shuffled every week, so that no one could follow who played for which team. NBA (National Basketball Association) fans would find it impossible to feel loyalty for a team that changes players so quickly. A world without change is inconceivable, and a world in constant, rapid, and unplanned change can be chaotic.

Change is nonetheless important and inevitable. Change is often a component of progress; viewed with hope, it provides not just different, but better, ways of doing things. Sport organizations are perfect illustrations of the importance of change and the negative results accruing from overly rapid or poorly planned change.

To grow and thrive, a sport organization must be able to change and adapt to its environment. Factors in the environment include its size, members, competition, strategy, and technology (Byers, Slack, & Parent, 2012; Chelladurai, 2014). As the size or membership of an organization grows, it changes to best serve its constituents. The organization defines strategy based on its competition and adapts to effectively utilize technology. Consider the National Olympic Committees (NOCs) in Chapter 10. The United States Olympic Committee (USOC) is a good illustration of an NOC that changed its operating structure to effectively deliver its mandate. As the Olympic Games evolved from a world festival of sport into a multi-million-dollar extravaganza and a stage for political agendas, the USOC changed to accommodate this new environment, while still effectively delivering services to its members. The importance of winning Olympic medals as part of the national political agenda of United States was one factor providing impetus for organizational change. This organizational change involved a substantial reduction to the size of the USOC Board of Directors, changes to the Executive Committee powers and the focus of the Olympic Assembly.

One major concern to sport managers as their organizations undergo change is the pressure of future economic survival. The world economy fluctuates. During a recession like 2008, government and institutional spending on high school and college or university athletic and recreation programs is in jeopardy, as well as funding for city and municipal recreation programs. Political changes result in new priorities (such as the new leadership in the US which has decided to cut funding to USAID, an organization which supports development through sport around the world), leaves some sport organizations scrambling for budgets. Professional sport, as well as Olympic and Paralympic sport, which rely on corporate sponsorships, also feel pressure as corporations make decisions about how much to invest in sport properties. Increased financial pressure, coupled with changing economic environments, present sport managers with a complex future.

This chapter completes our look at the governance of sport organizations. Its purpose is to look at the future of governance in the sport industry segments described in this text. Predicting the future, of course, is risky business. However, the future surely involves the continued evolution of sport organizations to meet the needs of their various stakeholders. The globalization of business practices, including the business of sport, has resulted in unprecedented change evolving faster than ever before (Covell & Walker, 2013). We hope such change will be planned change, as opposed to forced change.

CHANGE WITHIN ORGANIZATIONS

Structures and governance policies of sport organizations evolve to improve effectiveness. The importance of change for sport organizations is in keeping with business and other organizations worldwide. Beer and Nohria's (2000) earlier comment is still relevant today: "The demands of an ever competitive and changing environment are increasing the need for knowledge about how to lead and manage organizational change rapidly, efficiently, and effectively. The management mantra as we enter the 21st century is 'lead change'" (p. ix). Change should be planned and strategic, not some revolving door, constantly shuffling in new ideas while bouncing out the old.

According to Slack and Parent (2006), planned change can occur in four different areas of a sport organization: (1) the structures and systems of the organization, (2) the conduct of the organization's personnel, (3) the products and services delivered through the organization, or (4) the technology supporting the organization. So where do the pressures for change originate?

Pressures for Change

Pressure for organizational change may originate from three sources (Brill & Worth, 1997):

1. events occurring within the organization
2. factors arising outside the organization
3. an interaction of external and internal factors

For example, the National Collegiate Athletic Association (NCAA) membership provided the impetus for restructuring the organization into divisions based on the changing philosophical perspectives of its members. In the past, changes in legislation and rules were made at the organization's annual meeting, where members from all divisions met together. When voting on issues, every school had one vote, and all divisions voted on all issues. Today the Division I, II, and III categories are taken for granted in the governance structure of the organization. In 2015, the NCAA granted autonomy to five "Power" conferences including the ACC (Atlantic Coast Conference), Big Ten, Big 12, Pac-12, and SEC (Southeastern Conference), allowing them to pass legislation through their own voting process (Trahan, 2015). The changing perspectives of various institutions within the organization provided the impetus for this change.

NCAA sanctions on Penn State as a result of the Jerry Sandusky child abuse case is illustrative of change resulting from outside the organization. In 2012 Jerry Sandusky, former assistant football coach at Penn State, was convicted of 45 counts of criminal child sex abuse, with some aspects covered up over the years by university officials. The NCAA fined the institution $60 million, banned competition in all postseason play for four years, reduced initial scholarships, vacated the institution's 112 wins from 1998 to 2011, and served the university with a five-year probationary term.

For an example of a combination of internal and external pressures, one could look at the 2012 decision to institute an NCAA Division I national football championship play-off with four teams. Many people, including fans, some lawmakers, and even the President of the United States, were unhappy with the Bowl Championship Series (BCS) system to determine a national champion, and there was a continued outpouring of sentiment to have a play-off. The NCAA thus moved, albeit slowly, to implement a four-team, three-game playoff that incorporates the major bowl games.

The new format will take effect for the 2014–15 season, incorporating two national semifinal games that will rotate among the major bowl games, and a national championship game hosted at a neutral site.

Sport organizations work within fairly complex environments, both internally and externally. What are the goals of planned organizational change?

Goals of Planned Change

Planned change involves the systematic development and initiation of new modes of operating to gain competitive advantage. As stated above, it may be prompted by the need for action resulting from events internal or external to the organization or both. The goal of planned change within a sport organization likely involves either matters of finance or organizational capability (Byers, Slack, & Parent, 2012). The impetus for change often results from financial belt-tightening within an organization. Specifically, a goal often involves increasing revenues or decreasing expenditures, or both, in an effort to balance the budget or enhance organizational services. When finances are not at the root of planned change, improving the organization's effectiveness usually is. In this case the purpose of planned change is to enhance the organization's capacity to respond better to its environment. Furthermore, the goal might be to move from *responding* to the environment to proactively *shaping* the environment. Achieving this second goal allows an organization to exercise more control over future directions and be on the cutting edge of the industry. Understanding the goals of planned change within an organization is important in determining a strategy for change. How is such change initiated, and what procedures are used to invoke organizational change?

Procedures for Organizational Change

Planned change occurs when several stages of activities result in organizational action (Byers, Slack, & Parent, 2012). Change carries the most influence when it comes simultaneously from sources both within and outside the organization. Often the request for change is either initiated by or blocked by senior management depending on their perspectives of organizational needs. If change is supported, a consultant may be used to initiate planning and to overcome hesitancy to change. Second, the specific problem prompting change is diagnosed and recognized throughout all the levels of the organization. Third, solutions to the problems are proposed, and a commitment to a course of action is sought by testing several possible solutions. Finally, change is implemented through a number of small-scale decisions serving to reinforce a course of action and acceptance of larger-scale associated changes. This change process is presented in Exhibit 15.1.

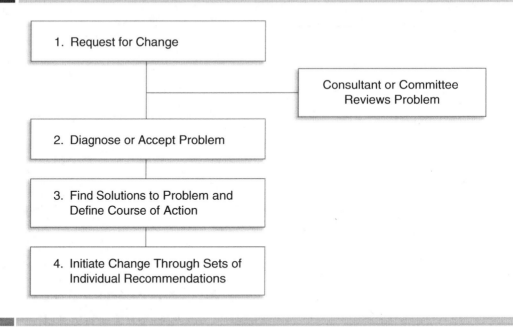

exhibit **15.1** Organizational Change Process

1. Request for Change

Consultant or Committee Reviews Problem

2. Diagnose or Accept Problem

3. Find Solutions to Problem and Define Course of Action

4. Initiate Change Through Sets of Individual Recommendations

FUTURE INDUSTRY SEGMENT ISSUES

Change within organizations is often slow and difficult. The previous chapters of this book outlined governance structure and policy development for several segments of the sport industry. Let's look briefly at some of the issues that might cause change within those segments.

Scholastic Sport

Today's youth has more opportunities than ever to participate in organized sport, from year-round traveling soccer teams and Amateur Athletic Union (AAU) basketball competitions, to sports offered in the European club model, Little League Baseball, summer camps, and more. While having such opportunities to participate is very positive, it also creates a more competitive climate for scholastic sport. Should a child play on a year-round soccer team or for the local high school team? Club sports, particularly AAU volleyball, soccer, and basketball, are becoming increasingly popular and are often the venue where young athletes showcase their talent for college coaches. Should a young athlete specialize in one sport all year, or change sports every season? Although even coaches at the professional level say they prefer multi-sport athletes to those who specialize, parents often feel the pressure to do what they think will help their child succeed. Often these choices are driven by the thought that the more visible the competition level is to college coaches, the more likely it is that the young athlete will have an opportunity for a college scholarship. But what is most important is sometimes lost—what does the child him/herself actually want to do?

These considerations lead to another key issue—what is the purpose of high school sport? Is it participation, healthy activity, and socialization, or is it preparation for intercollegiate athletics? A college education is a basic expectation, but these days as tuition costs rise and the world economy stumbles, parents are looking for alternative ways to finance their children's education. Although the odds are against it, many parents in the United States see athletic scholarships as a way to cover these costs, and they see high school sport as the platform for their child's future success.

Sometimes high school sport becomes an even higher platform. Increasingly, high school athletes consider jumping directly into the professional ranks. National high school rankings and national high school All Star tournaments are now commonplace. High school sport governing bodies must make decisions about which types of tournaments to sanction and must examine more closely their definitions of *amateurism*. Athletes in baseball and hockey have the opportunity to sign professional contracts directly out of high school and then move on to the minor leagues to hone their talents. This is not the case with football or basketball. The NBA's rule on higher age restrictions for rookies has stemmed the tide of high school athletes trying to go directly to the NBA. In the future, high school sport governing bodies, in concert with college and professional sport organizations, will need to continually revisit important philosophical questions about the basic nature of high school sports.

The Dear Colleague Letter issued in early 2013 by the US Department of Education has also opened the doors for high school students with disabilities to have competitive opportunities. As mentioned in the chapter on high school sport, these guidelines have been hailed as the Title IX for individuals with disabilities. It will be interesting to see how state high school athletic associations, school districts, and individual schools creatively respond. A number of state high school athletic associations are now offering sanctioned competitions for athletes with disabilities, a positive step that was quite overdue.

Finally, the issue of funding for high school sports needs to be addressed. More and more corporate dollars are being invested in interscholastic sport. In addition, some individual high schools are selling naming rights to their stadiums and entering into deals with companies such as Nike and Under Armour. In many ways, the intercollegiate financing model is trickling down to high school sport. The implications of high school sport becoming more commercialized and reliant on outside funding through sponsorship are twofold. First, it will impact the competition for sponsorship dollars as sponsoring organizations have another sector seeking external funding and sponsorship beyond amateur, collegiate, and professional sport. Second, it may result in elevating high school competitions to levels expected of entertainment properties such as professional sport, which involves high costs and may further contribute to potential budget pressures for administrators. Some may question this increasing commercialization of high school sport and whether it will influence the basic premise for why high school sport exists, which is to augment the education experience. Yet without these alternative funding sources, some students may lose out on the opportunities for these experiences.

Amateur Sport in the Community

Amateur community sport is the grassroots of competitive athletics. However, individuals in administrative positions will very likely be challenged to maintain the current breadth of programming. Kids are playing more and more hours of digital games in place of physical activities and sports. At the same time, sports groups are challenged to compete for resources. Regardless of age group or type of sport, it takes significant human and financial resources to deliver programs. Competition for facilities is fierce. Finding people to coach, officiate, and organize programming is becoming more and more difficult, and requires criminal record checks for volunteers. While public sport organizations will continue to strive to deliver recreational sport leagues, a lack of funding coupled with deteriorating infrastructure will create a major impetus for change. Policy decisions at the municipal or state level will unsuccessfully attempt to create larger sources of funding to renovate facilities, and thus sport organizations will focus more time on securing facilities in addition to program delivery. Current user fees will likely be increased to produce a larger revenue source. Personnel recruitment will be given higher priority, along with volunteer training. Competition among public and private groups will create an environment more accepting of change, spurred on by the importance of making use of every opportunity. Programming innovations and offerings will need to adapt to changing demographics, as the populations of seniors and racial and ethnic minorities continue to increase. The future success of the Y, YWCA (Young Women's Christian Association), JCC (Jewish Community Center), Boys & Girls Clubs, and city parks and recreation departments will depend largely on their leadership and the ability of their Boards of Directors to understand the competition, to harness new forms of financial and human resources, and to enact policy that will take advantage of and accommodate shifting interests and trends for amateur athletes.

Campus Recreation

The leaders of campus recreation programs will oversee unprecedented change in the next decade. The future will be one of balancing service and customer-care issues in state-of-the-art facilities, while managing all user groups. Innovative programming will be critical for success as the recreational interests of the various user groups change. In the past, campus recreation programming and facilities were primarily for constituent groups of the campus, including students, staff, faculty, and perhaps immediate family members. This mandate will continue to broaden as programs include members from the community. This might well involve parallel changes to organizational structures to include representatives from the community and their interests in campus recreation governance. It will surely include changes to campus recreation policies aiming to involve and protect the interests of an expanded group of constituents. Service will be the mantra, and unprecedented growth will create opportunities and challenges. Constructing additional facilities, expanding the numbers of professional staff, and increasing programming will be balanced with maintaining firm priorities so that the interests of university users, especially students, are not lost. Many universities will consider contracting the management of recreation facilities to private firms. The ongoing struggle over shared facilities at smaller institutions among campus recreation, intercollegiate athletics, and physical education departments will also continue. However, at larger institutions, the development of state-of-the-art recreation facilities for non-athletes will result in the need to include various user groups, especially as the demographics of the dwindling college-age population become better understood. The governance structure and policy-making procedures of future campus recreation programs, especially relating to risk management and access for people with disabilities, will be more important than ever before. Shrinking resources will also dominate the agenda, and more campus recreation programs will engage corporate sponsorship to fund particular programs or events. This may create conflict with intercollegiate athletics at smaller colleges and universities.

Intercollegiate Athletics

Although the commercial mandate of recreation programs on campus is generally accepted and supported, intercollegiate athletics policy makers will continue to confront negativity associated with commercialization in college football and basketball in the United States. It is more likely than ever that real change is on the horizon. The issue, of course, will revolve around the role of college athletic programs in higher education. For example, are athletes at Division I colleges playing football and basketball really "students"? The increase in the number of "one and done" basketball players who become professionals after one year of college competition certainly makes that question relevant.

NCAA Division I athletes more closely resemble professionals, except they are not directly paid to play. Why not? Colleges and universities make significant sums of money from their athletes. How is it that our colleges and universities, supposed collectives of truth and light, have created a system so incongruous with their mandate and their purpose? The questions go on and on and include issues of fairness, equity, scandal, and control. There will be extensive discussion supporting college athletes receiving pay from outside sources, like from sales of sports memorabilia or use of their likenesses in video games. No other students are restricted. How about athletes receiving a cut of revenues made by institutions from image and name sales from jerseys and other merchandise? The commercial nature of college sports is here to stay, and it is inevitable that large amounts of revenues accruing from star college athletes get shared with those athletes. This may be change prompted by the legal system as opposed to the sports system.

A related issue is the impact of technology and changes to technology rapidly occurring. Soon digital technology will overtake television as far as the consumption of college sports events is concerned. The decline of cable television will impact institutions and leagues through reduced revenues from championships. Next up will be efforts to corner the market in digital transmission and other commercial endeavors related to big time college athletics.

Finally, there is the ongoing issue of scandals occurring within intercollegiate athletics. Institutions such as the University of North Carolina, the University of Louisville, and Baylor University have made headlines for disreputable behavior by coaches and athletes. Athletic Directors need to know how to respond when these events occur, but more importantly, need to find ways to create healthy cultures where scandals will not develop.

The Major Games

Managerial activities associated with major games policy development will receive considerable attention and will be the focus of governance activities for hosting events in the future. Two important issues are at stake. First, organizers will focus on the development of policy to ensure the safety and security of participants and spectators. World events such as the Pan American Games, Commonwealth Games, Special Olympics, World University Games, and the FIFA (Fédération Internationale de Football Association) World Cup are major events, receiving considerable attention from the media, spectators, and television. Organizers must plan for every contingency to ensure security and safety are not compromised by any group attempting to use the event for political gain. Sport managers have certainly kept a more wary eye on this after the attacks in Paris outside the Stade de France and also the bombing at Manchester Arena. Major games administrators must be prepared to deal with issues of security, given the events confronting the world in the 21st century. Second, the governance structures in place for organizing major games must be able to deliver effective policy to manage the issues of the day in a timely manner. The committee structures are considerably large, requiring massive support to make change and allowing only a few members to effectively block the ability to move on issues quickly. Also, the procedures for developing policy and initiating change are unwieldy; inertia resists change, and thus the old, conservative way of doing things prevails. Organizers of major games will be forced to manage issues such as security, and it will be paramount that they have the governance structure and technology in place to set policy in a timely manner.

The Olympic Games

The IOC will continue to evaluate and endeavor to strengthen the Olympic Games with a view to longer-term partnerships with sponsors and increased transparency of operations. Olympic Agenda 2020, the IOCs Strategic Plan, will be enacted as the Games move from a sports-based to an events-based program. Work to ensure non-discrimination of athletes and coaches because of sexual orientation will proceed slowly. Efforts to decrease the costs of hosting an Olympic Games will likely fail. A major policy area demanding considerable attention of IOC members involves the size and "greening" of the Games.

A major issue facing the IOC is the future of host cities. Over the past years, the number of cities putting together final bids has dropped. For instance, only two cities—Beijing and Almaty—vied for the 2022 Winter Games. This also occurred with the 2024 Games, with only Los Angeles and Paris left after Hamburg, Rome, and Budapest withdrew their bids. As of the writing of this chapter, the IOC is considering, for the first time, awarding two Games at once time—the 2024 and the 2028 Summer Games. Time will tell how this strategy will work.

The current Olympic Games are considered by some the "overgrown Games," which have too many sports and too many athletes, and cost too much money to deliver, not to mention the Games' large ecological footprint. In 1948 the London Summer Olympic Games involved 17 sports, 136 events, and 4,104 athletes (IOC, 2017a), whereas the Rio 2016 games had 28 sports, 306 events, and 11,237 athletes (Rio 2016 Olympic Games, 2017).

The number of Olympic sports seems to rise with each Olympiad: 2012 saw 26 sports contested, 2016 included 28 sports, and 2020 will engage 33 sports. Thus the anticipated move to focus on numbers of events as opposed to number of sports reduces some events in retained sports. For example, athletics (track & field) will likely be reduced from the current number of 24 events which will be considered too large. Sports/events are voted on for inclusion on the program at the Sessions. For a sport to become an Olympic sport, a simple majority vote is needed at an IOC Session. Managing sports in the Olympic Program through this policy will continue to be an item on the IOC's agenda. An assessment of the overall governance structure of the IOC, namely practices to enhance transparency, efficiency, shared responsibility, democracy, and rights to appeal decisions, should parallel that process. Moving sports off the Olympic competition roster, however, will continue to be challenging and controversial, as seen by the 2013 vote on wrestling.

One more issue of importance to the Olympic Movement is environmental sustainability or greening the Games. The IOC has deemed the environment a fundamental objective of the Olympic Movement, along-side sport and culture (IOC, 2017b2). Efforts are made to ensure each Olympic Games operates with a minimal carbon footprint. Sustainability in areas such as design and construction, carbon management, sustainable transport, ethical supply chains, food vision, and waste management will be essential deliverables. The environmental impact of the Games will be continually monitored and reported to the public.

The Paralympic Games

The Paralympic Games are gaining international recognition as an elite sport product. Along with this growth, numerous questions will arise regarding the Paralympic Movement. For one, as pointed out in the Paralympic chapter, developing new talent for the Games is essential. To quote Sir Phil Craven, Past President of the International Paralympic Committee (IPC):

> We must increase the numbers practicing para-sports from the grassroots right through to the elite level, improving the depth of talent coming from each country Together we need to expand the pool of women athletes and athletes with high support needs. The Agitos Foundation will support this process through its various programmes of work, in particular to those countries and sports that need the most developmental and financial assistance. (IPC, 2015, p. 4)

Just like Olympic athletes, Paralympic athletes start at the grassroots levels and work their way up. The opportunities must be there for all athletes with a disability to have that access.

Another major issue facing the Paralympic Games involves illegal performance enhancement. Just as this is an issue in the Olympic Games, so too is it an issue in the Paralympic Games; elite athletes are always looking for an edge over the competition. Just before the Rio 2016 Paralympic Games, the IPC made the bold decision to ban all Russian athletes from competition after the McLaren Report revealed systematic, state-supported programs which supported drug cheats. The decision was celebrated by many who supported clean sports but criticized by others who thought the organization had over-reached its bounds. Cooperation between the IPC and organizations such as the World Anti-Doping Agency (WADA) will be critical in this area.

Advances in technology will also impact the Paralympic Games. As the technology of prosthetics advances, this will be reflected in the performances of athletes with disabilities. Racing chairs will be made out of lighter-weight materials, and prosthetic limbs will be made stronger and more flexible. Athletes will begin to achieve performances never seen before, and world records will be broken, establishing new standards. While examining the impact of technology, one must ask three questions: (1) Is the technology safe? (2) Is the technology fair? and (3) Is the technology accessible to all? These questions pertain not just to the Paralympic

Games, but also to the policy-making bodies of any sport governing body dealing with advances in technology.

Finally, just as with the Olympic Games and professional sport, security will continue to be important for the Paralympic Games. Whenever there are large gatherings of elite athletes from many nations, security and risk management become critical for the athletes, spectators, and workers.

As the Paralympic Games continue to grow, the governing bodies associated with the Games, including the IPC, National Paralympic Committees (NPCs), and International Federations (Ifs), will need to adjust to an ever-changing environment. They will need to be responsive to governance decisions made by able-bodied sport organizations that may impact events, rules, and eligibility for athletes with disabilities.

Finally, the United Nations General Assembly's adoption of the Treaty on the Rights of Persons with Disabilities will have long-term effects on the Paralympic Movement. The Treaty contains language specific to sport in Article 30.5, thus sport and physical activity clearly fall under the umbrella of this Treaty. It may take some time for the document to be put into practice, but the long-term result will be increased opportunities for athletes with disabilities (Wolff, Hums, & Roy, 2007).

www

UN Treaty on the Rights of Persons with Disabilities
https://www.un.org/development/desa/disabilities/

Professional Sport Leagues in North America

Professional sport leagues, teams, and players associations need to step up their stances on misconduct by athletes, coaches, and officials. Incidents such as the New Orleans Saints' Bounty Gate, the New England Patriots' De-Flate Gate and athletes being arrested for domestic abuse or sexual assault, or firearm possession seem to be in the news almost every day. The seemingly rampant behavioral problems, ranging from boorishness to unlawful activity, beg for leagues to take truly strong stands against misconduct.

Professional sport managers need to keep up with the latest technology in order to keep up with the desire of the fans to consume sport in ways never thought possible. Interactive stadium experiences are a requirement and stadiums must be equipped to sufficiently handle the increasing volume of Internet demand and phone use by fans in attendance. Slow Internet connections and dropped calls are no longer acceptable for today's fans, particularly the millennial fans who thrive on personal connectivity. Advancements in technology show no signs of slowing down. If today's big "thing" is SnapChat, well, by the next edition of this book, SnapChat may have vanished from our technological toolbox, having been replaced by the next generation of high-tech devices and software.

While athlete misconduct and rapidly advancing technology remain at the top of the list, other issues are constant in professional sport. Although the Big Four has recently avoided major periods of labor unrest, leagues and PAs will continue to debate collective bargaining agreements. The new MLB collective bargaining agreement (CBA) is now set to expire in

December 2021 and measures designed to speed up the pace of play were a hot topic. The NBA signed a seven-year CBA agreement in late 2016 with both sides recognizing the league's strong financial position. The National Football League (NFL) CBA expires in 2020 and discussions will likely revolve around guaranteed contracts, the discretionary powers of the Commissioner, and issues related to head trauma. The National Hockey League's (NHL) CBA is slated to expire at the end of the 2021–22 season. Hopefully these long-term deals will keep the product on the field and on the court running smoothly. Labor issues in sport will always be with us, and leagues and Players Associations (PAs) will continually hammer out new policies regarding everything from performance-enhancing substances to athlete misconduct.

Professional sport in North America has begun to take on a more international flavor. The number of athletes from around the world is increasing, with numerous athletes from South America, Central America, and Japan playing Major League Baseball (MLB) and many European players filling the rosters of the NHL and the National Basketball Association (NBA). In fact, many of today's biggest pro sport stars come from outside North America, including Yu Darvish (Japan) and Jose Altuve (Venezuela) in MLB; Kyrie Irving (Australia), Giannis Antetokounmpo (Greece), and Kristaps Porzingas (Latvia) in the NBA; and Evgeni Malkin (Russia) and Henriq Lundqvist (Sweden) in the NHL.

League and play-off games are being broadcast to different nations and in different languages as the professional leagues become a more global product. Each of these leagues is taking further advantage of this relatively new global market by scheduling regular season games in international cities, such as the NFL holding annual regular season games at Wembley Stadium in London, England. In addition, international "best-on-best" tournaments such as the World Baseball Classic and FIBA (Fédération Internationale de Basketball Association) World Basketball Championship showcase their respective games to the world, helping the game to grow even more.

Global #NBArank: Top 50 International Players in the NBA

www.espn.com/nba/ story/_/page/nbararik_ international_2016/ global-nbarank-ranking-nba-top-50-players-born-us

Best NHL Players from 5 Hockey Nations

www.flohockey.tv/ article/57265-5-best-nhl-players-from-5-hockey-nations

Individual Professional Sport

Over the past two decades, the participation rate for Golf among 18 to 34 year olds continues to decline. Time and financial constraints are primary reasons deterring millennial golfers and posing greater challenges for the Professional Golfers' Association (PGA) TOUR (NGF, 2015). Young PGA TOUR professionals under 30 such as Jordan Speith, Rory McIlroy, Jason Day, and Bryson DeChambeau, will face challenges with the number of spectators, media coverage, and sponsorship opportunities when compared to the Tiger Woods' era. The 2017 Masters at Augusta National Golf Club drew an historically low TV rating of 7.6 for the final round. The rating dropped 11 percent from 2016, and 21 percent from 2015

(Beall, 2017). A similar viewership decline was also found in the US Open in 2016 (Paulsen, 2016). The decline in traditional viewership is not entirely negative, as spectators are finding other media outlets such as online streaming, mobile apps, and social media sites to follow the events. Just as any other sports, the Tours will have to find creative ways to reach greater fan base.

While traditional viewership continues to struggle, virtual reality (VR) technology introduced game changers for individual professional sports fans. Technology companies are pairing with major tournaments to offer closer than courtside views to fans who could not afford to travel or purchase the tickets. In 2016, the United States Tennis Association (USTA) and NextVR company aired the 2016 US Open women's and men's singles semifinals and finals, providing a 360 degrees view of the stadium and behind-the-scenes views of the hallways and locker rooms (NextVR, 2017). The XFINITY virtual reality experience also provides fans with the on-track experience that NASCAR (National Association for Stock Car Auto Racing) drivers face on the day of race (NASCAR, 2016). The closer view and behind-the-scene features of the VR technology will attract new fans and provide greater opportunities. However, the price of the device and physical limitations VR users face, such as wearing goggles, is unavoidable. Additionally, policies regulating VR technology are still being discussed as fans continue to adopt new ways to view sports.

Grassroots development remains a focus for individual sports. These sports rely heavily on an athlete's ability to master the skills necessary to reach the highest level of competition. The missing components of camaraderie, team support, and sport popularity in individual sports are challenges to attracting young fans and athletes. In an effort to support grassroots development, the USTA adopted the QuickStart Tennis format for players aged 10 and under using lower compression balls, smaller courts and racquets, and a modified scoring system in the hopes of making the sport more welcoming to children (USTA, 2017). Similarly, the First Tee youth organization promotes the game of golf through local golf courses, elementary schools, and youth centers for golfers aged 7–18. More than 1,200 chapters around the US introduce golf during physical education class or through the activity-based program (The First Tee, 2017). NASCAR also promotes its Drive for Diversity program to bring more women and minorities to the sport. The organization also promotes its events as family entertainment, and these efforts may help attract potential drivers.

The concept of fair play in individual sport also represents another significant challenge. In comparison to team sports, drug use in professional individual sports is far less common as organizations strive to present a pristine image for the sport. In 2018, the PGA Tour will tighten their anti-doping policy by adding blood testing protocols and several new banned substances to their current list (Skiver, 2017). Since the adoption of the policy in 2008, the Tour's policy was criticized for being too lenient as they did not exactly follow the WADA protocols. The USTA also has been criticized for unfairly random testing of players, not testing winners under 18 at the US Open, ambiguity in their testing methods, and failing to suspend players who tested positive (Fish, 2016; Robson, 2015). On the contrary, NASCAR's own multi-tiered substance abuse program keeps their drivers on the edge. A driver who tests positive is suspended immediately following the zero-tolerance policy. The suspended drivers then could go through the NASCAR Road to Recovery program and may be reinstated upon completion of the program. The entire process from testing to recovery could be quite lengthy and difficult (Macwatters, 2012).

Finally, the financial requirements associated with some individual sports represent another future challenge. Golf and tennis are costly endeavors, given the need for equipment, coaches and lessons, club memberships, and tournament entry fees. The financial investment in NASCAR is even greater as drivers may require one or more vehicles, support staff and personnel, plus the expenses associated with traveling to and entering races. The ultimate rewards remain high for successful athletes who receive millions in prize earnings, yet the initial costs may represent a barrier to entry for interested athletes.

Professional Sport Beyond North America

It is interesting to speculate on the future of professional sport internationally. Political and economic factors will no doubt impact the sport industry. International sponsors will continue to reexamine their choices for investing in sporting leagues and events. Accordingly, sport governing bodies will have to make decisions regarding financial matters in order to maintain and improve operations in the coming years. Because of the interrelationship of IFs such as FIFA with the operation of international professional leagues, these organizations will be considering policies related to garnering sufficient financial resources, just as the professional leagues in North America will. Internationally, professional sport will continue to grow. Soccer will remain the most popular sport globally and a viable investment for corporations despite ongoing problems with racism and scandals involving high-level officials. In addition, eSport is here to stay. Whether one considers eSport competitors to be athletes or not, the fact is this multi-billion-dollar part of the professional sport industry is growing and shows no signs of slowing down. The fan base is rapidly expanding, with major sponsors hopping on board.

It seems that people in the United States are tuning in and slowly becoming more interested in and knowledgeable about international sport leagues. Current technologies and the proliferation of social media for transmitting sport allow for easier access and greater consumer choice, resulting in opportunities for some sport leagues, while presenting obstacles for others.

SUMMARY

T he future of sport will be full of changes! How sport governing bodies respond to these facts will determine their success in the future. Some people resist change, while others welcome it. In each segment of the sport industry, sport governing bodies will face change. Some of these changes will be unique to one industry segment, while others will cut across a number of segments.

As a future sport manager, how will you choose to face this future with all its uncertainties, questions, and changes? As they say, "The ball is in your court."

CHAPTER questions

1. Choose three industry segments from the textbook and identify two additional future issues for each. With a class mate, debate why (and why not) your future issues will come true.

2. Using the model presented in this chapter, analyze the steps for change for one of the following:

   a. a professional athlete being accused or convicted of criminal behavior

   b. a state high school or provincial association creating a wheelchair division for track & field competition

   c. a campus recreation program facing declining participation numbers

3. Choose one sport organization you would like to see experience changes in membership, eligibility, or organizational structure. Describe the changes you would like to see take place and how these changes will improve the organization.

FOR ADDITIONAL INFORMATION

For more information check out the following resources:

1. Ben Jervey. Will Climate Change Threaten the Future of the Winter Olympics?: Climate Change Threatens the Future of the Winter Olympics: https://news.nationalgeographic.com/news/2014/02/140221-climate-change-winter-olympics-global-warming-science/

2. Campus Rec Mag: Is the Future of Recreation and Wellness, Medical?: http://campusrecmag.com/is-the-future-of-recreation-and-wellness-medical/

3. Video. Hosting Healthy Sport Events: www.everactive.org/hosting-healthy-sporting-events-video

4. Video: the Future of the Paralympic Movement: https://www.paralympic.org/video/future-paralympic-movement

5. Is the future of high school football on the line?: https://www.usatoday.com/story/sports/highschool/2015/11/17/high-school-football-participation-california/75899218/

6. The 25 Players Who Will Define the Future of the NBA: www.foxsports.com/nba/gallery/nba-best-young-players-top-25-under-25-prospects-031917

REFERENCES

Beall, J. (2017). The Masters had its lowest TV rating in 13 years. Why? *Golf Digest.* Retrieved from www.golfdigest.com/story/the-masters-had-its-lowest-tv-rating-in-13-years-why

Beer, M., & Nohria, N. (2000). *Breaking the code of change.* Boston: Harvard Business School Press.

Brill, P. L., & Worth, R. (1997). *The four levers of corporate change.* New York: American Management Association.

Byers, T., Slack, T., & Parent, M. (2012). *Key concepts in sport management.* Thousand Oaks, CA: Sage.

Chelladurai, P. (2014). *Managing organizations for sport and physical activity: A systems perspective* (4th ed.). London, UK: Routledge.

Covell, T., & Walker, S. (2013). *Managing sport organizations: Responsibility for performance* (3rd ed.). London: Routledge.

DePauw, K., Driscoll, J., Fay, T., Hums, M. A., & Joukowsky, A. (2003). The Boston Marathon: Breaking barriers. Paper presented at the Disability Sport Symposium, Boston, MA.

Fish, M. (2016). Tennis has a clean record of PEDs, and that appears to be no accident. *ESPN.* Retrieved from www.espn.com/espn/otl/story/_/id/17693288/tennis-pristine-image-performance-enhancing-drugs-which-no-accident

Grevemberg, D., Hums, M. A., & Wolff, E. A. (2001). Integration of Paralympic sport into International Sport Federations: Comparative international models. Paper presented at the Annual Meeting of the North American Society for Sport Management, Virginia Beach, VA.

Han, M. (2017). Virtual reality headsets could be a game changer. Retrieved from www.afr.com/business/sport/virtual-reality-headsets-could-be-a-game-changer-for-tennis-fans-20170106-gtn0cj

Hyman, M. (2002, April 29). Security issues rise to the top of the docket for sport lawyers. *Street & Smith's SportsBusiness Journal.* Retrieved from www.sportsbusinessdaily.com/Journal/Issues/2002/04/20020429/This-Weeks-Issue/Security-Issues-Rise-To-The-Top-Of-The-Docket-For-Sports-Lawyers.aspx?hl=security%20issues%20rise%20to%20the%20top&sc=1

IOC. (2017a). London 1948. Retrieved from https://www.olympic.org/london-1948

IOC. (2017b). Sustainability. Retrieved from https://www.olympic.org/sustainability

IPC. (2015). *Strategic plan 2015–2018: Strategic outlook for the International Paralympic Committee.* Bonn, Germany: Author.

Klayman, B. (2009). Tiger's troubles seen swiping sports sponsorship market. *International Business Times.* Retrieved from www.ibtimes.com/tigers-troubles-seen-swiping-sports-sponsorship-market-3533

Macwatters, S. (2012). NASCAR's drug policy: Is it too strict? Bleacher Report. Retrieved from http://bleacherreport.com/articles/1258595-nascars-drug-policy-is-it-too-strict

NASCAR. (2016). Fans get closer to race action with virtual reality experience. Retrieved from www.nascar.com/en_us/news-media/articles/2016/3/4/virtual-reality-experience-brings-fans-closer-to-race-action-xfinity.html

NextVR. (2017). USTA teams with NextVR to offer US Open highlights from the men's and women's singles semifinals and finals for the first time in virtual reality. Retrieved from www.nextvr.com/usopenpress

NGF. (2015). #Golf and the Millennial generation. Retrieved from www.golf2020.com/media/62433/millennial_report_ngf.pdf

Olympic Golf News. (2012). Barra region to be Olympic golf site. Retrieved from http://olympicgolfnews.com/barra-region-to-be-olympic-golf-site

Paulsen (2016). US Open ratings low for third straight year. Retrieved from www.sportsmediawatch.com/2016/06/us-open-ratings-low-fox-golf-viewership/

Rhoden, W. C. (2012, October 7). Amid successes, WNBA is still facing challenges. *New York Times*. Retrieved from www.nytimes.com/2012/10/08/sports/basketball/amid-successes-wnba-is-still-facing-challenges.html?pagewanted=all&_r=0

Rio 2016 Olympic Games. (2016). Rio 2016. Retrieved from https://www.olympic.org/rio-2016

Robson, D. (2015). US Open doping loophole creates drug testing gap for US Players. *Sports Illustrated*. Retrieved from https://www.si.com/tennis/2015/09/04/us-open-doping-looping-usta-drug-testing

Skiver, K. (2017). PGA Tour makes drug testing more stringent with blood tests starting in 2018. Retrieved from www.cbssports.com/golf/news/pga-tour-makes-drug-testing-policies-more-stringent-starting-in-october-2018/

Slack, T., & Parent, M. (2006). *Understanding sport organizations: The application of organization theory* (2nd ed.). Champaign, IL: Human Kinetics.

Slezak, C. (2002, September 8). Sporting a different look. *Chicago Sun-Times*, p. 123.

The First Tee. (2017). About the First Tee. Retrieved from https://thefirsttee.org/about/

Trahan, K. (2016, May 12). Should Grambling State, Southern, and other HBCUs drop out of Division I football? Retrieved from https://sports.vice.com/en_us/article/should-grambling-state-southern-hbcus-drop-division-i-football

USTA. (2018). Jr recreational tennis. Retrieved from http://www.louisville.usta.com/Jr_Recreational_Tennis/Quick_Start_Tennis_Progarm/

Wolff, E. A., Hums, M. A., & Roy, E. (2007). *Sport in the United Nations Convention on the Rights of Persons with Disabilities*. Boston, MA: International Disability in Sport Working Group/United Nations Office of the Special Advisor of the Secretary-General on Sport for Development and Peace.

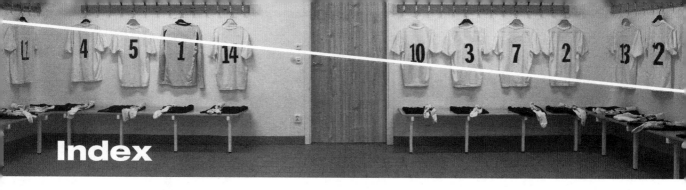

Index

Information in tables, boxes, exhibits and figures is indicated in *italics*.

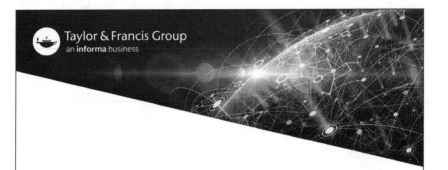